I0187760

CHANGING SIDES

CHANGING SIDES

UNION PRISONERS OF WAR WHO JOINED THE CONFEDERATE ARMY

★ ★ ★ ★ ★

Patrick H. Garrow

THE UNIVERSITY OF TENNESSEE PRESS | KNOXVILLE

First Edition.

Library of Congress Cataloging-in-Publication Data
Names: Garrow, Patrick H., author.
Title: Changing sides : Union prisoners of war who joined the Confederate Army / Patrick H. Garrow.
Description: First edition. | Knoxville : The University of Tennessee Press, [2020] | Includes bibliographical references and index. |
Summary: "Garrow's book investigates the experience of imprisoned Union soldiers during the final years of the American Civil War, including their captivity and their repatriation into Confederate ranks. Patrick Garrow's research stems from the archaeological excavation of Florence Prison in 2006 and subsequent archival research in the *Official Records of the War of the Rebellion* and other primary records. Garrow's deeply researched portrait will fill a significant gap in our understanding of Union POWs, since Dee Brown's lengthy work, *Galvanized Yankees*, dating back to the 1960s, largely focused on Confederate POWs that fought for the Union"—Provided by publisher.
Identifiers: LCCN 2020029312 (print) | LCCN 2020029313 (ebook) |
ISBN 9781621906179 (hardcover) | ISBN 9781621906186 (pdf)
Subjects: LCSH: Confederate States of America. Army—History. | Prisoners of war—Confederate States of America. | United States—History—Civil War, 1861–1865—Prisoners and prisons, Confederate.
Classification: LCC E611 .G37 2020 (print) | LCC E611 (ebook) |
DDC 973.7/71—dc23
LC record available at https://lccn.loc.gov/2020029312
LC ebook record available at https://lccn.loc.gov/2020029313

CONTENTS

ILLUSTRATIONS

ACKNOWLEDGMENTS

THIS BOOK GREW OUT OF archaeological research conducted on a Confederate guard camp at Florence Prison in 2006. That research was conducted for the National Cemetery Administration of the Department of Veterans Affairs through a contract with MACTEC Engineering and Consulting, Inc. of Knoxville, Tennessee. This author served as Principal Investigator for the project, with Paul Avery as the Field Director. Paul did the hard work in the field and wrote most of the report of findings. The Florence project was part of a 10-year professional collaboration with Paul at MACTEC and later at Cultural Resource Analysts, Inc., and I am indebted to him for his fine contributions at Florence and many other projects.

Military historian John Lundstrom contacted the author in August 2014, and asked to join the book project as a coauthor. We signed an agreement to that effect in September 2014. John focused his efforts on the 10th Tennessee and the 5th U.S. Volunteer Infantry. He also agreed to rewrite sections produced by the current author so that the book would have a single, consistent writing style. He produced drafts of several chapters, all of which lacked citations. The collaboration ended at John's request in August 2018 following long delays and a disagreement over the content of the manuscript. I honored John's stipulation that none of the chapters he wrote be included in the book.

Dr. Earl Hess of Lincoln Memorial University reviewed an early draft of the manuscript. It is difficult to express the debt I owe to Dr. Hess for helping me during this project. The generous use of his time to help someone who was not a recognized part of the community of historians researching Civil War history and the encouragement he gave for the research came at a critical time in the project.

Dr. Lorien Foote of Texas A&M University provided encouragement for the project and reviewed the manuscript for the University of Tennessee Press. Her thoughtful and detailed review materially improved the manuscript, and I am grateful for the time and effort she devoted to this project.

Dianna and Eric Haney of Cave Springs, Georgia, provided encouragement through this long and difficult project. They welcomed me into their home, built by Captain Wesley O. Connor of the Captain Van Den Corput Company of Light Artillery (Georgia) shortly after the Civil War. Captain Connor was captured at Salisbury along with elements of the 2nd Foreign Battalion (8th Confederate Infantry), and left a diary which was critical to understanding events that led up to the battle. Dianna and Eric alerted me to the diary, and Eric provided insights into military life that helped me better understand the men of the Union and Confederate armies.

The staff of the Louisiana Historical Association Collection of the Howard-Tilton Memorial Library at Tulane University in New Orleans provided every courtesy to the author during research on the George W. Brent Papers. Their detailed knowledge of the Special Collections facilitated that research and enabled me to complete the research in an efficient manner.

Steve Cox, Head of Special Collections and University Archivist of the Lupton Library of the University of Tennessee at Chattanooga, researched the Garnett Andrews papers in October 2011 and sent me documents pertinent to Andrews' command of the 2nd Foreign Battalion (8th Confederate Infantry). His kindness saved me a trip to Chattanooga, and I am indebted to him for his help. Jennifer Berzin, Processing Archivist at the same library, sent the image of Garnett Andrews in November, 2019, that is used in this volume, and once again saved me a trip to Chattanooga. Her assistance is also appreciated.

Norman V. Turner shared his publication on military executions at Savannah and the trial of General Mercer that was critical to completing the story of the Brooks Battalion. The information he provided was the product of his detailed research on local sources that would have been difficult to duplicate.

Bruce S. Allardice shared information he had gathered on Col. John G. O'Neill, Col. Martin Burke, and Col. William H. Wier that was not included in his book *Confederate Colonels*. His assistance is gratefully acknowledged.

Glen Swain has provided support and encouragement throughout this project. He has never hesitated to share information and that is greatly appreciated.

Thomas Wells, acquisitions editor at the University of Tennessee Press, offered encouragement and helpful advice through the long publication process. Lydia Gay was the content editor for the manuscript and did a tremendous job turning the manuscript into a readable book. Jon Boggs turned my manuscript into a finished book, and I am indebted to the whole staff of UT Press for their assistance.

My family has enabled me to devote the thousands of hours this book has consumed over the past 13 years. My wife Barbara has borne most of that burden, and I am grateful for her understanding and support.

★ INTRODUCTION ★

THERE ARE VERY FEW unexplored topics concerning the history of the American Civil War. Thousands, and probably tens of thousands, of volumes and articles are in print about the war, but not one deals with the Union prisoners of war who joined the Confederate Army in more than a superficial manner. Two published volumes focus on men who changed sides during the war, and both of those focus on Confederate prisoners of war. Dee Brown's classic work *Galvanized Yankees* deals with six regiments raised almost entirely from Union prisons and sent to the western frontier to protect settlers from American Indian attacks during the Civil War. Four companies of a single regiment were composed in part of Union prisoners of war who had joined the Confederate Army. Those men, captured in arms at Egypt Station, joined the 5th United States Volunteer Infantry. Brown devoted a single chapter to Union prisoners of war who changed sides.[1]

A second published volume that deals with former Confederate soldiers who had changed sides was *Galvanized Yankees on the Northern Missouri* by Michelle Tucker Butts. Her volume deals in depth with the 1st United States Volunteer Infantry (USVI), and remains the only substantive published work on a single galvanized Yankee regiment. There are other scattered references and at least one honor's thesis devoted to Civil War soldiers who changed sides, but most references are brief and in some cases in error.[2]

The term "galvanized Yankees" historically described men from both armies who changed sides during the war. "Galvanized" is a term used to describe a base metal that is coated with zinc to prevent corrosion. "Galvanized" soldiers were thus men not made up of true, incorruptible metal. The term "galvanized Yankees" in this study only refers to Confederate prisoners of war who joined the Union Army. The historically incorrect term "galvanized Confederates" refers to Union prisoners of war who joined the Confederate Army. This volume uses the term "galvanized Confederates" in the same way Dee Brown did in his book *Galvanized Yankees* in order to avoid the confusion that using the same term for both groups would create.

The term "enlisted Federals" also refers to galvanized Confederates in some instances.[3]

The idea of men changing sides to fight for the enemy was nothing new to the senior command of either the Union or Confederate armies. The officers had sorted themselves into one side or the other as the war began, but they shared the lesson of the San Patricios, learned during the Mexican War. Most of the senior command of both sides had fought in the Mexican War and had the opportunity to observe the effectiveness of the San Patricio Battalion. It is sufficient to point out at this point that they were an artillery battalion made up largely of deserters from the American Army that became one of the most effective fighting units the Mexicans had to oppose the American invasion. The San Patricios were primarily Irish Catholic immigrants subjected to severe persecution by nativist American officers. The position taken by Confederate leaders late in the war—that it was appropriate to recruit Union prisoners of war, and more specifically that the recruits should be foreign-born—may have been derived in part from their experience with the San Patricios.[4]

The official recruitment of galvanized Yankees began a year before the recruitment of galvanized Confederates. Unofficial recruitment of galvanized Yankees started even earlier when Col. Mulligan of the 23rd Illinois Infantry recruited prisoners from Camp Douglas to fill losses from his own regiment. Mulligan left camp with the new recruits despite the disapproval of the War Department.[5] Galvanized Yankees from northern prisons filled out at least two regiments in experiments that failed because of desertions.[6] One guard unit recruited at Fort Delaware from among the prisoners was successful and served until the end of the war. It is not the purpose of the current research to identify and discuss every Federal unit that included galvanized Yankees. It is clear that recruitment of Confederate prisoners of war went beyond the six regiments sent to the western frontier.[7]

Confederate officials did not consider recruitment of Union prisoners of war until late in 1864. That may have been due to the hatred most southerners felt for the north and northerners, and the belief that Yankees were inferior to southerners in almost every way. That belief, which originated years before the war, held that Yankees were cowards and morally unfit barbarians who could not replace the superior fighting men of the south.[8] The initial recruitments resulted from both the need for additional manpower, which had become critical by late 1864, and the large numbers of prisoners who expressed a desire to change sides. Those men were mainly collected at Florence Prison and organized into what became the Brooks Battalion. The rest stayed in Charleston and joined commands defending the city. The Brooks Battalion did not have enough officers to ensure adequate command and control or sufficient training, and the soldiers of the battalion attempted to mutiny while part of the Savannah defenses. It was no surprise that the Brooks Battalion failed.[9]

Four hundred prisoners enlisted in Confederate units around Charleston. The 47th Georgia Infantry and Captain Daniell's Battery were two units identified during the current research that received some of those men. The hundred men sent to the 47th Georgia were returned to prison because of their high desertion rate, and the 60 men sent to Captain Daniell's Battery simply melted away after playing their role in the defense of Savannah. The prisoners allocated to commands around Charleston proved to be a failed experiment.[10]

The Confederate government eventually authorized several individuals to enlist prisoners and form new commands. The 1st Foreign Battalion, which became the Tucker Regiment, was a pioneer regiment under the command of Col. Julius Tucker. That regiment, held together by draconian discipline, survived in reduced form until the end of the war. The 2nd Foreign Battalion, renamed the 8th Confederate Infantry, the most well trained galvanized unit, largely met its end at an April 1865 battle at Salisbury. The men of that battalion arrived at Salisbury after the battle was already lost, but fought well in a losing cause.[11]

Col. John O'Neill raised as many as a thousand men to fill out depleted regiments in the Bates Division of the Army of Tennessee under an authorization from Gen. John Bell Hood. Most of those men went west in December 1864 to join the Army of Tennessee, but over 250 were captured under arms at Egypt Station during a raid through Mississippi led by General Benjamin Grierson. Most of the captured men joined the 5th United States Infantry from prison. Over half of those men deserted during their term of service from April 1864 to October 1865. The 5th United States Volunteer Infantry was part of the Union experiment that sent six regiments made up mostly of galvanized Yankees to the western frontier to protect the frontier from warring American Indian tribes. That experiment was generally a success, although the desertion rate among the galvanized Confederates in the 5th was very high.[12]

Col. John O'Neill made the last serious attempt to enlist Union prisoners for the Confederate Army in January and February 1865. He was successful in recruiting men at Andersonville Prison, but it was too late in the war for his recruits to be used to any real effect. Those men appear to have melted away as the war ended.[13]

There were doubtless many examples during the war of men changing sides as individuals. It was not possible to track more than a few cases of men changing sides at that level during the current research.

The current research was the result of an archaeological investigation that focused on a part of a guard camp at Florence Prison.[14] That research excavated a nine-acre area that was between the southern boundary of Florence National Cemetery and the northern boundary of the Florence Stockade. The National Cemetery began with the cemetery established to bury those who died in the Florence Stockade. The Cemetery has expanded south since that time to the point that the latest addition brought it virtually to the walls of the stockade. Historical research undertaken to create a historic context for the archaeological investigation revealed the story of the galvanized Confederates that first unfolded at Florence. The guard camp excavation revealed important information on the shelters built by the guards and their diet, which provided useful comparisons with the plight of the prisoners inside the stockade learned from documentary sources. Additional research began on galvanized Confederates after that project was complete, and has continued to the present.

The galvanized Confederate units doubtless included many deserters, thugs, bounty jumpers, and other unsavory types. Those units also contained men who enlisted as a means of saving their lives or their sanity. Civil War prisons in both the North and South were deathtraps, where large numbers of men died of untreated or poorly treated wounds, malnutrition, dietary diseases such as scurvy, rampant epidemic or endemic diseases, inadequate medical care, exposure, or nothing more than deep despair. Prisons in the North offered shelter, which the open pens of the South did not, but those shelters were not adequate to protect the men from severe winter conditions. Sanitary conditions were at best inadequate and at worst nonexistent, and in many cases there was no safe drinking water. Those conditions were coupled with the failure of the exchange system at a time when battles on all fronts were flooding prisons with new prisoners. Enlisting in the army of the former enemy offered a way out for men who were out of options. It is not surprising that both sides found fertile ground for recruiting and so many men changed sides.[15]

After the war, the Pension Board classified former galvanized Confederates as deserters when assessing pension applications. That followed a law passed during the war, and it was not until 1891 that their status changed under new legislation that allowed their approval for pensions. The 1891 ruling did not change the statuses of men who had deserted their units and then joined a galvanized unit, but it was certainly a step towards welcoming galvanized Confederates back into society. Chapter 9 discusses the fate of a number of galvanized Confederates after the war, but the overwhelming majority of them had become invisible in the records even prior to that time.[16]

The research conducted for this volume was extremely difficult and time consuming. It began with the service records, such as they were, for each galvanized unit. The service records were abstracted and entered into sortable Excel databases. Confederate service records are largely incomplete, and the records for the galvanized units were no exceptions. Beyond miscellaneous clothing receipts in separate files, the only service records that have survived for the galvanized 10th Tennessee, as an example, were compiled by Union authorities and included only those men captured at the Battle of Egypt Station. It was not possible to identify three fourths of the men in that unit with any certainty. Either most of the 400 men allocated out to Confederate units around Charleston did not last long enough with their assigned units to be included on muster rolls or the muster rolls from the time of their assignments did not survive. The only identifiable men of that group from service records were the 60 men of Captain Daniell's Battery. The service records of the men of Tucker's Regiment and the 8th Confederate Infantry were much more complete, but still lacked some detail.

The *Official Records of the Rebellion*, which are available online, provided valuable information about Confederate prisons and prisoners. Confederate decision-making could be determined from numerous telegrams, letters, and reports exchanged within the Confederate command structure. Reports from both sides were invaluable in reconstructing the events surrounding the battles of Egypt Station and Salisbury, as well as better understanding troop movements and logistics. The research attempted to identify and assess every document pertinent to the galvanized Confederates in both the Confederate and Union armies.

Pension records and published government documents were excellent sources of information on some of the men who served as galvanized Confederates.

Prisoner accounts were consulted during this project, with the greatest emphasis placed on those published immediately after the war or on diaries written during the war. This does not mean that other prisoners' accounts lack value for research on Civil War prisons, but the accounts written well after the war tend to be derivative of earlier accounts and also tend to be less accurate.

The online service *Newspapers.com* provided an effective way to research newspaper accounts. Newspaper articles, when used with care, provided information unavailable in any other way. Obituaries for former galvanized Confederates tended to be somewhat burnished accounts of their lives. Most did not mention that they had changed sides during the war.

The online service *fold3* provided most of the archival documents used to tell the story of the galvanized Confederates. The available service records for the Confederate Army, plus a number of different record types, were available through that service. The Union records are less robust through that service, and service records for several northern states are only available in index form at this time. The service has a search feature linked to names, but it is a feature that has to be used with care. Links are often broken, and a search that may work on one day may not work on another. Further, the names for that feature came from using OCR technology, which is not always effective on handwritten entries. Despite the negative aspects, the service worked well enough to track individuals identified through service records, which yielded far more information than would be possible to find using traditional research methods.

Census records provided excellent information on some galvanized Confederates, but were difficult to use. *Ancestry.com* proved to be the best source for census records along with some other record types. There was insufficient information on most galvanized Confederates to be able to track them through the census records.

The research used many published sources. The online search tool *Google Books* identified many of those sources. Goo*gle Books* made it possible to identify pertinent sources, including many of the earlier sources downloadable as pdf. documents. A large reference library was built in that manner, and more recent sources were identified and acquired.

The South Carolina Department of Archives and History proved to be the most important source of unpublished records found during this project. Those records were fragmentary and dealt with Florence Prison, but provided important contextual information for the research. The search for other archival sources housed in private research facilities largely came up empty. The author visited Tulane University and the George W. Brent Papers at the Howard Tilton Memorial Library provided valuable information on the movements of the galvanized 10th in Mississippi immediately before the Battle of Egypt Station. The historical collections at the University of

Tennessee-Chattanooga and the University of North Carolina-Chapel Hill also provided limited sources that were important to the current research. No other private archival collections were identified that could further inform the research.

The few thousand men who changed sides and enlisted in the Confederate Army did not alter the course of the war. It is important, however, to attempt to understand their story and what motivated them to abandon their oath and duty to join their former enemy. The motivation, or more likely motivations, of those men is a complex issue that may be impossible to fully address absent direct and honest witness from the men who made those decisions.

It is also important to understand the motivation of Confederate officials who turned to that source of manpower late in the war. The use of their former enemies to fill out the depleted ranks of some of the Confederate Army was, given the southern distrust and hatred of Yankees, an act of desperation in its own right. That action was tempered by the instruction to only recruit foreign-born prisoners, but many native-born men ended up in the galvanized units.[17]

The story of the galvanized Confederates is a part of the larger story of Civil War prisons, which is another poorly understood topic in the available literature. The Civil War was definitely "a rich man's war and a poor man's fight," a slogan that was never more true than for the enlisted men isolated and abandoned to their fates in Civil War prisons on both sides, who faced the decision to either abandon their comrades or to stick with them and potentially die. Most of all, the study of galvanized Confederates is a study of violated expectations of loyalty, duty, and oaths by men who, in some cases, ended up facing their former comrades in battle in support of their former enemy.

⋆ CHAPTER 1 ⋆

Changing Sides

WHEN THE CIVIL WAR BEGAN, there were no protocols on either side for the proper treatment of prisoners. The handling of prisoners had varied in America from the Revolutionary War through the Mexican War. The British had refused to recognize American prisoners as enemy combatants, and had instead considered them traitors until close to the end of the Revolution. The British kept captured Americans in jails, factories, warehouses, and even prison ships in American harbors. Thousands of prisoners died under the harsh treatment of the British, with most dying of disease. American forces treated British prisoners as prisoners of war, while they treated Loyalists fighting for the Crown as traitors. Insufficient rations, forced marches to prisons, and disease caused the death of many of the British and Loyalist prisoners. Limited exchanges of prisoners began as early as 1776, with an exchange system based on rank used by 1781. The British finally agreed to the full exchange of prisoners in 1783. The exchange system initiated in 1781, where prisoners were exchanged by rank (a general under this system was worth 1,066 privates), became the model for an exchange system instituted during the War of 1812 and, for a time, during the Civil War.[1]

Both sides treated prisoners as enemy combatants during the War of 1812. Both sides paroled captured soldiers and sailors during the first year of the war, but held them because of the lack of an official exchange system. The British Commissary General of Prisoners handled their prisoners of war, a position specifically created for the task during the war. John Mason filled that role for America, and was instrumental in establishing and negotiating an agreement with the British. The American Congress quickly approved the *Cartel for the Exchange of Prisoners of War Between Great Britain and the United States of America*, signed on May 12, 1813. The Crown did not officially approve the cartel, but the British agent for prisoners considered it to be in force and implemented it. The exchange was a rank-based system, much like that during the Revolution, but in this case they exchanged generals and admirals for just forty enlisted men. The agreement included specific directions for the proper treatment of prisoners and the right of inspection of prisons by each side. The issues of the treatment of captives that were "free persons of color" and, to a greater degree, the legal status of captured Americans who had formerly been subjects of the Crown, led to suspension of the cartel for several months. Both sides reinstated the cartel in May 1814. The prisoners of war during the War of 1812 received better treatment than they had during the Revolution, but suspension of the cartel also underlined that such agreements were fragile and subject to interruption.[2]

Field commanders largely handled the treatment of prisoners of war during the Mexican War. The war took place mainly in Mexico, and the field commanders paroled the captured Mexican fighters soon after capture. President Polk ordered all Mexican officers held without parole. He offered no alternatives to the mass parole of the thousands of captured Mexican soldiers.[3]

The Mexican-American War of 1846–1848 provided the first example in American history where significant numbers of American soldiers deserted and formed an effective fighting force for the enemy. The San Patricio or St. Patrick Battalion was composed mainly of Irish and German Catholics who were recent immigrants to the United States. Most of the men in the unit were deserters from the American army but also included some Protestants, Irishmen, and Germans who had migrated to Mexico.[4]

Stevens and Miller published the most thorough histories of the St. Patrick Battalion. Stevens provided considerable background on the "ethnic and religious bigotry" faced by Catholic immigrants to America prior to the Mexican-American War. The potato famine in Ireland, coupled with a policy of land clearances by landlords, led to the death or outmigration of millions. The potato famine, caused by the spread of the potato blight, began in 1845 and continued for several years. Many of those immigrants, who had been laborers or farmers in Ireland, came to America and brought their Catholic religion with them.

While ethnic and religious bigotry had always (and certainly still does) existed in America, anti-Catholic hatred was fanned in the 1830s and 1840s by those who sought to "preserve America as a Protestant nation." Groups such as the Protestant Association, which published the inflammatory newspaper *The Protestant*, spread anti-Catholic propaganda. A published work titled *Foreign Conspiracy Against the Liberties of the United States* (published with the author as "Brutus" in 1835) ignited intense bigotry aimed at Catholic immigrants, which fueled the formation of the "Know Nothing" Party.

Samuel F. B. Morse, the inventor of the telegraph, first published it in the *New York Observer* in 1834. The book was widely read, with over 100,000 copies in print by 1845. The large wave of Catholic immigrants from Ireland who were fleeing starvation and death in their own land encountered the growing bigotry inflamed by the "Know Nothings."[5]

The large influx of Irish Catholics coincided with events that led to the Mexican-American War. Mexico saw the annexation of Texas by the American government in 1845 as a provocative act as Mexico had not recognized Texas independence.

The American army numbered only 8,613 officers and men on the eve of hostilities. That number included eight infantry regiments, four of artillery, and two of cavalry, all assigned to posts that extended across the continent. Mexico, in contrast, had 30,000 to 50,000 regulars under arms, concentrated in a much smaller area. Clearly, President Polk needed a greatly expanded army if he was going to be able to undertake his war. Polk's army heavily recruited Irish and German immigrants, who both tended to be Catholics. The recent immigrants lacked much in the way of job opportunities in Protestant America and joined by the thousands.[6]

One of the Irish immigrants recruited into Polk's army was John Riley, who had been born in County Galway in Ireland. Riley had apparently served in the British army and risen to the rank of sergeant despite his decidedly anti-British views. He had mustered out of the British army in 1843 at age 27 and had moved to Mackinac Island in the United States in the same year. He took a job working on the Mackinac Island docks within a community that was much less anti-Catholic than the rest of the country.[7]

John Riley joined the 5th U.S. Infantry on September 4, 1845, and was assigned to Company K. Half of the men in the 5th were either Irish or German. The 5th began their journey south to the Gulf Coast two days after Riley enlisted.[8]

Many officers in Polk's army held anti-Irish or anti-Catholic views. Those views caused the officers to exact harsh discipline on the Irish-born for the smallest of infractions. The harsh discipline was coupled with food that was often rancid. The nativistic officers verbally and physically assaulted the Irish enlisted men far out of proportion to their numbers. One of the worst offenders, Braxton Bragg, faced two attempts on his life by his own men as the Mexican War continued.[9] Desertions in large numbers from the American Army began on April 1–2 when 36 soldiers swam across the Rio Grande to Mexico. About 30 more men followed the next night. The commander of the Mexican garrison at Matamoros encouraged the desertions. Leaflets bearing a message encouraging immigrants to desert from the American Army were produced and distributed at the direction of General Pedro de Ampudia of the Mexican Army and Francisco R. Moreno, the Adjutant of the Commander in Chief.[10]

John Riley joined the growing number of deserters on April 12. He swam across the Rio Grande and was captured by Mexican soldiers and taken to Matamoros. Riley offered to raise a company from the deserters from the American Army for the Mexican Army. General Ampudia accepted his offer and made Riley a lieutenant in the Mexican Army.[11] Beyond the abuse visited on the immigrants in the American Army, the nativistic Americans were Protestant and were about to go to war with the Catholic country of Mexico. This made the idea of changing sides to fight for a country that valued the Irish and German immigrants' religion even more attractive, and it was a powerful lure to the badly abused soldiers. Riley soon enlisted 48 men in his company, and began their training as an artillery unit. A pamphlet was distributed in the American camp that offered immediate Mexican citizenship and free land to any American soldier who would come over and help fight against the upcoming American invasion. At least 200 men had deserted by the end of April.[12]

A state of war existed between America and Mexico as of April 25, 1846, although Congress did not declare war on Mexico until May 13. May 13 was a critical date for those who deserted, as desertion on or after that date was a capital offense. The war began on May 2nd as an artillery duel between Mexican batteries and batteries under the command of Braxton Bragg at Fort Texas (later Fort Brown and the site of Brownsville, Texas). Riley and his men took part in that battle, and the artillery barrage continued for several days. Defeats led the Mexican army to abandon Matamoros, which the American army occupied on May 18.[13]

Riley's company, along with what was left of the Mexican Army that had retreated from Matamoros, reached Monterey in July 1846. Riley added a second company to his unit, filled largely by deserters from the American Army. The Mexican government offered land and instant citizenship to those who joined in the hopes of enticing even more men to desert.[14]

The battle for Monterey began on September 20, 1846, and ended with the Mexican surrender of the city on September 25. Gen. Zachary Taylor, the commander of the American forces, gave the Mexican Army safe passage from Monterey, which included Riley and his men. Their former comrades-at-arms recognized some of the deserters, who jeered and cursed them as they rode by.[15]

The Mexican Army retreated to San Luis Potosi, which was about 225 miles from Monterey. Santa Anna joined the retreating Mexican Army at San Luis Potosi, where he met Riley and approved his artillery company composed of deserters from the American Army. He also turned over the heaviest guns in his army to Riley. The November 1846 payroll records listed Riley's unit as the Irish Volunteers. While at San Luis Potosi, Riley had nuns sew a unit flag that became emblematic of the "Irish Volunteers." The flag carried images of the Irish harp and the Mexican coat of arms, as well as the slogan "Liberty for the Mexican Republic" in Spanish and "Ireland Forever" in Gaelic. The reverse of the flag had an image of St. Patrick with his staff resting on a serpent over the words "San Patricio." San Patricio or the St. Patrick Battalion was to become the name of Riley's unit. His unit increased in strength to between 100 and 150 men, which included Irish, French, Germans, and others.[16]

A series of battles followed, all of which ended in defeat for the Mexican Army. The end for the San Patricios came at the monastery Santa Maria de Los Angelos during the Battle of Churusbusco, which was five miles from Mexico City. The San Patricio Battalion suffered 60 percent casualties during the battle, and Riley and 84 of his men were captured.[17]

The courts-martial that followed sentenced 71 men from the San Patricio Battalion to hang for desertion. Gen. Scott reviewed the findings and upheld 50 of the death sentences, but pardoned or reduced the sentences of 20 more. John Riley and 15 others had their death sentences reduced to 50 lashes and to be branded on the cheek with the letter "D." Five additional men received pardons. Riley and six others escaped the death sentence because they had deserted prior to May 13, 1846, and the declaration of war on Mexico. Riley received 59 lashes and a brand on both cheeks. The American authorities released him after his punishment. He may have eventually returned to Ireland.[18]

American authorities suppressed the news of the San Patricios after the war, although individuals who later would have key leadership roles during the Civil War knew the story. Winfield Scott, U. S. Grant, Jefferson Davis, Robert E. Lee, Braxton Bragg, Thomas (later Stonewall) Jackson, P. G. T. Beauregard, William Hardee, Richard Ewell, D. H. Hill, Joseph E. Johnston, George B. McClellan, George G. Meade, and doubtless many others witnessed the phenomenon of the San Patricio Battalion first hand. Some of those same individuals were to have direct roles in developing or approving units made up of soldiers captured from their enemies during the Civil War.[19]

The San Patricios demonstrated that American soldiers could change sides and become effective fighting forces for the enemy. It is no coincidence that the Confederacy targeted the foreign-born, and more particularly Irishmen, when the recruitment of prisoners began in late 1864.

Groups in parts of northern Alabama, northern Georgia, western North Carolina, and eastern Tennessee most openly opposed the Civil War, but resistance existed in some form over most of the region.[20] The enslaved and free African Americans supported the Union military, and contributed nearly 200,000 soldiers and sailors to the Union cause. The Union raised white regiments or battalions in every southern state except South Carolina. The number of white units raised in the Deep South ranged from one each in Alabama, Georgia, and Mississippi to eight or nine in Arkansas. Tennessee, which had officially seceded from the Union, contributed thousands of recruits to the Union cause. Current has estimated that approximately 104,000 white troops served the Union from states that joined the Confederacy, with about 70 percent of those from Tennessee and Virginia/West Virginia.[21] If that figure is correct, it is equal to nearly 10 per cent or more of those who served the Confederate army as three-year recruits.

Strong pro-southern and/or antiwar sentiment also existed in the North.[22] The Copperhead movement was strong through the Midwest, and served as vocal and constant critics to Lincoln and the war.[23] Approximately 25 percent of those who served in the Union army were foreign born, while only a little over 44 per cent were born in the United States and were of British descent.[24] A significant number of the foreign-born were essentially impressed into the military soon after arriving in this country and had weakly developed ties to the United States government or to the principles that drove the war. The draft riots in New York City in July 1863, a response to the planned implementation of a draft, demonstrated how unpopular the war was in some areas. The Draft Riots targeted African Americans, and many were killed by roving mobs.[25]

The high numbers of desertions on both sides reflected weak or weakening support for the war as it progressed. There were many reasons that men elected to desert, but for the Confederates desertions increased to a flood as it became clear that the war was lost.[26]

Thousands of men changed sides during the war and joined their former enemy's army. Dee Brown, in his classic work *The Galvanized Yankees*, gives a thorough account of mainly former Confederates who joined six new Union regiments recruited from northern prisons. Those regiments amounted to approximately 6,000 men, sent to the western frontier to fight in the Indian Wars. The Union Army formed the first unit in September 1864, with the last unit mustered out in November 1866.[27]

Hundreds, and perhaps thousands, of Confederate prisoners tried to change sides early in the war. The capture of Forts Henry and Donelson in early 1862 left 12,000 Confederate officers and men in Union prisons. Camp Douglas housed most of those men, and many of those expressed an interest in changing sides. The 10th Tennessee Infantry, made up largely of Irish immigrants from Middle Tennessee, was among the units incarcerated at Camp Douglas. One of the guard units was the 23rd Illinois Infantry, a largely Irish unit commanded by Col. James A. Mulligan. Col. Mulligan was a charismatic figure from Chicago, and it was not long before members of the 10th Tennessee requested to join the 23rd Illinois. Mulligan began recruitment of soldiers from the 10th and other units, and requested permission from Major General Henry Halleck to enlist the prisoners in his unit. Halleck forwarded that request to the War Department for approval. Hearing nothing to the contrary in a few days, Halleck gave permission for the enlistments. The War Department eventually declined the request, but not before the enlistments were made in the 23rd and 65th Illinois Infantry, which was a Scottish unit.[28] Mulligan recruited 228 prisoners for his regiment, many of whom were members of the 10th Tennessee Infantry. The service records of the 10th Tennessee indicate that 731 officers and men were captured at Fort Donelson and reached prison. Of that number, 25 died, 11 escaped with no further record, 201 exchanged with no further record, 149 enlisted in U.S. units, and 56 took the oath of allegiance to move north of the Ohio River for the duration of the war. Only 289 members of the 10th Tennessee rejoined their unit after Camp Douglas.[29]

It is impossible to know, with the state of the surviving records, how many individual soldiers changed sides during the war. It probably involved hundreds of small groups with thousands of individuals.

President Lincoln lifted the War Department's ban on recruiting Confederate prisoners of war in mid-1863, despite resistance from Secretary of War Stanton. Captain George W. Ahl raised Ahl's Independent Company Delaware Heavy Artillery at Fort Delaware in July 1863. Captain George Ahl was the second in command of Fort Delaware and ran the prison. He and his assistant, Lieutenant Abraham G. Wolfe, were the focus of the ire of the prisoners. The first group of 147 prisoners enlisted in Ahl's unit on July 15, 1863, and mustered in on July 27. One additional prisoner enlisted on July 27. Twenty more men enlisted from February 1864 to March 1865.

The enlistees served as prison guards at Fort Delaware; some were even sent on detached duty to guard Confederate officers on the way to Hilton Head Island in South Carolina and to Fort Jefferson on Dry Tortugas. All of the prisoners joined as enlisted men, although Ahl recommended one sergeant for promotion to 2nd Lieutenant. The sergeant disappeared or deserted while on furlough before approval of his promotion. The number of desertions was low: 11, or 12 if the sergeant was a deserter. All of the desertions took place while men were on furlough or in transit from detached duty. Seven men from the unit died of disease, with smallpox the most common cause. Two men died from stabbings by other members of the unit in separate incidents. Court-martials acquitted both men of murder. One of the stabbing victims had been a member of the 10th Tennessee Infantry (Confederate). One man committed suicide by gunshot while on detached guard duty at Fort Jefferson. Health issues led to the discharge of 17 men from the unit. One man left the unit early to transfer to the navy. One hundred and twenty-three men mustered out with the unit on July 27, 1865.[30]

The place of birth and occupation was recorded for all but one of the enlistees, and 60 were born outside the United States. Thirty-nine men came from Ireland, eight from Germany, and one from France; and six foreign born men were natives of England, two each from Scotland, Canada, and Switzerland. Fifteen of the men born in the U.S. had been born in northern states, with Pennsylvania (7) and Delaware (3) providing the majority. The rest were born in southern states, with Virginia (18), Georgia (17), North Carolina (13), Tennessee (12), and Alabama (11) providing most of the men. Over two-thirds of the former prisoners in Ahl's Company were farmers (78) or laborers (30). The remainder represented a range of occupations from clerks (10) and teachers (2) to stevedore (1) and stonecutter (1).[31]

Ahl's Independent Company appears to represent a case where the recruitment and use of Confederate prisoners was a success. The desertion rate was low, and the men were reliable enough to be assigned to detached duty at other prisons. This unit succeeded because the men did not have to face combat or any real hardships.

Ahl's Independent Company was not the only guard unit that recruited Confederate prisoners of war at Fort Delaware. At least two prisoners from the Cherokee Artillery (Van Den Corput's Light Artillery) joined Independent Battery A of the Pennsylvania Volunteers, commanded by Captain Stanislaw Mlotkowski, in July 1863.[32] Stoneman captured many of the surviving members of the Cherokee Artillery near the end of the war at Salisbury, along with the majority of one of the battalions formed from Union prisoners of war.

Four of ten companies of the 3rd Maryland Cavalry that were recruited at the formation of the regiment during September 1863 included Confederate prisoners from Fort Delaware. Review of the 3rd Maryland Cavalry service records reveals that the recruits included 391 prisoners; 102 were placed in Company D, 99 in Company E, 96 in Company F, and 94 in Company G. The information recorded for the Confederates included the place of birth for all but 70 of them. Ninety-one men were foreign-born, most from Ireland (54) and Germany (14). The rest were born in the United States, primarily in North Carolina (28), Georgia (37), Virginia (29), or Tennessee (23). Every northern state but Minnesota was represented among the recruits.[33]

The galvanized Yankees in the 3rd Maryland had a broad range of occupations. As might be expected for the time, the largest number of recruits were farmers (132), and the second largest were laborers (41). Some of the prisoners had job skills that were valuable to the regiment. These included 12 blacksmiths, 10 shoemakers, and five saddlers. The remaining occupations were virtually a cross section of trained professionals of their day and ranged from engineers to watch makers to stonecutters to clerks.[34]

The duty stations of the 3rd Maryland Cavalry were in southern Alabama and Louisiana, and they were involved in the battle for Mobile and the capture of Fort Morgan. The regiment did garrison duty at Fort Gaines and later New Orleans. They were part of General Bank's Army during the unsuccessful Red River campaign. A soldier killed by guerillas was the only combat death among the galvanized Yankees. Those captured from the regiment included 14 galvanized Yankees. All were paroled back to the 3rd Maryland without punishment. The death rate from disease among the four companies was low. From their recruitment in September 1863 to the mustering out of the regiment in September 1865, only 24 were lost to disease.[35]

The desertion rate among the four galvanized companies was quite high. Almost all of the men deserted at one time or another, with a significant number arrested and returned to their unit. Punishment for some of the men was imprisonment at Fort McHenry or Fort Jefferson in the Dry Tortugas, followed by eventual return to their units. Lincoln's Proclamation #124, which on March 11, 1964, offered amnesty to those who had deserted if they returned to their regiment within 60 days, brought many of the deserters back to the 3rd Maryland. One hundred and eighty-four men deserted and did not return to their units, for a net desertion rate of

47 percent. There was a single execution for attempted murder, but none were executed for desertion.[36]

Given the extremely high desertion rate, recruiting a significant number of companies made up totally of Confederate prisoners of war within a regiment seems to have been unsuccessful in the case of the 3rd Maryland Cavalry. That discouraged the experiment on a larger scale until the recruitment of six volunteer infantry regiments late in the war.

Following the example of the 3rd Maryland Cavalry, the 1st Connecticut Cavalry mustered in a number of Confederate prisoners from Fort Delaware on October 5, 1863. Robert B. Angelovich puts the total number of enlisted at 120, but review of the roster of the 1st listed just 110 enlistees on that date.[37] It is possible that a few men enlisted before or after that date to make up his full 120. The majority of the men enlisted in Company G, and most of the rest in Company F.[38] The desertion rate among the enlistees was quite high, as 43 of the 110 had deserted by February 20, 1864. Four of those men deserted just a week after enlistment. Two men had died by February 20, 1864, of which one died of a heart attack and it is likely that the other died of disease.[39] Major Blakeslee, who took command of the 1st in January 1864, did not trust the enlisted Confederates. He consolidated them into Company G, which did not accompany the rest of the regiment into action. He had what was left of the enlistees transferred from his command to Camp Chase by late April, and the surviving 65 men of those recruited in October 1863 were made part of the 1st United States Volunteer Infantry.[40] The 1st United States Infantry mustered out of service in May 1866.[41]

One incident that became infamous toward the end of the war involved fifty-three men of Company F of the 2nd North Carolina Union Volunteer Infantry. A number of those men had been members of Confederate bridge guards or local partisan ranger companies in eastern North Carolina and had joined the 2nd North Carolina in late 1863 to avoid conscription into the 66th Regiment of North Carolina State Troops. Confederate forces under the command of Gen. George E. Pickett captured the men of Company F on February 2, 1864. Pickett decided to make an example of them and treated them as deserters. He executed 22 of the men and sent the remainder to southern prisons where most died.[42]

There is evidence of other small groups of prisoners recruited into Union units during 1863, but it is beyond the current research to attempt to identify all of them and research their service records. The choices made by some of the men of the 10th Tennessee Confederate when they were recaptured after their exchange from Camp Douglas and the rebuilding of the unit illuminates this issue. Of those captured after Camp Douglas, 14 joined the U.S. Navy, six joined unspecified U.S. service, four joined the 6th U.S. Volunteers, four joined Captain Ahl's Battery, and one each joined the 34th Kentucky and the 12th Michigan.[43] The experiences of the men of the 10th Tennessee were probably not representative of more than a few Confederate units, but does clearly underscore that the question of galvanizing by, at least, Confederate prisoners of war is more complex than it appears.

There is evidence that some Union prisoners of war joined Confederate units on an individual basis as early as late 1863. Frank McElheny joined Company F of the 24th Massachusetts Infantry in October 1861. He was tried at a General Court Martial and sentenced on August 7, 1862, to five years imprisonment for violent and insubordinate conduct towards a Captain Clarke and was held in jail at New Bern, North Carolina. His sentence included a dishonorable discharge and loss of all pay and allowances. McElheny, sent to Fort Macon near present Atlantic Beach, North Carolina to serve out his term, escaped on November 1, 1863. Confederate soldiers captured him and took him to Castle Thunder in Richmond, Virginia. General Winder ordered his release on December 8, 1863, and he joined the 19th Virginia Battalion under an assumed name. He deserted from the Confederate Army before Richmond and rejoined Union lines. Members of his former company recognized him and he was arrested as a deserter. McElheny was tried for desertion and sentenced to be executed on August 6, 1864, and was executed by firing squad two days later. It is not known how many, if any, Union deserters held at Castle Thunder were allowed to follow a similar path.[44]

The most well known Union regiments filled by former Confederate prisoners of war began recruiting in the fall of 1864. Those were the six U.S. Volunteer Infantry regiments recruited for service on the western frontier. Brown published an excellent history of those regiments, and his classic work is still available.[45] Galvanized Confederate members of the 10th Tennessee Infantry joined the 5th U.S. Volunteers. Chapter 8 discusses their history with that unit.

Brown devotes a short chapter at the end of his book to galvanized Confederates based on information from the *Official Records of the War of the Rebellion*.[46] There have been brief mentions of them before and since Brown's work, but no comprehensive history of the Union counterparts to Brown's galvanized Yankees existed until the current volume.

The Confederate army did not begin recruiting Union prisoners of war for more than a year after recruitment of Confederate prisoners had begun.

The Confederate government did not make a conscious decision to begin that recruitment; it resulted from circumstances following the movement of prisoners from Andersonville to the east. Andersonville prison, with 33,000 prisoners, almost emptied out after the fall of Atlanta. Those prisoners, sent mainly to Charleston and Savannah, quickly exceeded the ability of both cities to deal with them. The mass influx of prisoners, followed by a small-pox epidemic in Charleston, led to the decision to order a new prison to be built at Florence, South Carolina. Construction started on September 12. Camp Lawton in Millen Georgia had been under construction before the virtual abandonment of Andersonville, but it was not ready to receive prisoners until October 15. It was during the chaos following the mass removal of prisoners from Andersonville that the recruitment of prisoners for the Confederate Army began.[47]

★ CHAPTER 2 ★

Civil War Prisons

ON MAY 12, 1865, Pvt. Martin J. Buzzard slipped over the side of the steamboat *Jesse H. Lacy*, which was carrying him from Fort Leavenworth to the mouth of the Niobrana River in the Northwest Territories, and deserted from Company D of the 5th U.S. Volunteers. He swam across the river and eventually made his way back home to Lancaster County, Pennsylvania. He and three of his brothers formed the notorious Buzzard Gang after the war, which terrorized Lancaster County for the rest of the nineteenth century. He would spend the last 25 years of his life as a reformed criminal, and he died in 1921 at 80 years old.[1]

Buzzard began his military career with the 2nd Pennsylvania Cavalry, which he joined in Philadelphia on September 15, 1863. He rose to the rank of corporal before he was captured at Chickahominy, Virginia, on May 14, 1864, during Sheridan's raid to the James River. Buzzard went to Andersonville, and then Camp Lawton after the fall of Atlanta in September 1864. O'Neill recruited him from Camp Lawton into Company B of the 10th Tennessee during the fall of 1864, and Union forces captured him after a battle at Egypt Station, Mississippi, along with more than 250 former Union prisoners of war who had joined the Confederate Army. Buzzard joined the rest of the galvanized Confederates at Alton Prison in Alton, Illinois, where most joined the newly formed 5th U.S. Volunteers. That unit was composed mostly of former Confederate prisoners of war, sent to the west to fight hostile American Indian groups that threatened frontier settlers.[2]

Martin Buzzard was one of almost 410,000 soldiers captured and imprisoned during the Civil War. Many more were captured and paroled in the field; approximately 56,000 of those captured and confined from both sides did not survive. Buzzard was one of thousands who changed sides while imprisoned.[3]

Both sides were unprepared to handle prisoners of war when the Civil War began. Many people in both the North and South thought the war would be over quickly and were not ready for the long, hard struggle it became. Prisoners were initially paroled and released, sometimes by commanders in the field, and then later were paroled and held for exchange. Some attention had been paid to the issue of prisoners of war by the Confederate Congress prior to the incarceration of large numbers of prisoners. The Confederate Congress had passed an act on May 27, 1861, that had made the Secretary of War responsible for the safety of and for feeding prisoners. The Secretary of War, with the concurrence of the President, ordered the Quartermaster General to provide the same quality and amount of rations to prisoners as those given to enlisted men in the Confederate Army. The Confederate government did not plan for the establishment of prisons, and Richmond soon became the point in the east where prisoners of war were concentrated.[4]

The first major test for the South came in July 1861 when the first battle at Manassas netted 1,300 Union prisoners. The provost marshal of the City of Richmond, Brig. Gen. John H. Winder, who was in charge of the prisoners, initially confiscated the John L. Ligon and Sons Tobacco Factory to shelter the prisoners. Winder then confiscated the Howard and Ross factories to use as additional prisons. Mayo's and Taylor's factories were soon pressed into service, and additional factory and warehouse buildings were confiscated and used as the number of Union prisoners grew.[5] Libby Prison, in the former Libby and Son, Ship Chandlers and Grocers building, opened in March 1862. Libby Prison became the most notorious of the prisons in downtown Richmond, and one of the most infamous in the Confederacy, although conditions there were far better than enlisted men faced at Belle Isle and the other open prison pens later in the war. Libby Prison primarily held Union officers, as officials in both the north and south soon concluded that officers had to be separated from enlisted men as a security measure.[6] Prisoners continued to stream into Richmond at a rapid rate. Belle Isle prison for enlisted men opened on an island in the James River where it flowed through Richmond. Belle Isle housed 3,000 prisoners within two weeks after it opened in mid-June. There were 5,000 at the prison two weeks later. Belle Isle was an overflow facility abandoned and reoccupied as needed. The Richmond prisons were under the command of Captain Henry Wirz, of Andersonville infamy, as of August 1862.[7]

In the north, Gen. John H. Winder was perhaps the most hated man who was associated with southern prisons as the war progressed. Winder would have probably been executed at war's end, had he not died of natural causes at Florence Prison on February 6, 1865. John Winder's father, Gen. William Henry Winder, led the American forces in the disastrous defeat at the Battle of Bladensburg on August 23, 1814, which led to the capture of Washington, D. C. and the burning of the Capitol and White House. The Winder family suffered from the disgrace of William Winder, and John Winder pursued a military career with the goal of restoring the Winder name.[8]

John Winder entered West Point at 15 years old on August 5th, just 18 days before his father's disastrous defeat at Bladensburg. Some of the cadets treated Winder badly after the failed battle, and he took six years to graduate. He experienced academic difficulty at West Point in some subjects and exercised poor personal discipline for the first few years.[9]

Winder remained in the military except for the period from 1823–1828, during which he tried and failed to manage his father-in-law's plantation in Georgia. His wife died in 1826, and Winder returned to the army in 1828. He remarried in 1830 to a widow of substantial means. He had inherited a number of slaves from his former father-in-law before his remarriage and had invested in schemes that failed and left him in debt. Winder concentrated on his military career for the rest of his life and was stationed at a number of posts prior to the Mexican War. Winder joined the American Army at Vera Cruz in April 1847, where he was charged with organizing recruits. He joined the main body of Winfield Scott's troops after the Battle of Cerro Gordo. Winder's artillery battery took part in the Battle of Contreras but had a larger role in the Battle of Churubusco. It appears that Winder's men were under fire from the battery served by the San Patricio Battalion during that battle, and he must have been aware of the San Patricios and their role in the war. Winder was brevetted Major for bravery at Churubusco and to Lieutenant Colonel for bravery later at Mexico City. Winder served as Lieutenant Governor of Vera Cruz until the peace treaty was signed on July 29, 1848. The experience gained at Vera Cruz was to be helpful to him in filling a similar role in Richmond during the Civil War, but it did not provide him with diplomatic skills, which proved to be missing at Richmond.[10]

At the start of the Civil War, Winder travelled first to Montgomery and then to Richmond trying to gain a rank and station that he thought was appropriate to his military experience and achievements. Winder eventually won an appointment as Brigadier General and Inspector General of the Richmond military camps. Winder's autocratic nature did not serve him well at Richmond. The press reviled him and even accused him of being too lenient in his treatment of the prisoners of war held in Richmond. Winder, promoted to the post of Provost Marshall of Richmond on February 27,

1862, was also in charge of enforcing martial law in the surrounding Henrico County. His new role gave him authority over both civilians and members of the military.[11]

The Union was much better prepared to deal with prisoners of war than the South. The failure of the Union Army at the first Battle of Manassas had shown Union military leaders that the war was likely to be a protracted contest. Quartermaster-General Montgomery C. Meigs was first given responsibility for Confederate prisoners of war, and he recommended the appointment of a Commissary-General of Prisoners. This was something that the South did not do until late in the war. Colonel William Hoffman became Commissary-General of Prisoners in late September 1861.[12]

Hoffman was born on December 2, 1807, to Captain William Hoffman, a career military officer. Captain (and much later Colonel) Hoffman and his wife had 10 children and had no other means of support for their family than his army salary. Captain Hoffman had to be miserly with his small salary and large household to support, a trait later shared by his son. The younger Hoffman entered West Point in 1823 and was graduated 18th out of 46 in his class in 1829; he was in the same class as Robert E. Lee. Hoffman went on to the west to fight American Indians and Mormons under the command of Gen. Winfield Scott. He fought in every battle in the Mexican War and was wounded at the Battle of Churubusco. Hoffman was brevetted to Lieutenant Colonel for his courage at the battles of Contreras and Churubusco. He, like Winder, doubtless fought against the San Patricio Battalion at Churubusco. He must have been aware of who the San Patricios were and the role they played for the Mexican Army. Hoffman went on to fight in the west against American Indians after the Mexican War. He was promoted to Lieutenant Colonel and sent to Texas to command the 8th Infantry immediately before the Civil War began. Confederate forces detained Hoffman and his men as prisoners of war in April 1861 until his parole on April 24. He received a promotion to Commissary-General of Prisoners on September 30, 1861.[13]

Hoffman's first major test came after the capture of Forts Henry and Donelson in Tennessee. The surrenders in February 1862 left 12,000 Confederate soldiers in Union hands. They joined the 2,500 prisoners captured on Roanoke Island (North Carolina) just eight days before. Hoffman had devoted his time and attention to that point on building a new prison on Johnson Island, and his prison system was woefully unprepared to accommodate the large numbers of new prisoners.[14] There was insufficient space to house all of those new prisoners, and Hoffman turned to existing training camps refitted as prisons. He set up permanent prisons at Camp Douglas in Chicago,[15] Camp Chase in Columbus, Ohio, and Camp Morton in Indianapolis, Indiana.[16] He established temporary prisons at Camp Butler near Springfield, Illinois,[17] and Camp Randall at Madison, Wisconsin.[18] He also used the newly constructed prison at Johnson Island.[19] Fort Delaware, located on the Delaware River, housed prisoners in small numbers from the beginning of the war. Expansion of this prison in 1862 made it a major prison as the war continued.[20] These prisons along with Alton Prison housed the majority of the prisoners of war held prior to a cartel of exchange, which went into effect on July 22, 1862. Hoffman added prisons at Rock Island in Illinois,[21] Elmira in New York,[22] and Point Lookout in Maryland as the war continued.[23]

THE DIX-HILL CARTEL

The Dix-Hill Cartel resulted from months of negotiations aimed at codifying an exchange protocol. Exchanges began immediately after the exchange cartel was negotiated on July 22, 1862. The Union and Confederacy exchanged privates on a one-to-one basis, and full generals were worth 60 privates. Union prisons held 20,600 prisoners in June 1862, while the Confederacy released 16,000 prisoners by late August 1862.[24] The exchanges were hardly smooth, and numerous problems emerged as they proceeded. Camp Chase near Columbus, Ohio, housed Union prisoners from the western prisons, and Camp Parole in Annapolis, Maryland, housed those from the east. City Point, Virginia, was the eastern exchange point for Confederate prisoners, while Vicksburg, Mississippi, was the western point.[25]

General Halleck, then General in Chief of the Union Army, stopped the cartel on May 23, 1863. The prisoner exchanges were over by June. James M. Gillispie maintains that the reason for the collapse of the cartel was entirely because of the South's insistence on not exchanging black prisoners and their threats to return these prisoners to their former masters or auction them off as slaves and to execute their white officers.[26] It is Gillispie's view that the North was simply protecting their soldiers as they were obligated to do. There is a great deal of merit in Gillispie's argument, but others have ascribed additional motives to the North that led them to end the cartel. Lonnie R. Speer also states that the exchange issue over black soldiers was the major cause of the collapse, but there also had been a series of disagreements over exchanges that led up to the demise of the cartel.[27] Charles W. Sanders presents the argument that President Lincoln and Secretary of War Stanton used the stalemate over black prisoners as the excuse to end the cartel since the exchange benefited the South more than the North.[28] J. Michael Martinez acknowledges that the treatment of black soldiers was the major reason for the collapse of the cartel.[29] He also concludes that Confederate soldiers left prison in better shape than the Union prisoners and could rejoin their old units in much higher numbers. He maintains that General Grant believed that refusal to exchange southern prisoners had strategic value in that it denied sorely needed troops to the Confederate ranks. Whatever the reason or reasons for the collapse of the exchange cartel, it was to signal a grim, and often fatal, new chapter for Civil War prisoners of war.

The effects of the cartel had been dramatic in both the north and south. Hunter estimates that there were 19,000 Confederate prisoners at the start of the cartel. The end of the cartel forced Hoffman to open several new prisons to handle all the prisoners. The number of prisoners held in northern prisons had decreased to 5,012 by September 1862 and then to 1,286 by the end of the year. Hoffman had closed all but six prisons by that time, and three of those six held civilian prisoners. Hoffman used mainly Alton Prison, Camp Chase, and Johnson's Island to house Confederate prisoners of war after this point. The Dix-Hill exchange cartel gave Hoffman the opportunity to reorganize the Union prisoner of war system and allowed him to gain true control of the prisons for the first time.[30] He permanently closed both Camp Butler and Camp Randall in spring 1862, both of which had proven to be unsuitable.[31] The impact on southern prisons was much the same. Only the Richmond prisons, with the exception of Belle Isle, remained in use.[32]

An important difference in Union and Confederate prisons as the number of prisoners soared on both sides was that the Confederates lacked a plan for dealing with the crisis. Hoffman, on the other hand, provided the unified command and guidance needed to use existing resources and add resources as needed. Hoffman was in charge of all Union military prisons until he received a promotion to Brevet Brigadier General in October 1864. His new orders split command of the prisons, with General Henry W. Wessells in command of those in the east and General Hoffman in command of the prisons west of the Mississippi. General Wessells, captured with his entire command at Plymouth, North Carolina, first was held in Libby Prison and then prisons in Danville, Macon, and Charleston prior to his exchange. His military career mirrored that of Hoffman prior to the Civil War, but he had held responsible field command positions during the war. He brought a personal understanding of how Confederate prisons worked to his position.

General Wessells appears to have simply continued Hoffman's existing policies during his tenure, and General Hoffman resumed command of all prisons in February 1865.[33]

The collapse of the exchange cartel put the stopper back in the bottle, and prison populations north and south soon exceeded those from before the cartel. The South held 50,000 prisoners by August 1864, while the North held 67,000 Confederate prisoners.[34]

The number of prisons used by north and south totaled 150 by the end of the war. Speer has broken those prisons down into seven types: existing jails and prisons; coastal fortifications; old buildings converted into prisons; barracks enclosed by high fences; a cluster of tents enclosed by high fences; barren stockades; and barren ground.[35] The use of existing jails and prisons was common in both the north and south, and these were the first type used for holding prisoners of war on both sides. Alton Prison in the north, which had been an abandoned prison, was the most well known example of this type. The Union more commonly used coastal fortifications, and the only one of this type used in the south was Castle Pinckney in Charleston. Fort Warren and Fort Delaware were the most well known of this type in the north. Old buildings converted into prisons were more common in the south and included all of the Richmond prisons except Belle Isle. Gratiot Street Prison in St. Louis was the most well known of this type in the north. Several of the largest and well-known prisons in the north were barracks enclosed by high fences. Those included Camp Chase, Camp Douglas, Camp Morton, Johnson Island, Rock Island, and Elmira Prison. All but two of those, Rock Island and Johnson Island, had been military training camps. A cluster of tents enclosed by high fences or a berm, a rarely used type, included Camp Lookout in the north and Belle Isle in the south. The barren stockade type was exclusive to the south. Barren stockades were compounds surrounded by a stockade or a berm with a stockade; they were stripped of vegetation and shelter of any kind. Speer included the prison at Cahaba in this category, but the prison was primarily within an abandoned and unfinished warehouse that was partially roofed and surrounded by a plank fence.[36] Most of the most notorious prisons late in the war were barren stockades, which included Andersonville, Florence, and Camp Lawton. Barren ground prisons were often expedient answers to securing prisoners after a battle, and simply involved securing prisoners with a guard line. Camp Sorghum in Columbia, South Carolina, was the most well known longer-term example of this prison type.

THE RICHMOND PRISONS

The prisoner situation in Richmond became critical even while the cartel was in force. Union prisoners to be exchanged were sent to Richmond and then to the exchange point. Food was in short supply for the civilians in Richmond from early in the war, and the shortages made worse by the need to feed thousands of prisoners of war. A ten square block of Richmond was looted by a large mob when a riot broke out on April 2, 1862, over the food shortages and the resulting price hikes. Reserve troops ended the riot, and only the continued presence of troops kept another mob from forming the next day. The South lacked a centralized command structure for military prisons, and Gen. Winder only had authority over the Richmond prisons and later Salisbury Prison in North Carolina by the time of the cartel. This meant the South lacked a single voice like Hoffman who could order new prisons built when needed and oversee the logistics of caring for the increasingly large number of prisoners.[37]

The prison populations in the Richmond prisons grew rapidly after the collapse of the cartel. Isaac Carrington, in a report prepared for the Confederate leadership dated November 18, 1863, reported the Richmond prison population as "Libby, 1,044; Belle Isle 6,300; hospital 728; and 3,579 in the various warehouses."[38] The death rate at Belle Isle rose to over a hundred a month, and the prisoners suffered from a shortage of rations, violence inflicted on them by other prisoners because of the shortage of guards, severe overcrowding, and a raging smallpox epidemic. The number of prisoners at Belle Isle reached 8,000 by early 1864.[39] Secretary of War Seddon concluded that the only way to address those problems was to ship prisoners out of Richmond to the south, and he ordered Sidney Winder, son of Gen. John Winder, to go to Georgia to find a suitable site for a new prison. That set in motion events and decisions that led to the construction of Andersonville Prison, the most notorious of all of the Civil War prisons.[40]

Castle Thunder

Castle Thunder and Libby Prison were two of the most important prisons made from existing buildings in downtown Richmond. Castle Thunder included three buildings and opened in August 1862. Greaner's Tobacco Warehouse, which faced Cary Street, was the middle building, with Palmer's factory and Whitlock's Warehouse forming the two wings. A high fence linked Palmer's Factory and Whitlock's Warehouse and created a secure yard behind Greaner's Warehouse. The yard contained the sinks (latrines) and was also a space the prisoner's could use for exercise. Water for the prisoners came from the James River, and the prison had gas heat and lights. The three buildings that made up Castle Thunder housed different types of prisoners. Greaner's Warehouse held Confederate deserters, citizens arrested for disloyalty, and soldiers who had violated military rules and were awaiting sentencing. Whitlock's Warehouse held women facing various charges and African American prisoners. Palmer's Factory held deserters from the Union Army.[41] Castle Thunder (Greaner's Warehouse) had a capacity of 652 prisoners, Whitlock's Warehouse had a capacity of 350, and Palmer's Factory had a capacity of 400. Many Richmond residents criticized the guards of Castle Thunder, made up of over aged men (45–55) and under aged boys (16–18) from the Second Virginia Reserve.[42]

The women prisoners held at Castle Thunder deserve special mention. The reasons for their arrests and incarcerations included "treason, disloyalty, contributing to the demoralization of the soldiers, and a number of other offenses." Women who were caught "wearing men's clothing" were also jailed there under the assumption they were spies. These included women who pretended to be men so they could join and serve in the Confederate army. One woman, identified as Loreta Janeta Velazquez, took the identity Lieutenant Harry T. Buford and organized the Arkansas Grays, before she ended up at Castle Thunder. Women believed to be married to Union officers or have ties to the Union army, were also sent there with their children.[43]

Captain George W. Alexander commanded Castle Thunder soon after it opened. Captain Alexander was the focus of many rumors dealing with the cruel treatment of prisoners. A Congressional investigation into his behavior was authorized on April 4, 1863, and hearings began immediately. Captain Alexander exacted a number of types of punishment of prisoners, including killing two prisoners, which was attributed to guards. A report prepared by a majority of the investigative committee members cleared Captain Alexander of wrongdoing; although one minority report condemned the methods he had used but recommended no punishment. The second minority report "condemned his administration" and recommended the removal of both Captain Alexander and General Winder from their positions. The two guards escaped punishment.[44] General Winder removed Captain Alexander from Castle Thunder after a court of inquiry cleared him of new charges. Gen. Winder replaced him with Captain Lucien W. Richardson on December 19, 1963. Captain Alexander briefly showed up later as the Commander of Salisbury prison.[45] The saga of Captain Alexander is important in that there was rarely a public outcry by citizens of the Confederacy about conditions in southern prisons. This case was probably more motivated by dislike of Alexander than concern for the prisoners, but it did result in a Congressional investigation and discussions concerning prison conditions.

Authorities transferred large numbers of prisoners from Castle Thunder to Salisbury Prison by mid-July 1864. Castle Thunder held 954 prisoners when Richmond fell and the guards fled the city. The property ended up as a parking lot for the Phillip Morris tobacco company in the twentieth century.[46]

Libby Prison

The Libby & Son Warehouse, constructed between 1845 and 1852, housed Libby Prison. The owners of the building had 48 hours to vacate when General Winder seized it for a prison. It occupied an entire block in downtown Richmond and faced Cary Street. The building had a basement and three upper floors. Each upper floor had three rooms that measured 103 by 44 feet. The ceiling in each room was only eight feet high, and the building had running water drawn from the river. The two uppermost stories held prisoners, while the rooms on the first floor housed an office, a kitchen, and a hospital. The upper three floors had stoves and sinks in each room.[47]

Libby prison mainly held Union officers, but prior to the establishment of the Belle Isle prison camp it also housed Union enlisted men as well as private citizens thought to be disloyal to the Confederacy. Union prisoners awaiting exchange stayed at Libby prison while the Dix-Hill Cartel was in force. Life in Libby prison was never pleasant for the prisoners, but became decidedly worse after the collapse of the cartel. There were over 1,200 Union officers held there by the fall of 1863. Over 125,000 Union prisoners of war passed through Libby prison from March 1862 to the end of the war. [48]

The prisoners received fewer rations at Libby prison as the prison population increased in the fall of 1863. The reduction in rations coincided with severe food shortages in Richmond. Richmond prisons held 14,000 prisoners by that time. The authorities allowed Libby prisoners supplemental rations with food purchases from Richmond and food boxes from relatives and from Union government shipments. Wood to cook the rations and to heat the rooms was often in short supply. Despite those hardships, the prisoners at Libby were in far better shape than the enlisted men who tried to survive in the Belle Isle prison camp.[49]

The available documents list only 43 successful escapes from the Richmond prisons, primarily from the summer of 1864 through the end of the war.[50] Most of those 43 men took part in a single escape. Their names, added at the end of the individual alphabetical sheets in black ink, apparently were not originally part of the register. Those men took part in a mass escape from Libby prison on February 9, 1864. That escape was the most famous mass escape from a southern prison during the Civil War, when 109 prisoners managed to escape via a tunnel. Less than half of the men who escaped were recaptured. The incomplete official record listed 37 of the 59 who actually made their way to safety.[51]

The Libby prison building survived the fires set by Confederates as they abandoned Richmond on April 3, 1865. The fires consumed tobacco warehouses and flour mills along the Richmond waterfront, and spread through a good bit of the commercial district. Major Thomas P. Turner, who commanded Richmond prisons, burned the prison records and escaped Richmond to join Lee's army on the way to its surrender at Appomattox Court House. Major Turner, fearing punishment for his role during the war, left the country, only to return ten years later to spend the rest of his life as a dentist in Tennessee. Richard Turner, who had been the jail keeper at Libby, ended up in his own prison. Turner escaped after a short time; he was recaptured, tried, and spent a year in prison for his mistreatment of prisoners. Libby Prison held 3,000 Confederate prisoners for a period after the war. The prison building reverted to commercial use by the Southern Fertilizer Company after the war. It was dismantled in 1888 and rebuilt in Chicago as the Libby Prison War Museum. Interest in the museum waned and the venture failed. The building was torn down in 1899.[52]

Belle Isle

Belle Isle was the deadliest of all of the Richmond prisons. The prison was located on an 80-acre island in the James River that was used first as a resort area and then as the site of a mining company and an iron foundry. The currents in the James River were treacherous around the island because of its proximity to the fall line. The prison was located on low, level ground on the north end of the island, and encompassed six acres surrounded by a low berm that marked the dead line. Guards occupied the slope above the prison and guarded the only bridge to the mainland. The prisoners were sheltered in tents, but there were rarely enough tents for all of the prisoners. Belle Isle was visible from one of the windows of Libby Prison, and the view of it served as a reminder to the officers incarcerated at Libby Prison of the much harsher conditions faced by the Union enlisted men.[53]

The Belle Isle prison, established in June 1862, housed 5,000 prisoners by mid-July. It relieved much of the overcrowding in the other Richmond prisons, but closed by September 23, 1862, after prisoner exchanges under the Dix-Hill Cartel.[54]

The Belle Isle prison reopened on January 17, 1863, as a flood of prisoners reached Richmond from the Battle of Murfreesboro. Use of Belle Isle this time was to be brief again—it closed after further prisoner exchanges. However, the prison reopened on May 16 of the same year to receive prisoners from Virginia battlefields.[55]

The prison population at Belle Isle steadily grew after the prisoner exchange ceased. There were 6,300 prisoners by November 18, 1863, and 8,000 by early 1864. The death rate climbed to over a hundred per month, with rations and adequate shelter in short supply. The guard force on the island was inadequate to protect the weaker prisoners from the stronger, and both overcrowding and a smallpox epidemic took a high toll among the prisoners.[56] Andersonville Prison was constructed to relieve the overcrowding in Richmond, and prisoners from Belle Isle were sent south by February 25, 1864, before the new prison was even completed. The *Richmond Examiner* of March 30, 1864, reported a nearly empty Belle Isle because of the prisoners sent to the south and to the north.

After more battles, Belle Isle once again housed 6,000 prisoners by June 1864. The population at Belle Isle remained very high until October 1864, when most prisoners were shipped to Salisbury prison, though a small number were sent to Danville. Belle Isle closed as a prison at that time, and the property returned to its owners on February 10, 1865.[57]

ANDERSONVILLE PRISON

The Confederates built Andersonville Prison, or Camp Sumter as it was referred to by Confederates, on Stockade Creek, a branch of what was ironically named Sweet Water Creek. The prison, built to house 10,000 prisoners, confined 33,000 by August 1864. A small stockade, called Castle Reed, held Union officers within a half mile of the main prison until May 1864. The first prisoners, largely from Belle Isle, arrived at the main prison on February 25, 1864, before construction was finished. The original prison was an open stockade that covered 16 ½ acres, with Stockade Creek dividing the stockade into two sections. As prisoners continued to pour into the stockade, the authorities expanded the prison to 26 ½-acres, which meant that there were 1,245 prisoners per acre when the prison reached its peak population. The 55th Georgia Infantry initially served as guards at Andersonville, and they later served the same function at Florence Prison. Captain Henry Wirz replaced Col. Alexander W. Persons of the 55th Georgia, the first commandant of the prison, by order of Gen. Winder on June 17, 1864.[58]

Andersonville Prison became the symbol for southern brutality in the handling of Union prisoners: almost 13,000 men, or nearly 35 per cent of the 41,000 men held there, died.[59] A very large body of literature exists about the prison in the form of both prisoner accounts[60] and later histories.[61] Many of the prisoner accounts, particularly those written in the late nineteenth century, were both derivative of earlier accounts and exaggerations of conditions the prisoners had faced, but the reality of Andersonville was and remains an American horror story.[62] Sadly, the issues that surfaced at Andersonville were to recur, to different degrees, at the major prisons in Millen, Florence, and Salisbury as the war continued.

The human disaster that Andersonville became was the product of a number of issues that were both within and outside of the control of the Confederate officials. The size of the stockade was insufficient almost from the start, and yet the officials in Richmond insisted on sending more and more prisoners to the south. Gen. Winder assumed command of Andersonville and the Georgia and South Carolina prisons on June 3, 1864. He arrived on June 17, at a point when the prison population totaled 21,539. Gen. Winder added ten acres to the stockade by late June, but by then the prison population exceeded 25,000. As previously mentioned, the prison population reached 33,000 by late August 1864, shortly before the majority of the prisoners were moved east after the fall of Atlanta on September 2. The overcrowding at Andersonville was a major factor that led to the deaths of many prisoners. It was impossible to maintain any standard of sanitation within the stockade, and the sinks built along the creek were inadequate for the number of prisoners who were present.[63]

A second major factor that contributed to the high death toll at Andersonville was the lack of shelter provided to the prisoners. Andersonville was a barren stockade, with a dead line placed to prevent prisoners from approaching the stockade, and sinks constructed along the creek. Prisoners were left on their own to construct shelters and were not provided tools or building materials. Most of the men who survived did so by constructing shebangs; they dug holes large enough for those who shared the shebang and covered and water proofed it with whatever they could find. The lack of shelters was made worse by the inadequate supply of clothing and blankets among the prisoners. Many men died from exposure because they did not have even a rudimentary shelter. The lack of shelter was due in part to the Confederate officials' inability to purchase lumber, nails, and tools. Only a few open barracks were constructed inside the stockade late in its history.[64]

Lack of clean water was a major cause of death and disease in the prison. The flow of Stockade Creek was not sufficient to flush out the wastes from the sinks. Human waste from two upstream guard camps, as well as waste and grease dumped into the stream from the bakery and cookhouse that were upstream from the prison further polluted the creek. The authorities eventually moved the cookhouse to alleviate at least that part of the problem. Prisoners dug wells without proper tools to get clean water.[65]

The quantity and quality of rations served at the prison were contributing causes to the high disease and death rates within Andersonville. Green vegetables were not available to the main prison population. The prison sutler sold some vegetables at high prices to those who could afford them. Corn meal in raw or cooked form was the main food supplied to the prisoners. The mills that provided the corn meal to the prison lacked bolting cloth and so the prisoners received a mixture of meal and ground corncobs. The prisoners did not have sifters, and thus the ground cobs were eaten with the meal. The cobs aggravated the dysentery and diarrhea that was ubiquitous among the prisoners and doubtless contributed to deaths of men already weakened by disease.[66] The authorities originally believed that a steady supply of beef would be available for the prisoners from the herds in north Florida. That did not turn out to be the case, however, as it proved impossible to find drivers to deliver the cattle to the prison. Further, the cookhouse and bakery built a few months after the prison opened could not feed the steadily increasing number of prisoners. Prisoners complained about the quality of the food from those facilities, but lacked the utensils and often fuel needed to cook their own rations.[67] Thousands of prisoners suffered from scurvy because of the lack of fresh vegetables or antiscorbutics like vinegar. The prisoners received some supplies of antiscorbutics by late August, but not before many deaths had occurred, with scurvy as a primary or secondary cause.[68] Insufficient rations at Andersonville remained a problem, compounded by a supply and transport system that was failing as the Confederacy neared its end.

The overcrowding, exposure, contaminated water, inadequate sanitation, and both insufficient and poor quality rations caused widespread medical problems and eventually death among the prisoners. Lack of adequate medical facilities, inadequate or incompetent medical staff, and an insufficient supply of proper drugs to treat the prisoners compounded the other issues faced by the prisoners. The prison hospital was originally located within the stockade and soon proved to have insufficient space to treat all of the prisoners who needed medical attention. Further, the hospital did not practice proper sanitation, and patients often picked up additional infections. Part of this can be attributed to the state of medicine in the mid nineteenth century, but overcrowding and the lack of proper procedures even for the age were major causes. Gangrene, acquired in the hospital, spread easily and killed and maimed many prisoners, and it became worse with time. Medical supplies had become scarce in the Confederacy by 1864, and surgeons often relied on folk cures that did not work or actually harmed their patients. The authorities later moved the hospital outside the stockade, but overcrowding kept seriously ill men out of the hospital on a daily basis.[69] Speer attributed the "main causes of death" at Andersonville to "scurvy, diarrhea, dysentery, typhoid, smallpox, and hospital gangrene."[70]

The guard force at Andersonville originally consisted of the 55th, 56th, and 57th Georgia Infantry and the 26th Alabama Infantry. Some of those troops lacked guns, and no tents were available for their use. An artillery company from Florida joined the guard force when artillery pieces became available. The bulk of the guard force was made up of newly formed reserve units composed of those too young or too old for regular military service. Those men were untrained, poorly disciplined, and never received uniforms or many of the accoutrements provided to regular troops. By August the 55th Georgia and the Florida artillery company were the only regular troops stationed at Andersonville, and the 230 men present of the 55th Georgia were described in an inspection report as being "thoroughly demoralized, mutinous, and entirely without discipline." That same report described the reserve and militia guards as "totally without discipline, and their officers are incapable of instructing them, being ignorant of their own duties." The guard force at that time totaled 3,067, of which 2,282 were available for duty. The daily guard forced required 784 men. The artillery company was the only well trained and disciplined unit on post. There was adequate artillery to guard the post, but 452 of the men assigned to the post lacked weapons.[71]

Almost all of the prisoners left Andersonville within a month of the fall of Atlanta; those thought to be fit to travel were sent mainly to Charleston and Savannah. Most of the officers held at Macon were sent to Charleston in late July and then to Columbia, South Carolina, by early October. The transfer of prisoners from Andersonville began on September 5, and 7,700 were sent by September 10. Groups of prisoners continued to leave Andersonville through the month of September.[72] The prison population of Andersonville numbered 1,359 by the end of November. Gen. Winder transferred his headquarters to the newly finished Camp Lawton near Millen, Georgia, by October 9 and arrived there on October 11. He left Col. George C. Gibbs in command at Andersonville. Captain Wirz remained at Andersonville as the commander of the interior of the stockade. The prison did not completely empty of prisoners until May 1865.[73]

THE FLORENCE STOCKADE

Charleston was unprepared to care for the large numbers of prisoners sent from Andersonville. No existing prison at Charleston was large enough to hold the prisoners. The Charleston Fairgrounds, which included the Washington Race Course, became the Charleston prison. The Charleston Fairgrounds lacked sufficient shelter and water for the large number of prisoners it held, and the prisoners dug shallow wells to gain access to brackish groundwater. Yellow fever broke out among the prisoners on September 11, which threatened to spread to the city. The outbreak of disease, the overcrowding at the Fairgrounds, and the continuing flow of prisoners from Andersonville led Major-General Samuel Jones to order Major Frederick Warley to build a new prison at Florence, South Carolina. Florence sat at the juncture of three railroads and was remote enough to be safe from Union raids.[74]

What was probably the beginning of the recruitment of prisoners to join the Confederate army occurred at the Charleston Fairgrounds. The Confederates aggressively recruited men from the prisons to work on the Charleston defenses on Sullivan's Island, and over three hundred responded. The authorities targeted those whose enlistment had expired, particularly Irish prisoners. The authorities sent approximately a third of the recruits back to the Fairgrounds prison, presumably for refusing to work, and the effort was unsuccessful. Over 800 men at Charleston asked to join the Confederate Army. Those men went to the new Florence Stockade.[75]

Construction of the new Florence prison began on September 12, 1864, upon selection of the prison site. Major Warley impressed 1,000 slaves from nearby plantations to come with their tools in hand to construct the prison. The new prison, which was a barren stockade, formed an east-west oriented rectangle and followed the initial plan for Andersonville. The prison encompassed 23 ½ acres. A palisade was made of heavy, undressed timbers buried three to four feet into the ground that projected twelve feet above.

Dirt piled against the stockade from a five-foot deep ditch that was dug outside the stockade formed a continuous nine-foot high walkway for the guards. A deadline built ten to twelve feet inside the palisade was made of wooden posts and rails. The slaves cut the trees inside to form the palisade, leaving a stash on the ground for firewood and to build shelters. Prisoners had to build their own shelters inside the stockade. Pye Branch, like Stockade Creek at Andersonville, bisected the stockade into two parts. The main living area for the prisoners was to the east, with support facilities to the west. The swamp around Pye Branch amounted to about six acres within the stockade. Platforms were built on the four corners of the stockade for artillery pieces, although probably not all were used.[76]

The prison hospital was located in the northwest corner of the prison. A map drawn by Sergeant-Major Robert H. Kellogg depicts the hospital as five buildings.[77] However, a description of the hospital by Sydney Andrews, written during a trip he made to the stockade after the war, indicates that it included seven log buildings that were each 40x20 feet.[78] Oliver Gates, quoted by Rev. Albert H. Ledoux, puts the number of hospital buildings at seven, but says that each was 130 by 60 feet in size.[79] The hospital buildings had dirt floors, and according to Kellogg (1868:326) had shake roofs held in place by heavy poles. The original hospital was located outside the stockade, but moved inside the stockade in early November.[80]

The first 1,500 prisoners arrived at Florence on September 15, well before the stockade was finished. Guards held initial arrivals in a field near the stockade. The guard force assembled to contain the prisoners consisted of over 100 members of the reserves, who were insufficient to prevent escapes. The precarious situation led Warley to call for help from local citizens, and a cavalry and an artillery unit soon joined the guard force.[81] Many prisoners tried to escape and at least 21 made it to Union lines at that time, a large portion of the 53 known successful escapes over the complete history of the prison.[82] The prisoners moved into the unfinished stockade on September 18.[83]

Major Warley asked to be relieved of command of the Florence prison, and Col. George P. Harrison, formerly of the 32nd Georgia Infantry, replaced him on September 20. Harrison, like Warley before him, requested more guards, and the authorities told him that he could only have more guards if he took the 6,000 prisoners still held at the Charleston Fairground with their 600-man guard force. The guard force gradually increased as South Carolina reserve troops were posted to Florence.[84]

There were 12,362 prisoners at Florence by October 12, guarded by a guard force of about 1,600 that included 1,200 reserve troops. The guard force also included the 5th Georgia Infantry, detachments from artillery companies, and a small cavalry detachment. The prisoners included 860 men who were in the hospitals and 20 parolees. The 807 men who had asked to enlist in the Confederate army were not included in the total. The guard force reported the death rate in the prison as 20 to 50 daily, and the main diseases observed in the stockade were scurvy and diarrhea. The health of most of the men, covered with vermin and filth as they were, was poor. They also lacked blankets and were poorly clothed. Medical facilities in the prison were lacking, with only one medical officer present. Further, the men lacked shelter and did not have sufficient cooking utensils to prepare their raw rations.[85] This was a very bad start for a prison thought by some prisoners to be worse than Andersonville.

Florence Stockade had its own Capt. Wirz in the personage of Lt. James Barrett of the 5th Georgia Infantry. Barrett, appointed "Inspector General of Military Prisons" at Florence in November 1864, commanded the interior of the prison. The prisoner's accounts described Barrett in the worst of terms. It is perhaps natural for prisoners to focus their ire on the most visible representatives among their captors, but Barrett seemed to be more than that in terms of his cruelty and brutality.[86] Barrett stayed behind when the 5th Georgia left Florence on November 18, and he remained in charge of the interior of the prison until sworn in as a Captain and company commander in the 2nd Foreign Battalion/8th Confederate Infantry on December 27th. Barrett fled to Germany after the war to avoid prosecution for war crimes. He remained there until 1870, when he and the wife he met in Germany returned to a farm in the Augusta, Georgia, area. His 1910 obituary, published in *The Atlanta Constitution*, stated that he had been an officer under Major Wirz at Andersonville and had commanded Florence prison. Both statements were incorrect, but he had caused a great deal of misery while commanding the interior of Florence prison. Barrett was 75 when he died.[87]

The men held at Florence suffered from most of the same issues that had caused such a high death toll at Andersonville. Florence was never as overcrowded as Andersonville, and the peak prison population was probably not more than 15,000. The prison population moved up and down quite a bit with the arrival and departure of prisoners. During the period from November 27 to December 5, 1864, the number of prisoners in the stockade fluctuated from 8,904 at the beginning of the period to 10,584 at the end.

The number of men in the hospital ranged from 1,134 on November 27 to 768 on December 5. The number of men paroled on November 27 was 173, and 77 were listed as paroled on December 5.[88] The interior of the stockade, better organized than Andersonville, had laid out streets kept free of shelters.[89]

Florence was a barren stockade like Andersonville, and the prisoners had to fend for themselves. Some of the men were able to bring shelter halves they had used at Andersonville, but most had to build Andersonville-style shebangs with whatever material they could find. Andrews estimated that the stockade contained 2,000 to 3,000 shelters when he visited the prison on October 19, 1865, and that three-fourths were still in good shape at that time.[90] Men still died of exposure there for lack of shelter.

Florence lacked proper sanitation. Pye Branch, surrounded by swamps just as Stockade Branch had been at Andersonville, provided drinking water on the upper end, with sinks on the lower end. Guard camps north of the prison polluted Pye Branch before it reached the stockade, much as Stockade Branch had been at Andersonville.[91] The prisoners had to dig wells, largely without tools, to get drinkable water, a task that even the guard force, using tools, found to be extremely difficult.[92]

Poor quality and small quantity of rations was probably even more of an issue at Florence than it had been at Andersonville. Unbolted corn meal was the most common type of food given to the prisoners, but other rations such as beans were also important. The prisoners rarely had meat of any kind at Florence, and fresh green vegetables were absent. Cooking utensils and wood were in short supply among the prisoners, with rations issued raw. Ledoux, in his landmark study of Florence, uses numerous unpublished diaries and memoirs to weave his story of the prisoners who lived and died there.[93] First Sergeant John L. Hoster of the 148th New York Infantry kept the most useful unpublished diary identified during the current research. He recorded what he ate on a day-to-day basis, and how he prepared it. Sgt. Hoster was a member of the police force, called the "Police Club," which kept order in the prison from the time he was kept at the Charleston Fairgrounds until he resigned on November 28. Hoster received an extra ration and worked every other day for the Police Club. He was one of several hundred prisoners who worked at the Police Club or served as clerks, musicians, woodcutters, as members of the burial detail, or other jobs the guard force could not cover. It is significant that he not only received more rations but also received rations of better quality than other prisoners. As an example, he received multiple rations of beef at times when beef was not available to the other prisoners. Hoster nearly died after he resigned from the Police Club as his rations were reduced to those received by ordinary prisoners.[94]

Lt. Thomas Eccles, an officer in the 3rd Reserve Battalion that guarded Florence, said that the prisoners drew the same rations as the guards. Lost Cause historians in the South have made that same argument, and it continues in some quarters today. The organization of power at Florence was best compared to a pyramid where the officers and men of the guard were at the top, followed by those prisoners who worked for the prison administrators in varying capacities, and finally with the overwhelming number of regular prisoners on the bottom. The guards undoubtedly received more and better rations than their helpers, who we know received more and better rations than normal prisoners. Archaeological evidence extracted from a portion of one of the guard camps to the north of the stockade revealed the guards received rations of fresh beef and lived in well-constructed huts. Further evidence that the guards were better fed than the prisoners comes from the fact that the few deaths among the guards were caused by diseases such as mumps, measles, and typhoid fever, while the prisoners were dying of scurvy, dysentery, diarrhea, malnutrition, and a host of other diseases.[95]

The level of medical care was no better at Florence than it had been at Andersonville. Most of the prisoners who arrived at Florence were already suffering from malnutrition and other ailments, but Florence never had enough doctors to care for those who needed it. The hospital was first outside and later inside the stockade. Kellogg, who worked in the hospital as a steward, indicated that there was never enough medicine to go around and that what was supposed to be a month's supply seldom lasted more than two weeks. Medicine compounded from locally available herbs was of questionable utility. The U.S. Sanitary Commission sent some food, clothing, and bedding, and some prisoners in the hospital were fed bread from a prison bakery.[96] Scurvy was ubiquitous at Florence; starvation and malnutrition contributed to many deaths. The total death toll at Florence is unknown since the death book, and the one known copy of it, disappeared after the stockade was abandoned. Historian Tracy Power estimates the death toll at 2,800.[97] James F. Rusling, in a report sent to Brevet Major-General Meigs in 1866, estimated 2,322 prisoners were buried in the primary cemetery, with 416 buried in a second cemetery.[98] An unknown number of prisoners died at the smallpox hospital and at the site of a galvanized Confederate camp. Ten individual graves were located near the main cemetery. Ledoux estimates the number of known dead at Florence at 2,746, including five additional bodies recovered from within the stockade after abandonment.[99]

The guard force at Florence was the same mixture of reserve troops and regular units that created issues at Andersonville. The 5th Georgia Infantry went to Florence soon after the prison opened and remained there until November 18. A small contingent of the 55th Georgia Infantry, of Andersonville infamy, came to Florence in late November. The 5th Georgia officers who remained at the prison after November 18th commanded the prison. The 3rd, 4th, 5th, 6th, and 7th battalions of the South Carolina reserves provided most of the guard force, but many of the men in those units apparently never showed up. The reserves came without uniforms and remained in whatever clothing they had brought with them through the course of their duty at Florence. Some of the reserves arrived without shoes or overcoats, and they received no uniforms upon arrival. Columbia reportedly provided the reserves with 300 obsolete .69 caliber muskets and 12,000 buck and ball cartridges. The artillery provided to them included a 6-pounder Napoleon and a 6-pounder gun with ammunition and all needed tools. There were 1,828 troops and 1,528 effectives among the guard force as of November 5, 1864.[100]

The members of the guard force had to build their own shelters, as it was October 28 before members of the 3rd Battalion received even two tents. The guards built their own log cabins as protection from the weather as winter approached. The guard camps were log houses laid out into small villages on both sides of Pye Branch to the north of the stockade.[101]

Lt. Eccles indicated that even above the stockade water was in short supply and not drinkable.[102] He said that they had no tools to dig wells and that attempts to dig them failed. The archaeological investigation of what may have been his guard camp found and excavated three wells that were dug to a depth of 20 feet each. The excavation discovered a broken shovel that had been hand forged out of sheet metal, apparently by a local smith, at the bottom of one of the wells.[103] That find certainly underscored the lack of tools available to the guards at Florence as the war was beginning to wind down.

Brigadier-General Winder assumed command of all prisons east of the Mississippi River on November 29, 1864. Lt. Col. J. F. Iverson, who had been in command of the guard force at Florence, took over command of the prison from Col. Harrison on December 6, 1864.[104] Gen. Winder died of a heart attack at Florence on February 6, 1865. Assistant Secretary of War J. A. Campbell gave the order to evacuate Florence prison on February 13,

1865. There were 7,187 prisoners at Florence at that time, of which 3,000 were sick, with 700 too sick to travel. Lt. Col. Iverson first evacuated the prisoners to Goldsborough, North Carolina, and then sent them to Wilmington, North Carolina, for exchange.[105]

Ledoux places the death rate at Florence at 16.57 percent and estimates 16,569 prisoners passed through Florence.[106] Andersonville had a much higher death rate. He does point out that the rate at Florence would have been much higher was it not for the exchanges of sick prisoners that took place.

It is unclear exactly when the last prisoner left the Florence Stockade. Paul G. Avery and Patrick H. Garrow report a partial skeleton found in the dugout floor of a hut in the guard camp during the archaeological investigations.[107] Plowing destroyed the skull, the most diagnostic part of the skeleton, but the rest of the skeleton yielded a good bit of information. The individual was a white male, aged 20-35 years old. He was 5' 9 ¼" tall and was wearing what may have been a military jacket. The heavily corroded jacket buttons lacked insignias. He was also wearing a shirt with porcelain buttons. The contents of a buck and ball load found scattered near the body could not be directly tied to it. Isotope analysis of the skeleton indicates that he had spent at least ten to 15 years of his life living on the Gulf or southern Atlantic coast. No DNA had survived in his bones, and his ancestry could not be determined. The identity of this man could not be determined, nor when or how he ended up on the floor of the hut. His remains, buried in the old section of the Florence National Cemetery, received full military honors with a headstone that reads "Unknown."

CAMP LAWTON

The construction of Camp Lawton, named for Confederate Quartermaster General Alexander R. Lawton, was Gen. Winder's solution to the deadly overcrowding at Andersonville.[108] Gen. Winder ordered Captains W. D. Vowles and W. S. Winder on July 28, 1864, to find a suitable site for a new prison and to "secure by rent the land, water privileges, timber, and such houses adjacent as may be thought desirable." On July 30, he requested that Adjutant Inspector General Cooper give Captains Vowles and Winder the authority to "press negroes and teams and wagons." He also asked for a quartermaster, as it was "very important to build as soon as possible." Gen. Winder repeated the request to Gen. Cooper on August 7 and reported selection of a prison site five miles north of Millen, Georgia. Gen. Winder ordered quartermaster Lieutenant R. S. Hopkins to proceed from

Andersonville to attempt to hire labor from planters in Georgia and Florida in lieu of impressing slaves. Despite Gen. Winder's pushing, the prison still was not complete on September 5 when he began sending the Andersonville prisoners to the east.[109]

The site of Camp Lawton includes an artesian spring that today has a flow of up to nine million gallons a day. A stream fed by that spring flowed through the site of the stockade, and a railroad to Augusta was (and still is) located to the east.[110] C. R. Johnson, a medical doctor from nearby Waynesboro, Georgia, sent a letter to Secretary of War James A. Seddon on August 10, 1864, in which he tried to persuade Seddon to move the prison elsewhere. His arguments were worthy of "not in my backyard" groups today when he argued that the water from the spring was from "rotten limestone" and was not fit to drink and that no other water was available "within five miles." C. R. Johnson stated that a widow (Caroline E. Jones) with 150 slaves owned the property and that the crops she raised within a half mile of the site were too valuable to the Confederacy and the community to endanger. He also argued that there were 600 to 800 slaves on the nearby plantations and suggested a more remote location with good water. He charged unnamed interests with misrepresenting the location to Gen. Winder "entirely for pecuniary purposes." There was no reply from Seddon in the available documents, and construction of Camp Lawton moved forward.[111]

Camp Lawton still was not complete when Gen. Winder arrived on the site on September 17. He thought that the prison would be ready to receive prisoners in a week at that point. Prisoners had arrived at the unfinished Florence Stockade two days before, and the situation with prisoners in Charleston had become critical. Gen. Winder reported to Gen. Cooper on September 21 that Lawton still had not been finished because of a shortage of labor, tools, material, and funds. He reported in a second communication to Gen. Cooper on September 21 that he thought the prison might be ready to receive prisoners the following week. He planned to move his headquarters from Andersonville to Camp Lawton and to leave Colonel Gibbs in command at Andersonville. He had already removed eleven artillery pieces from Andersonville, and he planned to bring the rest of the artillery and the artillery company to Lawton. He described Camp Lawton as the largest prison camp in the world at 42 acres.[112]

Gen. Winder reported to Gen. Cooper on October 8 that the stockade was finished, but the bake house and cookhouse were incomplete. He reported on October 15 that prisoners had arrived from Charleston, including about 700 sick prisoners sent before completion of the camp hospital. Gen.

Winder estimated that Lawton could easily accommodate 32,000 prisoners, and that 40,000 prisoners could be accommodated "without inconvenience." The guard force at Lawton was an immediate problem. The 2nd and 3rd Georgia Reserves constituted his main guard force, and Gen. Winder called them "the most unreliable and disorganized set I have ever seen." He said they "plunder in every direction and are creating a very bitter feeling against the Government." Winder requested replacements, and that the reserves be sent elsewhere under the control of other troops.[113]

Gen. Winder modeled the interior of Camp Lawton after Andersonville. The northern part of the stream that ran through the camp provided drinking water and a place to bathe. The southern, or downstream, part contained the camp sinks. Gen. Winder had the northern portion of the creek modified with a sluice to wash out the wastes from the sinks. The stockade contained a deadline that was located thirty feet from the stockade, with frequent guard stands along the exterior of the wall.[114]

John K. Derden illustrates a number of sketches of Camp Lawton prepared by Robert Knox Sneden.[115] He uses information from Sneden's "diary" while discussing life at the prison.[116] Sneden, who apparently wrote his "seven volume diary" shortly after the war, is an excellent example of the need to use care when relying on prisoner's accounts. He completed his sketches and maps later, and they contain numerous errors. Fortunately, other prisoner's accounts were available from Camp Lawton (see William Giles's *Disease, Starvation & Death: Personal Accounts of Camp Lawton*[117] for a compilation of some of the diaries), as many of those prisoners had also spent time at Andersonville.

Derden points out that a critical detail in understanding the lives of the prisoners kept at Camp Lawton is that virtually all of them came from Andersonville or started at Andersonville and were then kept for a short time in Savannah or Charleston.[118] Their incarceration had weakened all of them to some extent, and many came bearing the diseases that had caused the astronomical death rate at Andersonville. No accurate accounting of the dead at Lawton exists; there are wildly different estimates of the Lawton butcher bill. Derden estimates 713 deaths at Lawton for the short time it was open, and his estimate is probably close to the actual figure.[119] Dr. Isaiah H. White, who later served as Chief Surgeon for prisons east of the Mississippi, went from Andersonville to Lawton to aid the surgeon in charge at Lawton to get needed hospital facilities constructed. He said that the situation concerning medical facilities was serious at both Andersonville and Lawton, and stated "thousands of sick both here [Lawton] and at Andersonville are in a state of suffering that would touch the heart of even the most callous." He further complained in an undated report that proper funds were lacking to care for the medical needs of the prisoners. Commissary General of Subsistence L. B. Northrop answered White's report on November 18, 1864, by saying his office had $35,000,000 in unfilled requisitions that the Confederate Treasury had not provided the money to fill. The Surgeon General of the Confederacy S. P. Moore then appealed to Secretary of War Seddon to try to address the situation. Seddon forwarded that appeal to Northrop who replied on November 22 that his department could not provide more funds to fill the needs. This issue was resolved by the time Northrop wrote his reply, with the almost complete evacuation of Lawton prisoners to Savannah by November 22. Many of those prisoners went to Florence from Savannah.[120]

Camp Lawton lacked the lethal overcrowding of Andersonville, but was otherwise afflicted with a number of the same issues. The prisoners had to construct their shebangs from whatever material they could salvage and the few items they brought with them. The slash left behind from felling trees to build the stockade was still on the ground when the first prisoners arrived and was used build shelters. The prisoners cut up logs left behind and used them for firewood. Archaeological evidence gained in excavations in the stockade indicates that some prisoners were able to appropriate brick for building fireplaces. That brick probably was part of the supply brought to the prison to build the bake and cook houses. The supply of building materials was quickly exhausted, and those who came late to the prison had to go outside the prison to get wood and material.[121]

The prisoners reported that the rations given at Lawton were generally better than those issued at Andersonville. The first beef ration given to the prisoners consisted of cow heads, while the carcasses were given to the guards. The prisoners received no rations at times, and utensils for cooking and serving rations remained in short supply. The standard ration appears to have been corn meal, supplemented by beef, rice, beans, and molasses. A sutler provided a full range of food choices, but only to those that could meet his prices. Sweet potatoes were apparently available at times, but green vegetables and other antiscorbutics were apparently absent.[122]

Camp Lawton had received 12,229 prisoners when Captain D. W. Vowles submitted his November 8 report to the Headquarters of Confederate State Military Prison on the status of the prison. Captain Vowles was commander of the prison. He reported that of the 12,229 prisoners received 486 had died, 349 had "enlisted in the Confederate service", and 285 were working at the prison. That left 9,394 regular prisoners still on hand.[123] According to these numbers, the death rate within the prison from October 11 until November 8 was 16.8 per day, compared to 16.6 deaths per day if Derden's estimate of 713 total deaths during the 43 days the prison was in operation is correct.[124]

The composition of the guard force at Lawton is difficult to determine. Gen. Winder transferred eleven artillery pieces and what was probably the Florida artillery company from Andersonville to Lawton on September 15, and the 1st and 2nd Georgia State Reserves were at Lawton by October 15. Gen. Winder asked that the 2nd Regiment of the Georgia State Troops replace the Reserves, but that may not have happened.[125] The guard force for the "World's Largest Prison" seems to have been too small and poorly trained to secure Lawton, but there were amazingly few escapes. There are conflicting reports on the number of successful escapes from Lawton. Derden quotes a Congressional Report on the treatment of prisoners compiled in 1869 that indicates there had been 14 successful escapes from the prison.[126] That same report stated that only 118 men had enlisted in Confederate Service at Lawton,[127] which conflicts with the 349 given in Captain Vowles' report of November 8, 1864, as well as with numbers derived from the current research. Lists of Union prisoners of war who successfully escaped and returned to Union lines are available for at least mid-1864 to the end of the war. Seven successful escapes from Millen (Camp Lawton) were included on that list during the time the prison was in use, as well as one escape with no date of escape listed. Three others who escaped from the town of Millen are on the list, with two of those in April 1865 and the other in December 1864. The escapes included two on October 11, two on November 3, and another two on November 30. The single escape came on October 10. None of the men who escaped were from the same unit.[128]

The order to evacuate Camp Lawton came from General Hardee in response to the advance of Sherman's troops. Gen. Winder reported to Secretary of War Seddon on November 19 that prisoners taken to Savannah would be sent to Ware County, Georgia.[129] Approximately half of those prisoners ended up at Blackshear Prison in Pierce County, Georgia, while the rest were sent to Florence. Blackshear was a barren ground type prison commanded during its brief history by Colonel Henry Forno. Colonel Forno had been the commandant of the guard force at Andersonville, and he was at Florence with Gen. Winder on February 6, 1865, when Winder had a heart attack and died. The men sent to Blackshear ended up at Andersonville and other prisons by the end of 1864.[130]

A scouting force of Union cavalry under the command of Captain Llewellyn G. Estes reached Camp Lawton on November 26, 1864. Lawton was empty by then as the prisoners had been evacuated four days earlier. Captain Estes burned Camp Lawton on December 3, and the "World's Largest Prison" came to its end.[131]

SALISBURY PRISON

Salisbury Prison resulted from a request by Confederate Secretary of War L. P. Walker to several states to provide space for a prison. Acting North Carolina governor Henry T. Clark was the only one who responded to the request. He first suggested a site in Alamance County and then one in Salisbury after the owners of the Alamance County site had declined to sell their property. Governor Clark selected the Maxwell Chambers Factory site, and the site was sold to the Confederate Government for $15,000 on November 2, 1861. That site comprised sixteen acres and a large factory building, six four-room tenements, a superintendent's house, a blacksmith shop, and two to three smaller buildings. The factory building and the tenement buildings were brick, while the superintendant's house was a wooden frame construction. The factory building measured 90 by 60 feet with three full floors, a reduced sized fourth floor and a tin roof. It had an engine room on one end that was 16 by 80 feet.[132]

A stockade secured the prison and initially enclosed five to six acres with 13 guard posts; it was ready to receive prisoners within a month. The prison was set up to accommodate about 2,000 prisoners. The first prisoners arrived from Raleigh, North Carolina, on December 9, 1861. They were the 46 prisoners captured at Bull Run and the 73 sailors captured on the ship *Union.* The prison population increased to 800 by February 7, 1862.[133] The prisoners included officers and enlisted men, as well as civilians and prisoners from the Confederate army. There were 1,700 prisoners at Salisbury by spring 1862.[134]

The first commander of the prison was Dr. Braxton Craven, President of Trinity College. Trinity College later became Duke University. Dr. Craven had formed the Trinity College Guards from among his students and had instructed them in military practice. The Trinity College Guards formed the first guard force at the prison and remained there until January 1862. Craven refused induction into the Confederate Army, and Major George C. Gibbs assumed command of the prison on January 11, 1862. Gibbs recruited his own guard force, made up of three or four companies of 300 officers and men. Gibbs and his men left Salisbury, after an exchange of 1,400 prisoners in May 1862, to assume the same role for a prison in Lynchburg, Virginia.[135]

Captain Archie C. Godwin, formerly the Provost Marshall in Richmond, was promoted to Major and replaced Major Gibbs on May 21, 1862. Requisitions for rations filed in June 1862 suggest that there was one guard company of 100 men under the command of Captain William Howard as well as six employees of the quartermaster department at the prison at that time. A second company of 100 men under the command of Lieutenant Mullens, left at Salisbury for six days without transportation, received the same rations as the guard company. Each company ration included bacon, flour, beans, rice, corn meal, sugar, vinegar, candles, soap, and salt. The guards distributed corn meal in lieu of coffee at the rate of eight pounds per 100 rations. The six employees of the quartermaster department received the same rations, except for the beans. There was no indication of the quantity of each foodstuff given, with the exception of the corn meal. Major Godwin left Salisbury by September 22, 1862. He commanded the 57th North Carolina Infantry and was promoted to Brigadier-General. He did not survive the war.[136] Command of the prison passed to Captain H. McCoy by September 22, 1862, and he remained in command until October 1863. Captain Swift Galloway, of the 3rd North Carolina Infantry, then took command of the prison.[137] Captain George Alexander of Castle Thunder fame commanded Salisbury Prison in May and June 1864. The Castle Thunder prisoners sent to Salisbury in April and May 1864 included 58 in April and 78 in May who were under court martial sentences.[138]

Colonel John A. Gilmer was in command of Salisbury Prison by June 23, 1864, when Lieutenant Colonel Archer Anderson wrote an inspection report on the prison. Gilmer, severely wounded at the Battle of Bristoe Station on October 14, 1863, was unable to return to duty with his old unit.[139] He was extremely limited by the effects of the wound and retired from the army on January 11, 1865. Anderson reported that Colonel Gilmer and his Assistant Commandant, Captain Fuqua of the 13th North Carolina regiment, were temporarily disabled by wounds during his inspection of the prison.[140]

Colonel Gilmer sent a letter dated July 27, 1864, to an illegible recipient, the first page of which has survived with his service records. He stated that he had found a captain and two lieutenants of the guard under arrest when he first arrived at Salisbury, which was apparently after Anderson's inspection visit. It is likely that the captain was Captain Allen who, according to Anderson, had not kept a muster role with the age of his recruits, and that the two lieutenants served in the guard companies despite being eligible for conscription. Gilmer asked that the charges against the officers be dropped. The final disposition of that matter was not recorded in the surviving records.[141]

Colonel Anderson's report gives an excellent picture of the prison after the exchanges of the Dix-Hill Cartel and before the mass influx of Union prisoners of war that occurred by the fall of 1864. According to his report, Salisbury Prison had held 3,802 men from the establishment of the prison until June 1864, with 1,176 of these prisoners treated in the hospital and 77 deaths during this period. That meant that the total death rate had been two percent, which reflects the excellent conditions in the prison to that time. At the time of his report there were 550 people confined to the prison, which included "soldiers, working out their sentences, political prisoners, deserters from the enemy, and prisoners of war." There were three guard companies: one raised in Alabama and the other two raised for local service, with 200 men. The prisoners received cooked rations that included flour, meat, rice, beans, and salt. There was a garden attached to the hospital to provide fresh vegetables. The conditions at Salisbury in June 1864 were unusually good for a Confederate prison but would change much to the worse by fall.[142]

Major Garnett Andrews, who would later command the 2nd Foreign Battalion/8th Confederate Infantry, visited Salisbury Prison on August 10, 1864, and reported that there were 777 prisoners present on that date. He stated the capacity of the prison as 2,500, and he said the prisoners were "well treated and were supplied with the usual army rations of good quality." He further said that the prison buildings, grounds, and the quarters of the guard troops were poorly policed. He criticized the guard force and said that the guards performed their duties very poorly and that most lacked ammunition. Some of the guards were on duty with unloaded guns. He felt that "able bodied men" joined the guard to avoid service in the regular army. Captain Allen, criticized in Colonel Anderson's report, had even set up a private bar in Salisbury. Andrews blamed the lax discipline on the frequent absence of Colonel Gilmer because of his poor health and on the inexperience and lack of will and energy of Captain John A. Fuqua.[143] Major John Gee of the 11th Florida Infantry replaced Colonel Gilmer on August 24, 1864.[144]

The situation changed drastically at Salisbury Prison shortly after Major Gee took command. Authorities in Richmond sent a large number of prisoners to Salisbury from Belle Isle, and the first of them arrived before Gee could complete arrangements to care for them. Water had always been in short supply at Salisbury, and the single well located within the prison was often dry before noon. Gee started several new wells and began expanding the stockade portion of the prison. Five thousand prisoners arrived at the prison on October 5, and the prison held 10,321 prisoners by the end of the month. Belle Isle was empty by then, and the deadliest phase in the use of Salisbury Prison had begun.[145]

Assistant Adjutant and Inspector General R. H. Chilton reported to General Cooper on November 11 that Surgeon Brewer conducted an inspection of Salisbury Prison and found conditions there to be unacceptable. Brewer found that the boards of the stockade were not adequately fashioned and that prisoners could easily dig under the stockade from the holes they had dug for shelter. He further said that the commander of the guard force disregarded orders from the commander of the prison, and in one instance one entire side of the prison was unguarded. Chilton's report reflected the chaos within the prison at that time, which he attributed to "irresponsible management."[146]

A group of prominent Salisbury citizens wrote a petition on November 15 that was sent on to Secretary of War Seddon. It asked that at least half of the prisoners at Salisbury be sent to other prisons to relieve overcrowding. The petition cited a number of issues from the mass movement of prisoners there in October. They pointed out that the prison was too small to accommodate the 10,000 prisoners that it held and that the water supply in the prison was insufficient. Thy further stated that the supply of available wood was insufficient to meet the need of the prison for the coming winter months. The Salisbury citizens pointed out that the wheat crop in the area was a third of that from a normal year and corn was no more than half of that in an average year. This meant that there would not be enough food in the region to sustain the prisoners. The petitioners made valid points, but there was no other place to send the prisoners, and they had to remain at Salisbury.[147]

The number of men who attempted to escape from Salisbury is not known, but a registry of prisoners who escaped from southern prisons between the summer of 1864 and the end of the War has survived. According to that registry, there were two successful escapes from "near Salisbury" in September, both of which occurred on September 18. There were 13 successful escapes in October and seven in November. Eight escapes were recorded for December (three had been erroneously recorded as November 18 on the escaped prisoners list) and an additional 28 in January and 37 in February. There were only four successful escapes in March, but 17 escapes in April before April 11. Stoneman's raid on Salisbury took place on April 12, a few days after closure of the prison. Twenty-two prisoners claimed to have escaped on the day of the raid, but five of those were members of the 2nd Foreign Battalion/8th Confederate Infantry. Eighteen prisoners claimed to have escaped from Salisbury from April 13 to the 25th, but five of those were also from the 2nd Foreign Battalion/8th Confederate Infantry. Some of the men from the galvanized Confederate battalion may have been among the 35 wounded galvanized Confederates left behind after Stoneman's raid. Three additional men claimed to have escaped in May, another two escaped in April, and no day or month exists for three additional escapes. A single escape from "near Salisbury" recorded for July 19, 1864, brought the total to 169 escapes from in or near Salisbury.[148]

There were three successful escapes on December 18 that particularly embarrassed the Confederate government. The prison held Union and Confederate civilians as well as Union and Confederate military prisoners at that time.[149] Three newspaper correspondents were among the Union citizens in the prison. Albert D. Richardson and Junius H. Brown were correspondents for the New York Tribune when captured on May 3, 1863. They had tried to run the Confederate batteries in Vicksburg when their ship exploded and sank. William E. Davis was a correspondent with the Cincinnati Gazette captured near Resaca, Georgia, on May 18, 1864. The three of them made their way through western North Carolina despite numerous hardships and across the mountains to Knoxville on January 16. They escaped by simply walking out of the prison.[150]

A mass escape attempt with more serious consequences took place on November 25, 1864. Major Gee's official report, dated December 15 of the same year, appears to be an accurate accounting of the event. According to Gee, the prisoners first seized the Confederate relief guard, composed of a sergeant and nine men, as they were leaving the prison and took "most of the guns." They used those guns to attack the guards on the guard towers, and about a thousand prisoners stormed the water gate and the part of the stockade where the sinks were located and where there was no guard camp. Some of the guards threw away their guns and ran at that point, although a few stood their ground and fired at the prisoners. The guards shot two canister rounds into the prison at that point; a third shell failed to explode and bounced into the town with no damage. Gee further reported that two prisoners and three Union deserters helped defend the prison and stop the attack. The casualties among the guards amounted to two killed, one who died later of his wounds, and eight to ten "slightly wounded." The toll among the prisoners was much higher, with 13 killed, three who died later of their wounds, and 60 wounded. This was the only mass escape attempt carried out in one of the main Confederate prisons during the war, and points out why, even with poorly trained and unmotivated guards, mass escape attempts were futile.[151]

Captain John Fuqua reported on December 14 that the daily average number of prisoners at Salisbury from October 12 to December 12, 1864, was 8,200. The death rate of 1,320 during that time averages to 22 prisoners per day. The death rate percentage for the 60-day period was thus 16.1 per cent.[152] That was a significant difference from the 2 per cent death rate at the prison from its founding in 1861 until the mass influx of prisoners in October 1864. It reflects the difference between a prison that was operating at or below its intended capacity and a prison with four times as many prisoners as it was capable of supporting.

Brigadier General Bradley T. Johnson arrived at the prison and took command of the Salisbury post on December 17, 1864. Major Gee remained at Salisbury as commandant of the prison and medical officer. Gee's responsibility was inside the prison, while Johnson commanded the whole facility and the guards. General Winder posted Johnson there to address the issue of reserve officers who outranked Gee and would not follow his orders.[153]

Conditions at Salisbury continued to deteriorate into the new year. Conditions were so bad by February 1, 1865, that North Carolina governor Zebulon B. Vance sent a telegram to Secretary of War Seddon that stated: "I beg to call to your attention to the condition of the Federal prisoners of war at Salisbury, N. C. Accounts reach me of the most distressing character in regard to their suffering and destitution. I earnestly request you to have the matter inquired into, and, if in our power to relieve them that it be done. If they are willfully left to suffer when we can avoid it, it would not only be a blot upon our humanity, but would lay us open to severe retaliation. I know how straitened our means are, however, and will cast no blame upon any one without further information."[154]

Governor Vance received a telegram from newly appointed Secretary of War John C. Breckinridge dated February 8. The telegram acknowledged his earlier letter and informed him of an ordered inspection of Salisbury Prison. Captain and Assistant Adjutant G. W. Booth had answered Vance's letter on February 3 and tried to gloss over the conditions at the prison. He did acknowledge that the prisoners had insufficient clothing and revealed that there were only two wells within the prison, with water brought in from a nearby stream. A postscript to the report said that an unstated number of blankets and shoes had arrived for the prisoners from Richmond. An enclosure stated that 118,468 rations had been due from January 20 to February 3 that included beef, flour, meal, rice, potatoes, peas, molasses, and salt, and that there had been an average of 5,500 prisoners. The enclosure further said they gave prisoners beef left over after feeding the guards.[155]

General Johnson returned to Salisbury on February 11 and sent a telegram to Governor Vance that followed up on Booth's report. He asked for clothing for the guards and wall tents for the prisoners. He reported that he had received 3,000 blankets for the prisoners. He said that he had recently visited authorities in Richmond with the intent of "laying before them the terrible suffering and mortality among them [the prisoners]." He further said that he was pressing for exchanging all prisoners from both North and South Carolina and that the prisoners were a "terrible burden" that were better sent "home at once on parole."[156]

Assistant Adjutant and Inspector General T. W. Hall conducted the inspection of Salisbury Prison ordered by Secretary of War Breckinridge and filed an extensive report dated February 17. Hall had previously inspected the prison on January 31 and February 1 while General Johnson was not present, and he returned on February 16. He indicated that the prison encompassed eleven acres, almost twice its original five to six acres. Hall felt that the prison was not suited for its use as of the fall of 1864. This was due to the lack of a good water source in the prison (despite the nine wells he says were present) and the distance to the nearest reliable stream, which he said was a mile and a half away. He also said that despite previous reports to the contrary, there was not adequate fuel for the prisoners and the sinks did not flush out due to the poor nature of the soil in the prison. Hall claimed that the cooked rations provided to the prisoners were comparable to those fed to their soldiers in the field. The lack of clothing led to a great deal of suffering among the prisoners, despite recent receipt of 3,000 blankets and 1,000 pairs of pants from the United States. Lack of shelter was another issue, despite the 300 tents that had been distributed in October 1864. Even with the reduced prison population in February, Hall said that a third of the prisoners lacked shelter and were "burrowing like animals in holes underground or under the buildings in the enclosure." There still was no separate hospital in the middle of February, but most of the standing buildings in the compound sheltered the sick. Bedding for the sick was absent, and no more than half of them had bunks. The death rate within the prison was very high. Hall stated that from October 20 to the time of his report 10,321 prisoners had arrived and 3,479 had died. That was a death rate of 33.7 percent in less than five months, as compared to Andersonville's 35 percent over a much longer period. A further issue at Salisbury, as reported by Hall, was the lack of discipline among the guards and maintenance of the grounds within the prison. Guards were no longer posted inside the prison after the attempted mass breakout in November. Prisoners paid for the lack of internal security—some were attacked by "muggers" and even murdered.[157]

General Johnson submitted a report on February 18 to Brigadier General William M. Gardner, who was then in charge of Confederate prisons, including those in North Carolina; this must have been in reaction to Hall's report of February 17. General Johnson blamed Captain Goodman, the prison quartermaster, for not providing a sufficient amount of wood to the three reserve regiments and the one battalion and for their poor rations. He said that the prison doctor was unable to get enough straw and bunks for those in the prison hospital and that 732 prisoners had died in the hospital during January. He further said that he had been trying to fix those problems for two months but that he was "powerless" and asked to be relieved of his command. General Gardner took note of General Johnson's issues and ordered Major Morfit assigned as post quartermaster.[158]

The exchange of the Salisbury prisoners began on February 19, with most of the exchanges completed by March 3. Major Gee submitted a summary report of the exchanges as an enclosure to a report that Colonel Forno submitted to General Cooper's Assistant Adjutant on March 10. Gee reported 370 prisoners of war sent to Richmond on February 19. Another 400 well and 357 sick prisoners of war were sent to the same destination the next day. The majority of the prisoners left on February 22: 2,822 prisoners of war and 48 citizens were sent to Goldsborough, and 938 sick prisoners of war were sent to Richmond. Forty-two well and 125 sick prisoners of war left for Richmond on March 3, along with 28 citizens and 19 "free negroes." Those removals amounted to 5,149 men.[159]

By the time of the Battle of Bentonville on March 19–21, plans had already been underway to remove prisoners for parole who were sent to Salisbury Prison after March 3. General Cooper stated in a March 18 telegram to General Gardner that he planned to remove the Union prisoners of war from the prison "in a few days" and turn the prison buildings over to the Ordnance Department. The next day General Gardner suggested to General Cooper that Salisbury Prison be used to at least temporarily hold "some 5,000" prisoners captured by General Johnston's forces, and said that he was going to contact General Johnston with his recommendation.[160]

The prison was property of the Ordnance Department by April 7, when Colonel Forno contacted Brigadier General Daniel Ruggles, who was Commissary-General of Prisoners. Forno indicated that he was still receiving "quite a number" of prisoners at Salisbury, and that he had no suitable place to hold them. Forno suggested a site for a prison near Columbia, South Carolina. Forno apparently moved the prisoners out of Salisbury for exchange shortly after his request to Ruggles and prior to Stoneman's raid on April 12.[161]

Salisbury Prison appears to have been deadlier than either Andersonville or Florence. The deaths did not stop on February 15, and the death rate percentage was almost certainly greater than the other two prisons. Major Gee was one of three staff from a Confederate prison tried for war crimes after the war. Major Henry Wirz of Andersonville, put on trial shortly after the war, was found guilty and executed. That may also have been the fate of General John Winder had he survived the war, as the victorious North clamored for someone upon whom to focus the blame for the treatment of their men in southern prisons. The second officer tried after the war was Private James Duncan, who served as a clerk at Andersonville. Duncan, sentenced to fifteen years in prison for deliberately withholding rations from prisoners and profiteering from sale of rations, escaped after serving a year of his sentence. Major John H. Gee, tried for war crimes detailed in seven specifications, was cleared on all counts.[162]

★ CHAPTER 3 ★

Recruitment

THE RECRUITING PROCESS

The Confederacy was suffering from a lack of sufficient manpower on all fronts by early 1864. The Confederate Congress passed a new conscription act in February 1864, which was placed in force through General Order No. 26 on March 1, 1864. The General Order, signed by Adjutant and Inspector General Samuel Cooper, expanded the existing draft from men aged 18 to 45 to all those aged 17 to 50 and forbade release of medically fit men aged 18 to 45 who currently served in the Confederate Army. It also pressed those who had previously served or who had hired substitutes back into service. The General Order allowed for a range of exemptions but attempted universal conscription of able-bodied men. Despite the sweeping General Order, the Confederate Army continued to be depleted and faced even more critical manpower shortages by the end of 1864.[1]

The manpower crisis was so acute that General Patrick Cleburne floated the idea of arming slaves and mustering them into the Confederate Army in January 1864.[2] The Confederate government soundly rejected that idea until just a few days before the end of the war. Jefferson Davis and General Lee endorsed the idea of enlisting a few slaves into the army in February 1865. The Confederate Congress approved the enlistments by a small margin on March 13, 1865. That approval was too late to have any effect on the outcome of the war.[3]

That lack of manpower was particularly acute among the southern prisons, which were most often guarded and administered by inadequate, untrained, and undisciplined reserves. A partial solution to that problem was to use prisoners to fill certain jobs that were critical to the operation of the prisons. The prisoners received extra rations for their labor, which were often the difference between life and death in a world of malnutrition and disease.

The prisoners were organized into thousands and then into hundreds for the distribution of rations at Florence and other prisons. Each hundred was the responsibility of a sergeant chosen by that 100. The sergeant called the roll each morning and distributed daily rations. The sergeants received extra rations for their service.[4]

Prisoners filled many other jobs at Florence. Sgt. John L. Hoster, of the 148th New York Infantry, was a member of the internal police force at Florence until his resignation on November 28, 1864. He stated in his diary on October 11th: "Our police company is on duty today and we get extra ration. There are four companies of 50 men each and one company gets all the 200 rations whenever it is on duty, which is every fourth day."

By October 15, two companies were on duty each day, and Hoster was drawing extra rations every other day. The members of the "Police Club" received meat rations not issued to the prisoners at large. Hoster reported that on October 15 that he was one of 12 members who received the "surplus" of beef that was intended for the sick.[5]

According to Warren Lee Goss, the duties of the "Police Club" were: " . . . seeing to the police duties of the camp, constructing shelter, procuring fuel for those not able to help themselves, and the carrying out of the dead."[6] Goss believed the "Police Club accomplished much good" within the prison, but in time and under new leadership it became a brutal extension of the Confederate guards.

The "Police Club" was not the only way that prisoners could earn extra rations. The prisoners at Florence had no access to firewood for cooking rations or keeping warm as the weather turned. According to Ledoux, 250 men received extra rations from among the prisoners to chop and haul wood to the prison. Additional prisoners served as hospital orderlies, clerks, and even as band members to entertain the Confederate officers. Up to 90 paroled prisoners worked outside the stockade in and around Florence in skilled trades such as barrel makers, blacksmiths, and carpenters.[7]

A series of morning reports that date from November 27 to December 5 reflect the magnitude of the parole/employment of prisoners at Florence. Those reports, found among the sparse Florence Military Prison records on file with the South Carolina Department of Archives and History, indicate that the number paroled at Florence fluctuated from a high of 312 on November 27 to a low of 173 on November 29. The number of "extra duty men entitled to extra rations" fluctuated from a high of 617 on December 5, to a low of 100 on November 29. The number of prisoners entitled to extra rations increased steadily from November 7 to December 5, with the exception of the low of 100 on November 29, which coincided with the parole for exchange of 989 prisoners. It is significant that the number of prisoners issued extra rations for work at the prison exceeded the number of guards on duty at any point of the day. According to a report by Assistant Adjutant General Captain John C. Rutherford, the daily guard consisted of "6 commissioned and 17 non-commissioned officers and 336 privates."[8]

Another way to survive and even escape prison was open to prisoners by September 1864. Major General Samuel Jones, who had ordered the construction of the prison at Florence, noted in a correspondence to General Braxton Bragg on September 13: "Many Yankee prisoners here now profess to be highly indignant with their Government for not exchanging them, especially since the report that it will exchange those whose terms have expired, and they express an earnest desire to take the oath of allegiance, and many of them to join our army if we will permit them. Can anything be done in that way?" Secretary of War John Seddon endorsed General's Jones statement on the same date and said, "A battalion or two might be formed of the foreigners—the Yankees are not to be trusted so far, or at all."[9]

It is clear that many of the prisoners, outraged by the breakdown of the exchange cartel, believed their government had abandoned them. Many Union prisoners of war believed their government had sacrificed them to protect African-American soldiers. A group at Andersonville sent a petition to President Lincoln and other northern officials that requested "speedy release, either by parole or by exchange." The prisoner's outrage translated into a desire to change sides after the move from Andersonville to Savannah after the fall of Atlanta.[10]

Gen. Jones reported to Seddon on September 30 that "about 260 foreigners have volunteered for our service," and he requested that Assistant Adjutant Major Henry Bryan and Captain J. H. Brooks "be ordered to Florence without delay to organize them into a battalion." Seddon endorsed the request by Jones and ordered the officers to report to Jones. It is appears from that exchange that both Seddon and Jones intended for Major Bryan to command the battalion, but that did not happen.[11]

The idea of appealing to foreign-born Union prisoners as a special class was not entirely new when the recruitments began. General Robert E. Lee wrote to Adjutant and Inspector General Samuel Cooper on July 19, 1864, and said that the enemy had tried to encourage desertion from the Confederate Army, and he suggested a similar effort to encourage desertions among the enemy. He further suggested that the Confederate effort include support for Union deserters to return to the north. Cooper issued General Order

65 on August 15, which was aimed at "foreigners entrapped by artifice and fraud into the military and naval service of the United States." It directed that those "coming within the lines of the Confederate armies," if desired, could be given assistance to return north to their homes. Lee indicated in a communication to Secretary of War James Seddon on August 23 that General Order 65 was beginning to work in terms of "encouraging desertions from the enemy." He suggested that it be "translated into German, and a considerable number of copies be sent to all our armies for distribution." Union Major General Augur raised an alarm in a correspondence to Lieutenant General U. S. Grant on September 5 that General Order 65 was encouraging desertions among "bounty and substitute men" and that according to the Richmond papers "they have several hundred such deserters who are to be sent off."[12] The attention of the Confederate high command shifted from General Order 65 to the recruitment of foreign-born prisoners in September 1864.

A view commonly held in the South was that the foreign-born who fought for the North were mercenaries who would fight for "good rations and pay." The foreign-born made up about a quarter of the Union Army, but many in the South thought that there were few real Yankees fighting for the North. Many of the southern leaders thought that Union recruiters had forced the foreign-born to join the Union Army as they arrived in this country, which would have further weakened their allegiance to the Union cause. Confederate leaders also remembered the willingness of the San Patricios to change sides and fight against their former comrades. All of this led the Confederate authorities to target the foreign-born among the prisoners of war when they began recruiting Union prisoners.[13]

Several officers had requested and received permission to recruit prisoners during September and early October. Captain, and later Colonel, Julius G. Tucker of the 10th Virginia Cavalry recruited "a battalion to be composed of foreigners among the prisoners of war confined in certain prisons." Tucker had recruited eight companies by November 21, and his battalion was in training in Columbia, South Carolina. Major Garnett Andrews, who served as General Gardner's Adjutant General, received permission to recruit on September 24. Major Thomas P. Turner, commander of the Richmond Prisons, and Lieutenant Virginius Bossieux, commander of Belle Isle, received permission to recruit on September 28. Colonel Leon Van Zinken had permission to recruit prisoners for the 20th Louisiana Infantry on October 11. Assistant Adjutant General Hoge stated in his November 31 letter there had been that six hundred men recruited for a battalion in

South Carolina with several hundred more sent to regiments "in and around Charleston," without the agreement of the Secretary of War.[14] Brigadier General Zebulon York received permission from Secretary of War Seddon to recruit replacements for the 14th Louisiana Infantry on November 21.[15]

There was disagreement among members of the Confederate high command concerning the recruitment of Union prisoners. They generally agreed that the recruitments, if they went forward, should be restricted to foreign-born prisoners. General Hardee, who replaced General Jones in late September, was the main advocate for recruiting prisoners for new battalions. He even suggested on October 15, in an endorsement of a report by Lt. Colonel W. D. Pickett on his inspection of Florence prison, that "1,500 to 2,000 additional recruits can be obtained by enlisting Western men." General Braxton Bragg had objected to placing recruits in separate units and wanted them used to fill out "depleted units," where they could be "closely supervised." Secretary of War Seddon apparently agreed with Bragg and said he had been using recruited prisoners of war to fill out companies of "like material." He asked President Jefferson Davis for approval. Davis responded: "The organization of separate battalions to be composed of Prisoners is impolitic on many accounts because it will tend to prevent their voluntary enrollment in old companies." The recruitment and training of separate battalions continued despite the apparent reservations of both Seddon and Davis, with some recruits raised for existing units.[16]

The number of recruits at Florence was up to 807 when Lt. Colonel W. D. Pickett inspected the prison on October 12. He said that he had inspected the recruits and found them to be "mostly foreigners and are generally good-looking men, and I doubt not will make good soldiers." He recommended their use in separate units or existing ones. He also said that 1,500 to 2,000 more could be raised from among "Western men" if they were recruited, an idea endorsed by General Hardee. He said there were 50 "old gunners and sailors" who wanted to go into the Confederate navy and recommended that they should be allowed to do so. He also included a list of mechanics that were "among the 'recruits.'"[17]

The recruits held at Florence lacked official status as late as mid-October. General Hardee sent a telegram to Secretary of War Seddon on October 14 requesting guidance on the Florence recruits. Adjutant and Inspector General Cooper on October 19 said: " . . . in regard to the enrollment of Federal prisoners at Florence, was shown to the Secretary of War, who directs that they may be detailed for work at their respective trades."

Seddon's response at that late date indicated that he did not understand

Hardee's intent for those prisoners, and it did nothing to clarify the status of the Florence recruits. Captain Brooks organized the Brooks Battalion from 600 of the Florence recruits. He led those troops to Summerville, South Carolina, on November 17 and mustered them into the Confederate Army.[18]

The 1st South Carolina Artillery

Col. Harrison, commandant of Florence, sent galvanized Confederates to join the 1st South Carolina Artillery in November 1864. Those men may have been among the 50 "old gunners and sailors" that Lt. Colonel Pickett noted wanted to join the navy during his inspection of Florence on October 12. Twenty-seven Union prisoners of war were sent. Of these, the 16 men assigned to Company A were listed as having come from Florence after being recruited by Col. Harrison. One soldier who joined Company E and 10 who joined C were listed as former U.S. soldiers who had taken the oath. The difference in listing the soldiers on the last muster sheet that survived for the regiment probably was probably due to different methods of bookkeeping by the company commanders. All probably came from Florence, with all recruited by Col. Harrison. There were only two instances of additional information for individual solders. Private J. W. Chapman, who had joined Company E, returned to prison by the time of the November-December muster roll "on suspicion of intention to desert." Private Francis Tibbles of Company C was among the prisoners paroled upon the surrender of Gen. Johnston's Army at the end of the war.[19] Private Tibbles, from Seneca, New York, had been a private in Company G of the 8th New York Cavalry. According to his muster summary he was captured on June 29, 1864, and was still absent on November 1, 1864. Pvt. Tibbles was captured during or immediately after the Battle of Sappony Church (Battle of Stony Creek Depot) after an unsuccessful raid on the Weldon Railroad in Sussex County, Virginia.[20]

The 47th Georgia Infantry

Gen Hardee, discussing Union recruits in a communication to Adjutant and Inspector General Samuel Cooper dated November 7, 1864, said that he had "distributed several hundred among the Rgts in and around Charleston."[21] An enclosure to a letter, dated November 11, 1864, to General H. W. Halleck, Chief of Staff of the Union Army, by Major General J. G. Foster stated that there were 400 Union soldiers who had taken the oath to the Confederacy, were in arms, and were on James Island at that time. A second enclosure to the same letter stated that a Sergeant James B. Salisbury of Company K of the 1st Massachusetts Cavalry, taken near Petersburg on May 24, 1864, had made it to Union lines by November 8. Salisbury had galvanized and had enlisted in the 47th Georgia Infantry, stationed on James Island. His explanation for his enlistment was that he had enlisted "to save his life and health," and he said was one of 150 galvanized Confederates in the same regiment.[22]

The service records of the 47th Georgia did not list a Sergeant James B. Salisbury or the other galvanized Confederates. An account of the service of the galvanized Confederates has survived, however, in the form of a memoir written by Captain Ben S. Williams. Williams served as regimental adjutant when the recruits reached the 47th on October 31. He stated that the 47th Georgia received 100 recruits to reinforce a regiment that was down to only 300 men. The recruits were from Andersonville prison by way of Charleston. Each company received ten galvanized Confederates. Captain Laurence of Company B told Captain Williams that he received "two Irishmen, two Germans, one Italian, one Swede, two Michiganders, and two d—d Pennsylvania Dutch." The galvanized Confederates became a closely watched part of the regiment. Captain Ben Williams included a poem that he attributed to soldier named Pomeroy, whose first name was indecipherable in his account. The only Pomeroy in the 47th Georgia was Confederate Private Abner Pomeroy, captured in May 1864. At any rate, the poem is worth repeating:

We ration them, clothe them
and them to drill
But we know they are Yanks
and our enemies still.

The galvanized Confederates manned picket posts after a while, and they began deserting in numbers after they learned "the lay of the land, our lines, and the position of their former comrades, our enemy." The last of the galvanized Confederates, less one, returned to prison on November 29. One recruit supposedly slipped away from the detail that was returning him to prison and made his way back to Captain Williams. Williams said he begged to remain and fight with the regiment in an upcoming Battle of Honey Hill. Williams gave his name as Hogan of Company C. Williams claimed that Hogan died at the Battle of Bentonville, still fighting with his company. William called "Hogan" "O'Brien" in another section of his memoirs.[23] The only soldiers with the surname Hogan or O'Brien in the 47th Infantry enlisted in 1862 and could not have been galvanized Confederates.[24] Captain

Williams embellished his memoirs to some degree, but his account is the only one of its type found to this point and is worth consideration.

At least one galvanized Confederate from the 47th Infantry was at the Honey Hill battlefield a few days after the battle and may have still been with the 47th. McKee stated that while the troops of the 144th New York Infantry were forming up to attack Confederate positions on Bee Creek on December 4 near Boyd's Landing "just as the formation for the attack had been made, a Union prisoner captured by the Rebels at Olustee, made his escape from the enemy and came running into our lines as we were waiting the order to advance. This man reported the works as very strong and well manned with three masked batteries in position to do great damage to an attacking force. As a result of this communication the troops were withdrawn without loss and returned to the camp."[25]

Emilio of the 54th Massachusetts Infantry, made famous by the movie *Glory*, wrote that the Union Army attacked the Confederate batteries identified on December 4 and again on December 5th. He went on to state: "Important information was gained from a 'galvanized Yankee' who deserted from the Forty-seventh Georgia to Potter's force. His regiment had a considerable number of men like himself—Union soldiers who enlisted to escape starvation while prisoners-of-war—numbers of whom deserted to us subsequently."[26]

It appears that McKie and Emilio were talking about the same man, and it is likely a number of those who had previously deserted from the 47th Georgia had simply taken the opportunity of the Battle of Honey Hill and its following actions to cross into the Union lines.

Captain Daniell's Battery

Capt. Daniell's Battery mustered into the Confederate Army on March 12, 1864, at Camp Pembrook on the Savannah River, south of the city of Savannah.[27] It took part in the defense of Savannah in December 1864 and disbanded soon after the surrender of the city. The battery consisted of four 12-pound brass Napoleons, and its short history was plagued with desertions and transfers. The depleted unit was very short handed by November 1864. Sixty galvanized Confederates mustered into the battery on November 4.[28] The enlisted Federals made up a significant percentage of the total strength of the unit, as records show that the unit only drew 129 rations on December 16.[29]

Lt. General Hardee removed six of the enlisted Federals from the unit on December 9 for special service, perhaps as recruiters. They did not return before the unit disbanded. Union forces captured four men in hospitals at Savannah and Pocataligo, Georgia. Fourteen men deserted, which included one on December 10—the day Sherman arrived at Savannah—twelve on December 18 and 20, and one on the 21st, when the fight for Savannah had been lost. Five additional men escaped from various places after December. One enlisted Federal was "present in arrest" at an unspecified date. One man transferred to the Barnwell Light Artillery on November 29, but he was not included on the roster for that unit. The remainder of the enlisted Federals were either returned to prison or managed to desert or escape without notice.[30]

One enlisted Federal from Capt. Daniell's Battery bears special mention. Union troops captured Pvt. Joseph Liptrot, who was suffering from dropsy, in a hospital in Savannah. Liptrot, formerly of the 53rd and 145th Pennsylvania Infantry, claimed to have escaped from Andersonville Prison. He filed for a pension as an invalid, which he received on March 1, 1870. He died on April 27, 1899.[31]

There was one apparent reference to the placement of the enlisted Federals posted to Captain Daniell's Battery. Brigadier General William M. Gardner stated in a letter dated November 2, 1864, to General Samuel Cooper: "Lieutenant General Hardee, without my knowledge, has give permission to Colonel Daniel, of the Fifth Georgia Regiment, to fill up his companies with such prisoners as should take the oath of allegiance and enter our service. About 1,000 of them enlisted and have been carried away to some place unknown to me by one of General Hardee's inspectors."[32]

No enlisted Federals mustered into the 5th Georgia, and it is clear that Brigadier General Gardner was referring to the 60 recruits of Captain Daniell's battery.

The Tucker Regiment

The Confederate high command allowed Captain, and later Colonel, Julius G. Tucker of the 10th Virginia Cavalry to raise eight companies composed entirely of foreigners and excluding both "natives" and "citizens" of the United States. Col. Tucker raised companies A-C at the Richmond prisons on October 12, 1864, and mustered the companies into the Confederate Army the following day. Col. Tucker recruited Companies D-H at Salisbury Prison on November 7, 1864, and Company I on December 1. Company K was raised from Richmond, Salisbury, and Florence at dates that ranged from October 12, 1864 to February 1, 1865. Tucker did not record the muster dates of those companies. The recruits from October 1864 were from

Richmond. Most of these were recruited on October 16, which was after the original companies had been recruited and mustered. Lt. James, formerly a student at Virginia Military Institute and 1st Lieutenant of Company B of the Tucker Regiment, recruited part of Company K at Florence. Lt. (later Captain) Wilkinson secured most of the Salisbury recruits. Wilkinson had been a clerk in the Quartermaster Department prior to joining the Tucker Regiment. He served first as a 1st Lieutenant in Company A and then as Captain of the same company. Col. Tucker recruited the Company K enlistees from Richmond, as well as a few from Salisbury. Col. Tucker mustered the Company K troops into the Confederate Army on February 17.[33]

It appears that Col. Tucker was not very selective when enlisting Union prisoners for his unit. There is no evidence to suggest that Col. Tucker raised more than the recruits that were mustered directly into the Confederate Army. He supposedly acted within his orders to recruit only foreign-born prisoners, but there does not seem to have been a process to evaluate the men over time so that the best were chosen to make up his command. The Tucker Regiment was in camp in Columbia, South Carolina, by November 21.[34]

The 2nd Foreign Battalion/8th Confederate Infantry

The authorization to raise what was to become the 2nd Foreign Battalion and later the 8th Confederate Infantry (as it will be referred to in this chapter) was given to Major (later Lt. Col.) Garnett Andrews in a letter from Major John Blair Hoge of the Adjutant and Inspector General's Office, dated September 24, 1864. Major Hoge was the Assistant Attorney General and was acting under orders from the War Department. Major Andrews was first authorized to recruit from prisons in Georgia. His instructions were quite clear: "In making such enlistments Irish and French are to be preferred. No citizens or native of the United States and few if any Germans should be enlisted. The battalion is designed for service elsewhere than in the armies of Tennessee and Northern Virginia. The enlistments will be for the term of three years and the understanding must be (indecipherable) that the officers will be appointed by the President and not elected."[35]

Major Hoge modified that order on November 10, 1864 in a letter to Major Andrews, which stated in part: " . . . your original authority. . . . is enlarged among the same class of prisoners confined in any of the military prisons under the control of Brigadier-General Gardner."

Neither General Jones nor General Hardee kept Brigadier General Gardner—in charge of prisons in North Carolina, South Carolina, Virginia, and Florida during the time the recruitment of Union prisoners of war—informed of the early recruitments. Major Andrews focused his recruiting efforts on Florence Prison in South Carolina and Salisbury Prison in North Carolina.[36]

Major Andrews stated in a typescript on file with the *Andrews Papers* at the University of Tennessee-Chattanooga:

> Our lines had now become frightfully thin, and among the last desperate effort to recruit them, was the plan of enlisting voluntary enlistments of foreigners among the Federal prisoners. I was authorized to raise a batallion [*sic*] of six full companies of the material, with powers to select my own officers from the army at large. I soon enlisted 1600 men at the prisons at Salisbury, N.C., and Florence, S.C., all, without exception, foreigners, principally Irish, with some German, French, and English. They were men who had enlisted in the U.S. Army immediately on arrival in this country, and some of them could speak little English. Out of 1600, after several months of careful study of them in camp under rigid drill and discipline, I cautiously selected 600 picked soldiers, got them thoroughly equipped and uniformed, and reported for duty in the latter part of 1864 or early in 1865. Was ordered to Charlotte, N.C. and promoted to be Lieutenant-Colonel. The War Department first designated the corps as the "Second Foreign Legion," but soon afterward changed the name to "8th Confederate battalion of Infantry." But the public humor gave us the expressive appelation [*sic*] of "Galvanized Yankees."[37]

Lieutenant (later Captain) Barrett recruited most of these "Galvanized Yankees" from Florence, while Captain Tabb recruited at Salisbury. Lt. (later Major) Fouche was also responsible for a number of the Florence recruits. Company A included men from both Salisbury and Florence, while the men of Company F were all from Salisbury. The rest of the men in the battalion came from Florence. Barrett, of the 5th Georgia Infantry, had been in charge of the interior of the Florence prison and had specifically requested permission to join the 8th and to conduct recruiting. Captain Tabb may have been William Kemp Tabb, who had been on General Winder's staff in Richmond and later commanded Camp Oglethorpe in Macon, Georgia. He had no additional involvement in the 8th Confederate. Lt. (later Major) Fouche commanded Company A as a Captain and rose in rank to Major within the 8th, becoming Garnett Andrews' second in command. The recruits, enlisted in December, mustered into the Confederate Army on December 27.[38]

The 8th Confederate Infantry was clearly the most carefully recruited and vetted unit raised among Union prisoners of war. They also received the longest period of training. The 8th Confederate became a fighting battalion, while the Tucker Regiment became a pioneer regiment.

Zebulon York

General Zebulon York was among those authorized to recruit prisoners of war by Secretary of War Seddon, although not until November 21.[39] General Robert E. Lee, in a letter to Seddon dated November 14, indicated that he had been informed by Brigadier General Martin, who commanded Salisbury Prison, that "2,000 to 3,000 foreigners now held as prisoners of war could be enlisted in our service." General Lee suggested those numbers could be increased to 7,000 to 8,000 by "proper management," and "they would make a valuable addition to the Army." Seddon answered Lee's letter on November 16:

> "For some time past my attention has been attracted to that mode of recruiting, and I have given to officers supposed to be competent, in several instances, permits to raise battalions, directing them to prefer Irish and French, and to enlist no citizens of the United States. The latter, especially native born, I hold in great distrust. I preferred to form battalions to regiments, because I doubted the expediency of having so many of this material together as a regiment required.
>
> While authorizing the formation of those few battalions as an experiment, I all the time preferred, and directed officers of prisons to promote general enlistments and the distribution of the men enlisted among the regiments of our different armies, selecting, as far as practicable, those which had been originally composed of foreign material. I have, too, authorized several officers, whose commands had been greatly depleted, to recruit for them from this source. Among others, General York, while wounded here, has obtained this permission and proposes to visit the prisons, taking with him one or more Catholic chaplains, whose influence, he thinks, may be profitably exercised upon those of the same religious persuasion. I shall be pleased to give similar authority to any officers in your army you may recommend, and who are willing in that way to replenish their command."

Seddon's letter to Lee was illuminating in several ways. It revealed his strategy for the enlistment of prisoners of war by mid-November and explained his decision making to that point. It also explained the manner in which General York planned to go about his recruitment. Lee's original letter also explained why York targeted Salisbury for his recruitment effort on behalf of the 14th Louisiana Infantry.[40]

General York was recruiting at Salisbury with Quartermaster Sergeant Charles Moss of the 14th Louisiana on January 17, when he informed General Lee that he had enlisted 600 to 700 prisoners, but that the officers recruiting for the Tucker regiments had hampered his efforts. He said he could raise a brigade if given the sole right to recruit at Salisbury and in other prisons. York also indicated that he was having a supply issue and requested assistance in dealing with the quartermaster department. Lee referred York's communication to the War Department on January 24. Assistant Adjutant General Blair Hoge answered York's letter on February 7. Hoge pointed out that Tucker's authorization to recruit predated York's, although he understood that Tucker had completed his enlistments "unless he be authorized to recruit another company to form a regiment." That communication was followed up by a letter dated February 11 to the Adjutant General from Assistant Secretary of War J.A. Campbell, which stated that Tucker had been authorized to recruit another company and said, "If that enterprise be deemed of less importance than the one herein mentioned, it might to proper to recall that order."[41]

A document in Quartermaster Sergeant Moss's service record indicates that he had recruited prisoners at Salisbury on February 8, 1865, and he provided a list of those recruits from "Camp Viola" in North Carolina. The copyist placed a cautionary note dated January 26, 1921, on the copied document that indicates the card he had copied should not be considered as "the basis of an official report" until it had been investigated. There was no further clarification in the file, and no evidence that galvanized Confederates joined the 14th Louisiana.[42]

Major Thomas Turner and Lieutenant Virginius Bossieux

Major Thomas Turner, commander of the Richmond prisons, and Lieutenant Virginius Bossieux, commander of Belle Isle, received permission to recruit on September 28. The prisoners held at Belle Isle went to Salisbury Prison beginning on October 5, and Belle Isle was empty by the end of the month. Tucker probably intended to recruit among what was left of the Belle Isle prisoners for his regiment in mid-October, but the pool of prisoners that Turner and Bossieux planned to recruit from was soon gone.[43]

Colonel Leon Van Zinken

Colonel Leon Van Zinken received permission to recruit prisoners for the 20th Louisiana Infantry on October 11. Von Zinken was serving as Commandant of Columbus, Georgia, at the time of his request. General Hood had assigned him to that post on September 5, 1864, after Von Zinken was wounded in battle. Von Zinken planned to recruit foreign-born prisoners he had access to from his position at Columbus. No information has been uncovered during the current research that any recruits joined the 20th Louisiana.[44]

The 10th Tennessee Infantry/Bates Division

There was one known recruiting effort that originated within the Army of Tennessee. Brigadier General M. J. Wright requested permission to enlist "1,000 or more" Irish Catholic prisoners on September 29, and Secretary of War Seddon endorsed his request the following day. [45] Brigadier General Wright commanded the post of Macon, Georgia, a city well placed to direct a recruiting effort among Union prisoners. His commanding officer was Major General Benjamin Cheatham, who took over the Second Corps of the Army of Tennessee and reported directly to General John Bell Hood, commander of the Army of Tennessee. On October 11, 1864, General Hood ordered Lt. Col. John G. O'Neill of the 10th Tennessee Infantry to proceed to "Millen, Ga, and such other prisons as they may deem necessary for the purpose of recruiting from the Federal Prisoners for that [Bates] Division." The same orders or orders to report for special service on the same date were issued to 1st Lieutenant and Adjutant Robert P. Seymour, Captain James McMurray, Captain Lewis Clark, Captain A. J. Dorsey, Captain J. L. Pendergrass, and Lieutenant Evans, all of the 10th Tennessee, as well as Captain Conrad Nutzel and Captain Henry Rice of the 15th Tennessee Infantry.[46]

Brigadier General Wright apparently took an active role in recruiting for the Bates Division. He ordered Captain James McMurray on October 22 to go to "Andersonville, Millen, and such other places where Federal Prisoners are confined for the purpose of enlisting foreigners . . . by order of General Hood." Captain McMurray attempted to recruit at Salisbury under that order on November 21, but the commandant of the prison denied him permission to enter the prison. He sought reimbursement from Augusta on November 30 for the cost of a telegram he sent to General Gardner in

Richmond to resolve the issue, but there is no indication in the available records concerning its outcome.[47]

Lt. Col. O'Neill established his base of operations for the recruitment effort in Augusta, Georgia. O'Neill submitted a special requisition for camp supplies "for 150 men" that was approved and received at Augusta on November 7, which included 20 mess pans, 20 camp kettles, 125 tin cups, 10 skillets, 10 tea pots, and 26 fry pans. The use of Augusta as a marshalling and training base sets O'Neill's recruiting effort apart from all of the other efforts that had taken place through Charleston and Florence.[48]

Perhaps the first recruitment stop that O'Neill made was in Charleston, South Carolina. Major G. S. Buford, Assistant Adjutant General posted in Selma Alabama, sent a communication to General Beauregard in Tuscumbia, Alabama, on November 2 that stated: "Col. O'Neal 10th Tenn Regt. telegraphs from Charleston as follows: 'Among the recruits they sent Hardee has just enrolled from the Federal prisoners are some Irish which I wish to get. He says if General Beauregard is more in need of them than he is, he will turn them over to me—answer at Macon.'"[49]

The recruited Federals were probably the 400-500 men offered to General Beauregard by General Hardee. Hardee planned to use those men in the defenses around Charleston, but there is no available evidence that that is what happened. McNeill may have used the 400-500 men to help fill out his 1,000 man unit.[50]

O'Neill recruited at Millen by November 8. Several prisoners' accounts have survived that describe his efforts at that post. The accounts generally agree that the recruitments took place around the time of Lincoln's reelection (November 8, 1864). A rebel Colonel, who was undoubtedly Lt. Col. O'Neill, spoke to prisoners assembled outside the prison. An account by Lessel Long said that the prisoners had been required to fill out rolls of those who were born outside the United States and who had completed their terms of service. The guards called most of the foreign-born prisoners outside the prison the next day. According to Lessel, as well as John McElroy (a prisoner at Millen) and the anonymous "A Returned Prisoner of War," the prisoners refused to listen to O'Neill and returned to prison. Prisoners John Vaughter (writing as "Sgt. Oates"), Henry M. Davidson, and John McElroy agreed that the recruiters took prisoners from Millen.[51]

John Vaughter and Sgt. W. Goodyear listed the inducements made to prisoners for enlistment. Vaughter said that the recruiters offered "a good suit and fifty dollars (Confederate) at once, and would take him out and put him on full rations, as soon as he would sign his name to their muster roll." Goodyear said the recruiters offered "three bushels of sweet potatoes, a suit of clothes, and one hundred dollars in Confederate scrip." Kellogg published his account in 1866, while Vaughter published his account in 1880.[52]

John A. Cain, captured in Virginia on February 22, 1864, was imprisoned at Richmond, Andersonville, Millen, and Savannah. Cain made a list of 134 prisoners who galvanized, which he called a partial list of those who left with O'Neill.[53] O'Neill left Millen with 349 recruits, all secured by November 8.[54]

O'Neill left Millen for Andersonville, and probably had his Millen recruits taken to Augusta. William Marvel claims that O'Neill arrived at Andersonville as part of a circuitous route that would have taken him back to the Army of Tennessee, and that O'Neill visited Andersonville as a result of detours he took to avoid "Sherman's presence."[55] Marvel offers no evidence to support that statement. O'Neill arrived at Andersonville on November 15. The charge under which O'Neill pursued the recruitments specifically included an attempt to gain recruits from Andersonville.

O'Neill found few able bodied men at Andersonville. Few prisoners remained at Andersonville by the time of O'Neill's visit, and the men left there were mainly those who were too ill to leave. Andersonville would later receive prisoners back from Millen by way of the temporary prison at Blackshear.[56] Marvel claims that O'Neill raised four recruits from Andersonville on the afternoon of November 15, which was the day he arrived at the prison and four more the next day.[57] An eyewitness account and Confederate records dispute Marvel's claim. Pvt. Michael Doherty of the 13th Pennsylvania Cavalry witnessed O'Neill's visit. He recorded the following in his diary, which he incorrectly dated as November 13 but was actually the 15th: "All the Irish who could walk were called to the gate this afternoon by a Col. McNeill of the 10th Tennessee (rebel) regiment, to see if any of them would take the oath to join the rebel service. Not an Irishman enlisted, but two Yankees did, one from Connecticut and the other from a New York Regiment; so you see the Irish are the most loyal."[58]

Dougherty, who won a Medal of Honor for bravery at the action around Jefferson, Virginia—where he and his comrades were captured—was at least partially correct about the number and origin of the few recruits gained by O'Neill from his visit to Andersonville. The register of prisoners who left Andersonville (by both death and departure) recorded that four Federals left Andersonville with O'Neill on December 16. Those prisoners were Sgt. J.

Beasley of the 63rd New York Infantry, Pvt. William Long of the 7th Connecticut Infantry, Sgt. Chas. Moore of the 158th New York Infantry, and Sgt. J. A. Shean of the 6th Michigan Infantry.[59]

There is little doubt that the officers assigned to recruit with O'Neill visited other prisons, although the only clear proof that has survived was Captain McMurray's attempt to recruit at Salisbury on October 22. It is likely that O'Neill had his 1,000 recruits by the end of November, and that he had assembled them at Augusta, Georgia.

O'Neill returned to Andersonville Prison to recruit replacements in January and February 1865. The prison then contained many able bodied men captured during Sherman's March to the Sea. Gen. Beauregard authorized that additional recruitment, and O'Neill visited Andersonville on January 23 and 25 and on February 20. O'Neill recruited 315 men, but the war ended before they could be trained and used.[60]

Major Michael O. Tracy and Major General Dabney H. Maury

Major Michael O. Tracy of the 13th Louisiana Infantry requested leave to recruit prisoners of war for his brigade at Cahaba Prison in a letter dated December 6, 1864.[61] His rationale was that his brigade was "much depleted" and that they had not been able to replenish its ranks through "recruiting or by conscription." His letter went through the chain-of-command to the Secretary of War, with the endorsement of Major General Maury, who commanded the Department of Alabama, Mississippi, and East Louisiana. Major and Assistant Adjutant-General John Blair Hoge answered his request in a letter to Major General Maury, dated January 10, 1865.[62] The Hoge letter authorized the requested recruitments on behalf of the Secretary of War, while referencing the failure of the Brooks Battalion. Hoge recommended that the recruits not be formed into new units or placed in large numbers into existing ones, but instead be distributed among several existing units. He also recommended that the recruitment should focus mainly on Irish Catholics and other Catholic immigrants with the help of Catholic priests. Hoge also stated: "Men born in the United States should not be received unless known to have sincere and positive predilections for the South. Natives of the Southern States may be received more freely."

There is little evidence that Major Tracy recruited galvanized Confederates for his brigade. The 13th Louisiana, Major Tracy, and Major General Maury took part in the defense of Mobile, Alabama, which was then under siege by Union Forces. William O. Bryant, in his history of Cahaba Prison, states that a Charles Schallon, a Union deserter, joined the Confederate Army from Cahaba Prison on January 18, 1865, but he offers no further details of Schallon's enlistment. Major Tracy's enlistment efforts, if any, remain a mystery.[63]

MOTIVATIONS

It is difficult, if not impossible, to know what motivated individual Union prisoners of war to change sides and join their former enemies. That probably could not have happened on any scale early in the war. The Union Army of 1861–1863 was a volunteer force who left home and family to do their patriotic duty. The Union Army of 1864, replenished through a very unpopular draft, included many men who joined to get a state bounty or were paid to be substitutes for others. Bounty jumpers, men who joined and collected their bounty and then repeatedly deserted and rejoined under assumed names to collect multiple bounties, exploited the system in large numbers. The problem of an army that included numerous men who had weakly developed or no discernible ties to the central government or the war it fought was compounded by the breakdown of the exchange system, which led to overcrowded prisons that became hellholes where prisoners of war died by the thousand.[64]

Desertion was a significant problem for the Union Army. The number of desertions increased as the war ground on and reached an estimated 200,000 men by the end of the war. An estimated 117,247 deserters were at large at the end of the war, while about 80,000 had returned to the army.[65] The reasons for the desertions varied, but all involved a choice for self-interest over duty. Self-interest also motivated Union prisoners of war to change sides. There is no evidence to suggest that the men who changed sides did so out of feelings of loyalty to the Confederacy. Quite the contrary, Major R. T. Fouche categorized the galvanized Confederates of the 8th Confederate Infantry after the Battle of Salisbury as "foreigners and mercenaries who would "serve any government for food and clothing."[66] At least some of the galvanized Confederates were deserters who faced possible execution if returned to the Union Army upon exchange or capture. Robert I. Alotta demonstrates that there were actually very few executions for desertion by the Union Army during the war, but the prospect of facing the military justice system was probably enough to make deserters avoid being returned at all costs.[67]

The threat of death from a myriad of causes within southern prisons was probably a major reason that many men chose self-preservation over duty. It was not by chance that Andersonville, Millen, Florence, Salisbury, and Belle Isle were the major recruiting grounds for Union prisoners of war. All shared a high death rate from nutritional diseases, epidemic and endemic diseases, gangrene, and exposure, and each prison triggered deep despair among the men who saw no way out but death. It is true that the vast majority of prisoners remained loyal to their oath and duty in the face of the horror of those prison camps. Each person has a different breaking point. Some became collaborators and worked for the Confederacy within the prisons. Others reached their breaking point and gave up and died or went mad. Some chose to galvanize and join their former enemies.

★ CHAPTER 4 ★

The Brooks Battalion

THE BROOKS BATTALION was an orphan unit through its short history. As discussed in Chapter 3, the Brooks Battalion consisted of recruits who wished to join the Confederate Army but had not been formally recruited or planned for by Confederate authorities. The *ad hoc* nature of the formation of the battalion and the lack of official attention to provide sufficient leadership to train the men and maintain military discipline planted the seeds for the unit's ultimate failure.

Lt. Blunt (G. M. Blount, 32nd Georgia Infantry) and Captain Ross (unit unknown) enlisted the men of the Brooks Battalion at Florence.[1] Major S. L. Black, who was on General Hardee's staff, mustered the men into service at Summerville, South Carolina.[2]

Second Lt. Octavus S. Cohen provided insights into the reasons the Union prisoners stated for enlisting in the Brooks Battalion. According to Cohen, who was serving as Ordnance Officer at Florence at the time of the enlistments, the prisoners said that their terms of service had expired, that their government would not exchange them, or that they had been drugged and shanghaied into the army. He further said that most applied to the recruiters to join the unit, and that a number of the recruits had been members of the internal police force at the prison. The recruits lived in a separate camp and sheltered under minimum guard in houses they had built for themselves. Cohen also said that the recruits received the same rations as before they left the prison camp, which included: "A pound of cornmeal, a pound of beef, and when they did not get beef, they got a third of a pound of bacon: and when there was no meat, they had syrup; sometimes a little beans or rice. The beans and rice were extra."[3]

The rations received by the members of the Brooks Battalion were not the same as those provided to the prisoners at large. They do seem to be more similar to the rations given to members of the internal police force at

Florence, as indicated in the day-to-day diary of Sgt. John L. Hoster, who had been a member of the police force.[4]

The reasons prisoners stated after the fact for joining the Brooks Battalion were different from those cited by Cohen. Edward McQuade was an 18-year-old corporal in Company D when mustered into the Brooks Battalion. He described himself as a native of New York and returned to New York City immediately after the war. He had been a member of the 5th Rhode Island Infantry (which became the 5th Rhode Island Heavy Artillery) when he was captured at Croatan Station, North Carolina, on May 10, 1864. He had endured imprisonment at Andersonville until shipped out with the majority of prisoners after the fall of Atlanta. He had been sent to Florence soon after. McQuade stated that the rations at Florence included about a pint of cornmeal, beans or flour, with a quarter of a pound of beef for the first three weeks, and the rations diminished after that time. He said he joined the Brooks Battalion to "get something to eat."[5]

Francis C. Shrenk (also listed as Schrenk) was captured at the battle of the Wilderness, Virginia, while serving in the 5th New Jersey Infantry. He was a prisoner at Andersonville before Florence. Shrenk claimed that he tried to escape from Florence but was recaptured. He also said he was told he would be shot if he refused to take the oath and join the Brooks Battalion, and he joined the Brooks Battalion "on account of starvation and lack of clothes." He added that he joined for "the purpose of getting into the Union lines." Shrenk reportedly joined the 5th New Jersey under the name Charles Geiplen or J. Charles Geislen. The closest match to his name in the New Jersey records was for 26-year-old Charles Geissler of Company C. Shrenk appears to have joined the Brooks Battalion as Charles Geisseler or Gesseler of Company A. He was a resident of New York City after the war, and the address he gave in a letter dated January 23, 1866, was 108 Forsyth Street in Manhattan.[6]

Kellogg, in his memoir published shortly after the war, reflects the view that hunger and privation were major reasons for joining the Brooks Battalion. He presented a more pragmatic view of the enlistments than many who later criticized the recruits:

> We found with surprise and sorrow that many of our men had really taken the oath of allegiance to the Confederacy and had gone into the Southern army, and that still more had the intention of doing it. Over at our left was a camp which we were told was occupied by those prisoners who had taken the oath. It was not hard to account for it. They

> were ragged, half starved, and death was staring them in the face. By entering the Southern army they, no doubt, expected to receive better food, and it was their hope and intention, also, to escape at the first opportunity. We all shuddered at the prospect of staying through the winter in the Confederacy, if, indeed, we should live so long.[7]

Many of those who joined were apparently survivors of Andersonville and fully understood what they could expect to face at Florence. The promise of better food, clothing, and shelter was a strong inducement for men facing extreme privation and perhaps even death.

An article written by 2nd Lt. Thomas J. Eccles, which appeared in the South Carolina *Yorkville Enquirer* on October 7, 1864, reflected the view of many Confederate soldiers towards galvanized Confederates. Eccles, who was a member of Company D of Gill's Battalion of South Carolina Reserves, was one of the guards at Florence. Eccles opposed the recruitment of the prisoners and said they should not be allowed to take the oath and join the Confederate Army. He later acquiesced and said, "it is probable they will be sent to such places as they may be made useful."[8] That was hardly a strong statement of support, but perhaps an acknowledgement of an accomplished fact.

The intent of the Confederate officials when recruiting prisoners for any galvanized unit or to fill in troops for existing units was to target foreign-born prisoners who might have a weaker allegiance to the federal government than those who were native-born. Key Confederate military and political leaders had been officers in the Mexican-American War, and they were aware that hundreds of recent immigrants had deserted and joined the Mexican Army to form the St. Patrick's Battalion during that war. Most those men had been Irish or German Catholics who deserted because of their poor treatment in the American Army.[9] Vincent F. Martin reported that a large number of native-born men joined the Brooks Battalion while claiming to be Englishmen, and that the battalion included Irish, Germans, Spaniards, and one Italian.[10]

A roster of the members of Brooks Battalion was compiled by consulting the National Park Service (NPS) website and the Brooks Battalion service records.[11] The roster, as compiled by the NPS, includes 788 names, while the service records roster was reduced to 620 during the current research. The actual number mustered with the unit was probably closer to 610, and several duplicates may be present on even the reduced list. At least part of the difference between the two resulted from eliminating variations of the same name given on the NPS list. No service records include the recruit's country of origin. The available service records list their names, rank, company, date enlisted, date mustered into the Confederate Army, age, who enlisted them, where enlisted, and clothing receipts.

An undated list of prisoners at Florence Stockade from the South Carolina Department of Archives and History contained the names of 132 prisoners and their countries of origin.[12] Forty of those names correlate with names on the roster of the Brooks Battalion. That correlation was strong enough to support the assumption that the list contained the names of at least some of the men who applied to join the Brooks Battalion. Analysis of the list indicates that only 11 were born in the United States, while the foreign-born were from Canada, England, Ireland, Scotland, Prussia, and France. The native-born on the list were from Virginia, Maryland, Tennessee, Indiana, and Kentucky, all of which were border states or had significant numbers of southern sympathizers.

Inspector General J. F. Lay had recommended on September 30, 1864, that the men raised for the Brooks Battalion be placed in a separate camp.[13] The location of that camp remains unknown, but may have been near the prison burial ground to the north at the same location as the later camp of the 8th Confederate Infantry.[14]

John H. Cosart (Joseph or Jasper Cozart of Company C in the service records) wrote an account of his experiences in the Brooks Battalion, published in the April 1875 edition of the *Neighbor's Home Mail.* Cosart first served in the 27th New York Infantry and then the 4th Michigan Cavalry. Cosart was in the 4th Michigan when captured. He was born in New York and lived in Lyons Village in Wayne County, New York, with his parents at the time of the 1860 census. He was also enumerated there in the 1870 census. He escaped from Goldsboro, North Carolina, on March 16, 1865, during transport from Florence to Wilmington. He was listed as a clerk on the 1860 census and as a shoemaker on the 1870. The 1900 census listed him as a "Manufacturer of Soles for Shoes," married to Louise Cosart for 17 years. He passed away in 1932. The list of 132 prisoners at Florence found in the South Carolina Archives included Cosart, and he may have been on the list because of his background as a clerk or shoemaker. His account appears to be factual and is the best account available from the perspective of one of the galvanized Confederates.[15]

Cosart said that eight companies of one hundred men each were recruited and moved from the prison to an external camp. He described the appearance of his fellow recruits as "grotesque in the extreme." He further said: "In due time we were shorn of rags and hair, properly clothed and fed, and gained so rapidly that in a few weeks we were deemed able to perform camp duties."[16]

Six companies (A-F) mustered into the Confederate Army at Summerville, South Carolina, on November 17, 1864. It is unclear if the battalion originally enlisted eight companies as Cosart indicated, but the service records only include six companies and a little over 600 men. A battalion of 600 men is consistent with the size of the 8th Confederate Infantry (2nd Foreign Battalion) raised by Garnett Andrews.[17] It is more likely that if eight companies were initially recruited, then men found unfit for service were returned to the prison and the battalion was trimmed to six companies prior to its muster in Summerville.[18]

The officers assigned to the Brooks Battalion came mainly from existing commands. John Hampden Brooks commanded the battalion. Brooks was a Captain when assigned to the command. His motive in accepting the command was to achieve the promotion to Lt. Colonel that he had long sought. He unsuccessfully sought that promotion in the late spring to early summer, when the post became available on the 22nd South Carolina Infantry, despite endorsements from highly placed Confederate military and political leaders. John Hampden Brooks was the younger brother of Rep. Preston Brooks, who gained fame in the south and infamy in the north for caning Senator Charles Sumner at his Senate desk in 1856. Preston Brooks, who nearly beat Sumner to death with his cane, died of natural causes in 1857, but he left a powerful legacy for his family in the south.[19] D. Augustus Dickert refers to him as "Captain" in his 1899 book, *History of Kershaw's Brigade*.[20] Brooks requested the promotion to Lt. Col. in a letter written from Charleston on January 10, 1865, after the Brooks Battalion had disbanded, again without success.[21] Brooks sent a letter to General P. G. T. Beauregard from Ninety-Six, South Carolina, on March 1, 1891, asking him to attest to Brook's assertion that a promotion was supposed to have come with his assignment to command the Brooks Battalion. He signed that letter as "Late Lt. Col. 2nd Batt., C.S.A." Beauregard answered Brook's request and said that he indeed had been entitled to the promotion.[22]

Brooks had a distinguished military career. He fought at both First Manassas and Bentonville, was on picket duty at Fort Wagner when it was first attacked, and was wounded three times at Drury's Bluff. He was detached from his unit, the 7th South Carolina Battalion, until his wounds healed. Brooks assumed command of what was to become the Brooks Battalion when he returned to duty. He commanded unattached troops in Charleston after the Brooks Battalion mutiny, but soon returned to the 7th

South Carolina Battalion at his own request. Brooks was a "prominent" planter in Edgefield County, South Carolina, when Vincent F. Martin wrote his history of the Brooks Battalion in 1897.[23]

Most, if not all, of the officers assigned to the Brooks Battalion assumed their posts at the direct request of Captain Brooks and most received promotions. Those assigned directly from active duty with other units had distinguished military records and were competent officers. Vincent F. Martin, who was to later write the most complete available account of the battalion from a Confederate viewpoint (published in Brooks 1912), joined the unit from the 1st South Carolina Infantry (Butler). Martin had been a Lieutenant in that unit and rejoined the 1st South Carolina Infantry at Fort Moultrie after serving with the Brooks Battalion. Martin was promoted to Captain when he joined the Brooks Battalion and placed in command of Company A. Martin described himself as a farmer and as the County Superintendant of Education in Oconee County, South Carolina, in his 1897 history.[24]

John C. Minott was a 2nd Lt in the 1st South Carolina Infantry (Butler) when Brooks requested his transfer to the new battalion. Minott, promoted to Captain, took command of Company B. He rejoined his old unit after the Brooks Battalion disbanded and joined Martin at Fort Moultrie. Minott survived the war, but died before Martin wrote his history in 1897.

J. Louis (or Lewis) Wardlaw was a 1st Lt. in the 1st South Carolina Infantry (Butler) when his transfer was requested by Brooks. Wardlaw also promoted to Captain and commanded Company C. He was in business by the time Martin wrote his history of the Brooks Battalion in 1897. Wardlaw, disabled by an old wound after his service in the Brooks Battalion, was in a convalescent unit when the war ended.[25]

No military record for Charles Goodwyn was found. He served the battalion as Lieutenant and Adjutant (or Assistant Adjutant in some accounts). The position of Adjutant in the Confederate Army was primarily an administrative position, and it is likely that Goodwyn was a civilian recruited for the job. Martin indicated that Goodwyn was in business in Columbia, South Carolina, in 1897.[26]

Eldred J. Simkins was a 1st Lt. in the 1st South Carolina Artillery when recruited by Brooks to command Company D. Simkins returned to that regiment after the Brooks Battalion disbanded. Martin indicated that Simkins died in Florida before he wrote his history of the Brooks Battalion in 1897, but that information was incorrect. Lt. Simkins ended up in

Navarro County, Texas, where he had a distinguished career as a judge until his death on June 23, 1903.[27]

First Sgt. James Johnson commanded Company E. Johnson, a 27 year old prisoner in the muster documents, had been recruited with the rest of the battalion at Florence Stockade. The assignment of a prisoner to command Company E reflects the difficulty Brooks had in recruiting Confederate officers.[28]

B. G. Pinckney joined the Brooks Battalion from his position as Acting Assistant Inspector General for General Trapier of the 4th Military District of South Carolina. He had previously risen as high as the rank of Major in the 2nd Battalion of South Carolina Sharp Shooters, a rank revoked "as mistake in the appointment." The authorities dropped Pinckney from the rolls of the 2nd Battalion, and he ceased to be an officer in the Confederate Army. He joined the staff of Gen. Trapier after that time, and continually petitioned for a commission. He enlisted in the Brooks Battalion as a Captain.[29] Captain Pinckney first commanded Company F and then commanded the Brooks Battalion soldiers left at Summerville when the main command left for Savannah. He then returned those men to the Florence Stockade. Pinckney was a prominent businessman in Charleston when Martin wrote his history of the unit in 1897.[30]

Second Lt. A. R. Toutant was the nephew of Gen. Pierre Gustave Toutant Beauregard, and he probably received his position on that basis. A. R. Toutant was an Aide-de-Camp for General Beauregard before he joined the Brooks Battalion and apparently returned to that role for a while after the battalion was disbanded. Second Lt. Toutant transferred from Gen. Beauregard's staff to the 1st Foreign Battalion, or Tucker's Regiment, and joined that unit on March 28, 1865.[31] That was just in time to surrender with General Johnston's command on April 28, 1865. A. R. Toutant was the only Confederate officer known to have served with two galvanized units.

The final officer listed for the Brooks Battalion was Lt. Ulysess Robert Brooks. U. R. Brooks was expected to join the Brooks Battalion from the 6th South Carolina Cavalry, where he had served as a private. It is unclear if he ever joined the battalion. He surrendered with the 6th South Carolina Cavalry as a part of Gen. Johnston's army in late April 1865. U. R. Brooks edited the volume that contained Martin's history of the Brooks Battalion.[32]

The details of the camp life of the officers or men while they were in Summerville are unknown. Cosart witnessed the burial of one member of the unit while stationed there. He was part of a burial detail for a man who had died in the camp hospital. He said that they carried the body to the burial site in the forest on a litter made of muskets. The single mourner was the brother of the deceased. The deceased man and his brother had joined an Indiana regiment to raise money for a payment on a home that they could not otherwise raise, and they had left their widowed mother at home alone when they joined the Union Army. Cosart did not give the names of the dead man and his brother, and their names could not be determined during the current research.[33]

The men of the Brooks Battalion were not entirely under the control of their officers during their stay in Summerville. Cosart said of their stay in Summerville: "Our stay in Summerville was prematurely terminated by the frequent incursions of our foraging parties. The citizens grew clamorous for our removal and we accordingly removed, having gained nothing by our sojourn there but the appellation of galvanized Yankees."[34]

The problem of theft by members of the Brooks Battalion apparently began soon after they arrived in Summerville. First Sgt. John L. Hoster, writing in his unpublished diary on November 21 at the Florence Stockade, noted that Personner (listed as John Perrse of Company C), who, along with Hoster, had belonged to Company A of the 148rd New York Infantry, had been returned early to Florence. Hoster stated in his diary: "He says the rations were about the same as here but by foraging, they got all the chickens, fresh pork, and sweet potatoes they wanted. Citizens and Negroes had to stand guard over their henroosts [*sic*] to keep the galvanized Yanks from stealing the chickens. He thinks his squad was sent back for stealing."

Hoster noted that more galvanized Yankees reached Florence on December 1 and December 12.[35] It is likely that Companies E-F, left behind at Summerville when Companies A-D pulled out, was the group returned to prison in December 12. Those companies, left under the command of Captain Pinckney, returned to Florence immediately after the main group left for Savannah.[36] The group returned to prison between November 21 and December 12 outnumbered those sent to Savannah, and it is likely that Companies A-D consisted of the best from all six companies. Further, the Brooks Battalion clearly did not have enough experienced officers to field all six companies (or even four) as an effective fighting force at that point.

Two hundred and fifty men of Companies A-D went to Savannah on December 10. The companies passed through Charleston and across the Ashley River, where they were loaded onto platform cars and taken by rail to Savannah. The men were reportedly in good spirits and sang Confederate patriotic songs early in the trip. The officers, who travelled in a passenger car at the rear of the train, joined the enlisted men for a time. The battalion unloaded at Savannah and passed through the city at night on the way to the front. The men received a meal of tea, coffee, sugar, and soft bread when they arrived at the front.[37]

The original purpose in sending companies A-D to Savannah was to use them in what became the Battle of Honey Hill, but they arrived after the battle was over. Their first position was behind earthworks near Monteith Swamp, under the command of General Mercer. They soon moved several miles to a new position in the center of the defenses held by General McLaws' Division. General Mercer, replaced by division commander General McLaws, assumed command of a 900-man force in McLaws' Division that included the Brooks Battalion.[38]

General Mercer was not familiar with the nature of the Brooks Battalion when it joined his command in Savannah, and he deployed it as he would have any other Confederate unit. That is how that unit came to occupy a highly sensitive part of the fortifications.[39] Gen. Mercer asked for volunteers to serve as pickets the first night the battalion was deployed behind Monteith Swamp, and 15 men, under the command of a sergeant, stepped forward. Cosart said that the men seemed overeager to volunteer and he and others were concerned about what that might mean. All fifteen men and their sergeant were missing the next morning and presumably had deserted. Five men from the Brooks Battalion rejoined Union lines on December 10. Those men included Theodore Berg or Burg (formerly of the 124th Indiana Infantry), Frank W. Cole (formerly of the 58th Massachusetts Infantry), Michael Lyons (formerly of the 27th Massachusetts Infantry), Thomas McKinna (formerly of the 1st Connecticut Infantry), and James Motley (formerly of the 15th U.S. Infantry). The men included two from Company A, two from Company C, and one from Company B. The desertion of those men apparently was the beginning point of the plot that would end badly for the men of the battalion.[40]

The battalion moved to a new position the afternoon of their first day in Savannah, reaching the new location that night. That position was in a dense forest in front of a large rice swamp crossed by a causeway at their front. Corporal McQuade, in his testimony during the trial of Gen. Mercer after the war, indicated that the men of the battalion were detailed to dig their own earthworks, and that they were completed despite the fact that some of the men refused to work.[41]

Research conducted by local Savannah historian Norman Vincent Turner indicates that the second position occupied by the battalion was on Lawton's

Farm near an area now known as Silk Hope. That position was west of what was then downtown Savannah. They probably reached that position by December 12.[42]

A Union sniper wounded one soldier after they took their position at Lawton Farm. He would prove to be the only casualty in the unit caused by enemy fire suffered. The men of Company C killed the sniper after he was located by Capt. Wardlaw.[43] The wounded man, shot in the right arm, lost the arm to an amputation. Cosart did not identify the wounded man, but said he had met him in Annapolis, Maryland, after the war and that he was in "good condition."[44]

The desertions continued after the battalion took their position on Lawton Farm. The number of men who deserted is difficult to determine; Captain Martin said that 60 men deserted at one time,[45] while McQuade put the number at over 100 in his deposition and at 100 to 150 in his testimony.[46] Cosart estimated the total number of desertions from the battalion between its muster and its disbanding was 75.[47] Federal Records listed 14 men who deserted on December 10 and 14. That does not match up with any of the number of desertions thought to have taken place. It is curious that a number of escaped prisoners of war rejoined Union lines at Savannah at the same time the desertions from the Brooks Battalion were taking place. It is possible that those men were members of the Brooks Battalion who had joined under assumed names and returned to the Union authorities under their real names, but that seems to be unlikely given available information.[48]

Nine men from the Brooks Battalion made their way to Union lines in Savannah on December 14. Those men were Zachariah Blake (5th Virginia Infantry), W. Cragan (111th Illinois Infantry), Sgt. John Dean (24th Massachusetts Infantry), Herbert Ege (or Ego) (1st U.S. Sharp Shooters, also called the 1st Michigan Infantry), Jacob A. Ege (or Ego) (5th Michigan Cavalry), Newton Heard (4th U.S. Artillery), Peter Norton (or Naughtan) (65th New York Infantry), William Winslow (16th Connecticut Infantry), and Lewis Young (or Youngs) (75th New York Infantry). Those who deserted on December 14 included one from Company A, three from Company B, two from Company C, and three from Company D.[49]

According to McQuade one man was caught trying to desert on December 14 and was held to be executed the next day. McQuade identified that man in his affidavit as a red haired man named Brannan. Brannan was probably James Brainard, a 20-year-old private from Company D. It is not possible to identify Brannan or Brainard further with available records.

McQuade managed to slip away during the confusion, but he claimed to have observed the aftermath of the mutiny from nearby. Martin claimed that two men were caught trying to escape instead of one. Martin, as a company commander, was probably in a position to better identify what transpired than McQuade. It is likely that the second one thought to have tried to desert or to be complicit in the desertions was George Montgomery. Montgomery was a 22-year-old private identified by McQuade as an orderly from Company D. McQuade said that Montgomery was relieved from his duty at a nearby cannon (probably the cannon under the command of Simkins, who commanded Company D) and arrested at the time of the attempted mutiny. Montgomery is a common name, and nothing definitive was found in the available records about George Montgomery.[50]

According to Cosart, the plan that ended with an attempted mutiny was hatched immediately after the battalion reached Savannah. He described the plan:

> Directly to our rear and only a few rods from us, was the headquarters of Gen. Mercer, who had moved with us. It was believed that these officers with our own could be taken with us without causing an alarm, and so it was decided. The plan was well understood and in the hands of a few leading spirits was bound to succeed. The movement was to commence at one o'clock, ten of the company was to seize the General and staff (amounting in all to only three), gag them, and march to the end of the causeway. A picked squad was then to march out as if to relieve the picket line, capture them, and move on across the swamp. As soon as this was accomplished the remainder was to follow in their wake. The plot was thoroughly practical and all were pleased with the arrangement.[51]

Francis C. Shrenk, in his affidavit, said the plan to mutiny was made soon after the battalion arrived in Savannah, with 12 men involved in the plot. The plot began as an escape attempt and developed into a plan to mutiny and take the officers hostage.[52]

Martin identified the pickets stationed on both ends of the causeway in front of the battalion's camp as members of a militia unit. There were apparently only two pickets at each end, which would have meant that the plan as described by Cosart would have had a good chance of success.[53]

The plan to mutiny was revealed to Captain Martin by Sgt. Sinner of Company A. Sgt. Sinner was described by Martin as "a splendid specimen of the Teuton, about six foot three inches tall, well proportioned, and with a handsome face, with blue eyes and golden hair." Shrenk said the men of the battalion feared Sinner because of his "courage and strength."[54]

No Sgt. Sinner was listed in the Brooks Battalion muster records, and the closest fit was Sgt. George Linner of Company A. Further research revealed a clothing receipt for Joseph Sinner, an enlisted federal of Company A in an undesignated unit; this information was found among *Unfiled Papers and Slips Belonging in Compiled Service Records* in the National Archives.[55] That was clearly the Sgt. Sinner of the Brooks Battalion, which means that "Linner" may have been a transcription error from the original rolls or a different man. Joseph Sinner entered the Union Army in the 4th New Hampshire Infantry as a private and was promoted to corporal before transferring to the navy.[56] He enlisted in the navy at Hampton Roads on April 29, 1864, as an Ordinary Seaman in General Service on the USS *Atlanta.* The enlistment record described him as 23 years old, a native of Germany, with hazel eyes and fair hair and skin. His height was given as 5' 10 ½", short of the 6'3" attributed to him by Captain Martin, but still tall for the era.[57] It is most likely he was a deserter, as the USS *Atlanta,* originally a Confederate ship, was never recaptured. Nothing is known of Sinner subsequent to the Brooks Battalion.

Sinner revealed the plot to Captain Martin shortly after the announcement that the battalion was going to be moved closer to Savannah starting at 8 PM. According to Martin:

> Just after the announcement Sergeant Sinner told Captain Martin that he wished to see him alone. They went into the officer's tent, and Sinner then said that the men had determined to desert in a body at half-past 7 o'clock, and that they intended to buck and gag the officers and take them with them, and if they resisted, which they expected them to do, intended to kill them and take them anyhow. Captain Martin asked him if he was certain, and remarked that when in the earthwork a few days before the men acted like men who intended to fight. Sinner replied: "They would have stood to you to a man that day, but General Sherman has sent an emissary among them and told them if they will come over he will spare them, but if they do not, when he captures the city he will shoot every one of them."

Sinner told Martin that the men would kill him if they found out that he was there with Martin, and Sinner asked to have the ordnance sergeant bring several bayonets so he could select one as a ruse to cover his presence. Sinner selected a bayonet in front of the men and returned to Company A.[58]

Martin's first action after learning of the plot was to call Captain Brooks to his tent to inform him of it. He and Brooks put together a plan to alert a nearby unit and to bring it in to capture the men of the battalion. While walking through the camp Brooks and Martin encountered Orderly Sgt. Foraker of Company B who, when asked by Brooks how he was feeling, responded to Brooks with the single word "bully" and kept walking without saluting. That convinced Brooks that Foraker was part of the plot. Further, they observed men breaking the stacks, taking their guns, and throwing cartridges into the fire. They heard "loud and boisterous" laughter from Company B while that was going on, while Company A remained quiet. Captain Wardlaw, who was the officer of the day, was unable to bring the men under control, and was unable to get the sergeant of the guard to arrest those causing the disturbance. Wardlaw eventually drew his sword and threatened to decapitate anyone who threw a cartridge into the fire.[59]

Captain Brooks sent Captain Minott and Assistant Adjutant Goodwin to get help, but they soon realized that other troops might be slow to respond to them. Brooks then left at the urging of Captain Martin to add his voice to the request for help. They sent Lt. Toutant, nephew of Gen. Beauregard, out of the camp to safety, which left Martin and Wardlaw to face the mutineers in the camp. Simkins turned his cannon at the head of the causeway on the camp. Simkins made several trips to the camp to check on Martin and Wardlaw. One of the mutineers said to another after one of the trips, "Why did you not shoot him?"[60]

Captain Brooks, with Captain Minott and Assistant Adjutant Goodwin, proceeded to General Mercer's headquarters to get help. General Mercer's headquarters were in the Lawton's house to the left of the position occupied by the Brooks Battalion. Mercer sent his Aide de Camp, Captain Stodard, to General McLaw's headquarters to request that he send men to help put down the mutiny, as Mercer's own command was stretched too thin to provide the needed force. The men that McLaws sent were members of the Georgia Militia, which was under the command Col. William M. Browne. Col. Browne conducted the court martial that followed the incident and, according to the affidavit of Francis C. Schrenk, members of the Georgia militia made up the firing squad.[61]

Captain Martin said that the main reason the mutineers did not kill Wardlaw and himself was that the plan to capture or kill them at 7:30 had been changed to wait until the companies were formed up at 8 PM and the officers took their places at the head of their companies. Martin led the men on to believe they would be forming up in a "few moments." The mutineers repeatedly asked if they would have time to boil rice before the move as an attempt to determine when they were going to leave. In the midst of this, Simkins insisted that he wanted to go check on the men tied to a log for attempted desertion. Martin dissuaded him because he was afraid that if Simkins was observed checking on them and they had already been released by the mutineers, it would confirm to the men that their conspiracy was known.[62]

The point soon came when the mutineers would wait no longer. Captain Martin, armed with a sword and pistol, and Captain Wardlaw, armed only with a sword, stood with their backs to a tree to fight as best they could. The men of Company B picked up their guns and began to advance on the two officers, but they suddenly stopped and began talking among themselves. They were concerned about the absence of the other officers in the camp and were afraid they were walking into an ambush. The mutineers faltered and a man identified only as a "German barber" stepped forward and urged Company B to follow him towards the officers. The men of Company B failed to follow him, and the mutiny was effectively over. About 30 minutes later, Captain Brooks led a relief party of armed men towards Company A and disarmed that company. Captain Minott then moved the Georgia Reserve troops he had brought as a rescue force forward to disarm Company B. Goodwin entered the camp with the rescue force he had assembled shortly after that and ended any prospect that the mutiny had of success. The German barber tried to urge Company B forward at 8 PM and again at 8:30, when the rescue force arrived.[63]

Cosart recalled a different timeline. He said that the camp remained silent until 9 PM, by which time a number of the men who were part of the conspiracy had fallen asleep. He said when "movements in the adjacent camp" indicated discovery of the plot, the guard force sent out on the causeway and the few men in the plot who were awake crossed the causeway to freedom. Those who remained in the camp were surrounded and taken prisoner.[64]

McQuade said that the plan was to "make a raid and escape" at 10 PM, but that the plan was revealed to the Confederates by Sgt. Senner [*sic*] and a "Spaniard called Fernandez." McQuade said 1st Georgia Militia surrounded the camp, and the cannon (commanded by Simkins) was pointed at the camp. His timing for the capture was between 8 and 9 PM, which closely agrees with Captain Martin. The Georgia militiamen ordered the battalion to "stack their guns and fall back."[65]

Martin, Cosart, and McQuade agree that seven members of the battalion were under arrest at the end of the mutiny. McQuade named Brannan and George Montgomery, arrested for attempted desertion the day before. McQuade further named Clifford, who was probably Charles Clifford of Company D shown in the muster roles as 2nd Sgt. of Company D. Alternatively, Clifford may have been Samuel Clifford of the same company, listed on the muster roles as a 5th Sgt. McQuade said that Brannan, Montgomery, and Clifford were all from New York. McQuade also named "Four Acres," who he said was from Massachusetts. "Four Acres" was the Sgt. Foraker of Company B, named by Martin as being part of the conspiracy. No one by the name of Foraker or a name remotely like Foraker was on the battalion muster role. The fifth man arrested was Sgt. James Wilson of Company A. Martin said that Brooks found him lying down reading a book after securing the camp. Brooks questioned him about his role in the mutiny, to which Wilson said "what mutiny?" That led Brooks to decide he was guilty of being one of the leaders of the mutiny.[66]

The two remaining men put under arrest were not identified. One was the unnamed German barber from Company B. Captain Martin indicated that four of the men arrested were orderly sergeants.[67] Sergeants Wilson and Foraker were apparently orderly sergeants for Companies A and B. while Clifford probably filled that role for Company D. That means that the unnamed orderly sergeant was from Company C. There were five sergeants in Company C at the time of the muster at Summerville. John Charles Murray was a 1st Sgt. while Anthony Bertrand, John Dean, William Francis, and James Moore were sergeants. Anthony Bertrand was originally from the 24th New York Cavalry. He later enlisted in the 8th Confederate Infantry, also called the 2nd Foreign Legion, and survived the war.[68] If the ranks remained the same in Company C, the most likely candidate to have been the fourth orderly sergeant arrested was John Charles Murray. One orderly sergeant described as a very small Englishman with rings in his ears was likely either Clifford or the sergeant from Company C.

Francis Shrenk, in his affidavit and during his testimony in the trial of Gen. Mercer after the war, said that he was one of only 12 men who were part of the plot. He further said that only one of the seven men arrested for desertion or mutiny was actually part of the plot.[69]

The trial of the seven men was apparently brief. Captain Martin said that the information given him by Sgt. Sinner was corroborated by Sgt. Hernandez, who was the "Spaniard called Fernandez" mentioned by McQuade.[70] Hernandez, listed as Pvt. Manuel Fernandez of Company A in the original muster roster, was 25 years old. Research among available service records indicated that a man of the same name had been a private in Company G of the 14th Connecticut Infantry, but it cannot be certain that the two were the same man. The Fernandez who was the member of the 14th Connecticut deserted around the time of the Battle of the Wilderness.[71]

The officers separated Sgt. Sinner and Sgt. Fernandez from the rest of the men, as well as Pvt. William Seymour of Company A, who was Brooks' orderly. Seymour was 16 years old on the muster roster.[72] Sinner, Fernandez, or Seymour disappeared after the mutiny and it is likely they changed their names and relocated to avoid retribution.

A firing squad executed the seven men arrested and found guilty of desertion or mutiny. Cosart said that Gen. Mercer was present at the execution and had the names of the seven men read off to him before he ordered their execution. He said they were marched into a thicket next to where the rest of the battalion stood under guard with their hands tied behind them. Cosart said that the condemned faced their execution bravely, and one said "let's die with our enemies in front, boys." The remainder of the battalion then left for Savannah and heard the sound of the rifles behind them.[73]

Martin said men from the Georgia reserves made up the firing squad, and two of the men survived the first shots. The execution squad fired at the remaining two men until an officer stepped forward and had them more carefully direct their fire. They buried the men in the field. The affidavits and testimony of both McQuade and Schrenk largely corroborated Captain Martin's account, which indicated that it took three volleys to kill the seven.[74]

The attempted mutiny and the removal of the battalion to Savannah took place on December 15. The officers of the Brooks Battalion took charge of the men then held in Savannah as prisoners on December 16. The men of the Brooks Battalion built the pontoon bridge used to evacuate Savannah, and it was clear by then that the evacuation was imminent. The battalion officers learned that the men were threatening to kill them as General Sherman entered Savannah, and Captain Brooks asked Gen. Hardee and Gen. Beauregard for orders to evacuate. Major Black, who had administered the oath of allegiance to the men in Summerville, finally ordered Brooks to be the first to evacuate his command across the pontoon bridge. The battalion crossed the pontoon bridge at about 4 AM on December 21, under guard by troops from Cook's Battalion of Infantry, which was a Georgia reserve unit. The battalion made the crossing without incident and stopped for breakfast after they had travelled several miles from Savannah. It was at that point that an anonymous voice yelled "Remember Sergeant Wilson of Company A" as Martin passed Company A. The officers were unable to identify that man.[75]

At least five men managed to desert after the battalion left Savannah. Pvt. J. Shelton of Company C escaped with Captain Wardlaw's knapsack, which contained his money and clothing. The clothing in the knapsack included a uniform that had cost Wardlaw $1,800. Shelton, of the 51st New York Infantry, turned himself in to Union authorities in Savannah on December 21. Four other men from the Brooks Battalion crossed into Union lines on December 21. Those men were Thomas Campbell (28th Massachusetts Infantry), Thomas Lee (7th Connecticut Infantry), Henry Lewis (20th Massachusetts Infantry), and William Smith (9th New Hampshire Infantry). One man, Anthony N. Montgomery (6th Tennessee Infantry), had rejoined Union lines on December 20.[76]

The scene at Hardeeville, South Carolina, was chaotic when the battalion arrived. Brooks intended to return the members of the battalion to Florence via the railroad, but space on the railroad cars was filled by reserve troops and the sick and injured. Company A was making the loudest threats at that time, and Captain Martin received permission from Brooks to load his company on the train even if it meant separating them from the battalion. Brooks ordered Company A to climb on top of a railroad car, and the roof of the car collapsed after a third of them had loaded. Martin reformed the Company and moved it to the next car, where he was confronted by a man who threatened to kill anyone who tried to get onto the car. Martin threatened the man with his own pistol, at which point room was made for the men in the cars. The surviving members of the Brooks Battalion returned to Florence.[77]

First Sgt. Hoster chronicled the return of the men to Florence in his diary.[78] His December 23 entry reads in part: "A lot of galvanized Yanks came in today from Savannah. Sherman took Savannah on the run. They had laid a plot to spike the guns and kill the officers in charge of them and make for our lines. They were betrayed, however, by one of their own men and in the night while they were asleep and their arms in stack they were surrounded by a regiment of genuine rebs and seven orderly sergts were taken out and shot without ceremony and the men kept under guard and sent here. Their blankets were all taken from them when they were turned into the stockade." Cosart tallied the cost of the Brooks Battalion in human terms. He reported that 75 escaped, three died, seven were executed, and one was wounded.[79]

A few of the men from the battalion did not return to Florence. As previously mentioned, Sinner, Fernandez, and Seymour were separated from the unit in Savannah, and nothing more is known about their fate. Brooks, in a report published in the *Reports and Resolutions of the General Assembly of the State of South Carolina* for the 1900 session, indicated that a few of the men were allowed to join the 1st South Carolina Infantry (Butler) and the 1st South Carolina Artillery.[80] A careful search of the service records for the 1st South Carolina Infantry (Butler) revealed several names that matched names from the Brooks Battalion roster, but all were common names.[81] The service records did not list any men from the Brooks Battalion. No muster rolls that postdate November-December 1864 survived for the 1st South Carolina Artillery, and it cannot be confirmed that former Brooks Battalion soldiers joined that unit. Galvanized Confederates from Florence joined the 1st South Carolina Artillery before the Brooks Battalion mustered in at Summerville. Only two men who joined the 1st Artillery had names that duplicated those listed on the Brooks Battalion roster. Both names were common names and may not have been the same men.[82]

As many as 38 members of the Brooks Battalion may have enlisted in the 2nd Foreign Battalion (the 8th Confederate Infantry). The actual number that joined that unit was probably smaller, as many of the names duplicated on both lists were relatively common names. Two names on both lists were recruited into the 8th Confederate from Salisbury, and it is unlikely they were veterans of the Brooks Battalion. The remaining 36 men came from Florence or an unspecified place. Excluding the two recruited from Salisbury, the Brooks Battalion companies represented in the 8th Confederate were fairly even. There were 8 recruits from Company A, 6 from Company B, 3 from Company C, 5 from Company D, and 5 from Company F. Five recruits were not listed by company.[83]

At least four members of the Brooks Battalion who were returned to Florence later escaped. Those men, who escaped on December 20, were Charles W. Buchanon (48th Illinois), Edward Kenepp (48th Illinois), Joseph Graham, (4th Kentucky Infantry), and Francis St. Francis (4th Kentucky Cavalry). All four men had enlisted in Company E. Two other men of Company E, Thomas Smith (99th Pennsylvania Infantry) and John Henry Coleman (2nd Maryland Cavalry) crossed Union lines at Savannah on May 5 and 6.[84]

The list of prisoners who died at Florence Stockade was lost or hidden away after the war. Rev. Albert H. Ledoux has devoted many years to reconstructing that list, and his *The Union Dead of the Florence Stockade* is the best source that is currently available.[85] Correlation of the names of those in the Brooks Battalion with Ledoux's list indicates that at least ten members of the battalion died at the prison. The real death toll of former Brooks Battalion members among the 2,800 or more who died at Florence was probably much higher.

Gen. Hugh W. Mercer, arrested on August 3, 1865, by order of Secretary of War Stanton and Gen. Grant, was tried for the execution of the seven members of the Brooks Battalion at Savannah. Mercer was held at Fort Pulaski in Savannah until his trial began on December 16, 1865. Historian Norman Vincent Turner wrote an excellent account of Gen. Mercer's trial based on contemporary newspaper accounts and the diary of George A. Mercer, son of Gen. Mercer.[86] Turner's account has been supplemented with information gained from the Turner-Baker Papers, which documents the affidavits of two former members of the Brooks Battalion brought to Savannah to testify against Gen. Mercer.[87]

George A. Mercer contended that his father's arrest resulted from a letter sent to the War Department by Brigadier General William Passmore Carlin who commanded the 1st Division of the XIV Corps in Sherman's Army. Carlin's letter apparently has not survived, but a partial file with correspondence about the accusations was found.[88] Carlin's letter, referred up the chain-of-command on June 24, 1865, apparently had been written shortly before that date. The defense questioned the long delay between the executions and Carlin's accusations without a response.

Carlin testified on December 18, 1865, that a group of 27 men deserted from the Confederate Army to his position on December 13 or 14, 1864, and that they informed him of the failed plot to mutiny and the arrest of the seven. He further stated that he learned of the executions from later deserters, and that Gen. Mercer had ordered the executions. The defense attacked Gen. Carlin's testimony as hearsay and objected to it. The objection by the defense was overruled, and the defense then stated that it objected to all subsequent testimony of the witness based on hearsay. A series of adjournments followed, as the prosecution tried to line up their witnesses. The government postponed the trial indefinitely on December 22.[89]

Prosecutors then advertised in newspapers in northern cities, asking former members of the Brooks Battalion who had information on the executions to come forward. Francis C. Shrenk (also spelled "Schrenk"), who then lived in New York, was brought to the attention of the Judge Advocate's office by Wm. H. Yancy of the Indemnity Fire Insurance Company. Shrenk had been a member of the 5th New Jersey Infantry and had joined the Brooks Battalion under the name Charles Geissler or Gesseler. Shrenk claimed in his affidavit that he had seen Gen. Mercer preside over the court martial after he had successfully deserted the battalion. The prosecution gave him travel money to come to Savannah, and he agreed to testify at the trial.[90]

The other former member of the Brooks Battalion who came forward was Edward McQuade, who then lived in New York City. He had been a member of the 5th Rhode Island Infantry and joined the Brooks Battalion under his own name. He also agreed to testify, and the prosecution gave him travel money to come to Savannah.[91]

McQuade could not say with certainty that Gen. Mercer was present at the court martial of the seven. Shrenk, contrary to what he had stated in his affidavit, said he thought Gen. Mercer was present, but he was not certain of his identification. They both agreed that the court martial took about twenty minutes, and both heard the gunshots when the men were executed. Shrenk stated a company of Georgia militia executed the seven.[92]

The next prosecution witness testified on January 20, 1866. William Evans said he was 25 years old and a native of Salmersville, Ohio. He said he had been a 2nd Lieutenant in the 210th Pennsylvania Infantry, but he was not in Union service at the time the executions took place. He said he was in Savannah on private business, heard that "certain soldiers were to be executed," and went to where the executions were supposed to take place. He saw a group of men and heard two volleys of musket fire about 30 minutes later. He did not hear Gen. Mercer order the executions and did not know if he had been present.[93]

The defense called three witnesses on January 20. The first witness was Octavus S. Cohen, who had been Ordnance Officer on Col. Harrison's staff when he commanded the Florence prison. He said he was present at the enlistment of the battalion, and that the men had enlisted on their own free will. He said that many of the men who enlisted had been on the internal police force at Florence. He said that the enlistees received the same rations as the other prisoners at Florence, which consisted of a pound of corn meal, a pound of beef, and a third of a pound of bacon when they had no beef. He said they received syrup when there was no meat and sometimes received beans and rice. He specifically said that those rations were not the rations given to the police force but was the food given to regular prisoners.

It is clear from Hoster's diary,[94] and archaeological and research on one of the Florence guard camps conducted by Avery and Garrow that Cohen's account of camp rations was not true,[95] but he was trying to prove that the members of the Brooks Battalion were there of their own free will.[96]

The second defense witness was William M. Gibbons, who described himself as a resident of Savannah and a clerk. He said that he had led the Brooks Battalion to their position in the Savannah defenses. He said he had talked to "about two-thirds" of the men in the battalion, and they said they had volunteered for Confederate service.[97] William M. Gibbons appears to have been a civilian wagon master who was paid $7.75 for 31 days of service from December 1 to December 31 in Savannah. The year of that service was probably 1864.[98]

The third, and final, defense witness was George A. Mercer, son of Gen. Mercer. He had been on Gen. Mercer's staff as Assistant Adjutant General when the executions took place. He was at the Division headquarters when officers from the Brooks Battalion came and reported the plot. Col. Browne of the Augusta (Georgia) Battalion was present, and it was apparently his unit, along with the 55th Georgia, which prevented the mutiny. Mercer testified that his father knew nothing about the court martial of the seven men until after the execution.[99]

Gen. Mercer, found not guilty of all charges, was acquitted. Martin explained the absence of the former officers of the Brooks Battalion at the trial by saying that Captains Brooks and Wardlaw were on the way to Savannah when the trial ended, while Captain Minott simply did not go. Captain Martin's father withheld his summons, although he followed the trial with "great interest." Martin had been the president of the court martial that had convicted the seven, and both he and Brooks were concerned that they would be tried for their actions. The acquittal of Gen. Mercer ended the matter.[100]

Gen. Mercer, although acquitted of the murder charge, paid a steep price for his role with the Brooks Battalion. Mercer had applied for amnesty on June 26, 1865. His application may have triggered the letter from Gen. Carlin, as Carlin's letter reached the army chain of command two days earlier. The Union government had already confiscated Mercer's northern property. The rest of his property in the south was apparently under the threat of seizure, which made it important that his amnesty request be granted. The government denied his June 1865 request in the midst of the accusations. His attorney, Cortlandt Parker, sent a letter dated July 26, 1866, asking for amnesty in light of his acquittal. He repeated the request in a letter to the

U.S. Attorney General dated October 11, 1866, and included copies of the newspaper clippings of the trial coverage as proof of the acquittal. Mercer sent a letter dated July 6, 1867, again requesting amnesty as the government was confiscating the property of those not granted amnesty in Savannah. He said that property worth $150,000 had already been confiscated in the north, and that if the rest of his property was taken he would be reduced to "absolute beggary." Edward B. Stanton, of the Washington law firm of Stanton and Worthington, asked on Mercer's behalf if amnesty had been granted. Mercer's file contained the simple notation "answered in the negative," which was dated September 19, 1876.[101] Mercer apparently died without amnesty, as he passed away on June 9, 1877.

★ CHAPTER 5 ★

The 1st Foreign Battalion/ Tucker Regiment

THE WAR DEPARTMENT authorized Julius G. Tucker, "late Captain of the 10th Virginia Cavalry," to recruit the men for the 1st Foreign Battalion on September 17, 1864. A letter from Assistant Attorney General Major John Blair Hoge, dated November 21, 1864, confirmed that original order. It authorized Tucker to raise eight companies composed entirely of foreigners and excluding both "natives" and "citizens" of the United States. According to Hoge's letter, Tucker had raised eight companies by November 1, 1864. Tucker was a Lt. Colonel by the time of Hoge's letter and a full Colonel on March 29, which reflected the expansion of his command and a change in its status from a battalion to a full regiment.[1]

Assistant Adjutant General Col. R. H. Chilton questioned the appointment of Tucker to command the 1st Foreign Battalion in a letter to Adjutant and Inspector General Gen. Samuel Cooper, dated November 3, 1864. Col. Chilton contended an Irishman should command the unit and suggested Major Riley of Haskell's Artillery Battery. Col. Chilton charged that Col. Tucker was appointing his own officers instead of allowing them to be elected and suggested that the "favoritism he was showing would erode discipline in the unit." He questioned allowing Col. Tucker to recruit foreigners of all nations, and he suggested that mixing Irishmen and Germans was like trying to mix "oil and water." He advocated a unit formed of Irish prisoners of war and commanded by Irish-born officers from Confederate Army units. Gen. Cooper apparently ignored his letter.[2]

Julius G. Tucker was one of two foreign-born Confederate officers to command one of the galvanized units. Lt. Col. John O'Neill of the 10th Tennessee Infantry, who was born in Ireland, was the other. Tucker was born in Holstein, Denmark (later Germany), in ca. 1832. He had been a steamboat captain, living in Memphis, before the war. He first joined Company G of the 10th Virginia Cavalry on August 5, 1861, and was promoted to Captain of Company E soon after. Captured near Knoxville, Tennessee, on October 24, 1862, he was exchanged on November 10 to rejoin his unit. He served as Aide-de-Camp to Gen. Fitzhugh Lee at Gettysburg; his company disbanded on February 28, 1864.[3]

Tucker moved first to New York City and then to Augusta, Georgia, after the war. He finally settled in Brownsville, Texas, where he raised stock and worked as a civil engineer. Appointed as U.S. Consul to Martinique, he served in that capacity from 1895 to 1899. Tucker died of stomach cancer while visiting his sister in Hamburg, Germany, on September 30, 1905.[4]

Tucker's Regiment, as referred to in this chapter, appears to have had adequate command and control staff in terms of numbers, although many of the officers had little or no command experience. This stands in contrast to the Brooks Battalion, which never had an adequate command staff to control its constituent companies. Each company in the Tucker Regiment had at least a Captain, a 1st Lieutenant, and two 2nd Lieutenants. The regimental headquarter staff included Tucker, an assistant surgeon, an adjutant, and later a quartermaster.[5]

The officers of the Tucker Regiment (see Appendix A) consisted of a few trained officers and a number of former enlisted men (mainly privates) from line companies, from the Virginia militia, and from local defense units. It appears that Tucker tried to recruit former drillmasters as commanders of several companies, and he chose officers based on their ability to impose and maintain discipline. Tucker honored political connections, and officers such as Capt. Boatright and 2nd Lt. Toutant probably were "elected" as officers based on their connections. Second Lt. Toutant was the only officer to serve in two galvanized units. He probably served as his uncle's (Gen. Beauregard) eyes and ears within the unit. The officer corps of the Tucker Regiment would have been inappropriate for a combat unit, but it was functional for a pioneer regiment.

The galvanized Confederates of the Tucker Regiment came primarily from the Richmond prisons and the prison at Salisbury, North Carolina. Col. Tucker raised companies A-C at the Richmond prisons (probably mainly Belle Island) on October 12, 1864, and he mustered the companies into the Confederate Army the following day. Col. Tucker recruited companies D-H at Salisbury on November 7, 1864, and Company I was raised at Salisbury on December 1. The muster date(s) of companies D-I were not recorded in the unit's service records. The recruits of Company K came from

Richmond, Salisbury, and Florence on dates that ranged from October 12, 1864, to February 1, 1865. The recruits from October 1864 were from Richmond; most of these were recruited on October 16, after the original companies had been recruited and mustered. Lt. James recruited the Company K enlistees from Florence Prison, while most from Salisbury prison were recruited by Lt. Wilkerson. Col. Tucker recruited the Company K enlistees from Richmond, as well as a few from Salisbury. The men of Company K mustered into the Confederate Army on February 17, 1865.[6]

Col. Tucker does not seem to have been very selective when enlisting Union prisoners for his command. The companies, with the exception of Company K, were recruited from October 12 to December 1, 1864, and there is no evidence to suggest that Col. Tucker raised more than the recruits mustered directly into the Confederate Army. He supposedly acted within his orders to recruit only foreign-born prisoners, but there does not seem to have been a process to evaluate the recruits over time so that the best were chosen to make up his command.

Captain Colonna's biographer wrote that he commanded a French and a German company within the Tucker Regiment, and he was able to communicate with both because he had learned French and German at VMI. Captain Colonna commanded Company D, and the roster of Company D included surnames that suggest German, French, Irish, Hispanic, and English heritage. The men of Company D came from Salisbury Prison, which seems to be the common thread that bound them together.[7]

Col. Tucker's command was in Columbia, South Carolina, when Maj. John Blair Hoge wrote a letter on November 21, 1864, confirming Tucker's authority to raise galvanized units. Maj. Hoge commented that that Col. Tucker had moved his unit to Columbia "for the purpose of completing its organization."[8]

An incomplete and undated (probably November 1864) response, written in reply to questions raised by the Secretary of War about both Tucker's and Andrews (2nd Foreign Battalion, 8th Confederate Infantry) units, stated in part: "They were . . . prohibited from enlisting any native or naturalized citizen of the U.S. In Tucker's battalion, most of the men are Catholics and have had the oath of allegiance administered by priests. But two attempted desertions to the enemy have been reported, and they were arrested and punished. Inspection reports and the testimony of Lt. General Hardee attest to the efficiency of this organization. It consists now of nine companies and application has been made with Genl. Hardee's approval for its increase to a regiment."[9]

Mary Chestnut, writing in her diary between October 28 and November 6, 1864, noted the arrival of the Tucker Regiment in Columbia. She wrote: "Next to our house, which Isabella calls 'Tillytudlem' since Mr. Davis's visit, in a common of green grasses and very level, beyond which comes a belt of pine trees. On this open space, within forty paces of us, a regiment of foreign deserters has camped. They have taken the oath of allegiance to our government, and are now being drilled and disciplined into form before being sent on to our army. Their close proximity keeps me miserable. Traitors once, traitors forever."[10]

Grace Brown Elmore shared Mary Chestnut's view of the men of the Tucker Regiment. Elmore wrote in her diary on December 4, 1864: "As I passed by the galvanized Yankee camp today, saw one fellow riding a rail and another bucked and gagged, hoped they were native born Yankees and not poor foreigners. I wonder if our authorities dream those men will fight for us. That men who have taken the oath whilst prisoners will do their best [for] us, against whom they fought but a few months ago. I can excuse foreigners and have some pity for them, but the Yankee who has taken the oath I despise if possible worse than those who stay true to the government for which they have fought and which they have sworn to protect."[11]

Riding a rail, or riding the wooden horse as it was known during the Civil War, and bucking and gagging were common punishments during the Civil War. Riding the wooden horse was a punishment where a soldier sat astride a fence rail for a prescribed period without his feet touching the ground. This was a painful punishment, as the fence rail was triangular in section and the soldier's full weight rested on one of the points of the rail. Bucking and gagging involved the soldier being bound and gagged, with his knees drawn up tight to his chin, and being forced to remain in that position for a long period of time. Elmore observed soldiers from the Tucker Regiment receiving relatively minor punishment for a unit held together through harsh discipline.

The level of discipline exerted by the officers of the Tucker Regiment was not sufficient to prevent conflict with citizens of Columbia. Walter Brian Cisco writes in his biography of Gen. Wade Hampton:

> In October of 1864 the First Foreign Battalion, commanded by Lt. Col. Julius G. Tucker, went into training in Columbia, South Carolina. They quickly gained a shady reputation. One citizen thought them "the lowest and most debased set of men I ever saw" frankly concluding that "I would rather have them in the Federal Army than in our

own." In late November, while Mary Hampton was in Virginia, her home near Columbia was burglarized. "General Hampton's house has been robbed," Mary Chestnut recorded, "all his wife's jewelry taken, everything valuable stolen." To make matters worse, the intruders left behind "derisive notes" reading "Hang Hampton," "Rebel," and "Cattle Stealer." All eyes turned to the Foreign Battalion. After more nighttime thefts, and even assaults, there was talk of forming a "Vigilance Committee" in Columbia. A petition circulated demanding the immediate removal of the experimental organization. After the battalion departed in January, at least some of Mary Hampton's stolen jewelry and silver was found in the abandoned tent of a "foreigner."[12]

Tucker sent a letter to Secretary of War Seddon on December 14, 1864, that stated in part: " . . . respectfully request that I be allowed to return to the Seccessionville prison such enlisted men of my Battalion who by their conduct prove themselves utterly worthless and a disgrace to the Confederate Service."[13]

Col. Tucker moved his command to Branchville, South Carolina, in January 1865. It is unclear if the citizens of Columbia, Gen. Hampton, or Secretary of War Seddon forced that move. The order for the move, dated December 30, 1864, directed Col. Tucker to report with his command to Gen. Hardee, who was at that time headquartered in Charleston. Gen. Samuel Cooper issued that order at the behest of Secretary of War John Seddon. Seddon informed Gen. Hardee of the order, and he pointed out that the selected regimental officers lacked commissions and that the War Department had not yet recognized the regiment.[14]

Col. Tucker added a company to his command on February 9 or 10, 1865. Assistant Secretary of War J. A. Campbell confirmed permission to add that company to Major John Blair Hoge on February 11, 1865. The addition of that company allowed Col. Tucker's command to become a full regiment. Tucker had anticipated that permission and had recruited the last member of what was to be Company K by February 1.[15]

Col. Tucker wrote to Major Hoge from Charleston on January 18 to request a quartermaster for his unit, as he spent all of his time running his command. The letter further stated: "Having great number of my men not show up to this time It has been impossible to properly drill and discipline them, and I am not prepared to take them into a fight at present but of course am willing and anxious to make myself as useful as I possibly can. General Hardee has ordered four hundred of my men to this place as pioneers and has left it optional with me to accompany them or not, but I expect to remain with the body of my command at Branchville."[16]

It is clear from Gen. Hardee's order and Tucker's response that the Tucker Regiment was not raised as a pioneer unit. The lack of a clear original purpose for the regiment reflects the *ad hoc* nature of the galvanization process by the Confederate authorities.

It appears that the Tucker Regiment was still in the process of moving from Columbia to Branchville on January 18. The last men in Company K officially mustered into the regiment on February 17, when the total number of troops mustered into the Tucker Regiment reached 878.

Col. Tucker addressed the state of discipline in his command in his January 18 letter to Major Hoge. He said: "I have been in Charleston since yesterday on a meet to General Hardee who treated me very kindly and has endorsed everything I have done in managing my Command. I have had to shoot four more since I wrote to you last for desertion & conspiracy, and he expressed himself highly pleased with the state of discipline my command is under."

The regimental service records do not contain documents related to even one court martial, and there is no mention of executions beyond the January 18 letter. A search of the records indicated no cause or exact date of death for nine soldiers; their personal effects were simply handed over to the Quartermaster upon their deaths. The cause of death and the hospital where they died was recorded in the service records for men who died of disease. Two of the nine men died in 1864 and the remaining seven in 1865. The two who died in 1864 were probably the two deserters mentioned in an incomplete and undated (probably November 1864) response written in reply to questions raised by the Secretary of War about both Tucker's regiment and the 8th Confederate Infantry. Four of the 1865 deaths were probably the four executions discussed in the January 18 letter. If this line of reasoning is correct, three men were executed after January 18.[17]

The one with an exact date of death was J. W. Thompson, no rank given, of Company A, who died on February 18, 1865, and left $8 in personal belongings. The other eight men were Pvt. Cyrus Hubbard, A. J. Page, and Pvt. John Ward of Company A; Pvt. Henry Lapoint of Company B; Ferdinand Graviate of Company D; Thomas Farrell and Chas. Sternby of Company G; and 2nd Sgt. J. Grainger of Company H. Their personal belongings at the time of their deaths consisted of currency (presumably Confederate) that ranged from $3 to $28.[18] Companies A and G accounted for six of the nine probable executions.

Nineteen men from the Tucker Regiment died of disease, mainly in Charlotte hospitals. Seventeen of the nineteen died of diarrhea or chronic diarrhea. One man died at the hospital after admission for hemorrhoids. No cause of death was recorded for the remaining casualty. The majority of the men in the Regiment were ill at one time or another, from ailments such as typhoid fever, diarrhea, pneumonia, rheumatism, tuberculosis, ascites, colitas, hemorrhoids, asthma, bronchitis, and undiagnosed fevers. There were numerous instances of men noted as being sick in camp. It is remarkable, given the health status of most Union prisoners in Confederate prisons, that none of the men were diagnosed with scurvy. Col. Tucker must have chosen his recruits carefully in regards to that disease and then made sure that the rations they received were fully adequate.[19]

The documented death rate within the Tucker Regiment was extremely low for a Confederate unit in the last days of the war. There were no recorded instances of men killed or wounded in battle. It is doubtful that those records reflect events during and after the Battle of Bentonville, which was the largest engagement the Tucker Regiment would have had an opportunity to engage in.

The lack of casualties of battle probably reflects the status of the regiment as a pioneer unit. The duties of a pioneer unit included:

> Pioneers facilitated their own army's movement, while attempting to restrict the mobility of their opponent. They made and improved roads, cleared a line of battle, and constructed and repaired bridges. Pioneers cleared lines of fire by cutting underbrush in front of artillery positions; dug hasty field defenses, such as parapets and breastworks; built all manners of fortifications; threw pontoon bridges across waterways; and prepared shelters for field hospitals. They were even known, on occasion, to clear driftwood from a ford, corduroy a swamp, construct a bombproof, build a signal fire, fabricate a coffin, and bury the dead. Some of these tasks exposed pioneers to enemy fire, although most did not. Conversely, to help thwart the enemy, they placed obstructions, such as fallen timber, in the middle of roadways, blockaded gaps to deny avenues of approach, and demolished bridging to hinder pursuit after the rear guard was safely across. Soldiers serving as pioneers carried their own firearms, although while serving in this capacity, their primary weapons of war were spades, picks, and axes.[20]

It is doubtful that the Tucker Regiment was armed. There was no ordnance list among the regimental records. The clothing requisition included

192 jackets, 153 pairs of pants, 310 caps, 312 pairs of shoes, 486 pairs of socks, 553 shirts, 283 pairs of drawers, and 361 blankets.[21]

Scharle confirmed the function of the Tucker Regiment in her biography of Captain Colonna of Company D:

> Captain Colonna's battalion was the advance guard of the Confederate Army as it retreated northward one day, and another battalion would be the rear guard. Benjamin wrote that these battalions 'frogged' each other. The advance guard would be busy repairing bridges and roads. The retreat was largely through pine forests. The roads were so swampy that trees had to be cut down and corduroy roads prepared. The engineers had to select a site the Army could camp at night. Then they would make a camp for themselves.
>
> The rear guard would set fire to the woods and everything else they could to impede the advance of the Union forces . . . Supplies were short. Colonna's troops got 1½ pounds of bread a day.[22]

Scharle's description does not reference this, but it is likely that part of the Tucker Regiment served as the advance guard and the remainder as the rear guard. The short rations she mentioned were while the regiment retreated north from Sherman's advance towards the climactic battle of Bentonville, and the description probably does not reflect the rations received while on station in Columba, Branchville, or Charleston.

Sherman's army had moved through Georgia and South Carolina virtually unchecked after the fall of Atlanta. The opposition they encountered could do little more than harass and delay. The weather and the poor southern roads proved to be more formidable opponents than the scattered Confederate Army. Gen. John Bell Hood moved what was left of the Army of Tennessee north from Atlanta to try to draw Sherman back north, and eventually squandered that army through a series of ill-advised attacks. It was not possible to consolidate the Confederate forces that did exist in Sherman's path as it was uncertain where Sherman would strike next.[23]

Gen. Lee appointed General Joseph E. Johnston to command the new Army of the South on February 23, 1865. This unified several commands responsible for the defense of various areas still under Confederate control. Added to those dispersed units was what was left of the Army of Tennessee.[24]

The Tucker Regiment had been part of Jackson's Brigade, under General John K. Jackson, as late as January 31, 1865. Jackson's Brigade was a Detached Command within the Department of South Carolina, Georgia, and Florida, which was under the overall command of General William J. Hardee.[25]

Gen. Hardee's command, which included the Tucker Regiment, had been on the move north from Charleston before creation of the Army of the South. He and his command were at Cheraw, South Carolina, on February 23, 1865, and were moving towards the North Carolina line. The vanguard of Gen. Hardee's command reached Fayetteville on March 8, and men of Tucker's Regiment led the way. Gen. Johnston decided to consolidate his forces at Smithfield, North Carolina, which is east of Raleigh and a little north of Bentonville. Gen. Johnston chose Smithfield because of its proximity to Raleigh, which was the last major supply depot for the Army of Northern Virginia and the Army of the South.[26]

The Tucker Regiment apparently took no part in the engagements leading up to the Battle of Bentonville of March 19–21, 1865, and their role at Bentonville is not entirely clear. The regiment probably served its pioneer function until Bentonville: preparing the way forward for Confederate units and doing what they could to hamper the pursuit by Sherman's army. They may have also helped prepare entrenchments and gun emplacements prior to the battle. The order of battle for the Confederate Army at Bentonville does not include a reference to the 1st Foreign Battalion or the Tucker Regiment.[27] There is a reference, however, to at least one galvanized company fighting at Bentonville. That company, discussed in Chapter 8, was probably a remnant of the "O'Neill Regiment," which was the galvanized 10th Tennessee Infantry.

After the Battle of Bentonville, the Tucker Regiment was in camp near Smithfield, North Carolina. On March 25, 1865, Col. Tucker wrote to Gen. Samuel Cooper to request his promotion to full colonel, following the muster of Company K. He requested that the promotion date from February 17, 1865, when Company K was officially included in his command. Col. Tucker made no mention of the Battle of Bentonville or the role that his regiment played in the battle. It is likely that the Tucker Regiment spent March 19–21 in camp at Smithfield and was probably engaged in strengthening the defenses around Smithfield at that time. A Register of Appointment included with his service records indicates that he received his promotion on March 15, with an effective date of rank of February 25.[28]

John C. Breckinridge, then the Secretary of War, had sent a recommendation for Tucker's promotion to President Jefferson Davis on March 6, 1865, and he also recommended that his command officially become "Tucker's

Confederate Regiment." He said that the men of Tucker's command preferred that name and had objected to the use of the word "Foreign" to describe their unit. Breckinridge further stated that the discipline in Tucker's Command had been "severe," but that the unit had done well. He included a recommendation from Gen. Hardee that Col. Tucker also command Andrew's 2nd Foreign Battalion (later the 8th Confederate Infantry) and that both units be used as "Engineer Troops." Breckinridge said that Andrew's Command was still at Florence, South Carolina, which was not correct. President Davis responded on the same communication and concurred with Tucker's promotion as a full colonel. President Davis also said that it was desirable to have foreign-born officers in command of foreigners. No action was taken on Gen. Hardee's recommendation.[29]

An abstract from returns of the army, organized by general staff, infantry, artillery, and pioneer staff, was prepared at the Confederate camp at Smithfield for the period that ended January 31, 1865. That abstract reflected what remained of Gen. Johnston's army after the Battle of Bentonville. Fifteen general staff were present for duty, which was also the total of aggregate present and absent. A total of 1,789 officers and 15,481 enlisted men from infantry units were present for duty, although the number of effectives present was 14,903. The aggregate number of infantrymen present was 20,921, while the aggregate present and absent was 90,088. A total of 1,060 officers and 16,436 enlisted men were prisoners of war. The total number of artillerymen present for duty included 39 officers and 814 men. The number of effectives present totaled 793, while the aggregate present was 959. The aggregate present and absent was 1,187, and four enlisted men were prisoners.[30]

It is curious that the Pioneer Regiment (Tucker's Regiment) was not included with the rest of the infantry. The men of the Tucker Regiment were probably noncombatants. The regiment included 25 officers and 326 enlisted men present for duty, with 318 listed as being effectives. The total present and absent was shown as 621. The 621 apparently included men hospitalized or absent sick. Those totals do not include any returns from companies A or D, which were on detached duty. Those two companies included about 80 officers and men. None of the men of the Pioneer unit had been captured.[31]

A clue to the location of companies A and D came from a letter written by Assistant Quartermaster Capt. J. S. Richardson to Col. W. H. Hatch, the Assistant Commissioner of Exchange at Salisbury, on March 29, 1865. Richardson said in the letter that Col. Forno had ordered him to turn over funds in gold that had been entrusted to him by a Capt. T. R. Stewart and that had belonged to Federal prisoners of war. He complained that the amount he turned over was well short of the amount he should have had, as reflected in paperwork that accompanied the funds. The importance of this letter is that he wrote it from Salisbury, which was one of the few remaining major depots for military supplies in North Carolina. It is likely that Richardson and the two missing companies were in Salisbury to work on fortifications around the town and to secure needed supplies in advance of an expected raid by General Stoneman and his large cavalry force; a raid that was to come later. The letter directed Col. Hatch to send his reply via Col. Tucker in Raleigh.[32]

The regiment left for Raleigh after the muster roll taken at Smithfield on March 27, 1865, and arrived by March 29th. The Tucker Regiment probably preceded the main body of Johnston's Army by at least several days in order to improve the roads and bridges along the route that the army was to take.[33]

The end of the Confederacy was near as Johnston's army rested at Smithfield. Lee ordered a desperate and unsuccessful attack on March 25, 1865, at Fort Stedman in the siege line at Petersburg to try to prevent Grant from extending his lines and outflanking the Petersburg defenses. Grant attacked and broke the right flank of the Petersburg defenses, which forced Lee to abandon Petersburg and leave Richmond defenseless. Jefferson Davis and his cabinet left Richmond on April 2. Johnston learned of the fall of Richmond from a press release on April 4. The fall of Richmond seems to have had little impact on the men in Gen. Johnston's army, although Gen. Johnston believed that it meant that Sherman would try to move into Virginia. Sherman did not move towards Virginia and delayed advancing on Smithfield until April 10.[34]

Johnston and his army left Smithfield on April 10, 1865, and began their retreat towards Raleigh. Unknown to Johnston at that time, Lee had surrendered to Grant at Appomattox Courthouse on April 9. Johnston learned of Lee's surrender on April 12 during a meeting with President Davis and his cabinet in Greensboro. That news convinced Johnston that the war was lost, and his goal was to secure the best surrender terms possible for his men. News soon spread through Johnston's army of Lee's surrender, and rumors began to circulate that Johnston planned to surrender. Both the surrender and rumor of surrender had a devastating effect on Johnston's army; wholesale desertions began, which did not end until the final surrender at Greensboro.[35]

Tucker's Regiment joined the garrison of the Post of Greensboro, under the command of Brig. Gen. Alfred Iverson. Iverson's command consisted of the 2nd, 4th, 5th, 6th, and 9th Kentucky Mounted Infantry; the 2nd

Kentucky Cavalry; Tucker's Regiment; and the Invalid Corps. The mounted infantry and cavalry units had been part of Breckinridge's Brigade of Dibrell's Division during the Battle of Bentonville, which had been the first division to engage Sherman's troops.[36]

The rest of Dibrell's Division that was posted at Greensboro following Bentonville was assigned as President Jefferson Davis' escort as he fled south after the fall of Richmond. Davis had first fled to Danville, Virginia, and reached Greensboro by train on April 11, 1865. He left Greensboro on horseback with his cavalry escort on April 15. The damage caused by Stoneman's raiders made Davis' escape more difficult. Stoneman had attacked and captured Salisbury on April 12, and his raiders had disabled railroad lines and damaged roads that Davis and his escort had to take on their way to Charlotte. Davis passed through Salisbury on April 17. He was to make his way to Charlotte and into Georgia before his capture.[37]

Brig. Gen. Iverson, who commanded the Post of Greensboro, said that on February 15, 1865, only 500 men assigned to the Post (including Tucker's Regiment) remained on duty and most of those were ready to desert. Greensboro was full of soldiers from Lee's army in addition to those from Johnston's. Quartermaster Maj. Samuel R. Chisman kept a mob from looting the North Carolina and Confederate warehouses on February 15. Chisman went into a Confederate warehouse with a lit torch and threatened to blow it up if the crowd did not disperse. Members of a second mob fired on North Carolina troops detailed to guard the warehouses, but the mob dispersed after an exchange of gunfire.[38]

The assassination of President Lincoln on April 16, 1865, incensed the soldiers under Sherman's command and helped to destabilize the situation within Johnston's army even further. Johnston estimated that 4,000 infantry and artillerymen, and nearly as many from the cavalry, deserted between April 19 and 24. Johnston and Sherman agreed to an armistice, and the terms of surrender offered by Sherman were sent to Washington for approval. The authorities in Washington rejected Sherman's terms. They ordered Sherman to end the ceasefire and renew hostilities. Much of Johnston's army had melted away by that time, and those who remained were unwilling to fight. Johnston and Sherman met again on April 26, and Johnston agreed to terms of surrender that were much less favorable to his men and to the South in general than the rejected terms.[39]

Johnston's army stacked arms on April 28, 1865. Johnston gave them their last pay at that time. Jefferson Davis left $39,000 in silver coins with

Johnston when he passed through Greensboro. Johnston evenly divided that sum up among the 32,174 men that were present, which gave each officer and enlisted man a share of $1.17. Johnston gave the men cloth, thread, and cotton yarn to trade for food on the way home. Sherman also provided rations from his own stores.[40]

Muster records for the Tucker Regiment indicate that it had shrunk to 72 men by the time of the paroles at Greensboro. Compilation of the service records for the Tucker Regiment revealed that the actual number was 74, as one man (Pvt. H. Wilcox of Company K) was added to the muster role on May 1, and a second (Pvt. G. Gasley of Company C) was added on May 3. Twelve enlisted men from Company A surrendered; no officers were present. 1st Lt. Charles W. Wilkinson of Company A was paroled in Nashville on June 5. Eleven members of Company B were present, including officers 1st Lt. F. W. James, 2nd Lt Ludlow Cohen, and Jr. 2nd Lt. J. T. Trezevant. Fourteen officers and men of Company C surrendered at Greensboro, including Captain William A. James, 2nd Lt. Fleming James, Jr. 2nd Lt A. N. Power, and Jr. 2nd Lt. Robert Brockenbrough.[41]

Company D was not present at the surrender. Company D was on detached duty while the regiment was at Smithfield and apparently had not returned by the time of the surrender. Capt. Benjamin Azariah Colonna received his pardon at Richmond on May 16. Edward A. Bentz (40th Missouri Infantry) and Charles H. Fundy (100th New York Infantry) both received pensions after the war, and they apparently served in Company D. Fundy had been captured near Petersburg on October 27, 1864, and, according to his service record, was released from prison on April 23, 1865. Those men likely deserted at Salisbury and joined the flow of prisoners released from Salisbury and/or Florence at that time. Alternatively, Capt. Colonna may have released his company from service when he realized that the end was very near for the Confederacy, or he may have been unable to rejoin the regiment for any of a number of reasons.[42]

Seven men from Company E surrendered at Greensboro. These included 1st Lt. Edward B. Cohen and Jr. 2nd Lt. John A. Crawford. Only five men from Company F were present, including Jr. 2nd Lt. H. H. Dinwiddie. Seven men from Company G surrendered, including Capt. William T. Duncan. Six men from Company H were present, including 1st Lt. J. Thompson Quarles and 2nd Lt. A. R. Toutant. Six men were present representing Company I, of which half were officers. Those officers from Company I were 2nd Lieutenants J. L. Brisbane and Julius Cohen and Jr.

2nd Lt. John L. Ligon Jr. Two enlisted men and Bvt. 2nd Lt. J. Mercer Keesee remained from Company K. Col. Tucker and Assistant Surgeon Charles stayed with the regiment to the end.[43]

The Tucker Regiment was successful. The few records that survive indicate that the men of that regiment performed their tasks at a satisfactory level. A majority of the men enrolled in the unit stayed at least until the encampment at Smithfield, although only 74 remained at the surrender at Greensboro. It is likely that the severe discipline that had held the regiment together was relaxed when it was apparent that the end of the war was near, and the regiment was largely allowed to melt away prior to the surrender. The example of Pvt. Charles Fundy indicates that at least some of those men were able to blend in with the released prisoners of war from one place or another and rejoined their original units.

Col. Tucker does not appear to have been particularly selective about those he recruited, beyond selecting men who were free of scurvy. Tucker probably recruited a majority of foreign-born prisoners of war, as he was required to do, but it is likely that a percentage of his regiment was native born or naturalized citizens. The men of the regiment were apparently non-combatants and did not take up arms against their former comrades, which was probably a factor in their success.

The Union Prison at "Belle Isle," Richmond. Charles P. Rees, photographer. Library of Congress.

The Confederate Prison at Salisbury as depicted in an 1886 lithograph. #P0001, North Carolina Collection Photographic Archives, The Wilson Library, University of North Carolina at Chapel Hill.

"Beavers and the Rebel Recruiting Officer." Prepared by an artist well after the war at the direction of Ezea Ripple, a prisoner at Florence Prison. From the collection of the Lackawanna Historical Society, used with permission.

“Counting Off the Camp.” Prepared by an artist well after the war at the direction of Ezea Ripple, a prisoner at Florence Prison. From the collection of the Lackawanna Historical Society, used with permission.

Andersonville Prison, Georgia. View from the main gate issuing rations to thirty-three thousand prisoners. Library of Congress.

Captain John Hampden Brooks, from U. R. Brooks, *Brooks Battalion: Stories of the Confederacy* (Columbia, SC: The State Company, 1912), 311.

Col. Julius G. Tucker, Tucker Regiment, from a photo by Rud Bachman, New York, "How We Came Through Guachi," *World Wide Magazine,* Vol VIII, No. 44 (November 1901): 182.

Lt. Col. Garnett Andrews, 8th Confederate Infantry. Courtesy of the University of Tennessee at Chattanooga Special Collections.

Lt. Gen. William J. Hardee. Library of Congress.

Gen. Pierre Gustave Toutant de Beuregard. National Archives.

Lt. Gen. John Bell Hood. National Archives.

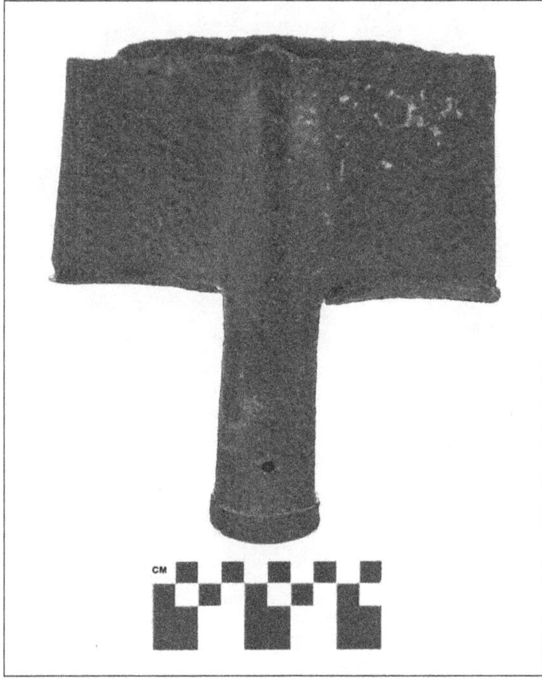

Shovel made of sheet iron that was probably made by a local blacksmith in Florence, South Carolina. Found during an archaeological excavation in the bottom of a well dug in one of the guard camps at Florence Prison. Photograph by the author.

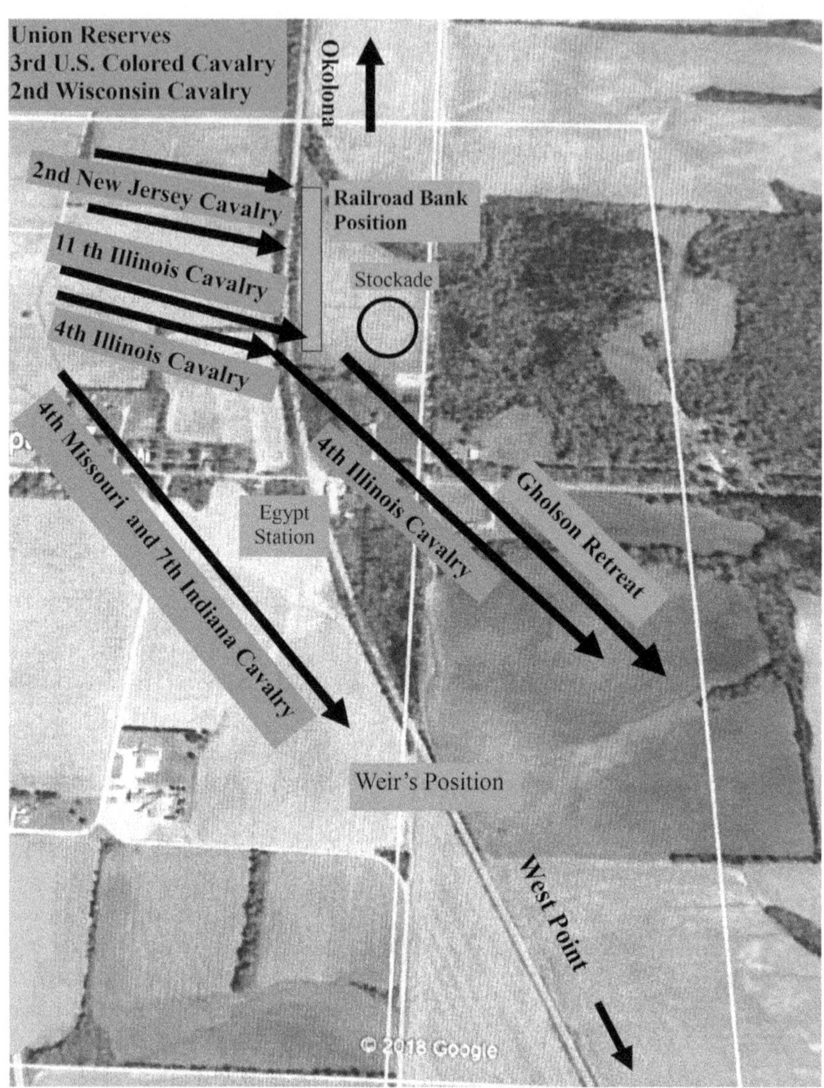

Battle of Egypt Station.

★ CHAPTER 6 ★

The 2nd Foreign Battalion/ 8th Confederate Infantry

THE AUTHORIZATION TO RAISE what was to become the 2nd Foreign Battalion and later the 8th Confederate Infantry (as it will be referred to in this chapter) was given to Major (later Lt. Col.) Garnett Andrews in a letter from Major John Blair Hoge of the Adjutant and Inspector General's Office, dated September 24, 1864. The letter authorized Andrews to recruit from Millen, Andersonville, and other points in Georgia. His instructions were quite clear and the letter stated in part: "In making such enlistments Irish and French are to be preferred. No citizens or native of the United States and few if any Germans should be enlisted. The battalion is designed for service elsewhere than in the armies of Tennessee and Northern Virginia. The enlistments will be for the term of three years and the understanding must be (indecipherable) that the officers will be appointed by the President and not elected."[1]

Major Hoge modified the order on November 10, 1864, in a letter that stated in part: " . . . your original authority. . . . is enlarged among the same class of prisoners confined in any of the military prisons under the control of Brigadier-General Gardner."[2] Major Andrews focused his recruiting efforts on Florence and Salisbury prisons.

The admonishment against recruiting Germans probably resulted from the stereotypic view of German character held by many in the mid-nineteenth century. Germans were believed to be less likely to truly change sides, reject feelings of duty and loyalty, and embrace the Confederate cause. Whatever the reason for that exception, German immigrants were recruited in significant numbers for each unit of galvanized Confederates.

Major Garnett Andrews was born in 1837 in Washington, Georgia, and was the son of a prominent judge. His sister, Eliza Francis Andrews, kept a diary of the events of the last two years of the Civil War, which was published in 1908 and has been reprinted many times since.[3]

There is somewhat more information available about Major Andrews than can be found about the other officers who commanded units of galvanized Yankees. Andrews' collected papers, archived at the University of Tennessee at Chattanooga, include two short documents that pertain to his actions during the war. The first source is a typescript that was apparently prepared for inclusion in a family history. According to that document, Andrews enlisted in the 1st Georgia Regulars in February 1861, and he was sent to duty posts at Savannah and Fort Pulaski. Andrews, elected 2nd Lieutenant, was an officer throughout the war. By June 1861, Andrews was Adjutant General and Chief of Staff, serving under General H. B. Jackson in the Army of Northwestern Virginia (later under the command of Gen. Robert E. Lee). Andrews fell ill while at that post and spent a year recovering from what was termed "camp fever" (perhaps typhoid fever or malaria). When he returned to duty in 1862, he joined Cutts Battalion of Georgia Artillery. Andrews, promoted to Captain, became the Assistant Adjutant General of Gen. Dayton's Brigade in Gen. Longstreet's Corps. From that post, he joined the Department of Richmond under the command of Gen. Arnold Elzey. While in Richmond, he organized a 400-man Local Defense unit, perhaps the same unit that would later produce officers for Tucker's Regiment and perhaps even the 8th Confederate Infantry. Captain Andrews, promoted to Major based on his work with the Local Defense troops, became an Assistant Advocate General. He resigned his commission in 1864 to join the 15th Georgia Infantry as a 2nd Lieutenant, and he fought with the 15th at the Wilderness, Spotsylvania, South Ana River, Second Cold Harbor, Bermuda Hundred, and Petersburg. Andrews was recalled to Richmond to his former office and rank while at Petersburg, and he remained there for several months. The War Department authorized him to raise what was to become the 8th Confederate infantry while at his post in Richmond.[4]

Andrews stated after the war:

> Our lines had now become frightfully thin, and among the last desperate effort to recruit them, was the plan of enlisting voluntary enlistments of foreigners among the Federal prisoners. I was authorized to raise a batallion [*sic*] of six full companies of the material, with powers to select my own officers from the army at large. I soon enlisted 1600 men at the prisons at Salisbury, N.C., and Florence, S.C., all, without

> exception, foreigners, principally Irish, with some German, French, and English. They were men who had enlisted in the U.S. Army immediately on arrival in this country, and some of them could speak little English. Out of 1600, after several months of careful study of them in camp under rigid drill and discipline, I cautiously selected 600 picked soldiers, got them thoroughly equipped and uniformed, and reported for duty in the latter part of 1864 or early in 1865. Was ordered to Charlotte, N. C., and promoted to be Lieutenant-Colonel. The War Department first designated the corps as the "Second Foreign Legion," but soon afterward changed the name to "8th Confederate battalion of Infantry." But the public humor gave us the expressive appelation [*sic*] of "Galvanized Yankees."[5]

As indicated above, Andrew's authority to recruit had been originally restricted to the Georgia prisons, but later included all prisons under the command of Brigadier-General Gardner. Camp Lawton at Millen was closed in late November 1864, and Col. O'Neill of the 10th Tennessee Infantry demonstrated that Andersonville contained relatively few able bodied men to be recruited at that time.[6]

As previously stated, the recruits for the 8th Confederate came from Salisbury, North Carolina, and Florence, South Carolina. A report filed by J. L. Tyerly, who was titled "Clerk of the Prison," which was dated February 1, 1865, gave totals of prisoners recruited at Salisbury to that point. According to that report, 653 men had been recruited for the First Foreign Battalion (which became Tucker's Regiment), 677 were recruited for Andrews Battalion (the 8th Confederate), and 407 were recruited for "General York's Battalion."[7] "York's Battalion" was apparently never formed, although Gen. York did have permission from Secretary of War Seddon in a letter dated November 16, 1864, to "visit the federal prisons and to recruit from them, for his Brigade, taking with him such Catholic clergy as he may select." The recruits raised by Gen. York apparently did not serve with any known unit. It is possible that York's intent was simply to pull Catholic prisoners from Salisbury to improve their chances of survival and not to actually recruit them.[8]

A typescript summary prepared by Andrews after the war for Goode, which is on file with the *Andrews Papers* at the University of Tennessee-Chattanooga, stated that he recruited 1,600 men in order to get 600 men that were fit and appropriate for duty in his battalion. If the report cited above from Salisbury prison is correct and comprehensive, 923 of the 1,600 men came from Florence.[9]

Comparison of the names of the recruits for the 8th Confederate and the Brooks Battalion found 36 names repeated on both rosters. The names of William Smith and William Walker, recruited for the 8th Confederate at Salisbury, were found on the Brooks Battalion roster. The surviving Brooks Battalion recruits returned to Florence, however, and it seems unlikely that two or more of the men then went to Salisbury. Further, a number of the men recruited at Florence, who had names that matched individuals on the Brooks Battalion roster, had common names and may not have been a part of the Brooks Battalion. All of the men with known recruitment dates were recruited before the Brooks Battalion companies went to Savannah. The names found on both rosters matched eight from Company A, six from Company B, three from Company C, five from Company D, five from Company E, and five from Company F from the Brooks Battalion. If indeed they were former Brooks Battalion recruits, they must have been among the men sent back to Florence from Summerville, who did not go to Savannah. All of the men with names on both rosters and with known companies ended up in Company F of the 8th Confederate.[10]

Captain Tabb recruited the men from Salisbury, while then Lt. Barrett recruited all but five of those from Florence. "Lt." Fouche recruited the remaining five men from Florence. A search through the records for the identity of Captain Tabb revealed a single individual of that rank and name who was associated with the Confederate prison system. That individual was Capt. William Kemp Tabb, who was on Gen. Winder's staff in Richmond for a good bit of the war, and who had been in charge of prisoners at Camp Oglethorpe in Macon during the spring of 1864. The prisoners hated Tabb, who was viewed by at least some of the prisoners in much the same manner as Lt. Barrett at Florence. Brigadier-General Seymour wrote to Col. Thomas Hoffman, Commissary-General of Prisoners, on August 11, 1864, that he had heard that Capt. Tabb, captured on a train south of Richmond, was in federal hands. He further stated: "The prisoners of war generally desire that steps be taken to visit upon Captain Tabb some of those indignities that he heaped upon them while in his hands. I am sure that a captain of our service was bucked and gagged by his order and in his presence at Macon, Ga., while I was confined there. If I can ascertain where he might be I will communicate with the commander of that prison, through you, more fully."[11] The report of Capt. Tabb's capture appears to have been in error, with no further mention of his capture.

The recruits from both Florence and Salisbury assembled at Florence, where 600 of the 1,600 recruits made the cut and joined the battalion. The exact location of the campsite they occupied at Florence is unknown, but it was probably the same camp used earlier by the Brooks Battalion. The campsite was probably near the cemetery established for those who died at the prison, which is the extreme northern end of the modern Florence National Cemetery. It is likely that the campsites of both units are now part of the National Cemetery, which has expanded well to the south since 1865.

The command and control staff of the 8th was adequate to train, lead, and maintain discipline. Andrews second in command and the commander of Company A was Captain (later Major) Robert T. Fouche. Fouche joined the 8th Georgia Infantry at his home town of Rome, Georgia, on May 18, 1861. He was elected 2nd Lieutenant on February 13, 1863. Fouche, seriously wounded in the right lung, was left for dead in the field at Dandridge, Tennessee, on January 27, 1864. He recovered from that wound and apparently went back on active duty in time to help recruit some of the members of the 8th Confederate Infantry. He also helped train and organize the battalion. He returned to Rome, Georgia, after the war, where he practiced law and served as president of the Citizens Bank. He died on March 1, 1908, at 74 years old.[12] Appendix B contains a discussion of the rest of the officers.

The 8th Confederate remained at Florence until late February. John Breckinridge, the Secretary of War, wrote a letter to President Jefferson Davis dated March 6, 1865, that stated in part: "A (indecipherable) was received last week from General Hardee, stating that Tucker's command had been on duty as 'Engineer troops' commending it and asking that 'Andrew's Battalion,' then at Florence, be placed under Tucker for the same duty."

President Davis did not respond to Gen. Hardee's request, but that likely forced the 8th Confederate out of camp to Charlotte, North Carolina, which became their duty station. The 8th Confederate had been far more selectively recruited than any other galvanized unit and had received a much longer training period. The handpicked men and officers of the battalion, and the training that the men received, probably made the 8th Confederate the most effective line unit recruited among the Union prisoners.[13]

There was a muster roll for the "month of March" at Charlotte among the records of the 8th. Members of the unit began showing up at Charlotte Hospital 11 with regularity in early March 1865, which probably coincided with the arrival of the battalion in Charlotte. The 8th probably became garrison troops at Charlotte.[14]

John B. Jones, a clerk in the War Department in Richmond, wrote in his diary on March 16, 1865, that the quartermaster at Charlotte complained in a dispatch to the Secretary of War that members of the "Foreign Legion" were committing crimes in Charlotte. He asked that they be removed from the city. It appears that no action was taken on that request.[15]

The situation was grave for the Confederacy when the 8th Confederate reached their duty station at Charlotte. Savannah had fallen to Sherman's troops in December 1864. Columbia, South Carolina, fell on February 17, while Wilmington, North Carolina, fell on February 25. Gen. Joe Johnston took command of what remained of the Confederate forces at Charlotte on the same day Wilmington fell, and he began gathering the forces that would oppose the advancing Union armies at Bentonville, North Carolina, on March 20–21. Sherman bypassed Charlotte, and Union troops did not occupy the city until early May.[16]

Garnett Andrews was still a Major and R. T. Fouche was still a Captain when the battalion moved to Charlotte. Major Andrews wrote to General Samuel Cooper on March 17, 1865, and informed him that he had successfully raised six companies of infantry from among prisoners of war, and his command at that point consisted of "nearly five hundred effective men" (men ready for duty). He requested a promotion to Lt. Col. for himself and to Major for Captain Fouche. His effective fighting force of nearly 500 from the 600 battalion meant that about a sixth of his command was unable to perform because of illness or had deserted. The service records of the battalion indicate that most of those who were not fit for duty were ill from a variety of ailments. Both Andrews and Fouche received their promotions.[17]

Desertion was apparently a problem for Andrews' Battalion. An article in the *Western Democrat* (Charlotte, North Carolina) on March 7 stated: "Six men (members of the Foreign Battalion or 'Foreign Battalion') were shot near this town for the crime of desertion. They deserted since their command has been encamped in this vicinity, were caught below here, and brought back and executed—four on Wednesday and two on Sunday." The identities of the executed deserters remain unknown.[18]

The overall health of the unit appears to have been good while at Charlotte. One man died in an accident at Florence prior to the muster. Fifty-nine men were hospitalized in Charlotte during the period from February through April, of whom four died and three deserted. Those hospitalized included two officers (1st Lt. Braxton and 1st Lt Marks) and 57 enlisted men. One of the enlisted men was a corporal and the rest were privates. The diseases listed for the men included 16 cases of typhoid fever, 14 cases of diarrhea of varying severity, 12 cases of intermittent fever (most of which was probably malaria), three cases of rheumatism, two cases of "catarrh" (inflammation of the mucous membranes), one case of dysentery, at least one burn, and single cases of diseases described as "ambustin" (a burn or scald), "ascites" (a fluid buildup from heart or kidney disease), "olianthus" (undefined), and "v.s." (syphilis). The reason for hospitalization was not given in four cases. The deaths included two from typhoid fever and single instances of chronic diarrhea and intermittent fever.[19]

The state of health of the 8th Confederate when it took the field appears to have been at least as good as other Confederate units and perhaps better. Major Andrews' careful selection process targeted men who were apparently free of scurvy and other nutritional diseases. The protracted training they received in comparison with other galvanized units meant they were better prepared for whatever they faced when they went on duty. The low death rate from disease is remarkable, as is the low desertion rate from those hospitalized. A check of the escaped prisoner of war records revealed an entry for one of the three members of the 8th Confederate who escaped while in the hospital, but no other deserters from the unit during March and April 1865.[20]

Gen. Sherman ordered Major General George Stoneman to undertake a cavalry raid into North Carolina as part of his strategy to bring Gen. Johnston and his troops to bay. After numerous delays, Gen. Stoneman launched his raid from Knoxville, Tennessee, on March 21, and sent his forces along the East Tennessee & Georgia Railroad, which ran through Greeneville and Elizabethton, Tennessee. An objective of the raid was Salisbury, North Carolina, where Gen. Stoneman hoped to free the prisoners at Salisbury Prison. He and his raiders crossed into North Carolina on March 27. Gen. Stoneman reached Mt. Airy, North Carolina, by April 2. His force split up and raided Wytheville, Salem, and Lynchburg, Virginia. On April 9 to 11, they also raided a number of towns in the North Carolina Piedmont. A portion of Gen. Stoneman's force made it to the vicinity of Salisbury by April 11.[21]

Col. Andrews rushed the 8th Confederate into action on April 11, 1865. Andrews, writing well after the war, described the events that transpired as follows:

> In the night of April 11, 1865, I was ordered by telegraph to report with the battalion at Salisbury, without delay, and to impress railway transportation beyond Salisbury, if necessary. The wires had been cut, and though fearful of impending disaster, we were ignorant of Lee's surrender at Appomatox [*sic*], on the ninth. I seized the first passing train, whose crew, including the engineer, promptly deserted it. I manned

it with another from our own ranks, and drew into Salisbury on one side, as Stoneman was entering it from the other. We were immediately ordered into action, and straightaway had all, and more, than we could do, for Stoneman had a magnificent division of cavalry and mounted infantry. The other Confederate troops, few and hastlin [*sic*] (hastily), had been dispersed before we arrived, and I was entirely without support. But, to my great relief, I saw that our men were not only true, but some of them devoted; for a sergeant, named Boothe, saved my life and was himself grievously wounded in the effort. It soon became a hand to hand encounter, a few in the midst of many, we lost severely in killed and wounded, and I was sabered through the neck and wounded in the right shoulder, was previously wounded slightly at Spotsylvania and Cold Harbor. We had to make the seemingly useless fight because I was ordered to hold Stoneman in check as long as I could, at all hazards, so that certain trains of valuable stores could be moved out, and to that extent we were successful.[22]

Erwin Ledyard, in the Philadelphia Weekly Times, wrote on June 16, 1865, "A remarkable feature of this engagement was the very effective fighting done by the battalion of "Galvanized Yankees" (who had just been telegraphed for from Charlotte). They stood up to their work like men, and only gave way when overpowered by numbers. They were commanded by gallant and efficient officers, of whom several were severely wounded, including Col. Garnett Andrews, commanding the battalion."

The Sgt. William Boothe mentioned by Andrews was a 2nd Sergeant of Company F. Boothe served in the 58th Massachusetts Infantry until captured near Poplar Grove Church in Virginia. According to his service records, he was 5'8" tall with a fair complexion, light hair, and hazel eyes, and he was from Bristol County Massachusetts. He rejoined his unit after his release from Union prison on July 17, 1865.[23]

Major R. T. Fouche, writing as Captain and commander of the 8th Confederate Battalion, submitted the following report of the battle, dated April 19, 1865, to Lt. Col. Kinloch Falconer, Assistant Adjutant General, Army of Tennessee:

In pursuance of order from Brigadier-General Gardner to this battalion, commanded by Maj. G. Andrews, arrived at Salisbury, N. C., at 7 o'clock in the morning of the 12th instant. Before the battalion could be fully armed the troops then defending the place began to give way. Major Andrews, as soon as four companies had procured arms

> and twenty rounds of ammunition, took them and hurried to the front, leaving Captain Napier in command of the two remaining companies. Upon getting near the scene of the action, it was discovered that the enemy had turned the flank, and our troops were met going to the rear in great disorder. Without staff officers or couriers to direct, Major Andrews threw the battalion into line to receive the cavalry which was coming down on us at the charge. The men stood well, and had there been troops enough in the field to contend with the enemy would have distinguished themselves; but being hemmed in on all sides, the most of the battalion was captured. Captain Fouché, commanding Company A, was sent to the right of the line and succeeded in getting out with a few men. Captain Napier, with the two remaining companies met the enemy in the streets, checked them, and then attempted to cover the retreat of four pieces of artillery which had taken the Gad's Hill road, but was unsuccessful. Captain Napier and Lieutenant Leftwich made their escape from the enemy two days after capture and are now present. This affair leaves the battalion at present with forty men present for duty, and should we be successful in getting back the wounded now at Salisbury, can reach seventy-five muskets. The men were all foreigners and mercenaries, and it is not probable that any of the captured will ever return. They will serve any government for food and clothing. Major Andrews was painfully wounded with the saber and pistol in the affair, and I forward this statement and respectfully submit that it would be in the best interest of the service to dispose of the men and officers at once.[24]

It is clear from the statements of Col. Andrews and Major Fouche that the men of the 8th Confederate put up a stiff fight at the Battle of Salisbury, with at least 35 men injured. Major Fouche made it clear that the loyalty to the Confederacy of those captured was weak, and they would not attempt to rejoin the battalion.

The Union reports of the battle at Salisbury were straightforward. Gen. Stoneman, in his report of April 13 to Gen. Thomas said the following about the battle:

> With the other two brigades, Brown and Miller's, and the artillery under command of Lieutenant Regan, we pushed for Salisbury, where we found about 3,000 troops under the command of Maj. Gen. William M. Gardner and Col. (late Lieutenant General) Pemberton, the whole formed behind Grant's Creek about two miles and a half from Salisbury. As soon as proper disposition could be made I ordered a general charge

> along the entire line, and the result was capture of 14 pieces of artillery, 1,364 prisoners, including 53 officers. All of the artillery and 1,164 prisoners are now with us; the remainder of the force was chased through and several miles beyond town, but scattered and escaped into woods.[25]

Gen. Stoneman further reported destroying a massive amount of military stores at Salisbury, including 10,000 stands of arms, 1,000,000 rounds of ammunition, 10,000 rounds of artillery shells, and 70,000 pounds of powder. The food he destroyed included 35,000 bushels of corn, 50,000 bushels of wheat, and 160,000 pounds of bacon. The other items destroyed included 100,000 uniforms, 250,000 army blankets, 20,000 pounds of harness leather, 10,000 pounds of saltpeter, medical supplies worth $100,000 in gold, and much more. He also burned the notorious Salisbury prison and four cotton factories.

Reports filed soon after the battle by Signal Corps member 2nd Lt. Theodore Mallaby Jr. and division commander Brig. Gen. Alvin C. Gillem paralleled Gen. Stoneman's report, and none of the three mentioned the role played by galvanized Confederates in the battle.[26]

The 8th Confederate's performance at Salisbury has been portrayed quite differently from the descriptions of Col. Andrews and Major Fouche since the Civil War. Civil War historian Chris J. Hartley describes the role of the 8th in the battle thus:

> "The Confederate artillery is said to have been handled effectively and the Artillery men fought gallantly until they were outflanked and compelled to leave their guns in the power of superior numbers," wrote the Reverend Beall. "Had they been adequately supported the result might have been different." As for the battery of galvanized Yankees, it simply fired its cannon over the heads of Stoneman's charging cavalrymen and greeted the victors with cheers. "Indeed, nowhere along the line did the Confederates hold out for very long. The invalid soldiers from the hospital were quickly pressed back. A few galvanized Irishmen fought well, but most went over to the enemy and thus abandoned the artillery. Some of the galvanized Yankees fired their guns in the air and gave three cheers for the Union."[27]

No artillery battery was part of the 8th Confederate, and they received only rifles and ammunition when they got off the train in Salisbury.

Hartley, however, based his description of the role of the 8th Confederate at Salisbury on an article by R. L. Beall published in the *North Carolina*

Review in 1910. Beall wrote letters describing Stoneman's raid soon after the war, but he was not present during the raid, and his description of the raid and the circumstances he described surrounding the raid are highly suspect. Beall, and the accounts derived from his version of events, placed the blame for the failure of Confederate troops to defend Salisbury on the galvanized Confederates, which exonerated the brave defenders of the city. Revisionist history like that was common after the war, in efforts to find scapegoats for the loss of the war by the South.[28]

Captain Wesley O. Connor of Captain Van Den Corput Company of Light Artillery (Georgia) was present at the battle and left diary entries that pertain to this discussion. He arrived in Salisbury on April 7, 1865, to join Johnston's Battalion, and the guns of that Battalion reached Salisbury on April 10. His diary entry concerning the battle was brief: "After a feeble attempt to defend the place, the few troops present were put to flight and nearly all captured. Johnston's Battalion artillery was taken. Were all put in barracks till 10 P.M. then marched three miles on the Morganton R.R."[29] Connor did not mention the soldiers of the 8th Confederate Infantry at that point or at any other point in his diary.

William H. Knauss, in his *The Story of Camp Chase*, claimed that Connor said of the battle: "Having no fortifications, of course this force offered but little resistance to the impetuous onslaught of General Stoneman's disciplined cavalry. Those 'galvanized' Yankees threw down their arms and refused to fight as soon as the Yankees made the charge on our lines, and they, with nearly all the rest of the command, were captured."[30]

Capt. Connor's observation of the battle is at odds with Knauss's statement, as Connor cast no blame on Andrews' men for the defeat at the time the battle occurred. Further, the Confederate artillery had two days prior to the battle to prepare fortifications, and it is inconceivable that they had neglected to fortify their positions at that stage of the war. No artillery battery was part of the 8th Confederate, and they only received rifles and ammunition when they exited the train in Salisbury.

Stoneman apparently left the wounded Confederate prisoners behind, which explains the discrepancy between the number of men captured and the number taken back to Tennessee by Stoneman's forces (1,364 captured versus 1,164 taken away). Major Fouche said 35 wounded men from the 8th Confederate were among those left at Salisbury. Col. Andrews was released on parole in late April, and Salisbury returned to Confederate hands after the battle.[31]

Eliza Francis Andrews, sister of Col. Garnett Andrews, kept a diary in

1864 and 1865 during the Civil War and from 1870 to 1872 following the war. Her entry for April 30, 1865, stated in part:

> We were all standing under the ash tree by the fountain after breakfast, watching the antics of a squirrel up in the branches, when Gen. Elzey and Touch [name by which the general's son, Arnold, a lad of 14, was known among his friends] came to tell us that Garnett was wounded in the fight at Salisbury, N. C. Mr. Saile brought the news from Augusta, but could give no particulars except that his wound was not considered dangerous, and that his galvanized Yanks behaved badly, as anybody might have known they would. A little later the mail brought a letter from Gen. Gardiner, his commanding officer, entirely relieving our fears for his personal safety. He is a prisoner, but will soon be paroled.[32]

The April 30 entry indicates that the rumor began soon after the battle that the galvanized Yankees had not performed well at Salisbury. Col. Andrews revealed the true actions of the men of the 8th when he returned home to Washington, Georgia. Eliza Andrew's May 4 entry stated in part:

> While we were in the parlor with these and other visitors, the carriage drove up with Fred and Garnett and Garnett's "galvanized" attendant, Gobin. As soon as I heard the sound of wheels coming up the avenue, I ran to one of the front windows, and when I recognized our carriage, Metta, Cora, and I tore helter-skelter out of the house to meet them. Garnett looks very thin and pale. The saber cuts on his head are nearly healed, but the wound in his shoulder is still very painful. His fingers are partially paralyzed from it, but I hope not permanently. Gobin seems attached to him and dresses his wounds carefully. He is an Irish Yankee, deserted, and came across the lines to keep from fighting, but was thrown into prison and only got out by enlisting in a "galvanized" regiment. I wonder how many of the patriots in the Union army have the same unsavory record! He is an inconvenient person to have about the house, anyway, for he is no better than a servant, and yet we can't put him with the negroes. Garnett says the report about his galvanized troops having behaved badly in the battle was a slander. They fought splendidly, he says, and were devoted to their officers. If the war had lasted longer, he thinks he could have made a fine regiment out of them, but somehow I can't feel anything but contempt for that sort of men, nor put any faith in them.[33]

Gobin was Pvt. David M. Gobin, captured along with Sgt. Boothe at Poplar Springs Church in Virginia on September 30, 1864. He had been a member of the 9th New Hampshire Infantry. According to a brief biography published in a history of Littleton, New Hampshire, he was born in New York in 1837. Pvt. Gobin, recruited at Florence, was a member of Company C. He left Col. Andrews and joined a contingent of Union soldiers at Washington, Georgia, on May 6 at Col. Andrews' direction.[34]

There appears to have been a very high expectation among civilians and certain elements of the Confederate military that the galvanized Confederates would fail under fire. There is no way to determine beyond all doubt if all, or at least most, of the members of the 8th Confederate fought or fought well at the Battle of Salisbury. The after action report of Major Fouche, the May 4 entry in Eliza Andrews' diary, and the description of the battle after the fact by Col. Andrews indicate that the unit acquitted itself well during the battle. After action reports by Gen. Stoneman, Gen. Gillem, and Lt. Mallaby did not even mention galvanized Confederates. Their actions would not have escaped the attention of the Union officers had they acted the way Beall later described. The 8th came to the battle too late to take part in the initial defense, and the battle was lost by the time they arrived.

More information is available about the men of the 8th Confederate than those of the Brooks Battalion or the Tucker Regiment. This is largely due to the Battle of Salisbury and the capture of a significant number of the battalion at that battle. The unit service records listed a total of 645 officers and men in the unit. The number of men who deserted prior to the deployment to Charlotte and the number who deserted subsequent to Salisbury could not be determined. The 8th Confederate lost 211 enlisted men who were captured and taken to Nashville or Camp Chase after the battle. Three officers were taken to a Federal prison from Salisbury by Gen. Stoneman, and all three (1st Lt McCorkle, 1st Lt. McKee, and 2nd Lt. Hanna) were taken to Camp Chase. The captured enlisted men came from all six companies of the battalion, which indicates that the battalion was fully engaged at Salisbury. The men captured at Salisbury came from 21 states, the District of Columbia, and Canada. Well over half of the men with known home states came from New York (101), Pennsylvania (31), or Massachusetts (22). Maine contributed eleven men to the unit, while Connecticut (9), Ohio (7), Maryland (6) Illinois (4), Michigan (4), Missouri (3), Virginia (3), and Vermont (3) each contributed more than one enlisted man. Canada, the District of Columbia, Georgia, Iowa, Indiana, Kentucky, North Carolina,

New Hampshire, New Jersey, Tennessee, and Wisconsin each contributed a single enlisted man.[35]

The men of the 8th came from many different Union military units. Three of the men were seamen and had served on the bark *Texandria*, the gunboat *Flambeau*, and an unnamed merchant vessel. It was common for two to three men from the same regiment to enlist in the 8th. There were seven men from the 35th Massachusetts Infantry in the unit, while the 51st New York Infantry, the 69th New York Infantry, and the 4th New York Heavy Artillery each had six members in the 8th. There were four men each from the 1st District of Columbia Cavalry and the 39th Massachusetts Infantry.[36]

The 8th Confederate Infantry was a carefully recruited and trained battalion that had sufficient command and control. It is difficult to assess the success or failure of this unit since it went into battle at a time when the battle was already lost. They fought well enough for 35 of their number to be wounded but, like the 10th Tennessee unit discussed later in this book, most ended up being captured during their one and only action. Perhaps the most significant thing about this battalion is that when thrown in to action they fought hard against overwhelming odds.

The enlisted men captured at Salisbury and taken to Nashville, Tennessee, were paroled in early July 1865. The three officers captured and taken to Camp Chase survived: 2nd Lt. Hanna and 1st Lt. McKee (captured at Napier, Virginia, on April 13) were paroled on May 2 and 1st Lt. McCorkle was paroled on June 11. The galvanized Confederates escaped prosecution for enlisting in the Confederate Army, although they were later denied pensions on the basis that they had aided and abetted the enemy and were treated as deserters.[37]

★ CHAPTER 7 ★

The 10th Tennessee Infantry

THE 10TH TENNESSEE INFANTRY

General John Bell Hood issued an order on October 11, 1864, that directed the recruitment of Union prisoners and their assignment to the Bates Division of the Army of Tennessee. The 10th Tennessee Infantry and the 15th Tennessee Infantry both provided officers for the recruitment under Hood's orders. Supernumerary officers in Macon, Georgia, and those on sick leave from the Division were probably also assigned to the task, and documentation has survived for four and perhaps six of those individuals. The first and second in command of the unit, when it was sent into the field, were from outside the Bates Division. Those officers were Lt. Col. Martin Burke of the 1st Missouri Infantry and Major MacPherson Berrien Eve, who had been on the staff of Brigadier General Henry C. Wayne. Brigadier General Wayne was the Adjutant and Inspector General of Georgia under an appointment by Governor Brown. Major Eve may have been Brown's eyes and ears within the galvanized unit.[1]

Despite General Hood's original intent to recruit for the entire division, the effort became most closely associated with the 10th Tennessee Infantry. That is appropriate as the original commanding officer and most of the other known officers were from that regiment. Further, Union officials designated all galvanized Confederates captured after the Battle of Egypt Station as members of that unit.

The 10th Tennessee was the subject of three articles written by men who served in the regiment and a recent book authored by Ed Gleeson. None of the articles written by former members of the 10th mention the galvanized Yankees raised to supplement that unit, and the Gleeson book almost completely dismisses the idea that such a recruitment took place. Captain Lewis R. Clark, who had served as an officer in the galvanized unit, wrote one of the articles, but he restricted his topic to events that transpired at Fort Donelson.[2]

Captain (later Colonel) Randall McGavock recruited the initial company of what was to become the 10th Tennessee Infantry into the Tennessee Militia in April 1861. McGavock's company, filled with Irish laborers from the Nashville area, was assigned to help construct forts Henry and Donelson after secession. His company joined recruits commanded by Colonel Adolphus Heinman, who was a native of Prussia. Heinman was a Colonel and engineer in the Tennessee Home Guards at the start of the war, and he was the first to command the 10th Tennessee. Most of the men under his command in the Home Guards were also Irish laborers. Recruits who joined the regiment at Fort Henry filled out the remainder of the 10th Tennessee. The 10th mustered into the Confederate Army on September 1, 1861.[3]

The battle for Fort Henry began on February 6, 1862 and lasted just two hours. Col. Heinman led most of the garrison, including the 10th Tennessee, in a retreat to Fort Donelson, 12 miles away. The garrison troops made it to Fort Donelson without major losses, and the siege of Fort Donelson began soon after.[4]

Union troops under the command of General Ulysses S. Grant began to close on Fort Donelson on February 12, and fighting was widespread by the 13th. The Confederate leadership at Donelson was chaotic. Col. Heinman took command of the post when he withdrew his command from Fort Henry. Brigadier General Bushrod Johnson took command on February 9, followed by Brigadier General Gideon Pillow from February 9 to 13. Brigadier General John Floyd commanded the post from February 13 to 16, and Brigadier General Bushrod Johnson resumed command on February 16 in time to surrender the post.[5] The Confederate command knew soon after Grant's army reached the fort that their position was untenable, despite beating back an assault by Union gunboats on the 14th. Attempts to break out of the fort and take the command to safety failed. The decision to surrender on the 16 was controversial. Generals Pillow and Floyd left the fort and escaped, leaving General Johnson to surrender to Grant. Then Lt. Colonel Nathan Bedford Forrest, who commanded the cavalry posted to the fort, insisted that the entire army could still escape but to no avail. He led his cavalrymen away from the fort to freedom. General Floyd managed to evacuate his Virginia regiments across the river before the return of Union gunboats. The remainder of the garrison surrendered, and the men were sent to Union prisons.[6]

The 10th Tennessee, despite being an engineer regiment and armed with obsolete flintlocks, acquitted themselves well in battle at forts Henry and Donelson. Patrick M. Griffin recalled that the 10th was part of the rearguard in the retreat from Fort Henry to Fort Donelson, and they helped hold off the pursuing Union forces so that all could reach Donelson.[7] Lewis R. Clark recalled:

> The fighting commenced at Fort Donelson on Feb. 13, 1862, with the enemy in overwhelming numbers. Our works were assaulted several times during the day, and shelled repeatedly during the night. The next day showed a steady continuance of the fight, which was rendered very trying by the bad weather, the ground being covered with snow in a slushy, half melted condition, freezing at night and thawing in the day-time. The third day we repulsed an attack of the enemy and drove them several miles. It was owing to the terrific losses inflicted upon the assaulting forces by our regiment that it earned the sobriquet of "The Bloody Tenth." Among the enemy's forces engaged in our front, the Second Iowa—which was a magnificent body of men—suffered the most severely. By that time our men were completely worn out. With three days of steady, hard fighting and two nights of sleepless exposure in the trenches to guard against an apprehended assault, we were thoroughly exhausted. Then rumors came that we were about to be surrendered.[8]

As Griffin remarked, "With all of their fighting ability, the 'Tinth' was surrendered at Fort Donelson without their knowledge or consent."[9]

Five hundred and fifty-four of the enlisted men went to Camp Douglas near Chicago, with the remainder sent to Alton Prison and Camp Morton. The Union captors sent staff officers to Fort Warren in Boston Harbor and the junior officers to Camp Chase near Columbus, Ohio.[10]

The service records for the men of the 10th reveal that 731 officers and men went to prison after the surrender of Fort Donelson. Of that number, only 289 rejoined the regiment upon parole to Vicksburg in September 1862.[11]

Members of the 10th expressed their dissatisfaction with the treatment of the 10th at Donelson and with prison life soon after the majority of them reached Camp Douglas in Chicago. Col. James A. Mulligan of the 23rd Illinois Infantry commanded the camp, and he led a regiment severely depleted by battle losses and their own imprisonment. Irishmen made up most of the 23rd, and Mulligan treated the men of the 10th well.[12] Col. James A. Mulligan wrote to Major General Hallock on February 27 and stated in part:

> Among the thousands of prisoners of war now in these quarters I believe there are many who became soldiers in the army of the rebels by compulsion or overwhelming necessity. From conversations which have been had by them by myself, my officers, and others I feel certain that many are loyal and abhor this nefarious war. This is especially the case with the Tennesseans, of whom large numbers express a desire to enlist in some of our companies now in camp. One Tennessee regiment, the Tenth, is composed almost exclusively of Irishmen and they desire to enlist in some of the companies in my regiment. I would willingly and fearlessly trust them. Should they be released, take the oath of allegiance, then enlist, and be sworn into some of my companies, would it be objectionable in any point of view?[13]

Major General Hallock forwarded Col. Mulligan's request to Brigadier General L. Thomas, Adjutant General of the Army on March 1. Governor O. P. Morton of Indiana sent a communication to Halleck on March 4 and said that there were prisoners at Camp Morton who also wanted to take the oath and enlist in the Union Army, as well as "a large number of Tennesseans who wanted to take the oath and be discharged."[14]

Major General Halleck responded to Col. Mulligan's request on March 10. He indicated that he had heard nothing from the War Department and authorized Mulligan to "fill up your unit in that way." He advised Mulligan to become "personally acquainted" with the history and character of each recruit, and to send the recruits to Benton Barracks in Arkansas and to not send them to Tennessee or Mississippi. The War Department replied to Hallock on March 15 and forbade the enlistment of prisoners. Col. Mulligan ignored the orders from the War Department and enrolled over 120 men from the 10th Tennessee, all but a few of whom later showed up on the roster of the 23rd Illinois. Additional members of the 10th joined the 65th Illinois, which was a Scots unit.[15]

The galvanized Yankees of the 23rd Illinois have largely escaped the attention of historians. The exception is an article written by David T. Maul for the *Journal of the Illinois State Historical Society* in which he follows five galvanized Yankees from the 10th Tennessee through the war. The 23rd went east after leaving Camp Douglas in June. Pvt. Patrick Carmody, who joined Company I, was the first to leave the 23rd and deserted somewhere in West Virginia before the roll call of October 2, 1862. Pvt. Patrick King, hospitalized for pneumonia on November 19, did not return to his unit until after Pvt. John Connor died. Pvt. Michael Joyce died in battle in April 1863. Pvt. Michael Crane, captured on January 28, 1864, died at Andersonville Prison on June 2, 1864. King spent the last few months of the war in the hospital and did not rejoin his unit until April 1865. He survived the war and worked for the B&O Railroad after the war. King lived to be nearly 88 years old and passed away in February 1920.[16]

The loss of men from the 10th while imprisoned after the surrender at Donelson was not limited to those who galvanized. Twenty-five men died, while 11 escaped before parole. One hundred and forty-nine men from the 10th enlisted in Union units, while 56 took the oath of allegiance to the Union. Four hundred and ninety men made the exchange at Vicksburg, but only 289 rejoined the 10th. The men of the 10th were among the first galvanized Yankees.[17]

The 10th Tennessee was not the only regiment captured at Donelson that included men who were unwilling to rejoin the Confederate Army upon release. A petition, dated March 7, 1862, was submitted by members of Tennessee regiments held at Camp Morton in Indiana who expressed "Union sentiments" and a "returning attachment to the Union." That letter from Lt. Col. William Hoffman to General M.C. Meigs referenced a communication from Col. Mulligan, who said that some of the prisoners at Camp Douglas had expressed a desire to enlist in the Union Army.[18]

Col. Richard D. Cutts, Major John J. Key, and 1st Lieutenant Charles W. Canfield, who made up a Military Board to determine the willingness of prisoners at Camp Butler to take the oath to the Union, reported their results to Assistant Adjutant General Col J. C. Kelton on March 19, 1862. The Union authorities required anyone who wanted to take the oath to post a $1,000 bond. Further, the oath taker had to remain behind Union lines in "Kentucky, Tennessee, Arkansas, and Mississippi for the duration of the war." Despite those conditions, they found that 1,640 men asked to take the oath, with 1,430 of those from Tennessee units. Five men from the 10th Tennessee made the request, but that was probably because only a small number of men from that unit were at Camp Butler.[19]

The men exchanged to Vicksburg who remained with the 10th first assisted in fortifying Vicksburg and then went to Port Hudson, Louisiana, to help build those defenses. The men of the 10th avoided the long siege at Port Hudson and went to Jackson in May 1863 to help defend the Mississippi capitol. They were engaged in the Battle of Raymond, Mississippi, on

May 12, where they lost Col. McGavock and suffered heavy casualties in killed, wounded, and captured. The 10th fought at Chickamauga, through the Atlanta campaign, and at Nashville and Franklin. Few of the regiment survived and remained with the unit after the Battle of Franklin. A number of the men of the 10th who were captured after their exchanged at Vicksburg, as well as new recruits gained after that time, continued to galvanize and join U.S. army and navy units. One man joined the 12th Michigan Battery, and four joined Captain Ahl's Battery at Fort Delaware. One joined Captain Richard's Battery at Fort Delaware and three joined the 6th U.S. Volunteer Infantry. Five more joined or attempted to join the U.S. Frontier Service, while four joined the navy. The service records indicate that a large number of other men joined Union units, but their enlistments could not be confirmed.[20]

THE 10TH TENNESSEE GALVANIZED

John Duane is emblematic of how difficult it is to understand the full story of the officers who joined the 10th Tennessee Infantry. Duane, captured at Egypt Station on December 28, 1864, during the Battle of Egypt Station, was a 2nd Lieutenant of Company B. He had not been a member of the 10th Tennessee Confederate prior to his service in the galvanized unit. He told his Union captors he served for four months in the summer of 1863 in Brown's South Carolina Battery and was made a 2nd Lieutenant by "Col. O'Neil." He further identified himself as a native of Ireland and his profession as "stone cutter." Duane stated that he had lived in New York until 1860, and he had travelled to Columbia, South Carolina, to visit his brother and attend school. He claimed that the Confederate authorities gave him the choice to enlist voluntarily in the Confederate Army or be conscripted. He described himself and his brother as "Union men," and he asked to take the oath to the Union. He took the oath at Johnson Island on May 13, 1865.[21]

There were some holes in Duane's story. There is no record of an artillery unit from South Carolina known as Brown's South Carolina Artillery. Second, the only record of prior service in the Confederate Army for a "John Duane" was as a private in the 5th South Carolina Reserves who served as guards at Florence Prison. The record of that John Duane indicates that he enlisted at 19 years old in the 5th on September 15, 1864, and was "sent to the front 1 Nov." The commander of the 5th Reserves was Lt. Col. Thomas R. Brown, who was probably the inspiration for Duane's "Brown's South Carolina Artillery." If indeed the John Duane who guarded prisoners at Florence Prison was the same John Duane captured at Egypt Station, it would not have served him well to admit that to his Union captors.[22]

It is not possible to reconstruct the roster of the galvanized 10th as no muster rolls are available. The Cain List, which is probably not entirely accurate, and the list of those captured by Grierson on December 29, 1864, at Egypt Station, Mississippi, provide the only enumerations of the galvanized Confederates for that unit. Further, no comprehensive list of the officers assigned to the galvanized 10th Tennessee is available.[23]

The current research identified a number of the officers assigned to the galvanized unit through related service records or other sources. Col. John G. O'Neill was the senior officer assigned to the unit. As previously mentioned, O'Neill had previously served in the 10th Tennessee Confederate, where he had risen to Colonel shortly before he commanded the galvanized 10th. He was a native of County Kerry in Ireland and was born in February 1841. Wounded at the Battle of Resaca in May 1864, he received his commission as Colonel on September 27 of that year. He was back with the 10th Confederate by the time of the Battle of Bentonville in March 1865. He married Nancy Drusilla Jackson of Warren County, Kentucky, after the war, and they moved to El Paso, Texas. He died in El Paso of a lung hemorrhage on October 29, 1884. He and his wife had two children who were both childless.[24]

Lt. Col. Martin Burke of the 1st Missouri Infantry was the second in command of the galvanized unit and was the officer who actually led the unit into action. Burke was a native of Galway, Ireland, and was 35 years old when he joined O'Neill. He had been a merchant living in St. Louis when he joined the 1st Missouri at Memphis, Tennessee, and he was a member of the local volunteer militia and a player for one of the best baseball teams in the city. He was elected captain in command of Company D for the 1st Missouri and promoted to Major in March 1862 and then to Lt. Colonel in May 1864. Burke fought in a number of engagements in the west with the 1st Missouri, including Shiloh and Corinth. He suffered a minor wound to the chest at the Battle of Kennesaw Mountain in late June 1864. General Hood detailed him and others to an inspection of hospitals south of Atlanta in August 1864, which took him to Macon, among other cities. It was probably during the inspections in Macon that he caught the eye of Major General Marcus Wright. General Beauregard ordered him to duty with the 10th Tennessee galvanized, also known as "O'Neal's" Regiment. Burke submitted a special requisition for 300 men in camp at Augusta, Georgia, on October 11 that included six axes, 40 camp kettles, 100 mess pans, 30 pots, 30 fry pans, six axe handles, 30 lids, 26 tents, and 250 tin cups. He signed the requisition as "M. Burke, Major comd'g recruits." Col. O'Neill followed with another requisition for 150 men on November 7 that included 20 mess pans, 20 camp kettles, 125 tin cups, 10 skillets, 10 teapots, and 26 fry pans.[25]

On November 3, 1864, Burke submitted expenses for travel from Augusta to Milledgeville and then to Macon, which took five days. That was apparently the same route taken by the recruits as they headed for the western front a month later. Again, he signed the travel request as a Major, but this time as Major of the 1st Missouri Infantry. Burke regained the rank of Lt. Col. before capture at Egypt Station in late December. That promotion probably came after Col. O'Neill decided that he could not lead the galvanized regiment into the field. Burke was released from Johnson Island on an oath of amnesty on May 16, 1865.[26]

MacPherson Berrien Eve served the galvanized unit as its major. Eve was born on August 13, 1846 to the powerful and wealthy Eve family of Augusta, Georgia. He briefly attended VMI as part of the class of 1867. His biography in the VMI Historical Rosters Database says that, according to an unofficial source, he attended "preparatory class at GMI (Georgia Military Institute), but ran off to army whenever possible." His official tenure at VMI was August 4 to October 7, 1863 "when dropped AWOL." His biography further states that he served as a drillmaster at Fort Johnson in North Carolina. He joined the staff of Major General Henry C. Wayne, Georgia's Adjutant and Inspector General and a close ally of Governor Joseph E. Brown, in 1864 with the rank of Major. Eve was hospitalized in Macon after suffering a wound at the Battle of Kennesaw Mountain in June 1864. Eve, for the most part, lacked military experience commiserate with his rank of major, and he was probably assigned to "O'Neill's Regiment" as a political decision to gain support from Governor Brown. Major Eve led a portion of the regiment to the west and was in Artesia, Mississippi, during the Battle of Egypt Station. He requested authority to "raise an Infty Bn or Reg from Among Federal Prisoners" on February 16, 1865, but no reply to that request was found among the available records. A note included on the record of that request stated: "Rt'd to ____? 3/22/65." His request may not have been sent up the chain-of-command for approval. Major Eve survived the war and was a planter until his death in Lillandale, Virginia, on June 28, 1886.[27]

Most of the remaining officers of the 10th galvanized are unknown. See Appendix C for a discussion of the rest of the known officers.

Col. O'Neill gathered his recruits at Augusta where they were clad in Confederate uniforms and trained. Gen. Hood authorized Major General

Wright to raise 1,000 recruits, and many were assembled at Augusta during October and November. The recruitments were likely enlisted men from Florence, Charleston, Millen, and Andersonville.[28]

The location of the camp in Augusta has not been determined, but a 1915 article in the *Atlanta Constitution* provides information that may point to the general area of the camp. According to that article, the camp was located two miles south of Augusta on the Central of Georgia Railroad. The story was about a woman who lived next to the camp. A galvanized Confederate approached her and asked to borrow a sifter. Sifters, used to sift either wheat flour or cornmeal, would have been valuable items at a time when bolting cloth was in short supply and cornmeal was a major part of military rations. Unbolted cornmeal, provided by the Confederate government to prisoners, was a mixture of both kernels and cobs. According to the story, the galvanized Confederate tried to return the sifter, but she told him he could keep it. He gave the woman his family bible in exchange, which her family still had in 1915.[29]

Elements of the galvanized unit started pulling out of Augusta and moving to the west in late November or early December. Col. George William Brent was the Assistant Adjutant General on the staff of Lieutenant General Richard Taylor who commanded the Department of Alabama, Mississippi, and East Louisiana. Brent sent a telegram on December 15 to Captain John Perry at Opelika and directed him to find out to which command "O'Neal's" Regiment belonged. The telegram further stated that that regiment was coming through Opelika by way of Columbus, Georgia.[30]

Two days later Brent sent a telegram from Montgomery to Lieutenant General Taylor in Meridian, which stated: "About 500 enlisted foreigners under Col. O'Neal of Hood's Command leave for field B. . . . —unarmed. If needed, they might be used between Corinth & Huntsville."

Brent sent a telegram on December 17 to Major General D. H. Maury, who commanded the Department of the Gulf and the defense of Mobile, and informed Maury that he had ordered the 500-man force of enlisted foreigners to Meridian. Brent further said that Taylor could arm them at Meridian and send them on to Mobile if needed. Mobile faced an imminent Union attack at that time, and all available units were sent to their aid. Brent sent a telegram to Lieutenant General Taylor at Meridian on December 18 that "O'Neal's" Regiment was leaving that day for Meridian and could be sent to Mobile for "immediate operations." Maury apparently asked for half of the men. Brent was apparently unaware that the 500-man force he was tracking was actually under the command of Lt. Col. Martin Burke.[31]

"O'Neal's" Regiment remained in Meridian until December 22. Lt. Col. and Assistant Adjutant and Inspector General William M. Levy informed Major General Maury on that date that he was sending 450 members of "O'Neal's" Regiment to assist in the defense of Mobile.[32]

Meridian and other key points in Mississippi had been under threat of a raid from Baton Rouge, Louisiana, led by Brigadier General John W. Davidson in late November to early December. Those portions of Mississippi still under Confederate control were vulnerable to raids from Memphis, Baton Rouge, and Vicksburg and there were few military units available to meet those threats.[33]

Another element of the galvanized unit was still in Georgia, making its way towards Macon, when the man body under the command of Lt. Col. Martin Burke was nearing Opelika. A letter originally published in the *Augusta Chronicle* (and republished in the *Richmond Whig* on January 6, 1865, and the *Cleveland Morning Leader* on January 13) told a curious story about 200 "galvanized Yankees" who were on the way to join Hood's Army on December 15. According to the story, the major in command turned the "galvanized Yankees" loose at the Mayfield, Georgia, railroad depot and told them to find their own food. Predictable chaos resulted: "They went off in quick time and scattered in every direction, killing hogs, and going into ladies' houses, demanding something to eat. They went around every farm. Some of them were seen fifteen miles from Mayfield, and in the lady's opinion they can never be picked up again. 'The major went to Sparta, fourteen miles from the depot, and the captain to Augusta.'" The letter further claimed that the major, offered rations for his men if he would keep them together, declined the offer.[34]

The major referred to in the story was Major MacPherson Berrien Eve, as he was the only one of that rank known to have served with the galvanized unit. It is impossible to confirm or deny the statements made in the letter, but the actions ascribed to Major Eve are consistent with what appears to have been his impetuous nature. As will be discussed, Major Eve showed up in Mississippi in late December with at least part of his command.

The small town of Mayfield was the terminus of the planned Milledgeville Railroad that was to link Warrenton and Milledgeville. Construction of the railroad, interrupted by the onset of the war, halted at Mayfield. Milledgeville is approximately 37 miles by road today from Mayfield. The Central of Georgia Railroad between Milledgeville and Macon was probably still inoperable in mid-December 1864, after Sherman moved on to Savannah. It is possible that the galvanized Yankee unit could have made at least part of that trip by rail. Lt. Col. Burke had made the trip from Augusta to Macon in five days during November by following the same route.[35]

The departure of Lt. Col. Burke with his 500 men (or 450) and Major Eve with his 200 men left about 300 men behind in Augusta. No reason for leaving that many men behind could be determined during the current research.

A new threat emerged from Memphis on December 21. Brigadier General Benjamin H. Grierson led a force of three brigades of about 3,500 men towards Corinth, Mississippi, along the Memphis and Charleston Railroad. Grierson had achieved fame for the successful raid he led through Mississippi from April 17 to May 2, 1863, which began in LaGrange, Tennessee, and ended in Baton Rouge, Louisiana. The path of that raid was west of the 1864 raid, and its main objective was to cut off the Southern Railroad east of Jackson. Grierson cut the railroad at Newton Station in 1863, and from there the raiders proceeded to Baton Rouge. The 1959 movie *The Horse Soldiers* was a fictionalized account of the raid, starring John Wayne as Grierson.[36]

Corinth was an important supply depot in northern Mississippi, and the feint towards Corinth represented it as the target of the raid. The actual target was the Mobile and Ohio Railroad, which was a critical link in the supply line of General Hood and his Army of Tennessee. General Grierson's raiders travelled without wagons, carrying supplies and 20 days of rations on pack mules. The raiders moved south while destroying stations, tracks, and war material in a number of small towns. They moved into Tupelo without opposition and then seven miles south to Verona Station, where they attacked a Confederate camp of 700 dismounted cavalry and destroyed "2 trains, 32 cars, and 8 warehouses filled with ordnance, commissary, and quartermaster stores; also 200 army wagons, most of which were marked 'U.S,' having been captured from Gen. Sturgis in June." The main force of the raiders left Tupelo on the 26th and followed the railroad to Okolona, where they first encountered the Confederate force under Lt. Col. Burke and then General Gholson on the 27th.[37]

Lt. Col. Burke's and his command's stay in Mobile had been brief—they were back in Meridian by the 26th. Major John S. Hope, Assistant Inspector-General of the Department of Alabama, Mississippi, and East Louisiana and a member of Lt. General Taylor's staff, submitted a report on the Battle of Egypt Station a day after the battle. He stated that 700 men and King's Battery of four guns arrived in Meridian by train on 26. Lt. Col. Burke was in command as the ranking officer. Burke requisitioned 17 boxes of .58 caliber ammunition, which amounted to 17,000 cartridges for the infantry, who had muskets but lacked ammunition. It was Major Burke's intention to take that force to Corinth, which Lt. General Taylor and Major General Franklin Gardner still believed was the target of the raid that had come out of Memphis.[38]

Burke's troops included his 500-man contingent and 200 men of "Metts' Battalion." The "Metts Battalion" was not part of any known unit. It is likely that they were reserve troops from various units. Lt. Col. D. W. Metts commanded the 5th Infantry State Troops, but that unit disbanded on September 22, 1863. These troops may have also been elements of the 1st Mississippi Reserve Cavalry.[39]

Upon arrival at West Point on the afternoon of December 26, Major Hope learned that Grierson's raid was not moving on Corinth but instead was threatening Verona and Okolona. He telegraphed Lt. General Taylor for new orders, which arrived at 9 PM. Those orders directed him to move as close as he could to Okolona, which was 28 miles from West Point. There he was to use the train to remove military stores from Okolona if the raiders were not already in the town. The orders informed him that he could expect 600 reinforcements on the 27th.[40]

Major Hope encountered delays on the way to Okolona, which would also effect the movement of his reinforcements a day later. His train did not leave West Point until 11 PM. At 3 AM the train engineer told him there was not enough water to run the train all the way to Okolona. This should have been a known problem as railroad employees had told Major Hope at West Point that there was no functioning water tank between West Point and Okolona. At that point the engine was detached from the train to go ahead to get water and then go back to pick up the train. Major Hope accompanied the locomotive to Okolona which he reached by 4:30 AM. Hope learned that the enemy with 2,000 to 2,500 men was camped a mere five miles away, and that the only force between Grierson's raiders and Okolona was General Gholson, with 250 cavalrymen who were armed but lacked ammunition. A box (1,000 rounds) of .54 caliber ammunition found for the Austrian (Lorenze) rifles that Gholson and his men carried amounted to only four rounds per man. The only thing Major Hope was able to save from Okolona was a train of fourteen cars, which he sent to Egypt Station. Major Hope decided that the terrain was too flat and open at Okolona for it to be defensible against a force the size of Grierson's raiders, and he decided to make his stand at Egypt Station.[41]

Major Hope returned to Egypt Station by train and he and Lt. Col. Burke worked out a plan to send Burke and 270 men to a point 2 ½ miles south of Okolona, where the railroad had tree cover and a bridge and trestle to provide a better defensive position. That place was the only defensible point along the railroad. Burke agreed to try to hold the position unless in threat of being flanked, and the train was left with him so he could evacuate his men to Egypt Station, if necessary. General Gholson and his 250 men fell back to Burke's position when the raiders came into Okolona, around 11 AM on December 27. The entire force retreated to Egypt Station that evening.[42]

Brigadier General Grierson had learned a good deal about the planned defense of Egypt Station by the time his raiders entered Okolona. His men had tapped the telegraph wires near Okolona and had intercepted communications between Major Hope and General Franklin Gardner, and Gen. Grierson knew that reinforcements were on the way from West Point. They also had direct human intelligence from deserters from the galvanized unit, and perhaps from others that had come over to his command on the evening of December 27. Colonel Joseph Kargé of the 2nd New Jersey Cavalry said that 15 deserters surrendered to his pickets, but only five from Lt. Col. Burke's were identified in the available service records. The five men from the 10th who can be confirmed as deserting on December 27 were privates Thomas Keltcher (Company E, 119th Pennsylvania Infantry), Francis Melville (Company A, 5th Iowa Cavalry), P.W. Murphy (Company B, 52nd New York Infantry), William Roberston (Company I, 10th Ohio Cavalry), and Patrick Runnels (Reynolds) (Company H, 9th New Hampshire Infantry).[43]

Col. John W. Noble of the 3rd Iowa Cavalry enumerated the war material destroyed by his men at Okolona as: "1 water tank, with steam-engine and fixtures attached; 1 turn-table; four switches; 1 depot filled with meat and meal; 1 building filled with 3,000 barrels of corn; 1 large lot of rebel uniform clothing, socks, shirts, drawers &c; 4 buildings filled with rations; and a lot of drugs and medicines." Col. Noble and his men missed the fight at Egypt Station, arriving there after the Confederate surrender.[44]

Confusion reigned at West Point where Lt. General Richard Taylor ordered Major General Franklin Gardner, commander of the District of Mississippi and East Louisiana, to send reinforcements to General Gholson and Lt. Col. Burke. Gardner had served as the commander of Port Hudson during what proved to be the longest siege of the Civil War. That siege ended immediately after the fall of Vicksburg. Gardner had left Meridian on December 27 with Lt. Col. William W. Wier and the 500 (600 in some communications) men of the 1st Confederate Veterans. They arrived at West Point between 9 and 10 that evening. Lt. Col. Wier and his men were the reinforcements promised to Gen. Gholson and Lt. Col. Burke, but Gardner allowed them to detrain at West Point so they could cook their rations. Gardner ordered Wier and his men back on the train at 11:30 PM, but the train did not depart until 2 AM. Gardner and Wier seemed to be unaware that Grierson's raiders had destroyed the water tanks between West Point and Okolona and that it would be necessary to load water from a cistern along the way. There were only three small buckets on the train, and the delay caused by getting and loading the water made it impossible to reach Egypt Station in time to reinforce the defenders. It also meant that the ammunition needed by Gholson and his men would not reach them in time.[45]

Major-General Gardner was court martialed and cashiered out for drunkenness in part because of his actions at West Point. The transcript of Gardner's court martial has been included with his service record and proved he was impaired on the evening of December 27. The outcome of the battle of Egypt Station may not have been different if the men and ammunition had reached the defenders in time, but it could have made the defense formidable enough for Grierson to bypass it and turn to the west.[46]

The attack on Egypt Station began at 7:30 AM on December 28, an hour before Lt. Colonel Wier and the reinforcements arrived. Grierson's force consisted of three cavalry brigades. Col. Joseph Kargé of the 2nd New Jersey Cavalry commanded the 2nd Brigade and led the attack on Egypt Station. He stated he encountered the enemy's cavalry two miles from Egypt Station and drove them in to the enemy's skirmish line. The skirmish line was composed of the 100 men under the command of Captain Nutzel. It is likely that many of those men were able to escape Egypt Station as the battle continued and that some of the men who deserted in the night were from Nutzel's company. The Egypt Station defenses were located half a mile north of the train depot known as Egypt Station. Kargé attacked the defenses with the 2nd New Jersey at the center and the left flank, and the 4th Missouri Cavalry and the 7th Indiana Cavalry at the right.[47]

Captain Thomas Brownrigg of Gholson's cavalry unit provided the only known Confederate eye witness account of the battle from within the Egypt Station defenses. He wrote his account of the battle in 1879. Brownrigg said about 200 cavalry under General Gholson and 300 enlisted Federals under Lt. Col. Burke manned the defenses. He did not mention the Metts Battalion although they clearly were within the defenses. He probably derived his numbers from the number of prisoners taken, and they were clearly undercounts of those actually present. Brownrigg stated that the officers present had concluded that their position could not be held against the raiders, but that Gholson had been ordered by Major General Gardner to hold the "to the last moment."[48]

The Confederate position was quite strong. The initial position was behind a railroad embankment, where Lt. Col. Burke held his and Gholson's men in a prone position until the Union attack, which came in columns, was 50 to 60 yards away. At that point, he had his men stand and fire into the columns, which shattered the heads of the columns. Lt. Col. Burke, wounded in the arm during the first attack, stood with his men during subsequent charges to direct their fire. The Union cavalry charged several times with the same results. The attackers withdrew after several unsuccessful attempts, and Gholson ordered Captain Brownrigg forward to determine what they were doing. Brownrigg said he found that the Union attackers had begun a flanking move that would overrun the position on the railroad embankment. It was this point, according to Brownrigg, that Gholson ordered Burke's men into a stockade to the east of the railroad, as they "could not escape." He ordered his cavalrymen to mount their horses and mules and retreat eastward across an open field. Gholson and his men were doubtless out of ammunition by this time, as they could not have had more than four cartridges per man when the battle began. Gholson was shot in the arm while trying to cross a ditch in the field. His aide, Captain Thomas W. Harris, fell while trying to cross this ditch, and the pursuing Federal column captured both of them. Brownrigg crossed the ditch on his mule and escaped eastward into woods, where the rest of the cavalry was waiting. He said that Burke and his men made a "valiant defense in the stockade," giving up only when they were out of ammunition.[49]

Col. Kargé included a brief discussion of the battle in his report of the raid. As previously mentioned, the 2nd New Jersey Cavalry occupied both the center and left of the attack columns, while the 4th Missouri Cavalry and the 7th Indiana Cavalry occupied the right. The 2nd New Jersey drove back the defenders on the railroad embankment, and the defenders retreated east to a stockade. The stockade, not described in any account, may have been a defensive strong point erected at some point in the war to protect the railroad at Egypt Station. One of the units on the right flank overtook and shot Major General Gholson as the battle continued, which confirms at least in part the description of the battle by Captain Brownrigg. Two squadrons of mounted troops attacked the stockade from the left, while two dismounted companies attacked from the right. The 4th and 11th Illinois

Cavalry from the 2nd Brigade, commanded by Col. Embury D. Osbond, joined the assault on the embankment as part of the right wing. They took cover behind houses to the right of the stockade, intending to attack it on foot. Grierson ordered them to make a mounted assault on the rear of the stockade and they took heavy casualties as they moved into position. The stockade surrendered before they were in position for the attack.[50]

Brownrigg claimed that the men of the stockade surrendered because they ran out of ammunition. That seems unlikely, as they started the fight with 17,000 rounds of .58 caliber ammunition, and the victorious raiders found 15,000 of these rounds left after the fight. Chickasaw, who observed the battle from the Union side, gave what appears to be a better explanation. According to Chickasaw, the mounted troopers of the 2nd New Jersey Cavalry were armed with Spencer rifles and managed to ride up to the stockade and concentrate their fire inside the defenses, forcing Burke, who was flanked on both sides, to surrender. Chickasaw exaggerated the number of prisoners taken; he claimed that 800 men, including both infantry and cavalry, were captured, while the actual number was more reliably reported as 500.[51]

Kargé specifically stated that the raiders captured 500 prisoners at the stockade, including a Colonel and 15 line officers. Kargé did not identify the prisoners by unit, but they almost certainly were members of the galvanized 10th and Metts' brigade. Gholson's unit largely escaped during the battle.[52]

Captain Anthony T. Search of the 4th Illinois Cavalry, in command of five companies of 260 men, told a slightly different version of the battle than Kargé. According to Search, he and his men took part in the battle and drove the defenders back from the embankment while attacking from the right. He maintained that his companies drove the defenders about 100 rods (550 yards) to woods, where a deep ditch made them break off their pursuit. Col. Osbond reported that the 4th Illinois was the unit that caused Gholson to retreat from the railroad embankment, and that they pursued his cavalrymen to a "road beyond." Osbond claimed that the 4th Illinois killed or wounded 15-20 of the fleeing cavalrymen using pistols and sabers, at a cost of two wounded from the 4th Illinois. It was the 4th Illinois that wounded and captured Gholson.[53]

Two other units of the 2nd Brigade were also present at the battle. Osbond reported that he moved the 3rd U.S. Colored Cavalry to the previous position of the 11th Illinois. Grierson moved two companies from that unit, in addition to two companies of the 2nd Wisconsin Cavalry, to the extreme west of the Union line. The battle ended before those units were able to press their attacks, although a few of their horses were wounded.[54]

The battle was not restricted to the embankment and stockade. The attackers received cannon fire from King's Battery on a railroad flat car about a half mile to the south at the railroad depot. Col. Kargé detached the 4th Missouri and the 7th Indiana to try to capture the battery, at which time Grierson arrived and took command of those units. Major Hope had remained with the train, and he decided to take the train towards West Point to try to find out why Col. Wier had not arrived. He encountered the second train four and a half or five miles from Egypt, where Col. Wier's men were unloaded and formed up to meet the enemy in full pursuit, then about a mile away.[55]

Wier, in his report, stated the following:

> About two miles below Egypt we met the train from above, having on board King's Battery. They reported the enemy in full pursuit, and that they had to leave part of their train behind; also that General Gholson with his entire command were captured. I immediately moved up the railroad at a double-quick to an eminence about a half a mile in front. When I gained this position the enemy were formed and moving down upon me, my skirmishers already firing on them. They then moved around to my right flank, causing me to change my front. From this position they bore down on me at a full gallop. My men were steady and cool, and with a well directed fire scattered them in every direction. They then fell back to their former position near Egypt, but in fill view. They immediately formed their line of battle across the railroad, two other columns moving out of the woods to join them. I took immediate steps to fortify my position, requesting Major Hope to take his train down to Prairie Station, get some water for the locomotive, and return with the battery immediately. The enemy remained in this position about two hours, then withdrew out of sight. Having no horse I could get but little information.

Wier learned at 4 PM that the raiders had left Egypt and gone to the west. He returned to West Point with his men on the 29th.[56]

Brigadier General Grierson took personal command of the troops dispatched to intercept Wier when he and his troops finally arrived. Grierson's brief account of that action stated: "while the fight was in progress two trains with reinforcements said to be under command of General Gardner, came in sight, but I threw a force between them and Egypt, which succeeded in capturing a train of cars, tearing up the tracks two miles and a half south of that point, and engaged the trains with re-inforcements, preventing them from joining the garrison at Egypt." Grierson went on to say that the total engagement lasted just two hours.[57]

The 1876 regimental history of the 7th Indiana Cavalry includes a somewhat garbled account of the Battle of Egypt Station, but it does provide some additional details about the blocking action of the reinforcements under Wier. According to that account, Grierson first attacked the train that contained King's Battery and forced the engineer to unhook 14 cars from the engine to escape with the battery. Detachments of the 7th and 4th Missouri Cavalry, under the command of Grierson's Adjutant General, continued to pursue the engine, while others burned the cars. They pursued the train for about a mile when two more trains with the reinforcements pulled up. The Union cavalrymen then tried to tear up track to keep the trains from approaching, but they only succeeded in removing one rail. The reinforcements then disembarked from the train, forming up in a cornfield behind a fence, and began firing on the Union cavalrymen. The pursuing cavalrymen reportedly consisted of only a hundred men, and they believed they were facing about 300 Confederates. Nevertheless, the 7th Indiana charged the position but could not get past a ditch located in front of the Confederate position. The casualties suffered by the 7th Indiana included two dead, 11 wounded, and 28 horses killed or disabled.[58]

Then butcher bill for the battle was quite high given the short (two hour) duration of the battle and the number of men involved. The 2nd New Jersey Cavalry suffered most of the Union casualties, with two officers and 16 enlisted men killed and three officers and 69 enlisted men wounded. The 7th Indiana Cavalry had two enlisted men killed and 11 wounded, while one officer of the 4th Missouri Cavalry was captured (thought to be wounded) and one enlisted man was wounded. The 2nd Brigade under Col. Embury D. Osmond also suffered casualties when they supported the right side of the attacking line. Two men of 4th Illinois Cavalry were severely wounded in the pursuit of General Gholson and his cavalrymen. The 11th Illinois had one enlisted man killed and two officers and 13 men wounded during their attack on the stockade. The total Union casualties numbered two officers and 19 enlisted men killed and six officers and 96 enlisted men wounded, for a total of 21 killed and 102 wounded. Wier claimed that his men found seven Union dead in front of his position.[59]

Surgeon F. H. Evans, of the Confederate Office of the Surgeon in Charge of Hospitals, visited the field hospital with both Union and Confederate wounded on January 1, 1865. The field hospital was set up in houses in Egypt for those too badly injured to travel. Union Brigade Surgeon Krauter and a hospital steward stayed with the wounded. Confederate Surgeon W. A. Evans, dispatched to Egypt immediately after the battle, helped Krauter care for 35 Union and seven Confederate wounded. W. A. Evans later attested that Krauter had shown the same level of care for the Confederate as the Union wounded. Before arriving at the hospital, F. H. Evans had left 15 of his litter bearers with the train to repair the tracks as far as possible towards Egypt. Evans evacuated the badly wounded from Egypt a mile and a half away to the train by litters. He left surgeons West and Wilkinson of the reserve corps, who were in transit from Corinth, with the train to oversee the evacuation. Surgeon L. W. Tuttle, left in West Point, prepared for the arrival of the wounded and arranged for their transport by rail to Columbus, Mississippi. The train arrived late at night, and the wounded were cared for on the train that night. The wounded then went to Columbus under the care of a Confederate medical officer, Surgeon Krauter, and his hospital steward. Twelve or fifteen of the wounded Federals died before F. H. Evans reached Egypt, and one more died in transit. One Confederate soldier, too severely injured to move from Egypt, presumably died, while a second died in transit.[60]

The Confederate commanders did not report their casualties, but they probably had fewer given the protection offered by their defensive positions. Gholson suffered a severe wound to his arm that necessitated amputation of the arm at the shoulder, but he did survive the battle. Chickasaw calculated the Confederate casualties as "no less than 60 or 70."[61]

A mystery that emerged from the Battle of Egypt Station, which was not addressed through the available records, is what happened to the balance of the soldiers of the galvanized 10th who escaped capture. It is clear that Lt. Col. Burke took approximately 500 men north towards Egypt from West Point on 26, in addition to 200 men in the Mettes Battalion. Grierson's raiders captured 500 men, leaving about 200 (less the killed and wounded) who escaped. The service records of the 10th galvanized list 262 enlisted men captured during the battle in addition to at least four officers. A few men escaped from their captors during the travel to Vicksburg or from the boat from Vicksburg to Memphis. General Gardner reported to Lt. General Taylor, "Col. Burke and most of his men reported captured," which means that at least some of the 500 had escaped.[62]

Major General Gardner, through his adjutant Col. Ed Woodlief sent the following telegram to Col. F. H. McDonnell from West Point on December 29: "I am directed by the Maj Genl Commdg to say to you that you will Immediately send out a detachment of unarmed cavalry to pick up all stragglers both infantry and cavalry in this vicinity and organize them. You will also establish a regular camp of direction at this Post and all men must be kept under control organized and armed as soon as practicable." Those stragglers were probably men who escaped at Egypt Station, and the admonishment that "all men must be kept under control" may have referred to those from Burke's unit. The cavalry and infantry were separated when both were sent to a camp of direction in Columbus, Mississippi.[63]

Not all of the men from the galvanized 10th who were in Mississippi at the time of the battle had been sent to Egypt Station with Burke. General Gardner stated in his report on Grierson's raid that he ordered a Major Eve to remain with his men at Artesia, Mississippi, on December 28. Artesia is located south of West Point where the spur line to Columbus meets the main line of the Mobile and Ohio Railroad. Gardner ordered Eve to remain there in case the raiders continued to the south. Major Eve may have been proceeding north from Mobile at that time. Eve's command was probably the same 200-man unit that reached Mayfield, Georgia, on December 15, as he had "180 U.S. Confederates" at that station on December 30.[64]

There seems to have been some confusion on the part of Acting Assistant Adjutant General (a Major when he served on Gardner's staff) Woodlief and Major General Gardner about Eve's name. Gardner's report on Grierson's raid was the only place found to this point that cited Eve's proper surname. Three different telegrams to Eve gave his name as Major McP. Bieres, Bires, or even Bevis.[65]

Eve was under the command of Col. C. H. Colvin, the commander of the post of Macon, Mississippi, on December 30. Colvin provided rations for Eve and his men on that date. Major Eve's welcome at Artesia seems to have worn thin by January 1. A telegram sent to him on that date by authority of Gardner ordered him to: " . . . remove your command to this place as soon as you can obtain transportation, provided you have not already received orders from the Lieut Genl Comdng Depart."

It appears that Major Eve was either unwilling or unable to control his troops, much as he had been at Mayfield. Gardner sent a telegram to Lieutenant General Taylor on January 2 that read in part: "Major Beries is in command of U.S. Confederates at Artesia telegraph is removed. I will order him by train tomorrow to proceed to this point (West Point) as citizens complain."

Major General Gardner issued an unnumbered Special Order on January 3 that read: "Lieut George Eames Ord officer will proceed by first train to West Point and Columbus to gather up the arms recently issued to the troops organized to meet raid of the enemy and bring them to this point." That order gathered the arms from at least some of the survivors of Burke's force that fought at Egypt Station, as well as from the 180 men under Major Eve.[66]

There is some confusion in the literature over where elements of the "O'Neill Regiment" were on January 1. William Pitt Chambers wrote in his memoirs that he arrived in Macon, Mississippi, at 9 PM on the night of January 1, 1865, and slept there overnight on the train he was taking north to West Point. He said he was unable to sleep well because of a "battalion of 'galvanized Yankees' aboard." He called them "the lowest and most debased looking set of men I ever saw." He further said the men were "ignorant, noisy and thievish, and are a discredit to any civilized army." He called them "good fighters," but he also said he would have preferred that they were in the Union Army and not that of the Confederacy. He mentioned Artesia, which he said was a spur line that led to Columbus, on the way to his destination at West Point. The enlisted Federals he mentioned were probably Eve's men, and Eve had probably taken his men to Col. Colvin's headquarters in Macon to arrange transportation to West Point. They arrived at West Point on January 2nd.[67]

Chambers joined the 1st Regiment of Consolidated Veterans at West Point, and he was sent to a post near Columbus, Mississippi, on January 4, 1865, to meet a rumored Federal raid from Alabama. Chambers and his unit returned to West Point on January 12 on the way to Tupelo. Along the way, Chambers commented on "soldiers recently enlisted from among the Federal prisoners." He said there was a "small battalion (about one hundred and 50 men) attached to his brigade." He reiterated his contempt for them when he said: "They belong to the criminal class, and more than twenty instances are reported in the past few days in which both whites and negroes have been robbed and in many cases personally assaulted. They are scattered all over the country through which we have passed, and are said to be committing all sorts of depredations. . . . Many have already deserted to the enemy and others say they will do the same at the first opportunity. . . . It is said some of them fought bravely at Egypt a few weeks ago before they were captured by Grierson. Perhaps so." [68]

Chambers reached Egypt on January 16, and remarked that was the place where "Consolidated Veterans" had fought Grierson and where Col. Burke's enlisted Federals and Major Phelps Reserves had been captured. The galvanized Confederates that Chambers met in that instance were probably those who escaped from Egypt Station.

Col. Kargé reported that the 500 prisoners taken in the stockade included a Lt. Col. and 15 line officers. The officers from the galvanized 10th included Lt. Col. Burke, Captain Conrad Nutzel, 1st Lt. Robert P. Seymour, 2nd Lt. George Wharton, and 2nd Lt. John Duane. It is not known if any of Burke's officers escaped between their capture at Egypt Station and their arrival at Memphis, where the official roll of the prisoners was recorded; they traveled through Vicksburg along the way. The official roll of the enlisted prisoners captured from the galvanized 10th included 262 enlisted men, of which as many as four privates may have always been Confederate soldiers and not enlisted Federals. The four men in question were James Eustace, Pat Wells, Henry W. Goodrich, and John Wilson. None of whom could be otherwise traced through available Civil War records. Those men may have functioned as sergeants despite the rank given in the Memphis list, or they may have functioned as Burke's eyes and ears within the unit to warn him of any impending attempts at mutiny or desertions.[69]

The remnants of the O'Neill regiment in Mississippi joined the Army of Tennessee after the Battle of Egypt Station. The Army of Tennessee moved east to join the command of General Johnston after the abandonment of Charleston and then marched towards surrender at Greensboro, North Carolina. It is unknown if what was left of the galvanized 10th at Augusta joined them or if that contingent remained in Augusta or some other post until the end of the war. The remnants of both the 10th and 20th Tennessee were part of Cheatham's Division at Bentonville, which included the former Bate's Division. Captain Lewis R. Clark, who was part of both the 10th Tennessee and the galvanized 10th, was on detached duty in command of the "Division pioneers" at the surrender at Greensboro. That command probably consisted of what was left of the galvanized 10th.[70]

It does appear, however, that at least some of the galvanized 10th fought in the Battle of Bentonville. Dr. W. J. McMurray in his *History of the 20th Tennessee Regiment Volunteer Infantry*, states: "Lieutenant Sanders commanded a company of 'galvanized Yankees'—(Federal soldiers who had joined our army to get out of prison) in this fight, and of course was not with his Regiment . . . Lieutenant Sanders was wounded in this battle. Those 'galvanized Yankees' gave him credit for being the gamest man that ever took them to battle. He certainly put them in and made them do splendid fighting."[71] Lieutenant M. M. Sanders was one of only three men from Company E of the 20th Tennessee Infantry who made it through the war to Bentonville.

McMurray explained the assignment of Lt. Sanders to command the "galvanized Yankee" company: "At the Battle of Bentonville, N. C., he was chosen to command a lot of 'galvanized Yankees' because of his daring and independent nature. At first they wavered and showed a disposition to lag back, but he got square with them, and actually 'cussed' them into desperation, and a more gallant fight was seldom seen than they made on that occasion."[72]

At least a few galvanized Confederates were present at the Battle of Bentonville. Three soldiers described as "galvanized Yankees" deserted during the first day of the battle on March 19. The Union captors took the three deserters to Gen. William P. Carlin, who commanded the 1st Division of the 14th Army Corps. At the time, Gen. Carlin accompanied the 2nd Brigade of his Division, commanded by Bvt. Brig. Gen. Carlos P. Buell. This placed Gen. Carlin on the extreme left wing of the 14th Army Corps when the Battle of Bentonville began, on the morning of March 19. His division fronted Clayton's Division, commanded by Maj. Gen. Henry D. Clayton.[73] Bates, quoting from a letter sent to him by Gen. Carlin, said:

> Immediately after this assault, three privates in Confederate uniform, deserted to my lines and were brought to me. One of them stated they were federal soldiers who had enlisted in the rebel army while prisoners of war to avoid starvation, with the intention of joining the federal army again as soon as possible. He told me all the rebel forces south of Virginia were in our front, and mentioned Generals Bragg, Hardee, Cheatham, Stewart, and Beauregard, with General Joseph E. Johnston in command of the whole rebel army. He said at that moment the confederate generals were riding among their troops making speeches and explaining to them their plans to destroy the left wing of Sherman's army, and then turn on the right wing and destroy that. This statement fully confirmed my previous conclusions, and was so important that I immediately put the man on my own horse and detailed my only staff officer present to take him to generals Davis and Slocum. Until that moment General Slocum had believed there was no force in our front but a little cavalry. Having now sent off every man belonging to my staff and headquarters, on duty of some kind, and being entirely alone, I stayed with General Buell's brigade, expecting to remain there until some officer of my escort should return to me.[74]

Major General Henry W. Slocum commanded the Left Wing of the Union Army, which was under attack at Bentonville. Bvt. Major General

Jefferson C. Davis commanded the 14th Army Corps. The unidentified galvanized Confederate was sent to those generals by Gen. Carlin to repeat the story he had been told. Gen. Slocum later recalled the meeting:

> About the same time one of my officers brought to me an emaciated, sickly appearing young man about twenty-two or twenty-three years of age, dressed in Confederate gray. He had expressed great anxiety to see the commanding officer at once. I asked him what he had to say. He said that he had been in the Union Army, had been taken prisoner, and while sick and in prison had been induced to enlist in the Confederate service. He said he enlisted with the intention of deserting when a good opportunity presented itself, believing he should die if he remained in prison. In reply to my questions he informed me that he formerly resided in Syracuse, New York, and had entered the service at the commencement of the war, in a company raised by Captain Butler. I had been a resident of Syracuse, and knew the history of the company and regiment. While I was talking with him one of my aides, Major William G. Tracy, rode up and at once recognized the deserter as an old acquaintance whom he had known in Syracuse before the war. I asked how he knew General Johnston was in command and what he knew as to the strength of his force. He said General Johnston rode along the line early that morning, and that the officers had told all the men that 'Old Joe' had caught one of Sherman's wings beyond the reach of support, that he intended to smash that wing and then go for the other. The man stated that he had no chance of escaping till that morning, and had come to meet me to warn me of my danger. He said there is a very large force immediately in your front, all under the command of General Joe Johnston.[75]

Major Tracy had first enlisted in the 12th New York Infantry, and later transferred to the 122nd New York. It is likely that the galvanized Confederate had belonged to one of those units. Major William Tracy, cited for a mission he carried out behind enemy lines at Chancellorsville on May 2, 1863, received the Congressional Medal of Honor on May 5, 1895.[76]

Gen. Slocum's officers soon corroborated the information provided by the galvanized Confederate. The Battle of Bentonville lasted for three days and resulted in a Union victory. Gen. Johnston's army retreated to Smithfield after the battle and spent several days reorganizing and preparing for its last retreat.

Major Eve did not remain with the galvanized 10th to the end; he requested the authority to "raise an infantry Bn or Reg from among Federal Prisoners" on February 16, 1865. The request did not indicate the recipient. O'Neill was already in the process of recruiting by then. Eve probably had tarnished his reputation by his poor handling of the troops of the galvanized 10th, and he was no longer trusted to recruit, train, and lead a battalion or regiment.[77]

Col. John O'Neill successfully requested authority to recruit prisoners on January 16. O'Neill's authorization was signed by Major and AA J. N. Eustis by command of General Beauregard. That order read:

> Special Order No. 8
>
> Col J G O'Neil 10th Tnn Regt is directed to proceed to the several depots for Federal Prisoners in Georgia, North and South Carolina and Virginia for the purpose of enlisting such Irishmen and other Foreigners who may be willing to join the Confederate Service. He is ordered to direct transportation rations and clothing for the enlisted men.
>
> The time employed by Col O'Neil on this duty will not exceed ninety days.
>
> He is also authorized to request Brig, General Mackall commanding at Macon to cause twenty supermunary [*sic*] officers to report to him to aid the enlistment and organization of the recruits.
>
> He will report every week in writing to these hd qrs his proceedings.
>
> Brig general [*sic*] Winder is respectfully asked to give Col O'Neil every facility in his power. By command of Genl Beauregard.

Col. O'Neill personally recruited Andersonville Prison on January 23 and 25, where he took out 175 men. On February 2, Brigadier General Mackall, in command of the Macon, Georgia, Post, reported to General Beauregard that Col. O'Neill had requested clothing for his "200 enlisted Irishmen" and presented him with the January 16 Special Order No. 8. Mackall did not have enough clothing in stock to fill the request and took the clothing from General Cobb's supplies for his State troops. Mackall asked for the replacement of Cobb's stock of clothing from Montgomery or Columbus. General Beauregard approved the request. The request made by O'Neill was for 25 more men than he recruited at Andersonville, and the extra men may have represented recruits from other posts as authorized in the January 16 Special Order No. 8.[78]

McNeill returned to Andersonville on February 28 and recruited 140 more Federals. It is unclear how he clothed and equipped them. There is no record of prisoners recruited from other prisons at that point. [79]

The fates of the men O'Neill recruited at Andersonville during January and February are largely unknown. The war was near its end at that point, and little time remained to equip, train, and deploy them. Chapter 9 discusses the effects of the recruitment of some of those men after the war.

Mrs. F. G. DeFontaine reported seeing a company of galvanized Confederates fleeing Columbia, South Carolina, on February 16, 1865, on the last train to leave before the surrender of the city on the 17th.[80] "The passengers on this train, which was the last of sixteen already ahead of us, were an odd mixture, consisting of the Governor of this State, several ex-Governors, the Treasury Department which had been moved from Richmond to Columbia, a number of colored prisoners, and a company of 'galvanized Yankees,' as deserters from the Union army were then called."

That was probably the same unit of enlisted Federals noted by "C.Q.M.," a correspondent of the *Buffalo* (New York) *Commercial Advertiser*, when he was travelling between Columbia and Augusta. His article ran on April 3, 1865, with the date he wrote the article noted as February 1865. "C.Q.M" did not say when he passed through Lexington. He noted that he had camped "not far from a battalion of galvanized Yankees" across the Congaree River and "well on towards Lexington."[81]

The origins and fates of the enlisted Federals noted by DeFontaine and "C.Q.M." remain unknown. It is likely they were provost guards assigned to Columbia, kept on post until the last possible moment to help keep order at the railroad depot. Their position in Lexington when "C.Q.M." passed through suggests they may have been on their way from Augusta to Columbia at that unspecified time. They may have been among the prisoners recruited at Andersonville by Col. O'Neill during late January, but that seems unlikely given the short time that would have been available to clothe them, equip them, and provide them with some basic training. It is more likely that they were a company of the galvanized 10th from Augusta.

★ CHAPTER 8 ★

The 5th U.S. Volunteer Infantry

SIX INFANTRY REGIMENTS with about 6,000 men recruited from Union prisons went to the western frontier. Dee Brown presents an excellent summary of the sixth regiments in his classic 1963 volume *The Galvanized Yankees*, and each regiment had its own story and role in the Indian Wars during 1865–1866. This chapter focuses on the story of the 5th U.S. Volunteer Infantry, and more specifically on the galvanized Confederates who became part of that regiment. All six regiments were interrelated and in some cases interdependent in the larger tapestry of the history of the western frontier at that time.[1]

Private Hiram Jepperson was among the members of the galvanized 10th captured at Egypt Station. He was born in Lisbon, New Hampshire, and was an illegitimate child left in the care of his grandfather. In August 1862, with his grandfather's consent, he enlisted at 16 years old in the 5th New Hampshire Infantry as Hiram Jefferson. He survived Gettysburg and other battles but apparently deserted at Cold Harbor, eventually ending up with eight others from Cold Harbor who enlisted in the galvanized 10th. Only one other known member of the 5th New Hampshire Infantry who was captured at Cold Harbor joined the galvanized 10th; however, it is likely that all nine of the Cold Harbor captives went to Andersonville at the same time. Col. O'Neill recruited Jepperson, recording him as Hyson Gypperson. Marvel claims that Jepperson was one of eight prisoners recruited at Andersonville. The official record of departures from Andersonville, however, lists only four taken from there by O'Neill prior to 1865, and does not include Jepperson, who was more likely recruited at Millen. It was common for prisoners after the war to claim recruitment directly from Andersonville as the northern public considered that prison to have been the worst of the worst in the Confederacy.[2]

Jepperson enlisted in Company C of the 5th U.S. Volunteer Infantry as Hiram Jefferson (his name as used on the 5th New Hampshire roster), although his real name of Jepperson was on the muster rolls. He was 19 years old with grey eyes, fair hair, and fair complexion and was 5 feet 6 inches tall when he enlisted. His occupation, listed as tanner, was blacksmith on his enlistment document. His date of capture was given as June 3, 1864, and he was mustered into the 5th US on April 14, 1865. The only duty station mentioned in Jepperson's service record was Fort Kearny, although as part of Company C he would have taken part in the Sawyers Wagon Road Expedition and spent time at Fort Reno. An undated note in his file from the Adjutant General's office indicates that he had deserted from the 5th New Hampshire Infantry between June 8 and December 28, 1864, and had enlisted in the 5th USVI in violation of the 22nd and later the 50th Article of War. Despite that, Jepperson received an honorable discharge.[3]

Hiram Jepperson lived his life after the war under the name Thomas Mulvey. Marvel states that Mulvey had been a deserter from the 5th New Hampshire Infantry, although his name does not appear on the roster of the 5th New Hampshire. His former unit was the 12th New York Cavalry in his 5th USVI service record. Mulvey was from Lancaster, England, and deserted from the 5th USVI on April 10, 1866. The pension records consisted of two entries, in one of which Hiram Jepperson was listed with the alias Thomas Mulvey and in the other Thomas Mulvey was listed with the alias of Hiram Jepperson. The date of both pension records was November 14, 1892. It is unknown how Jepperson picked his alias, but it is clear that he had one. He wandered the west until his death in 1926, having lived in five different states. The government denied his pension application based on his desertion from the 5th New Hampshire.[4]

The roster of the prisoners from the galvanized 10th taken at Egypt Station and recorded at Memphis, included four officers and 262 enlisted men. Four of the enlisted men were probably not enlisted Federals, which left 258 enlisted Federals on the roster. Those figures were from the muster rolls of the complete 10th Tennessee and should be accurate. An unknown number of officers or enlisted men may have escaped during the trek from Egypt to Vicksburg or during the boat voyage from Vicksburg to Memphis.[5]

The captured men of the galvanized 10th transited from Vicksburg to Memphis and reached Alton Prison on January 17, 1865. Brigadier General Roy Stone, who was commander of Alton Prison and the post of Alton, Illinois, sent a "special roll" of the prisoners to Brigadier General H. W. Wessells, Commissary-General of Prisoners in Washington, D.C., on

January 24. That communication referenced the enlisted Federals as former Union "prisoners of war at Andersonville, GA." It transmitted a letter from Colonel John W. Noble of the 3rd Iowa Cavalry, whose unit had destroyed war materiel left at Okolona, but had arrived at the Battle of Egypt Station too late to take part in the fighting.[6]

Col. Noble had been in charge of the captured enlisted Federals on their trip by water between Vicksburg and Memphis and between Memphis and Cairo, Illinois. He had a chance to interact with the prisoners and learn their stories. Col. Noble wrote his letter while aboard the *E. H. Fairchild* on the way to Cairo. He said he had written the letter at the request of Captain Samuel Wilson, of the post of Memphis. The official roster of the captured members of the galvanized 10th was prepared in Memphis. It was given to Brigadier General H. W. Wessells on February 9, 1865, by Lt. Col. and Provost-Martial W. R. Lackland of the 108th Illinois Infantry.[7]

Noble tried to minimize the role played at Egypt Station by the captured enlisted Federals in his letter when he said: "On the evening previous to the engagement at Egypt several of these men designated on the rolls deserted the rebels and, coming into our lines, gave information of the force opposed to us and reported that many of these men would not resist us in battle. In the engagement which ensued in the morning this proved true in many instances, although the fight was a severe one and required great valor on the part of Colonel Kargé's cavalry to gain the victory."

It is likely that the pickets driven back by Col. Kargé's attack accounted for most, if not all, of the enlisted Federals who did not resist the attack. They probably accounted for many of the galvanized 10th who escaped capture. All available evidence indicates that the enlisted Federals captured in the stockade at the conclusion of the battle had fought hard and inflicted numerous casualties on the attacking force.[8]

Col. Noble further claimed that all of the captives had been "prisoners of war at Andersonville, Ga., when they enlisted in the Confederate service." That certainly was not true, as only four prisoners are known to have been been recruited from Andersonville. Col. Noble also said that Col. Burke had recruited all of them and had served as their commanding officer since that time. Noble claimed that it had been the stated intent of the enlisted Federals to desert Confederate service at the first opportunity, but they had not been trusted and had been kept under close guard. The captives claimed they did not receive muskets until the day before the battle, but archival sources suggests they were armed at Meridian before going to Mobile on December 22. They did not receive ammunition until they reached Egypt.[9]

Noble acknowledged that his regiment did not take part in the battle and that his information about the battle was secondhand from other officers en route from Egypt to Vicksburg. As previously mentioned, he did have firsthand knowledge of the captives; he offered this assessment of their character:

> . . . from my intercourse with these men, I believe that most of them are worthy of clemency, a few of special favor, but many at the same time are not to be trusted. As to the more general effect of the treatment of these men upon other prisoners in the rebel prisons, and again upon the rebel Government, I am not called upon to express, and Brigadier General Grierson (now under orders to report to Louisville, Ky.), Colonel Kargé, Second New Jersey Cavalry, at Memphis, Tenn., and Captain S. L. Woodward, assistant adjutant general on General Grierson's staff, can give more definite information in reference to the peculiar status of these men and the acts of particular individuals than is my knowledge.

Captain Woodward had been in charge of prisoners on the march between Egypt and Vicksburg, and he probably had a better knowledge of the individual prisoners than anyone besides Noble. There evidently was a discussion underway at the time Noble wrote his letter concerning the effects that clemency for the prisoners might have on Union prisoners of war still held in Confederate prisons. That would have been a serious consideration for the Union officials, but they allowed prisoners to join a new Federal unit in lieu of punishment.[10]

Major General Grenville Dodge made the argument in favor of allowing the prisoners to rejoin the Union army in a letter to Assistant Adjutant General Captain Joseph M. Bell, dated March 5, 1865. He informed Bell of the enlisted Federals being held at Alton Prison and gave their number as 250 men. He identified them as former members of Burke's Battalion, who, he said, "in the recent raid deserted on the approach of our forces to us." He further said they asked to rejoin their former units, but they could not for their own safety, in case of capture by the enemy. He further argued:

> There are also 1,000 prisoners of war and conscripts who refuse to be exchanged—claim to be deserters, unwilling conscripts, &c. These men have applied to enlist in our army. I respectfully submit if we had not better organize a regiment of these men and put them on the plains, where they can be made of use to our Government, relieve our prisons,

> and I have no doubt in most cases make better men and good soldiers. They are now a burden and expense to us. We cannot exchange them, and if I am authorized I am confident I can form an effective regiment from them by placing old reliable officers over them. I have 3,000 miles of overland mail and telegraph route to guard, and every regiment of infantry that I can put along it will relieve that number of cavalry to use in offensive operations against the Indians, who, I am satisfied, are determined to make aggressive war upon all our overland routes this spring and summer. Many of the "galvanized Yankees" I know were captured in the battle of July 22 before Atlanta, Ga., and have been good, earnest soldiers.[11]

The facts of the Battle of Egypt Station had already been distorted by Noble to make the enlisted Federals appear to be more dedicated to the Union cause than they seem to have been. It appears there was never a thought given to exchanging the galvanized 10th back to the Confederacy. He did reveal the reason he wanted to recruit infantry for the Plains, where mobility was key to cornering and combating American Indian warriors. His plan was to garrison the infantry at key posts to act as deterrents to raids, a strategy of limited utility as the Indian wars continued. Enlistment of the galvanized Confederates was underway by mid-March, and continued into April.[12]

Major and Judge Advocate A. A. Hosmer argued in a May 13 letter to the Secretary of War that the captured enlisted Federals should be "held and tried as deserters." Hosmer recommended leniency for the six men (five identified from the service records) who had crossed over the Union lines the night before the battle and gave information useful to Grierson. He stated: "It is submitted whether or not they may not be properly restored to their regiments, with forfeiture of all pay due at capture, in consideration for valuable services rendered."

Hosmer's letter claimed that the "better part" of the captured enlisted Federals had been on the "skirmish line" and had opened fire when the Union troops came into range. The "skirmish line" probably referred to the position behind the railroad embankment, and he did not mention that the enlisted Federals had shifted their position to the stockade for the final fight. Hosmer did correctly state that the men had not received ammunition until the day before the battle. He further stated that the battle resulted in the deaths of three Union officers and 20 enlisted men and left 74 wounded. He repeated the fiction that the men had enlisted at Andersonville, and that most had enlisted with the intention to escape to Union lines. Hosmer was skeptical of the prisoners' stories because of how hard they had fought and the casualties they inflicted. He stated that it was the opinion of General Hoffman that the men did not deserve clemency. Hosmer gave the total number of enlisted federals as 254, versus the 257 calculated from the available service records. The difference in the numbers may in part reflect deaths that had come to Hosmer's attention, although the actual number of deaths between capture and before May was five. Hosmer's letter appears to have been too late to influence the manner in which the prisoners were treated.[13]

Desertions began shortly after men of the former galvanized 10th enlisted in mid-March. Fifteen deserted on or before April 14, the day the men mustered into the 5th. Ten additional men enlisted but did not join the regiment. Seven of those men were sick in the prison hospital, and one was held for the civil authorities. One man awaited a court martial, while the tenth man was "absent." This means that of the 218 former Federals who enlisted in the 5th USVI, only 193 joined the regiment and left Alton Prison with their assigned companies. The four enlisted men suspected of not being enlisted Federals did not join the 5th. Four of the five men identified from the service records as having deserted to Grierson's raiders the night before the battle joined the 5th. The fifth man, Patrick Runnels, left the army on June 27, 1865, upon taking the Oath of Allegiance to the Union. Five of the enlisted Federals died at Alton Prison of smallpox—four in February and the fifth in early March. Most of those who did not join had been hospitalized for smallpox or other ailments and were not fit for further service. At least ten men, released upon taking the oath on dates that ranged from April 16 to June 27, had probably refused to join the 5th.[14]

The authorities placed the galvanized Confederates of the 5th USVI in companies A, B, C, and D along with galvanized Yankees. The men of the galvanized 10th made up about 20 percent of the regiment.[15]

Officers appointed to the 5th USVI for companies A-D were a mixed lot of professional officers, former enlisted men, and civilians (see Appendix D). Col. Henry E. Maynadier commanded the regiment. He was born into a military family in Hampton, Virginia, in 1833, and was graduated with the 1851 class at West Point. He was mustered into the regiment on March 7, 1865, in Washington, D.C. Maynadier had a distinguished Civil War record and had commanded the mortar flotilla on the Mississippi River that played a key role in the Battle of Island No. 10. He spent the war in the 12th U.S. Infantry, which he returned to after his duties in the west were completed. He was probably selected for this duty in the west because of his special duty experience escorting immigrants who were trying to reach Idaho in 1861.

That immigrant train reached Sioux City Iowa before halting because they lacked guides who could help them continue west. Maynadier's service on a board, scheduled to adjourn in April, delayed his departure for the west. Maynadier, arrested at Fort Leavenworth by May 12, proceeded after his release to Fort Riley on May 27. The nature of his offense is not clear, but appears to have involved a verbal exchange while at Fort Leavenworth. He arrived with eight companies at Fort Riley by May 29 and took command of the post. Companies C and D had already been deployed to take part in the Sawyers Wagon Road Expedition. He attributed the late arrival at Fort Riley to the "inferior condition of the mules provided for the transportation of the Regiment and the scorbutic [*sic*] condition of many of the men." Scurvy was not a disease suffered by many men of the galvanized 10th, and it probably was more common among the galvanized Yankees.[16]

Immediately after reporting to that post, Col. Maynadier went from Fort Riley to Fort Laramie to take command of the District of the Upper Arkansas. He apparently returned to Fort Riley and took command of that post again while commanding the District of Upper Arkansas. He was at that post when he was relieved from command of the District of Upper Arkansas and reported, "without delay," with men of the 5th USVI to Fort Kearny in Nebraska Territory. Maynadier reported to Brevet Major General Wheaton, Commander of the District of Nebraska, for further orders when he reached Julesburg. Wheaton appointed him to command the West Sub District of Nebraska on October 7, 1865. Maynadier replaced General Wheaton as Commander of the District of Nebraska in April 1866, with command of the District of the Platte. Maynadier joined a Commission to deal with the American Indians at Fort Laramie on May 13, 1866. Col. Maynadier received his promotion to Brevet Major General on June 22, 1867. He commanded the Post of Savannah with the rank of Major after he completed his duties in the west and rejoined the 12th US Infantry. He died of consumption at Savannah on November 3, 1868, leaving a wife and five minor sons. The Pension Board agreed that his consumption resulted from his military service and granted his wife a widow's pension. He was 37 or 38 at the time of his death.[17]

The need for replacement soldiers was becoming desperate by the time the men of the galvanized 10th mustered into the 5th USVI. General Lee surrendered the Army of Northern Virginia on April 9, and General Johnston surrendered his army on April 26. Practically everyone on both sides knew the end was near after Lee's surrender, and the thoughts of the men in the Union Army turned to home. Many of the men of the 5th USVI had no desire to continue in the military; 18 deserted at Alton Prison between their enlistments, as early as mid-May, and the regimental muster in April. Fifteen of those who deserted at Alton were from the galvanized 10th Tennessee, while only three were galvanized Yankees.[18]

The men who deserted from Alton Prison do not seem to have been representative of those who joined the regiment from both sides. Most of the members of the 5th USVI were farmers or laborers, but the 18 who deserted included two cigar makers (from Germany and Prussia), a hostler, a butcher, a cooper, two tanners, a tailor, a moulder (mold maker), a silversmith, a blacksmith, a harness maker, and only five farmers and one laborer. The men with trades would have had marketable skills that would have made it easier to find work with few questions asked.[19]

Assistant Adjutant General Joseph M. Bell sent a letter to Brevet Major General Sully on April 20, 1865, that directed him to send the available companies of the 5th USVI to Fort Leavenworth "without delay." It stated that Colonel Maynadier, who would command the 5th, was then at Columbus, Ohio, "organizing companies for the regiment."[20]

Companies C and D of the 5th, sent ahead of the rest of the regiment to Fort Leavenworth, had a special assignment. Company C lost six members to desertion prior to leaving Alton Prison, while none deserted from Company D.[21]

The desertions accelerated after companies C and D left Alton Prison and went first to Fort Leavenworth and then to the mouth of the Niobrara River, where they joined the Sawyer Wagon Road Expedition. That expedition attempted to build a wagon road from the Niobrara, in Nebraska territory, to Virginia City. Five men deserted on the way to or while at Fort Leavenworth, while 17 more deserted from the *Jesse H. Lacey* while on the way to Niobrara or after the men arrived there. Two of those men, privates Miles Shay and S. A. Myers, deserted on June 13, the day the expedition began. Only five of those men were, or possibly were, galvanized Yankees, while the remainder had been galvanized Confederates. Colonel James A. Sawyers, who commanded the wagon road expedition, reported that only "about" 118 men were present between the two companies of the 5th USVI sent as his escort for the expedition.[22]

The men of the 5th USVI, armed with .58 caliber Springfield muskets, lacked the fire rate of some of the units with more advanced cavalry carbines, but they offered accuracy at a longer distance. Their equipment included a waist belt and plate, cartridge box, cap pouch, wiper, tampion, screwdriver and cone wrench, canteen, haversack, knapsack, and half a shelter tent. Their clothing included a uniform with a cap, greatcoat, drawers, socks, and shoes. Each man received a blanket. The enlisted men were destitute after their term in prison and most had nothing more than their government issued items. Most of the men who deserted did so with full gear, which was charged against any pay they may have accrued.[23]

An Act of Congress passed on March 3, 1865, and signed by President Lincoln, funded the Sawyers Wagon Road Expedition and three other wagon roads. The proposed Sawyers Road Expedition received $50,000 for construction of the section from the mouth of the Niobrara to Virginia City. A representative from Iowa who represented business interests in Sioux City and hoped to benefit from the road's location introduced the act. Col. Sawyers, a resident of Sioux City, lead the expedition that was to bear his name. He had served in Millards Company Sioux City Cavalry and as a 1st Lt. in the 7th Iowa Cavalry. It is unclear how he received the rank of colonel.[24]

Accounts written about the Sawyers Wagon Road Expedition include a diary by John Colby Griggs, who was a galvanized Yankee in Company D of the 5th USVI.[25] The official report of the expedition, written by Colonel Sawyers; a report prepared by Dr. Tingley; a report submitted by Captain George W. Williford, who commanded the 5th USVI escort; and Albert M. Holman's (who had served as a teamster) reminiscent account of the expedition all provide detail about the expedition. None of the reports, save the one by Griggs, provides much insight into what the men of the 5th USVI did while on the expedition.[26]

Griggs reported that about 150 men of companies C and D were present for escort service for the expedition at the mouth of the Niobrara River. That is more accurate than Sawyers estimate of 118, given the initial enlistments less the desertions and the number of men who could not leave Alton for the deployment for other reasons. Dee Brown states that 159 officers and men left Fort Leavenworth on the *Jesse H. Lacy* on April 30 for the mouth of the Niobrara River—a figure confirmed from service records during the current research. He further states that 90 of those men were former Federals, while 69 were enlisted Confederates. Seventeen men deserted from the ship, leaving 142 men to serve as the infantry escort for Sawyers expedition. Two of the remainder deserted after the expedition was on the road.[27]

Captain Williford (see Appendix C), in command of companies C and D, was unable to acquire the clothing and shoes that his men would eventually need while in the field. He brought a three-month supply of food and clothing from Fort Leavenworth and tried to purchase additional clothing and shoes at Sioux City, to no avail. This would eventually cripple his command as his men quickly wore out their shoes and clothing on the march. That would be the major factor that caused his command to leave the expedition in late August. Williford tried to remedy the situation by sending 2nd Lt. Dana, the Acting Quartermaster, with an escort to Fort Laramie to bring back clothing. Lt. Dana, however, returned empty handed; he had left the wagonload of clothes with a cavalry detachment for delivery, but it never reached companies C and D.[28]

Companies C and D were not Col. Sawyers choices as escorts for the expedition. He had requested "at least" 200 cavalry with two pieces of artillery to accompany his wagon road endeavor. Sawyers found the inadequately supplied and provisioned galvanized companies poor substitutes for the needed cavalry. He requested additional support from Major General Pope, who commanded the District of the Northwest. Pope directed Brigadier General Sully, commander of the sub-district, to do what he could to support Col. Sawyers. Sully sent a detail of 25 men from the 1st Dakota Cavalry Battalion and six months worth of rations. Gen. Sully sent no additional transportation, and Captain Williford had to arrange transport through a contractor. Gen. Sully did send 40 additional Springfield muskets to arm civilians who accompanied the expedition. Sawyers took with him 53 men of his main road building detachment. "Five emigrant teams and a private freight company of 36 wagons" accompanied the expedition."[29]

Relations between Col. Sawyers and Captain Williford were strained from the beginning of the expedition and did not improve en route. The expedition began at the mouth of the Niobrara on June 13, 1865, and Col. Sawyers observed about his escort:

> It will be seen at a glance that the escort detailed for the expedition was wholly inadequate to protect a train of over eighty wagons passing through the heart of the most hostile Indian country in the territories. It consisted of only 143 men [actually 167 at that point]; and as the train was marched mostly in one column, to form a prominent well-marked road, it could not protect the whole length from Indian assaults, and small parties of Indians could make dashes and be away before infantry could get within shooting distance of them. Some emigrants and some men I had hired, turned back and would not make the trip on account of the insufficiency of the escort.[30]

Albert M. Holman, in his reminiscent account of the expedition, claimed that the relationship between Sawyers and Williford was dysfunctional to the point it endangered the expedition. He stated: "As to this escort we may as well have had none. There was constant friction between the officer Captain Winniford [Williford], commanding the soldiers and Colonel Sawyer commander of the entire expedition all the way through to Fort Connors where the escort left us. So marked was this friction that the escort made and broke camp when and where they wished and we men in the train hardly realized that we had an escort for our safety, as we did our own guard duty."[31]

Grigg's account does not reflect the poor level of performance in the field by the galvanized companies that Holman claimed. Holman undoubtedly exaggerated that portion of his account as he was trying to prove the importance and success of the wagon road, while the escort, as demonstrated by Griggs, did not share that view.

Col. Sawyers compensated for his infantry escort with a plan that spread the infantrymen through the column. Sawyers led the column with a platoon of infantrymen and one of the two artillery pieces. The escort's wagons came next, followed by another platoon. A third platoon followed the expedition's wagons, followed by the emigrants and the freight wagons, and then the remainder of the infantry and the second artillery piece. The guides and pioneers advanced in front of the column to find a good line of advance and to prepare the way for the column to follow. This was an efficient arrangement that provided the best possible protection while moving the column day-by-day.[32]

The only members of companies C or D who deserted during the expedition left on June 16. Two men of Company D, identified by Griggs as Richard Sneath and James E. Wilson, deserted from a camp near the Ponca Indian Agency. Wilson was in confinement at Fort Kearney in August 1866. Sneath was captured in Denver in January 1866 and was back on duty with Company B of the 5th USVI.[33]

The men of companies C and D largely stuck to their duties through the course of the expedition. Captain Williford reduced two men in rank on July 3 for being drunk, and he followed this with an order to empty out two barrels of whiskey to prevent a recurrence. The two men were Sgt. Henry D. Marshall and Cpl. Homer Worden of Company D. Henry Marshall, captured at Egypt Station along with the galvanized Confederates, had been a Confederate soldier. He deserted from Fort Reno on June 6, 1866. Homer Worden was a galvanized Confederate and eventually mustered out of the 5th with his company. A second incident occurred on August 11, 1865. H. P. McGinnis (a former member of the galvanized 10th) of

Company D hit Uriah J. Breshears (a Confederate) of Company D on the head with a gun and severely wounded him. McGinnis had suffered a sunstroke on July 2, and it is unclear if that contributed to whatever disagreement he had with Breshears. Breshears deserted from Fort Reno on June 6, 1866, while McGinnis followed on June 16.[34]

Sawyers' fear of an attack did not materialize until the expedition was near the Powder River. A guide had exchanged shots with a small group of Native Americans and captured two ponies prior to that time, but there had been no other trouble. The trouble came on August 13, when the expedition was 15 miles short of the Powder River. The march from August 9 to August 12 had been over broken and waterless terrain, and the company had heard reports of large numbers of Native Americans in the area. A detachment of cavalry sent out on August 12 reported that water was 15 miles ahead, but that the terrain was not suitable for wagons. Sawyer then decided to turn back to their camp of August 9. They began moving back on August 13, only to encounter a war party after just five miles. The Indians drove off some of the cavalry horses and killed Nathaniel D. Hedges, a civilian member of the freight line that accompanied the expedition. Hedges left the security of the emergency encampment and was killed while looking for water in a nearby clump of trees. The attackers left, going toward the Powder River, and the expedition continued for another 10 miles that day. The expedition continued on the march for three more miles on August 14, when the war party again tried to run off the cavalry horses. The members of the expedition drove off the attackers at that point with no loss of livestock. The Native Americans surrounded the camp in large numbers on August 15, but did not attack in force. Small groups and individuals charged the camp from time to time and exchanged shots with members of the expedition, and the escort used their artillery to apparently good effect. The attackers had lost about 10 warriors at that point and proposed a parlay after a few hours. Sawyers gave them a wagonload of provisions and tobacco, and they exchanged moccasins for tobacco with the barefoot men of the 5th USVI. A gunshot terminated the parlay, after which a soldier of the 1st Dakota Cavalry was found dead and a second one was missing. Captain Williford identified the dead trooper as Private Anthony Nelson, a native of Norway. Nelson was the only expedition member killed during the fight. The missing trooper was Private Orlando Sous, who was on the muster role as John Rouse. Griggs identified Sous as "Luse" and said he was a Mexican. Those men were the only members of the escort lost during the expedition, and only a few were slightly wounded. A few members of the war party tried to raid the expedition camp on August 16, but were unsuccessful. That was the last attempted raid until after the 5th USVI left the expedition on August 24.[35]

Sawyers claimed that Williford refused to escort his wagon train any further on August 23. The men of the 5th USVI were barefoot and their clothes were in tatters after 2nd Lt. Dana's failed attempt to bring supplies for the escort from Ft. Laramie. Williford's brief report of August 29, 1865, simply said that he received orders from General Connor to proceed to Fort Conner (later moved and renamed Fort Reno and henceforth referred to under that name) with his command for duty.[36] Griggs reported that the order from General Connor to report to the fort came on August 25. His diary entry for August 26 read: "Preparations were finished today to dissolve our connection with Sawyer's [*sic*] expedition, and a few cavalry, together with our cavalry and one of our pieces of artillery, accompanied him on his pleasure excursion to Virginia City in the afternoon. At the same time Sawyer's [*sic*] wagons started, we struck camp and removed just on the outside of the stockade of the fort, where we encamped for the present."[37]

That was the end of the participation of the 5th USVI in the Sawyers Wagon Road Expedition. Sawyers made it to Virginia City, without completing the road. He faced severe criticism for his shortcomings as a road builder from both the military and civilians. They considered the road to be impractical because of the terrain and the lack of water and grass. Sawyers planned and conducted an expedition the next year to upgrade the road and build or repair bridges. The route took him past the new and improved Fort Reno, a few miles south of the original Fort Conner. The situation in terms of military manpower in the west had changed since his expedition a year before—troop numbers were drastically reduced. Sawyers, denied a military escort for his second attempt, had to arm the civilians who were part of the expedition for security. His second attempt made it to Virginia City with a road he claimed was over 100 miles shorter than the original. The road was no longer needed after construction of the Union Pacific Railroad and more feasible routes. Companies C and D remained at Fort Reno for most of the rest of their term with the regiment.[38]

Members of Gen. Connors' expedition built Fort Reno just a few days before Captain Williford took command of the post. The fort was little more than a stockade at that point, and companies C and D completed the interior buildings before the onset of winter. The men spent a hard winter at the fort, during which a number of diseases, including scurvy (from the lack of fresh vegetables), spread through the companies. Four men died over the winter at Ft. Reno. The cause of death in each case was different: one death by scurvy, one by typhoid fever, one by consumption (tuberculosis), and one by "congestion of the lungs." All of the deceased were enlisted Confederates. The inventories of the four men who died provide insights into the severe poverty of the enlisted men of the 5th USVI. The inventory of 20-year-old Pvt. Ephraim McClure, who died of scurvy, included one great coat, one pair of flannel drawers, one woolen shirt, and one pair of shoes. All of his clothing was apparently government issue, and others in the company had likely claimed the rest of his government issue clothing prior to his death. Pvt. M. K. Leggett (Liggitt), who was 20 years old and died of consumption, had one hat, one cap, a great coat, a blouse, one pair of trousers, three pairs of flannel drawers, two flannel shirts, one pair of shoes, and two pairs of socks. His clothing probably represented a full issue of government clothing. Cpl. Thomas C. Kelly, who died of typhoid fever, had one cap, one great coat, two pairs of flannel drawers, three flannel shirts, one pair of shoes and one pair of boots. Pvt. James Holt, who was from Hardin County, Kentucky, and died of congestion of the lungs, had a great coat, a blouse, one pair of trousers, one pair of flannel drawers, two pairs of boots, and two blankets. It is unclear if the boots in the inventories of Kelly and Holt were government issue.[39]

The contrast between the property of the enlisted men at death and that of Captain Williford, commander of Ft. Reno, when he died on April 28, 1866, is emblematic of the wide social and economic divide between officers and enlisted men during that period. The origins of the enlisted men and the fact that they had entered the regiment with little more than the clothing they wore likely exaggerated the divide in the case of the 5th USVI. That divide between officers and enlisted men still would have existed in every regiment to a marked degree. Captain Williford died of a heart attack at Ft. Casper. His possessions that were with him at Ft. Casper included: one (indecipherable) belt, one pistol and holster, one whip, one buggy, one saddle bag, two gloves, one overcoat, one treasury note of $875, currency of $3.39, and specie of $.25. Williford's other possessions included: one portfolio with private papers, three pairs of cavalry pants, one pair of officer's dress pants, one pair of buckskin gloves, one case of surgical instruments, one gentlemen's pin cushion, one officer's dress coat, one kit of shaving utensils, one officer's silk sash, one copy of Lt. Col. J. N. Simpson's engineering report, five woolen shirts, four c.f. drawers, seven pairs of wool socks, one pair (calf) fine shoes, one army and navy journal, one volume of McClellan's Tactics, one pass book, one horse, one Colt Army revolver, one uniform officer's vest, one pocket bible, four tea cups and saucers, one sugar bowl, four knives and forks, three tin table spoons, three tin tea spoons, three tin milk pans, three cup plates, one iron frying pan, one tin dish, one tin coffee pot, three tin plates, and one deep earthenware dish. Williford's possessions accumulated over his career, but probably were typical of its age.[40]

There were 24 desertions while companies C and D were at Ft. Reno. Nine of the desertions were from Company C and 15 from Company D. Sixteen of the deserters were galvanized Confederates, while eight had been galvanized Yankees. The ratio of former Federal and former Confederate deserters reflects the relative composition of the companies. One former Federal was found dead just six days after he deserted, but the cause of death was not given. Nine of the men were recaptured—one at Ft. Randall and the rest at or near Ft. Laramie. Two men deserted again after their capture. Some of the men, and perhaps even all of those recaptured from companies C and D, mustered out of the 5th USVI with honorable discharges. The leniency shown deserters from the 5th USVI was in response to General Order No. 46, issued by order of President Andrew Johnson and dated July 13, 1866. That order read: "Ordered: That all persons who are undergoing sentences by military courts, and have been imprisoned six months, except those who are under sentence for the crimes of murder, arson, or rape and excepting those who are under sentence at the Tortugas, be discharged from imprisonment and the residue of their sentences remitted. Those who belong to the military service, and their term unexpired, will be returned to their command, if it is still in service, and their release is conditional upon their serving their full term and being of good behavior."

None of the members of companies C and D who had deserted from Ft. Reno met the six-month requirement by July 13. It appears the prisoners benefited from the spirit of the order and subsequent pension records identified several as honorably discharged.[41]

General Dodge issued Special Order No. 117 through the Headquarters Department of the Missouri on May 3, 1865. It ordered Col. Maynadier and the other officers of the 5th who were at Alton, Illinois, to go to Fort Leavenworth by steamer and report to Brigadier General R. B. Mitchell, who commanded the District of North Kansas. That order brought eight companies, including companies A and B (the other two companies that contained former members of the galvanized 10th), to the west. General Dodge reported to Brigadier General Mitchel at Fort Leavenworth that the 5th USVI was ready to move on May 11, with seven of the companies under the command of 1st Lieutenants. Colonel Maynadier, who commanded the 5th, assumed command of newly created sub-district No. 1 on May 27, which included "Fort Riley, Ellsworth, and the stations of Saline and Lake Sibley." He still commanded the 5th, which presumably headquartered at Ft. Riley.[42]

The condition of the regular soldiers posted on the western frontier was grave by the time the 5th USVI reached the area. Major General John Pope reported to Colonel R. M. Sawyer, Assistant Adjutant General, on July 11, 1865:

> Reports received from Major General Dodge, commanding on the plains, comprise what has already been made known to me from various official sources in regard to the troops serving in that region. Already all the regiments are in a mutinous condition, claiming that they are entitled to a discharge from the service, and refusing to do duty. Wherever regiments are concentrated such insubordinate conduct can be dealt with, but it is very difficult to do so at small posts on the frontier. The five regiments of U.S. Volunteers (enlisted from rebel deserters) are our main reliance, and must therefore be retained in service.[43]

The regiments whose term of service had expired were mustered out as soon as they could be spared, and officers of the 5th USVI, such as Captain McDougall and 1st Lt. Charles Coloney of Company B and Captain George M. Bailey of Company D, all served as acting commissary of musters for various posts. The discharges of so many regiments left the military thin on the ground in 1865 and 1866, and it was unable to perform many of the tasks that had previously been under their charge.[44]

Companies A and B had nearly equal numbers of enlisted Confederates and former members of the galvanized 10th. Company A had three officers and 103 enlisted men, 40 of which were enlisted Confederates and 63 were former members of the galvanized 10th. Company B had three Federal officers and 105 enlisted men: one of unknown origin, 51 enlisted Confederates, and 53 former members of the galvanized 10th. Both companies suffered losses from desertions and illness, and one man was rejected for service. Those losses, except those by desertion, were minimal.[45]

Fifty-six of 103 men of Company A deserted during their term of service; most desertions occurred between March and September 1865. The post with the highest number of desertions was Lake Sibley, with 13. Three men deserted from Alton Prison, while most of the rest came while the company or components of the company were on the march from one post to another. Company B lost 66 of 105 men to desertions. Most of those desertions also took place in 1865 and began with nine men deserting from Alton Prison. Half of the desertions took place while on the march from one post to another. While at their posts, Company B lost three at Fort Kearney, nine at Ft. Leavenworth, 13 at Ft. Riley, and eight at Denver City. When recaptured, many of the men of both companies were subject to court martial. Sentences were often light, and some men deserted again.[46]

None of the men of companies A or B took part in hostile actions against American Indians, and the only deaths were caused by disease or by wounds inflicted by unknown parties, other members of the 5th USVI, or through accident. Pvt. Samuel Brady, an enlisted Confederate, died of an unstated disease while on a boat on the way to Ft. Leavenworth. Pvt. N. B. Brown, a former member of the galvanized 10th, died of an accidental gunshot wound while at Ft. Leavenworth. Pvt. Albert C. Cobbs, an enlisted Federal, froze to death in a storm near Ft. Halleck. 2nd Lt. A. C. Dutcher was the only other member of Company A who died while serving in the regiment. Dutcher was shot by an unknown person while in Denver City and passed away as the result of his wound. The single member of Company B who died while in service was Pvt. James B. Tuggle, an enlisted Confederate. He died at Fort Leavenworth on July 15, 1865, of heart disease.[47]

Other incidents among the men of companies A and B reflected friction among and between the men and the Union authority. Pvt. Henry Peters of Company B, a former member of the galvanized 10th born in Zurich, Switzerland, was court martialed for "rejoicing after the death of the President of the United States." His offence had occurred on April 15, 1865, a day after Lincoln's assassination. Peters' charge was "disloyalty to the prejudice of good order and military discipline." Referring to the deaths of both President Lincoln and the Secretary of State, he allegedly said that "he was damned glad of it, that they ought to have been killed two years ago, and that they, meaning the President of the United States and Secretary of State, had done nothing for the past two years but kill and murder men. That he was not fighting for Lincoln but for the Union, and Lincoln was not, but for the negro and other language of like tenor and import." Peters pled not guilty but was found guilty by the court martial. Peters received a dishonorable discharge with forfeit of all pay and allowances, and a two-year sentence term in the state penitentiary at Jefferson City, Missouri.[48]

There were numerous arrests and convictions for disloyalty based on speech during the war. None of the galvanized Confederates were arrested for disloyalty despite the fact they had taken up arms against the U.S. government.[49]

Pvt. Patrick Redman of Company B (a former member of the galvanized 10th who was born in Dublin, Ireland) was charged for refusing to go to camp when ordered by his superior officer. The incident occurred at Salinas, Kansas, on July 27, 1865. Redman called his superior officer a "God damned Rebel Sgt. son of a bitch" while refusing his order and struck him several times. The superior officer was Sgt. Moses W. Province, an enlisted Confederate formerly of the 10th Missouri Regiment. Redman, charged with conduct prejudicial to good order and military discipline, deserted on August 30, 1865, at Clay Center, Kansas, before his trial.[50] The actions and arrest of Redman reflected a level of tension and mistrust between the galvanized Confederates and the galvanized Yankees of the 5th USVI. Redman, back in his element as a Union soldier, resented taking orders from a former Confederate soldier, which may have reflected a sense of guilt for his own past actions.

Pvt. George McDonald—an enlisted Federal, drummer of Company B, and native of New York—faced a court martial for a second offense that occurred at Salinas, Kansas, on July 27, 1865. McDonald's charges included conduct prejudicial to good order and military discipline and destruction of government property: he had thrown his drums, drumsticks, and Fife into the Smokey River and had declared his intention to desert. The witnesses against him included Sgt. Pierce Pendergrast, a former member of the galvanized 10th, to whom McDonald had confided his intention to desert. Sgt. Moses W. Province was another of several witnesses against Pvt. McDonald. His court martial, like that of Patrick Redman, was apparently not held because he deserted at Fort Riley on August 27, 1865.[51]

Companies A and B found duty in small detachments, escorting mail coaches and the like or serving in static defense forces throughout the west. Company B served in a supply depot in Denver City for part of their enlistment; this duty was far superior to service in the frontier forts and cantonments, which was the fate of others in their regiment. The men of the 5th USVI mustered out of service on October 11, 1866.[52]

⋆ CHAPTER 9 ⋆

After the War

AT LEAST 4,000 Union prisoners of war become galvanized Confederates during the war, and the actual number was probably much higher. Some of those men, such as the 400 men assigned to units around Charleston and the 60 men of Captain Daniell's Battery, either deserted or quickly returned to prison. The total number of galvanized Confederates includes the 620 men of the Brooks Battalion who went back to prison before deployment or returned to prison after an attempted mutiny in Savannah. Some of them—such as members of the Tucker Regiment, members of the galvanized 10th Tennessee who were not captured at Egypt Station, and perhaps a few of the recruits taken by Col. O'Neill from Andersonville in January and February, 1865—remained with their Confederate units until the end of the war. Others, such as members of the 8th Confederate Infantry captured at Salisbury and the members of the galvanized 10th captured at Egypt Station, were in Union prisons as the war ended.

Each man who had served as a galvanized Confederate and survived the experience had an important decision to make as the war ended or upon release from prison. Each faced the possibility that he would be treated as a turncoat by his former neighbors and friends, and some simply made the decision to move elsewhere and start a new life. Those who made the decision to return home either found acceptance back into their former homes or the difficult homecoming they had dreaded. It is impossible to gauge what kind of reception each man faced upon return home in the absence of diaries and other types of personal recollections and documentation. It is possible to look at individual cases as well as documentation concerning pensions and pension policy to gain insights into how the men were treated.

Some former galvanized Confederates simply neglected to tell their home communities that they had served in the Confederate Army. A good example of this is the life story of John H. Cosart, who published the only substantive account of the Brooks Battalion and his service in it. Cosart published his account in the *Home Mail* in April 1874. The *Home Mail* was a monthly publication with a newspaper format dedicated to "Home Affairs, Temperance, Army Sketches, Education, &C." It was available by subscription and was first published in 1874. Cosart's article, "Brooks Battalion," was a straightforward account of the recruitment, deployment, and demise of the battalion. Cosart lived a very long life and died in Lyons, New York, which had been his home since 1848, on April 11, 1932. Despite his publication in the *Home Mail*, his obituary presented a slightly different story of his life; it discussed his Union service during the Civil War but omitted his service in the Brooks Battalion. The obituary acknowledged his capture at Lovejoy Station on August 24, 1864, and his confinement at Andersonville Prison (he joined the Brooks Battalion at Florence Prison). It stated that he had been a founding member of Post Wayne 44 and A.D. Adams Post 153 of the Grand Army of the Republic, and that he had enjoyed a successful career in the shoe business.[1]

Edward McQuade was a member of the Brooks Battalion who volunteered after the war to testify in General Hugh Mercer's trial. Union authorities tried Mercer and attempted to convict him for the execution of seven galvanized Confederate deserters and mutineers. The Union prosecutor put out a nationwide call for witnesses to come forward, and McQuade and Francis Shrenk (Schrenk) were the only ones who responded. Both McQuade and Shrenk lived in New York City and traveled to Savannah to take part in the trial. McQuade had first joined the 51st New York Infantry in October 1861. He claimed to be 18 in 1865, which means he had joined as a minor at 14 years old. He joined the 5th Rhode Island Heavy Artillery on January 17, 1862. McQaude, captured at New Bern, North Carolina, on May 5, 1864, ended up at Florence Prison by way of Kingston and Wilmington, North Carolina, as well as Augusta, Macon, and Andersonville in Georgia. He was at Florence for four weeks before enlisting in what became the Brooks Battalion. His gave his reason for changing sides as "being nearly starved, naked, and filthy, I, with others, threatened with starvation or being shot, was forced to take the oath of allegiance to the rebel Confederacy." He went with his battalion to Summerville, South Carolina, and then to Charleston and Savannah with the companies selected for duty. He escaped during the failed mutiny in Savannah.[2]

His testimony in the trial of General Mercer was not helpful to the prosecution, and McQuade returned home to New York City after the trial. The 1870 census shows him living in New York City and working as a clerk in a store. He married by 1880 and had a five-year-old daughter named Mary. He was a 32-year-old salesman in 1889, living in Brooklyn at 18 Ainslie Street. He and his wife were born in New York, but both their parents were born in Ireland. He did not appear in the 1890 census, but a July 27, 1889, article titled "Bush's Blow Was It Responsible for Edward McQuade's Death?" in *The Brooklyn Daily Eagle* explains his absence. McQuade, who resided at a boarding house at 157 Myrtle Avenue (Brooklyn), was working as a "second man on a wagon" for the Knickerbocker Ice Company and got into a dispute with Lawrence Bush, whose job it was to select ice for McQuade and others. Bush struck him in the face with an unknown weapon. McQuade returned to his boarding house without realizing the severity of his injury, but later went to City Hospital because of the pain of the injury. McQuade had a broken jaw and died from his injuries. Bush was arrested for murder. The article stated that McQuade was single and did not mention his wife or daughter.[3]

Francis Shrenk (Schrenk) was the other witness who came forward for the trial of General Mercer. He joined the 5th New Jersey Infantry on August 9, 1863, under an assumed name and was captured at the Battle of the Wilderness on May 6, 1864. He was sent from Gordonsville to Lynchburg, then to Danville, and finally to Andersonville and Florence. He enlisted in the Brooks Battalion in Florence, still under an assumed name, and said he had enlisted after he was "informed that we must take the oath of allegiance or be shot." He claimed, "It was starvation or be shot," and he alleged that he had agreed with others who took the oath to enlist so they could escape and that they would not fight. He further claimed to have escaped at Savannah, and that he witnessed the trial of the seven executed there. He was positive in his affidavit of General Mercer's role in the trial and execution, but much less so in his testimony. Shrenk was 29 years old, a resident of New York City, and recently married at the time of his testimony.[4]

Francis Shrenk may have been a bounty jumper given the fact that he had enlisted under an alias. The length of time between his enlistment and capture argues somewhat against that, but bounty jumpers and deserters would have had extra incentives to enlist as galvanized Confederates, since an exchange would not have been to their benefit. Desertion was a capital offense during wartime and bounty jumping was a criminal offense. There is no way to determine with the available records how many galvanized Confederates were deserters or bounty jumpers, but the number was probably significant.

Pvt. John Kirkwood enlisted in the galvanized 10th and the 5th USVI.

He wrote a letter to General Grant on behalf of himself and 49 other Galvanized Confederates at Fort Reno on April 24, 1866. They requested an honorable discharge from their former companies so they could receive their "back pay and bounty" from the Union. He said that while imprisoned in "rebel prisons at different stations" they lacked enough and the right kind of food, did not have sufficient clothing, lived in filth, and were infested by vermin. He further said that many men were sick and a number of them died every day. Kirkwood claimed the guards coerced them into enlisting in the Confederate army by threatening conscription if they did not join. Kirkwood claimed they finally gave up on November 20 and took the oath, although none enlisted or mustered into the Confederate Army. The plan formed by each of them was to desert and rejoin the Union Army at the earliest opportunity. Grant did not reply to his letter and did not release the men from service with the 5th USVI. Kirkwood deserted from the 5th USVI on September 9, 1866, at Fort Kearny.[5]

Kirkwood's service in the Union Army did not end with his 1866 desertion. His pension records indicate that he served at least brief terms with seven Union units in addition to the galvanized 10th. Kirkwood had been born in Scotland, and he was 21 years old when he joined the 5th USVI. Captured at Petersburg while serving with the 42nd New York Infantry, he gave his occupation as "clerk." After the war, he joined the 3rd U.S. Cavalry on April 14, 1868, and was discharged on June 24, 1871. He joined the 5th U.S. Cavalry on June 17, 1872, and apparently transferred to the 1st U.S. Cavalry on October 20, 1872; he was discharged from that regiment on June 17, 1877. Kirkwood was a member of the 21st U.S. Infantry from April 1, 1882, to June 24, 1884. He also served undated terms in the 1st Battalion Pawnee Indian Scouts and in the U.S. Marines. Kirkwood died on February 5, 1920.[6]

Elias Bare, who served in Company A, followed Kirkwood's example after the war. He was mustered out of the 5th USVI on July 14, 1865, because of physical disability (the nature of which was not given in his service records). He then went on to join the 12th U.S. Infantry. The 12th was reorganized and became the 21st U.S. Infantry on December 7, 1866, which means that Bare's transition from the 5th USVI to the 12th must have been very soon after he was mustered out of the 5th USVI. Bare went on to serve in the 21st U.S. Infantry for an unknown term. The 21st served in southeast Arizona for the next three years, providing escorts for mail runs and performing various tasks that often sparked hostile contacts with Apaches. After three years, the 21st transferred to Fort Vancouver in Washington

Territory, where the companies dispersed—much like elements of the 5th USVI had been sent to serve posts throughout the territory. Bare filed for and received a pension on April 15, 1902, where he listed his service in the 5th USVI, the 12th Infantry, and the 21st Infantry, and he claimed that he had been discharged from the 87th Pennsylvania on October 13, 1864. The Pension Board discovered Bare had lied on his pension application about his discharge from the 87th Pennsylvania. He had, in fact, been captured at Harris Farm in the Battle of Spotsylvania and had been sent first to Belle Island and then to Andersonville, where he had joined the 10th Tennessee Infantry. He joined the 5th USVI after his capture at Egypt Station and was mustered out for physical disability. The Pension Board revoked his pension for "fraudulent representation." Bare lived in Maricopa County, Arizona, in 1907 and later moved to an Old Soldier's Home in Louisiana, where he is buried in a National Cemetery.[7]

Franklin Bannon adopted a different strategy than Kirkwood and Bare after the war. He had been a member of the 11th Indiana Infantry upon his capture and ended up in Florence Prison. The notorious Captain Barrett had recruited him for the 8th Confederate Infantry at Florence, and his service to the Confederacy ended with his capture during Stoneman's raid on Salisbury. The single service record that survived after capture indicates that he had been a resident of Adams County, Pennsylvania, and that he had been released from Union custody on July 5, 1865. His wife's obituary of March 11, 1904, stated that she and her husband had been married in Indiana and moved to a Kansas farm in 1877. They had eight children, and she was 71 at the time of her death. United States Senator John Ingalls of Kansas introduced a bill to grant a pension to Franklin Bannon on January 15, 1890, but Bannon was still applying for a pension as late as 1908. He apparently remarried, as his widow applied for a widow's pension in 1927. Bannon died on July 10, 1921. It appears that Bannon and his wife chose to start over in a new place after the war, and he managed to become a respected member of his new community. There is no documentation of what he and his wife faced when he returned to his old community, but given that he was captured in arms, fighting against Union troops, it is likely that his service to the Confederacy was known in that community.[8]

Martin Buzzard took a different path after the war. Buzzard enlisted in the 2nd Pennsylvania Cavalry and was captured on June 29, 1864. He joined the 10th Tennessee Infantry and was among those captured at Egypt Station. Buzzard mustered into the 5th USVI on March 22, 1865. He was born in Lancaster County, Pennsylvania, and was listed as a carpenter in his service record. Later in life he would describe himself as a basketmaker. One document in his 5th USVI service records listed his age as 20 years old, while another listed it as 28. Both documents described him as having grey eyes, light hair, and a fair complexion, with his height listed as 5' 8" in one and 5' 7" in the other. He deserted from the steamer *Jesse H. Lacy* while on the way with his company from Fort Leavenworth to the mouth of the Niobrara River on May 12, 1865, and had no further military record. Buzzard chose a life of crime after the war and, with his brothers, terrorized the Lancaster, Pennsylvania, area for the rest of the century. It is sufficient to say at this point that he was probably the most famous, or more appropriately infamous, of all of the galvanized Confederates after the war.[9]

George Dietz filed for a pension on March 22, 1910. He had been a member of Company C of the 4th New York Heavy Artillery upon capture at Weldon Railroad on August 21, 1864, and he was sent Richmond. Enlisted men sent to Richmond at that time went to Belle Isle Prison. Dietz went to Salisbury Prison on October 19, 1864, when Belle Isle Prison emptied out for the last time. He joined the 8th Confederate Infantry on December 27, while being held at Salisbury. Dietz, captured at Salisbury, was released on July 6, 1865. He individually mustered out of the 4th New York Heavy Artillery on September 26, 1865. A report on his service issued by the War Department on October 25, 1902, ruled that he had received his muster out and discharge from the 4th New York through "misrepresentation and misapprehension of the facts of record in the case." The War Department ruled that his discharge was void and without effect, his final record being that of a deserter on December 13, 1864. A second report issued on April 4, 1910, stated that nothing could be determined of Dietz's whereabouts from the time of his release from Nashville until September 26 when he was apparently at Rochester, New York. He had apparently made no effort to rejoin his unit until the unit mustered out and disbanded on October 5. Dietz appealed the rejection of his pension application on January 28, 1911, contending that he "did not voluntarily enlist or serve in the Confederate Army." Deitz submitted a curious statement with his pension application that distorted the facts of his enlistment in the Confederate Army in his favor. The Pension Board paraphrased his response to the rejection by stating:

> The claimant's statement is that he was a prisoner at Salisbury, N.C. 'with scant rations and no care' until sometime in January or February 1865 [1866]; that he was then 'a walking skeleton,' sick and discouraged

and willing to do almost anything to save his life and get out that he might get enough to eat; that he and other prisoners talked the matter over and concluded that they would be justified in offering to enlist in the Confederate Army in order that they might get food and thereafter escape to the Union Army at the first opportunity; that a 'compact' was made for the purpose of carrying out that plan, but it was agreed among the parties thereto that they would not bear arms or fight against the United States Government; that pursuant to such 'compact' and agreement he enlisted in the Confederate Army and was sent with other recruits to Florence, S.C., where they were kept under guard, but fed, until Stoneman's last raid. when they were returned to Salisbury and given guns for the first time, and marched towards the skirmish line; that when they got within running distance of the Union line they, in accordance with their agreement and plan, dropped their guns and rushed into the Union lines; that he immediately told the federal officers that he was a Union soldier and how he happened to get into the Confederate ranks, and was not put under guard, but sent to the rear and marched (not under guard) to Greenville, East Tennessee, where he was detained until sometime in June (not under guard) to New York City, to a Soldier's Rest, and remained there until his brother came to take him home; and that some time [*sic*] in August he went to Rochester and was honorably discharged.

The Pension Bureau rejected Dietz's explanation. The only "proof" he offered was affidavits from his three brothers, who stated his statement was "substantially the same story" he had told them when he returned home after the war. That part is likely true and represented his cover story for his actions during the war. It is likely many of the Galvanized Confederates offered their own cover stories when they returned to their communities to prevent their friends and neighbors from ostracizing them.[10]

Peter J. Knapp must have been well received when he returned home to Iowa after the war. Knapp was a 22-year-old farmer who had been born in Sandusky, Ohio. He joined Company H of the 5th Iowa Infantry and was captured at Missionary Ridge on November 25, 1863. He enlisted from captivity in the 10th Tennessee Infantry and was then captured by the Union Army at Egypt Station. He then joined the 5th USVI, where he was eventually promoted to sergeant. He was trusted enough to be granted a furlough in the summer of 1866 and mustered out of the 5th with the regiment on

October 11, 1866. The Iowa Legislature passed a resolution on April 2, 1868, "in relief of Knapp." That resolution, directed to the Senators and Congressmen from Iowa, read in part:

> Whereas Peter J. Knapp, a private of Company H, 5th Iowa volunteer infantry, was captured by the rebel army at the Battle of Missionary Ridge, Tennessee, on November 25, 1963, and remained a prisoner until nine of his company captured with him had died of want and exposure; and whereas the same soldier was captured in December, 1864, by Grierson at Egypt Station, on the Ohio and Mobile Railroad in company with Union prisoners who were then regarded as deserters and treated as such by military commanders, but it being known that the said P. J. Knapp never took an oath of allegiance to the so-called rebel government, and that his loyalty and fidelity is and always was unquestionable; and whereas the said Peter J. Knapp has endured great hardship, and did honor to himself and flag on many a battle-field, both before and since his long captivity: there be it *resolved by the general assembly of the State of Iowa.* That we instruct our Senators and request our representatives in Congress to secure such legislation as will authorize the honorable muster-out of said P. J. Knapp and the full payment of all back pay and allowances due him as a soldier of the company and regiment above stated. . . .

Knapp's story, as relayed in the resolution, asserted that he had never sworn an oath to the Confederacy, which implies that he had not enlisted and mustered in to the Confederate Army. His story implies that he simply showed up with the galvanized 10th at Egypt Station and was captured. That was not a credible story, but it sanitized his experience for the Iowa Legislature. It is unclear if he ever received a pension, as the most definitive pension record for him was in the pending files.[11]

Most of those who became Galvanized Confederates simply slipped back into anonymity after the war. Those men did not seek pensions or show up in available federal records in any way. David M. Gobin was born in New York in 1837 and enlisted in Company G of the 9th New Hampshire Infantry on December 9, 1863. Captured at Poplar Springs Church, Virginia, on September 30, 1864, Gobin joined the 8th Confederate Infantry at Florence Prison on December 10, 1864. Gobin served as Col. Garnett Andrews' "attendant" and cared for Andrews' wounds after the battle at Salisbury. Gobin accompanied Andrews to his home in Washington, Georgia. Andrew's sister, Eliza Francis Andrews described Gobin: "Gobin seems attached to him and dresses his wounds carefully. He is an Irish Yankee, deserted, and came across the lines to keep from fighting, but was thrown into prison and only got out by enlisting in a "galvanized" regiment." Gobin finally left Andrews in the care of his family and joined Union soldiers who were then in Washington. Gobin disappears from the historic record after that time, but it is likely he simply disappeared to avoid arrest and punishment for desertion.[12]

Many men who had been held in southern prisons were broken in mind and body by the time the war ended. Those who became galvanized Confederates did not all escape that fate, although many used that as a rationale for changing sides when recaptured or after the war. John McFarland may have been an example of those who were left permanently damaged by their experiences. McFarland joined Company E of the 64th Ohio Infantry on October 19, 1861. He fought with his company at Shiloh and contracted typhoid fever four weeks later. McFarland was wounded and captured at Chickamauga on September 19, 1863. He was held at Libby Prison, then Danville, followed by Andersonville, and finally at Florence, where he enlisted in the 10th Tennessee. He had spent 14 months in prison by the time of his enlistment, and he had survived the worst of Andersonville and the first few months of Florence. Most of the prisoners enlisted in the various galvanized units had spent much less time in prison than McFarland, and he must have been in bad shape by the time of his enlistment in November 1864. Captured at Egypt Station, McFarland went to Alton Prison with the rest of the prisoners. Unlike most of the other prisoners, the authorities released him from Alton upon taking the oath on January 29, 1866. The War Department denied McFarland an honorable discharge from the 64th Ohio based on the interpretation that his enlistment in the 10th Tennessee constituted desertion. McFarland (or his advocate) filed a petition with the Senate Committee on Military Affairs requesting an honorable discharge, a necessary step in securing a pension. The Senate Committee denied his first appeal in a decision approved on February 21, 1876. It stated the basis of his appeal and their response as:

> The petitioner states that he became so much reduced by disease and starvation while in prison in Andersonville, Ga., that he saw no other way of saving his life than by enlisting in the rebel army, which he did with a view of "saving himself from starvation, and with the intention of making his escape to the Union lines at the first opportunity. "We have here a clear case of desertion that should not be confounded with honorable conduct by any lapse of time, and to grant the relief prayed

for would be an injustice to the surviving loyal men who suffered all the hardships enumerated by the applicant rather than abandon their colors and array themselves on the side of the enemy."[13]

McFarland submitted a second petition to have his record changed so he could receive an honorable discharge; this petition was referred to the Committee on Military Affairs as S. 2553. The Committee on Military Affairs responded favorably to that request based on additional information presented in his petition. Affidavits from friends and men who had served with him in the 64th Ohio accompanied McFarland's second petition. The report noted from the affidavits of three men who knew McFarland well: "McFarland's brain and weakened constitution rendered him a fit subject for an asylum at the time he took the oath to the Confederacy." The former 1st Lt. of Company E of the 64th Ohio, who had known McFarland almost all of his life, said "that he saw him after his captivity and return home, and that he was then a complete wreck, physically and mentally; that he did not have control of his mental faculties." The Committee, in a report dated April 28, 1890, found that McFarland was "*non compos mentis*" when he took the oath and joined the Confederate Army based on the assessment of his mental abilities from all of the affiants.[14]

John McFarland returned to his father's farm in Lucas, Richland County, Ohio, after the war. He applied for and received a pension on November 12, 1895. McFarland, born in Monroe Township in Richland County on May 27, 1844, spent his life, less the three years of military duty, in that county. He was a farmer and purchased his father's farm after the war. He married on January 10, 1867; this marriage lasted until his wife's death in 1902. He and his wife had six children, all of whom survived to adulthood. He remarried in 1904 and died on November 11, 1918. He left his second wife, the six children, 23 grandchildren and two great grandchildren. He was a member of the McLaughlin Post of the Grand Army of the Republic in Mansfield, Ohio.[15]

Joseph Liptrot mustered into Company L of Daniell's Battery on November 4, 1864, and served while it was engaged in the defense of Savannah. He had served in the 53rd and 145th Pennsylvania before capture, and he claimed to have escaped from Andersonville when recaptured. He was left in a hospital in Savannah suffering from dropsy (now referred to as edema), when his Confederate unit was dissolved and was captured there by Union troops. He was 35 years old and living in Philadelphia in 1870, where his occupation was "attendant at Asylum." He did not appear on the 1880 or 1890 census roll. Liptrot applied for a pension on March 1, 1870. His pension was not approved until November 12, 1897, when he was in the Soldier's and Sailor's Home in Erie, Pennsylvania. He received an increase in his pension a month later and died on April 27, 1899.[16]

An unknown number of the galvanized Confederates did not make it home after the war, and their fates were unknown to their loved ones. Michael Nelligan, a 21-year-old laborer who had been born in Ireland, first served in the 8th Massachusetts Infantry and then enlisted in the 20th Massachusetts Infantry on August 7, 1863, as a substitute for Hiram H. Barrows. Nelligan, captured at Reams Station, Virginia, on August 25, 1864, was sent to Belle Isle Prison and then Salisbury Prison on October 9, 1864. Nelligan had suffered from diarrhea at Belle Isle in September before his transfer, and he must have entered Salisbury in a weakened condition. His Union service records tracked him to the Salisbury Prison, but no further. He enlisted in the Tucker Regiment on November 7, 1864, and died a week later at the General Hospital in Columbia, South Carolina. There was a "Memorandum from Prisoner of War Records" included in his Confederate records, which noted his enlistment in the Tucker Regiment but did not record his death. An investigation by the Attorney General's Office of the War Department conducted in 1876 failed to track Nelligan past Salisbury Prison. That investigation was on behalf of his widow, who was seeking a widow's pension. There is no evidence in the records that his fate was later determined, despite the surviving reference in the Tucker Regiment service records.[17]

Prisoners of war in Confederate prisons had few ways to maintain a level of personal control over their lives. This is true of men enlisted in any army, but especially acute in the case of prisoners. The men at Andersonville, Millen, and Florence were in open pens without shelter or potable water to drink. The rations for the general prison population were, in most cases, of poor quality, too small, and distributed raw. Wood and vessels for cooking rations were in short supply. Medical care was virtually nonexistent, and the men were exposed to numerous diseases made worse by malnutrition, contaminated water, and lack of shelter. Worn out clothing was not replaced. In the face of so many obstacles, many men in these prisons simply gave up, wasted away, and died, or crossed the deadline to be killed by the guards as a form of suicide. Many men lost their sanity and any real chance to exert enough control over the prison structure in order to survive.[18]

The men who survived found ways to exert agency in some form. Men built shelters out of whatever they could find or shared shelters with others. They dug wells to get clean water to drink and for cooking. There was little that could be done about the rations, but men who had retained some money or items for trade supplemented their starvation diets by buying food from the camp sutler. Some even prepared any excess food they could find into dishes, like plates of bean soup, to sell to others for a return on the money they had used to buy more food. Prisoners also made items such as rings from rubber buttons or bone to sell to the guards, despite the fact that contact between prisoners and guards was forbidden in most cases. The guards were, for the most part, too young or too old to serve in the army and lacked any semblance of training or discipline. Some guards took bribes to look away during an escape attempt or when contraband was introduced into the prisons. The prisoners could buy or trade for wood, and those with cooking utensils could use them to cook rations for others for a share of the food. Finally, some men preyed on their fellow inmates, stealing whatever they could use to extend their own lives or to live in greater comfort within the prison. That was a dangerous strategy, if caught, as the raiders at Andersonville discovered.[19]

Successful escape was perhaps the most significant way of exerting agency for prisoners of war. Escape presented an honorable option for prisoners to return their former units or a way to disappear to avoid further involvement in military duty. At least 3,000 known successful escapes did occur during the Civil War, of those who reported to Federal authorities. An unknown number of men died in the attempt, with many more recaptured. After the war, at least a few of the galvanized Confederates, like Joseph Liptrot, tried to deny their service in the Confederate by claiming to have escaped directly from prison. At least some of the men who were left behind because they were wounded after the Salisbury raid or who deserted from the 8th Confederate Infantry were listed as escaped prisoners of war in the Federal records.[20]

Exchange was the most desired method of escaping prison, but it became unlikely after the collapse of the exchange protocol. Exchange simply returned the healthy to the restrictive military life they had been in before prison. Exchange was potentially lifesaving for the unhealthy, who might receive a medical release from service and return to their families.[21]

There were other ways that prisoners could exert agency and improve their chances of survival. Men who had skills needed by the Confederacy could volunteer for work out of prison and thereby enjoy more (and probably better) rations and be able leave the unhealthy prison for outside work. The Confederacy badly needed the skills of cobblers, blacksmiths, farriers, and mechanics. The Confederates did not have enough manpower to do many of the jobs needed to operate their prisons. Those jobs included grave diggers, wood cutters, clerks, hospital attendants, and internal police officers (to maintain discipline inside the prisons). The men who helped the prison function received extra rations and even extra clothing, as in the case of the internal police force. Those who collaborated with the Confederate authorities and made it possible for the prisons to function were a short step away from those who enlisted, but there is no evidence of punishment for that collaboration after the war. Some survivors who wrote their memoirs criticized members of the internal police force for their brutal behavior, but even they escaped punishment.[22]

Enlisting in the Confederate Army was a way to exert agency that presented a number of potentially positive outcomes, such as immediate release from prison and sufficient rations and clothing. Further, there were men in the Confederate prisons who had no desire to be exchanged back their unit. There were criminals, deserters, and bounty jumpers among the men who enlisted, who faced punishment (including execution) if recaptured. As examples, Joseph Sinner and Manuel Fernandez of the Brooks Battalion were probably deserters who had no desire to be exchanged or returned to their units, had the planned mutiny of the Brooks Battalion succeeded. They revealed the mutiny plot in the Brooks Battalion and probably did so to keep themselves out of Union hands. Both men disappeared after the mutiny failed.[23]

The men who enlisted and became galvanized Confederates did so for a number of reasons. The most common reason cited for changing sides was so they could escape and return to their units. Many of the galvanized Confederates did desert their new units and return to the Union lines, but many more performed their tasks as pioneers or took up arms and fought with their Confederate units when put into battle. Most of the men of the 8th Confederate Infantry and the galvanized 10th Tennessee Infantry fought hard when their time for battle came; they inflicted casualties on Union forces, even when faced with impossible odds.

A second reason given by galvanized Confederates was that they had changed sides to escape almost certain death from exposure, starvation, or disease. It is difficult to argue with that given the state of Confederate prisons late in the war, but many more men stayed true to their oath to the Union and still survived the war. It is impossible for those who did not experience what those men went through to fully judge their behavior. They faced each day covered with lice; with little to eat, and much of that indigestible; with inadequate shelter from rain, snow, heat, or cold; with inadequate clothing; with one or more of a catalog of illnesses for which there was no real access to effective medical care; and experienced comrades dying around them every day. It is little wonder that some chose to enlist in the Confederate Army as a way out.[24]

A third reason given by at least a few of the galvanized Confederates is that the Confederate authorities coerced them into enlisting. Francis Shrenk went so far as to claim that the Confederate authorities threatened to shoot him if he did not join. That line of reasoning had far less merit than the other two, as the enlistments seem to have been voluntary.[25]

There were men who changed sides to have an opportunity to escape and return to their units. Given the miserable conditions and high mortality in southern prisons, there were doubtless also many men who became galvanized Confederates in order to improve their chances of survival. Some men may have felt Confederate authorities coerced them into enlisting, whether it was actually happening or not. A few men probably enlisted because they supported the Confederate cause, but no one stated that reason in the available records after the war. It is clear that men who changed sides did so out of self-interest and a need for self-preservation that overrode their sense of duty and sworn oath.

The decision to galvanize was no longer a way for the galvanized Confederates or Yankees to exert agency after the war. It was a decided negative for those who wanted to return to their communities and resume their lives. One immediate strategy used by many galvanized Confederate was to claim they had enlisted at Andersonville. Andersonville was then, and remains even now, the worst of the worst of the southern military prisons in the eyes of the public. The death toll at Andersonville was certainly worse than any other prison in terms of sheer numbers, and the overwhelming majority of prisoner accounts soon after the war and of reminiscent accounts written well after the war dealt with that prison. The majority of the galvanized Confederates, however, joined at Florence and Salisbury, and those from Salisbury came from Belle Isle and not Andersonville Prison. The idea of having been in Andersonville, whether true or not, did not fail to illicit pity and sympathy for those who made the claim.[26]

A second strategy used by those who returned to their home communities after the war was to create their own narrative to explain why they galvanized. Peter J. Knapp did that when he said that he had been in a galvanized unit but had never taken the oath of allegiance to the Confederacy. The Iowa State Legislature bought Knapp's explanation and directed their Congressional delegation by act to sponsor legislation to secure an honorable discharge for him with back pay and allowances. It is likely that few men had the political connections that Knapp had to try to relieve their situations, but it is also likely that many of the men used false narratives to escape the scorn and ostracism by their neighbors.[27]

It is impossible to say if the mental disability claimed for John McFarland was a ruse or really was a case of a mental breakdown. Friends and those who had served with McFarland submitted affidavits to show that McFarland was mentally ill because of the conditions he had survived in prison when he enlisted in the galvanized 10th Tennessee. McFarland won his appeal in 1890 on that basis, but the documentation suggests that he began living what appears to have been a normal life soon after the war. He married in January 1867, bought his father's farm, and joined the McLaughlin Post of the Grand Army of the Republic in Mansfield, Ohio. McFarland's case may well have been true as submitted, but it is likely that at least some men used the mental stress of prison to explain their decisions, whether it was true or false.[28]

An unknown number of men simply vanished after the war and did not leave any further traces in the historical record. Their invisibility in surviving records may simply be due to the anonymity of the common man after the war, but it may also be the result of a conscious effort by some men to shed their identities and with them any consequences for their decisions during the war. The western frontier certainly offered opportunities for men to disappear under new names and identities, or even under their own. John Jepperson, captured at Egypt Station and a member of the 5th USVI, may be an example of a man who chose to vanish under a new name after the war.[29]

What appears to have been a small number of men rejoined Union units after the war. That may have been a way for those men to escape the ostracism and scorn they would have encountered had they returned home. John Kirkwood served in several post-war units of the frontier despite his desertion from the 5th USVI. Elias Bare served in units in the Southwest after he mustered out of the 5th.[30]

Enlisting in the Confederate army as a galvanized Confederate was an act of desertion, following a law passed on February 4, 1862. That law, used to deny pensions to former galvanized Confederates under a joint resolution of Congress in 1867, applied under the following terms: "No money on account of pension shall be paid to any person, or to the widow, children or heirs of any deceased person who, in any manner, voluntarily engaged in, or sided, or abetted the late Rebellion against the authority of the United States."[31]

That policy was reviewed by the Department of Interior in 1891 at least partially as a result of an appeal filed by Russell S. Cole, who had been one of the men taken from Andersonville Prison by Col. O'Neill in his final attempt to recruit soldiers for the 10th Tennessee Infantry. Before being captured by the Confederates, Cole had served with Company E of the 1st New York Veteran Cavalry and Company D of the 27th New York Infantry. After he had mustered out of the 27th New York, he joined the 1st New York Veteran Cavalry on September 13, 1863. Captured at Leetown, Virginia, on July 30, 1864, Cole was sent to Andersonville. Col. O'Neill recruited him on January 23, 1865. He returned to his unit on June 5, 1865. The Secretary of War removed the penalties against him for enlisting in 1881, but he continued to be ineligible for commutation of rations and his record of becoming a galvanized Confederate remained. Cole provided additional information in support of his appeal on June 10, 1889:

> I was taken prisoner at Leetown, Va., July 30, 1864, stripped me of all I have, and took all of my clothes and left me with an old pair of pants and an old blouse. In this situation I served an imprisonment of something over seven months, covered with sores and lice. In my last extremity I took the oath, not with the intent to help the rebels, but solely to save my life and get out of the stockade, so I could make a break for our lines, which I did in about two weeks after taking the oath, and reached our lines in Charleston, S.C. From there I was sent to Hilton Head, from there to Governor's Island, from there to my regiment, and was mustered out with my regiment receiving an honorable discharge.[32]

Cole's appeal was used to respond to the findings of a pension application filed for William Dawson of the 2nd West Virginia Cavalry, for a dependent's pension for the mother of Frederick Thatcher of the U.S. Navy, for Rueben Lightner, and for John Van Fossen; none of these men, besides Dawson, could be linked to a galvanized unit. The Thatcher application is of particular interest since he disappeared over the side of the U.S.S. *Tennessee* in May 1863. That was before formation of any of the galvanized Confederate units. Documents in his service records alleged that he served under the alias George Ryder and that he had joined a Confederate unit and moved to New Orleans prior to its capture by Union forces. A further allegation was that he had left New Orleans as a crewmember of a merchant ship. The pension application claimed he was dead, having drowned when he accidently fell overboard from the *Tennessee*. His mother, Hanna Thatcher, who died on February 22, 1906, received his pension.[33]

William Dawson left Andersonville Prison with Col. O'Neill after enlisting on January 25, 1865. He claimed to have escaped from Andersonville Prison when he rejoined his unit and received an honorable discharge when that regiment mustered out. The Pension Board denied Dawson a pension based on his enlistment with O'Neill in a decision rendered on May 21, 1885.[34]

Changes in pension law, which resulted from the review of the appeal of Russell S. Cole and other rejected pension applications in 1891, were based on several principles. One important principle was that enlistment in Union services constituted a contract between the government and the enlistee:

> Enlistment in military service is held everywhere and always as a voluntary contract between parties, inasmuch as such enlistment in its true meaning and intent, is necessarily based upon mutual consent and upon a lawful consideration. The violation of a contract is the highest ground on which to base an action for damages in judicial tribunals inasmuch as it involves personal honor, fidelity, and responsibility, no less than other foundation principles of civil society. Out of this doctrine grew the fact that the *violation of a contract for military service* is held to be the most heinous offense known to the Articles of War, the act of *desertion* being punishable not only by imprisonment but by *death*. But was the case of Dawson one of desertion? And is this case now under consideration? To those questions the answer is No! The papers show that Dawson, *while in the line of duty while on the battle-field* was captured by the enemy. He was not only captured, but imprisoned by the Rebel authorities; and it is admitted his *temporary* enlistment in the Rebel army was not a *bona fide* engagement, nor a voluntary contract for service, but a mere *device* whereby he intended to procure "an early opportunity to escape to the Federal lines"; and the conclusion seems inevitable that the prisoner of war who thus temporarily joins the enemies forces as a measure of *escape* from captivity, and who does escape sooner or later—whether or not the method adopted be a wise is discrete one—can not [*sic*] be held to have "voluntarily engaged in or aided and abetted the late Rebellion."[35]

A later statement opened the door for galvanized Confederates who had not escaped and rejoined their units: "It is clearly apparent that the Government has no scales in which to weigh either the motives or the necessities of the prisoner of war while remote from its dominion, seeking a way to *escape* from the hands of its alien captors under which the Government itself possesses no control."[36]

The galvanized Confederates joined the rest of the survivors of the Union army or their surviving dependents after the 1891 decision and were finally eligible for government pensions. The war was finally over for those who had changed sides.

APPENDIX A

Officers of the Tucker Regiment

ASSISTANT SURGEON HENRY B. CHRISTIAN

Col. Tucker's Assistant Surgeon was Henry B. Christian. Christian served as an Assistant Surgeon throughout the war and moved from hospital to hospital in Augusta, Georgia, as well as in several cities in Virginia. His assignment prior to joining the Tucker Regiment was at General Hospital No. 21 in Richmond. He apparently served with the regiment until paroled at Greensboro on April 26, 1865.[1]

ADJUTANT 1ST LT. J. THOMPSON QUARLES

J. Thompson Quarles was elected 1st Lieutenant of Company C and appointed Adjutant on Col. Tucker's staff. He served as a private and chief clerk in the Signal Corps in Richmond as late as June 1864. He doubtless had skills that were useful to a pioneer unit such as Tucker's Regiment. A note in his service record, included with the Tucker Regiment records, indicates that he had been a conscript assigned to the 14th Tennessee Infantry, but he does not appear among the service records for that unit.[2]

ASSISTANT QUARTERMASTER J. S. RICHARDSON

J. S. Richardson served the regimental staff as an Assistant Quartermaster. His prior military service, if any, is unknown.[3]

COMPANY A

Captain John B. Johnson of Company A had been a drillmaster of the Army of Northern Virginia when he was recruited to join Tucker's command. He resigned his command with the Tucker Regiment in a letter dated January 31, 1865, to rejoin the Army of Northern Virginia as drillmaster of cavalry. He stated in his letter that the position with the Army of Northern Virginia was one that "I greatly prefer to the present one."[4]

Second Lt. Ed Manes, wounded at Gettysburg, was an officer of Company A. Tucker filed charges against Manes on February 3, 1865, stating that he had been AWOL from January 29 to February 1. Manes submitted a letter of resignation on February 10, 1865, stating that the wound he sustained at Gettysburg made it impossible to carry out his duties. There was no record of how that matter was resolved.[5]

First Lt. Charles W. Wilkinson of Company A initially served as a private in the 7th Tennessee Infantry and then as a clerk in the Quartermaster General's office. Immediately prior to joining the Tucker Regiment, Wilkinson served as a clerk for the 2nd Auditor and a private in the 3rd Virginia Infantry Local Defense Troops. Upon the departure of Captain Johnson, Wilkinson replaced him as Captain.[6]

Second Lt. George Place may have been a private in the 2nd Virginia Artillery until released from the service under a surgeon's certificate of disability in 1862. That George Place was born in Ireland and was 22 years old in 1862.[7]

COMPANY B

Captain Louis Power, commander of Company B, had served as a Lieutenant in a Richmond guard unit prior to transferring to the Tucker Regiment. Second Lt S. M. Levin had been a private in the 3rd Infantry, Local Defense Force, before joining Tucker and had previously been with the Treasury Department. He resigned his commission on October 17 1864. John L. Ligon, elected a 2nd Lt., had previously been at Libby Prison. He was promoted to 1st Lt. and transferred to Company I. Second Lt. Ludlow L. Cohen had been a private in the 2nd South Carolina Cavalry prior to his service with the Tucker Regiment. First Lt. F. W. James was a member of the VMI cadet corps stationed at Fort Lee, Virginia. No record of prior service was found for 1st Lt. F. W. James or 2nd Lt. John L. Trezevant, although it is likely that they were drawn from Richmond guard units or state reserves. [8]

COMPANY C

Captain William A. James commanded Company C. Captain James was a somewhat shadowy character who had served as a conscription officer, drillmaster, and most recently as a train guard prior to accepting command of Company C. Captain James, a 1st Lieutenant before joining the Tucker Regiment, travelled extensively through the Confederacy during the war.[9] J. Thompson Quarles, initially a 1st Lieutenant of Company C, was named regimental Adjutant by Col. Tucker. No information was found concerning the prior service of 2nd Lt. Alex N. Power or 2nd Lt. James J. Russell of Company C.[10]

COMPANY D

Captain Benjamin Azariah Colonna commanded Company D. Captain Colonna was a student at Virginia Military Institute (VMI) and a captain of Company B, which was entirely comprised of VMI students at the time of the Battle of New Market. He led his company into battle when the company commander was unable to take charge. The VMI cadets played a role in the Confederate victory, but the school barracks were lost to fire by the time the cadets returned to campus.

Colonna was graduated from VMI in July 1864. He was a 2nd Lt. and drillmaster in Staunton, Virginia, when he was placed in command of Company D of the Tucker Regiment. After the war, Colonna went on to a varied and distinguished career. He spent several years after the war as a teacher and then joined the Coast and Geodetic Survey. He travelled much of the country while working for the Coast and Geodetic Survey, and mapped both coastal areas and mountainous areas of the far west. He went in with his brother to establish the Colonna Shipyard in Norfolk, Virginia, a private shipyard that is still in operation today. Colonna, severely injured while on a survey trip to the west, suffered the effects of the injury for the rest of his life. He was placed in charge of the Washington office of the Coast and Geodetic Survey in 1885, but he left that post in 1895. He remained active in scientific affairs in his later life and was a close confidant to President Theodore Roosevelt. Colonna died at home at age 82 on March 12, 1924.[11]

B. W. Barton, elected 1st Lt. of Company D, appears to have been a member of the VMI cadet corps prior to joining Tucker's Regiment. [12] Philip L. Cohen served as a 2nd Lt. of Company D and had served with the 7th South Carolina Cavalry prior to joining the Tucker Regiment. His service records from that unit indicate that he had experience on signal duty.[13] James K. Cleary, elected Jr. 2nd Lt of Company D, had prior service as a private with Captain Moore's Company Light Artillery, which was a Virginia unit.[14]

COMPANY E

Captain D. M. Cleary commanded Company E. Captain Cleary was apparently a Lieutenant in the Confederate army prior to his assignment with Tucker Regiment, but his prior service record did not survive.[15] First Lieutenant Edward B. Cohen had served as a private in Captain Walter's Company of the South Carolina Washington Artillery prior to joining Tucker's Regiment.[16] An Edward Cohen was also an officer in Companies H and K. Edward Cohen in Company H was a 2nd Lieutenant from the 3rd Virginia Infantry, Local Defense Troops, prior to joining the Tucker regiment. A further annotation to his service record indicates that he transferred to Company K as a 1st Lieutenant. This information indicates there were two Edward Cohens among the officers of the Regiment. Two other Cohens, Philip L. Cohen, a 2nd Lieutenant of Company D, and Ludlow Cohen, a 2nd Lieutenant of Company B, were also on the rolls.[17]

H.S. Kennedy served Company E as a 2nd Lieutenant, and he served as a private in the 3rd Virginia Infantry, Local Defense Force. The 3rd Virginia Infantry, Local Defense Force, organized in September 1864, was composed of staff (largely clerks) of the departments of the Confederate government in Richmond. The service records for surnames that begin with A through E are not available, but several of the available names do match with officers of the Tucker Regiment. These include C. W. Wilkinson (1st Lt Company A), Kennedy, S. M. Levin (2nd Lt Company

B), and J. M. Keesee (2nd Lt Company K). All were privates in the 3rd Virginia Infantry, Local Defense Troops. It is likely that the list would be much longer if the A-E records were available.[18]

John A. Crawford served as a Junior 2nd Lt of Company E. His prior service was with the 2nd South Carolina Infantry, where he had served as a Sgt. Major. Lt. Crawford served with the 2nd South Carolina Infantry for most of the war and was one of the few officers of the Tucker Regiment who had served with a line unit.[19]

COMPANY F

Tucker offered Collier H. Minge a promotion from 2nd Lieutenant to Captain and command of Company F. Lt. Minge, a drillmaster for the Virginia Reserves and graduate of VMI, commanded the Cadet Corps 3-inch rifled section of artillery during the Battle of New Market. He was the first cadet to command the Corps artillery in the field and distinguished himself during the battle. Minge declined the appointment to the Tucker Regiment, and he chose instead to transfer to the Alabama Reserves.[20]

1st Lieutenant, and then Captain, S. O. Kirk Commanded Company F. Kirk had served as Lieutenant of the Provost Guards in Winchester, Virginia, in 1862. He drew expenses for rental of quarters on September 30, 1863, while serving on Gen. Winder's staff in Richmond. General Winder, first appointed Provost Marshall General of Richmond in 1862, was later responsible for Richmond and a 10-mile radius around the City. Winder created a police force and imposed harsh control methods on the citizens of Richmond, which were extremely unpopular. Winder was also responsible for the Union prisoners of war housed in the Richmond prisons, and he was put in charge of all Confederate military prisons east of the Mississippi River on July 26, 1864. Captain Kirk's background would have prepared him for the harsh disciplinary role that Col. Tucker seems to have expected of his officers.[21]

W. H. Heyward served as a 2nd Lieutenant of Company F. No record of prior service could be found for Heyward.[22]

H. H. Dinwiddie was a 2nd Lieutenant of Company F. An 1868 letter, filed among letters received by the Office of Adjutant General, from an H. H. Dinwiddie of Lynchburg, Virginia, supported reopening a military school in Bostick, Texas. Dinwiddie was a proposed professor for the school, under the direction of Major John J. James. It is unclear if the H. H. Dinwiddie who wrote the letter is the same man who served with the Tucker Regiment, or if Major John J. James was related to 1st Lt. F. W. James of Company B or W. A. James of Company C.[23]

The remaining officer in Company F was 2nd Lieutenant W. L. Lewis. Individuals by that name appear in Confederate military records, but it is impossible to tell if any of them was the officer in the Tucker Regiment.[24]

COMPANY G

Captain W. J. Duncan commanded Company G. Captain Duncan had served (no rank indicated) in Lieutenant Moorehead's Company, Virginia Local Defense, which was previously designated Captain William H. Bosang's Company of the Provost Guard in Dublin, Virginia. His appointment was yet another example of officers of the Tucker Regiment being drawn from local defense forces and provost guards.[25]

The 1st Lieutenant of Company G was initially John L. Boatright, who had a long and somewhat checkered history in the Confederate Army. He had enlisted in the 2nd South Carolina Infantry as a private in Company C at age 18. He took an appointment as a cadet from South Carolina that lasted from September 26 to October 21, 1861. Boatright's father requested that his son be assigned to Gen. Ripley's staff in Charleston on October 26, 1861. John L. Boatright was mustering officer for the 3rd South Carolina Cavalry by March 19, 1862. Promoted to 1st Lieutenant, he served as an ordnance officer for the 4th Military District under Gen. Trapier from January 15 to October 16, 1863, and he served as an ordnance officer for the 4th Military District under Gen. Trapier. Boatright unsuccessfully requested a promotion to Captain of Artillery on June 20 and 30, 1863. Assigned to duty under Captain Harden, the Chief Ordnance Officer for the Georgia District, on December 20, 1863, his duty station was Savannah by December 31. Lt. Boatright's career took a turn for the worse in April 1864, when Lt. Col. J. R. Waddy requested that Boatright be "transferred elsewhere." He was relieved of duty in the Ordnance Department on June 9, 1864, and ordered to report, with a demotion, to the commanding general of the Department of Georgia, South Carolina, and Florida. Major John B. Hoge recommended him for appointment as a 2nd Lieutenant on October 27, 1864. Boatright joined the Tucker Regiment on November 22, 1864. He was elected 1st Lieutenant and then promoted to Captain and placed in command of Company K on February 28, 1865. Capt. Boatright gained his assignment to the Tucker Regiment through the political influence of Major Hoge, and he was one of the few officers of the regiment who came to his position from the regular army.[26]

John Setze was a 2nd Lieutenant of Company G. He had previously been a private in Captain Walter's Company of the South Carolina Washington Artillery, along with 1st Lieutenant Edward B. Cohen of Company E. Setze joined Tucker's Regiment in Ridgeville, South Carolina. M. Ezekiel was offered a commission in Company G as 2nd Lieutenant but declined and remained with the VMI cadets serving in the defense of Richmond. He became a renowned sculptor after the war, and died in Rome, Italy, in 1917. William J. Hubbard Jr., elected Jr. 2nd Lt. in November 1864, left the company in January 1865 at the insistence of his guardian and returned to VMI. No record of his tenure at VMI was found. No information was found on 2nd Lt. J. G. Penn or 1st Lt. C. W. Hardy (who declined the appointment).[27]

COMPANY H

Captain Charles H. Byrne commanded Company H. Byrne had been a member of the English Army and had graduated from the Royal Military Academy Sandhurst. He joined Maj. General Patrick Cleburne's staff as volunteer Aide-de-Camp and served as an unpaid volunteer for two years prior to joining the Tucker Regiment. Cleburne had also served in the British Army prior to coming to America, which may be the reason, in part, for the bond between the two men. Major General Cleburne, a division commander in the Army of Tennessee, personally recommended Byrne for a position as a field officer, which resulted in Byrne's election as Captain of Company H. He joined Tucker's Regiment on November 18, 1864, in Columbia. Within a month, he sent a letter to Judge John A. Campbell seeking an assignment as a major in a new cavalry unit in Alabama. He did not receive the transfer and promotion, and remained with the Tucker Regiment. He commented in his letter to Campbell that the men in the regiment had not received arms, equipment, or clothing, despite an order from the Secretary of War that the regiment be supplied with "everything it needed" from Augusta. He was complimentary of the progress that had been made organizing and training the regiment, and he said that with "about two months more drill, we will make one of the finest Regiments that ever entered the field."[28]

2nd Lieutenant Edward Cohen was a private in the 3rd Infantry Local, Defense Troops, of Virginia prior to joining the Tucker Regiment. Junior 2nd Lieutenant Robert L. Brockenbrough was a member of the VMI Cadet Corps at Camp Lee, Virginia, before accepting his assignment. He ended the war as a 1st Lieutenant with Company H. Second Lt. A. R. Toutant joined Company H on March 16, 1865. Toutant had previously served in the Brooks Battalion and had served as Aide-de-Camp for his uncle, Gen. P. G. T. Beauregard. At the time of his parole, Toutant was 20 years old, 5' 8 ½" tall, and had dark hair and blue eyes. Although paroled in April 1865, at the end of the war, with Gen. Johnston's Army, he was arrested and not officially paroled until May 1. His parole listed his residence as San Antonio, Texas. L. Royster and Corey Weston declined commissions with Company H. Nothing more was found about 2nd Lt. Wm. Clarke who served with the company.[29]

COMPANY I

Captain Charles B. Day commanded Company I. Nothing more is known about Day or his prior service. Julius Cohen served Company I as a 2nd Lieutenant. His service prior to the Tucker Regiment was as a private in Captain Walter's Company of the South Carolina Washington Artillery, along with Edward Cohen of Company H, later of Company L. John L. Ligon Jr., added as a 1st Lieutenant after John L. Tunstall declined to serve, had previously been a private in the 1st Virginia Infantry and had served as a guard at Libby Prison. He was apparently the son of John L. Ligon, owner of a tobacco warehouse in Richmond that was appropriated by the

Confederate government to be used as a prison and later as a hospital. 2nd Lt. J. L. Brisbane previously served as a private in the 4th South Carolina Cavalry.[30]

COMPANY K

Company K, formed in February 1865, allowed Tucker's Battalion to become a regiment. The leadership of that company was partly from the existing officer corps, with John L. Boatright of Company G promoted to Captain and put in command of the company. The 1st Lieutenant was Edward Cohen from Company H. L. Crieger (Cruger) Trezevant of Company B was one of the two 2nd Lieutenants. Nothing was found concerning his prior service, if any. Brevet 2nd Lieutenant J. M. Keesee was a private in the 3rd Virginia Infantry, Local Defense Troops, prior to joining the Tucker Regiment.[31]

APPENDIX B

Officers of the 8th Confederate Infantry

COMPANY A

Captain, and later Major, Robert T. Fouche was discussed in the body of the report. The remaining officers of Company A included 1st Lt. J. L. Lyerly and 2nd Lieutenants John F. Hanna and J. P. Herndon. 1st Lt. Lyerly was at Salisbury Prison as late as January 4, 1865, where he perhaps was part of the prison guard. 2nd Lt. John F. Hanna was born in Philadelphia in 1843, attended both Gonzaga College and Georgetown University, and enrolled in VMI in January 1862. He graduated from VMI in June 1864, shortly after he had taken part in the Battle of New Market as cadet 1st Lt. of Company D of the VMI cadet corps. He was one of several former VMI cadets chosen by Andrews to be officers of the 8th Confederate. He studied and practiced law in Washington, D.C., after the war, and he died following a riding accident in 1885. 2nd Lt. J. P. Herndon was the remaining officer of Company A, and no information was found about his background.[1]

COMPANY B

Captain James Barrett commanded Company B. Barrett initially enlisted in the 8th Georgia Infantry on June 7, 1861, but he had to leave that regiment due to disability. He joined the 5th Georgia Infantry at Tyner, Tennessee, on August 18, 1862, and was elected 2nd Lt. of Company C in June 1863. 2nd Lt. Barrett was one of two "Inspectors" of the prison after the 5th Georgia became a guard unit at Florence Stockade in October 1864. Barrett became "Inspector of Military Prisons" in November 1864, a title he retained until he joined the 8th Confederate Infantry. The 5th Georgia left Florence on November 18, 1864, leaving Barrett and other elements in command of the prison behind. Barrett wrote a letter to then Major Garnett Andrews the next day and requested permission to recruit a company for the 8th at Florence. That request was approved, and he joined the 8th as Captain and commander of Company B.[2]

Barrett was the most hated of the Confederate guards at Florence. Most prisoner accounts published after the war mention Barrett, including those that appear to be the most accurate accounts of what transpired at the prison. Ezra Hoyt Ripple described Barrett as: "A braggart and bully when armed, among unarmed men his general style and manner made me believe he was a coward at heart. He was Lt. Barrett, and he was known throughout the prison as a redheaded devil."[3]

Judge Advocate General J. Holt, in a letter to Secretary of War Stanton, singled out Barrett shortly after the war for prosecution for war crimes: "That Lieutenant Colonel Iverson, Forty-Seventh Georgia Volunteers, and his subordinate, Lieutenant (or Captain) Barrett should be arrested and brought to trial for their treatment of our soldiers when prisoners of war at Florence, SC. The testimony fixes upon them not only a series of most cruel and inhumane acts or neglect, abuse, assault, robbery &c, but a considerable number of homicides. In these Barrett was the principal agent, but Iverson, as his commanding officer, was clearly no less criminal."[4]

Barrett fled to Germany after the war to avoid prosecution. He married while in Germany and returned the United States in 1870, after interest in the prosecution of those guilty of war crimes had waned. He had a farm in the Augusta, Georgia, area until his death in 1910. His obituary, published in the *Atlanta Constitution* and the *New York Tribune,* stated that he had been an officer under Major Wirz at Andersonville and had commanded Florence prison. Both statements were incorrect.[5]

The 1st Lieutenant assigned to Company B was William Beamish Crawford. Lt. Crawford was part of the class of 1867 at VMI, and apparently fought at the Battle of New Market. He was born in 1845 at Staunton, Virginia, and died in 1892 at Nelson, Nebraska. J. S. Hanna and Charles Pratt served as 2nd lieutenants of Company B, but nothing more is known about them. A list of officers assigned to the 8th Confederate that was dated January 4, 1865 contains a notation by J. S. Hanna's name: "care Col. Shriver Richmond," but no additional information could be found.[6]

COMPANY C

Captain John W. Kerr commanded Company C. Kerr had served as 1st Lt. of Company I of the 5th Texas Infantry, and the January 4, 1865, list of officers of the 8th Confederate indicates that he had also served as Assistant Adjutant and Inspector General of the Texas Brigade of the Fields Division prior to joining the 8th. The Texas Brigade was engaged in many of the major battles of the Civil War, and sustained heavy casualties. First Lt. A. M. Braxton served Company C as a Captain in the Virginia Light Artillery prior to joining the 8th Confederate. The remaining officers of Company C were 2nd Lt. James Martin, and 2nd Lt. E. D. Christian, but nothing more could be found about them.[7]

COMPANY D

Captain John Shotwell, who commanded Company D of the 8th Confederate, served in the 1st Texas Infantry as a Captain in command of Company B, prior to his service with the 8th. The 1st Texas had been part of the Texas Brigade. He reported that his reason for requesting to serve with the 8th Confederate was that his company had "been destroyed by the casualties of battles." Captain Kerr of

Company C may have accepted the assignment to the 8th for much the same reason. Both Shotwell and Kerr came to the 8th with extensive experience as line officers, hardened by numerous battles. C. H. Marks, who served as 1st Lt. of Company D, had been a cadet at VMI prior to his service with the 8th. Second Lt. R. C. Braxton apparently served at the Richmond prisons on Major Turner's staff prior to joining the 8th, as one notation says that he was from "C.S. Military Prisons Richmond," while a second said "care of Major Turner Libby Prison."[8]

COMPANY E

Captain Edward Napier commanded Company E, and had previously spent the entire war as a 2nd and then 1st Lieutenant with Company C of the 60th Georgia Infantry. The 60th Georgia took part in many major battles, and surrendered with the Army of Northern Virginia at Appomattox. Captain Napier transferred to the 8th Confederate in time to be on the January 4, 1865, roster; he was at Florence with the battalion at that time.[9]

James W. McCorkle, the 1st Lieutenant of Company E, entered VMI in December 1862, and he resigned to accept a commission with the 8th Confederate on February 18, 1865. McCorkle was made an honorary graduate of the VMI class of 1867 based on his appointment to the 8th. He enlisted in the 9th Virginia Battalion soon after the start of the war and was a sergeant when the 9th merged with the 25th Virginia. McCorkle, elected 2nd Lieutenant of the 25th, was wounded at the Second Battle of Manassas on August 29, 1862. He resigned his commission with the 25th to enter VMI. He followed a career as a merchant after the war and died in Roanoke, Virginia, on October 27, 1914.[10]

Company E had three 2nd lieutenants. A receipt dated September 13, 1864, shows that 2nd Lt. H. C. Mosely was a civilian clerk employed by the Southern Express Company. The receipt was for the delivery of $80,000 from Macon to Augusta, Georgia. No service record was found for Mosely, but it is likely that his service to the government, which justified his appointment as an officer, went beyond that of a simple clerk. 2nd Lt. Charles W. Turner had been a private in Capt. W. P. Carter's Company of the Light Virginia Artillery prior to joining the 8th Confederate. 2nd Lt. James B. Crawford had been a private in the 7th Battalion Virginia Reserves prior to the 8th Confederate, and he took his parole with that unit in April 1865. He may have rejoined his old unit prior to the end of the war, but his parole with that unit may have been a record keeping error.[11]

COMPANY F

Captain Samuel Sprigg Shriver commanded Company F. Shriver commanded VMI cadet Company C during the Battle of New Market. Shriver, wounded during that battle, graduated first in his class in June 1864. The 8th Confederate appears to have been his first regular army post after his graduation. 2nd Lt. John F. Hanna of Company A was graduated 10th of 14 in the class of 1864. Captain Shriver was born in Wheeling, West Virginia, in 1843, and his father was Jacob Sherman Shriver. Samuel Shriver was a farmer and legislator after the war. He never married and passed away in Suffolk, Virginia, in 1881.[12]

Henry C. Stacker was the 1st Lieutenant of Company F. The only record of 1st Lt. Stacker that could be found outside of his records with the 8th Confederate were two parole documents dated June 11, 1865, which referenced his service with Company A of the 2nd Kentucky Cavalry. No record of his service was found with the 2nd Kentucky Cavalry.[13]

Edward Lumpkin Hamlin served as a 2nd Lt. in Company F. Hamlin was born in Athenia, Mississippi, on January 24, 1845. He attended VMI and was part of the class of 1867. He took part in the Battle of New Market as a member of Company D of the Corps of Cadets. He apparently served on Major General Marcus J. Wright's staff after he left the Cadet Corps and before he joined the 8th Confederate. He was an attorney in Memphis after the war and was killed in a duel on August 27, 1870, by Major Ed Freeman. The cause of the duel was never publicly stated. He never married and was childless at the time of his death.[14]

"H. Leftwich" was one of the 2nd Lieutenants of Company F. That individual was Alexander H. Leftwich, who entered VMI in 1864 and was made an honorary graduate of the class of 1867 in 1875. That entry indicates that he fought at New Market as a private in Company B and joined the Confederate Army on January 14, 1865. He joined the 8th Confederate at an unknown date. Leftwich escaped capture at Salisbury during Stoneman's raid, and was paroled in Hamburg, South Carolina. He died in Baltimore, Maryland, on August 11, 1908.[15]

The remaining two officers listed under Company F were 1st Lt. John S. Hanna and 2nd Lt. Meade Bernard. First Lt. John S. Hanna is probably the same person as 2nd Lt. J. S. Hanna listed for Company B. No information was found on Lt. Hanna, and it is not known if he is related to John F. Hanna of Company A. No information was found on Lt. Bernard.[16]

APPENDIX C

Officers of the Galvanized 10th Tennessee Infantry

ADJUTANT 1ST LT. ROBERT P. SEYMOUR

First Lieutenant Robert P. Seymour served as Adjutant of both the 10th Tennessee and the galvanized 10th. Gen. Hood ordered Seymour to join the 10th Galvanized under Special Field Order #130 on October 11, 1864. Mathes, in his brief biography of Conrad Nutzell, describes Seymour as "an old soldier from the Crimean War." Seymour accompanied Lt. Col. Burke into battle at Egypt Station and was captured. Seymour was 34 years old with light hair and eyes and was 6 feet tall. His place of residence was Cleveland, Ohio. He swore an oath of allegiance to the United States at Johnson's Island on June 17, 1865.[1]

CAPTAIN JAMES MCMURRAY

Gen. Hardee declared Captain James McMurray of Company A of the 10th Tennessee a supernumerary officer on December 4, 1864, and ordered him to report for duty to Major General Wright, who then commanded Atlanta. He apparently remained under Wright's command after the fall of Atlanta, when Wright assumed command of Macon, Georgia. Wright ordered McMurray on October 21, 1864, to proceed to "Andersonville, Millen, and such other points where Federal prisoners are confined for enlisting foreigners under orders of the Sec. of War." It is not known if McMurray preceded Col. O'Neill at Millen, or if he assisted in O'Neill's recruitment effort at that prison. The available records indicate that there was a single recruitment effort there by O'Neill, who left the prison on November 8. McMurray attempted to recruit at Salisbury prison; he sent a telegram to Brigadier General William M. Gardner on November 21, which said he was refused entry to the prison to recruit and requested orders from Gen. Gardner giving him permission to recruit there. It appears that he did not receive that permission. One J. L. Tyerly, Clerk of Prison, prepared a tabulation of prisoners recruited from Salisbury on February 1, 1865, which showed that no Salisbury prisoners had been recruited for the galvanized 10th to that point. McMurray was in Augusta by November 30, where he requested a reimbursement of $21 for the telegram he sent to Gardner. He was apparently also at Augusta on December 18, when he requested reimbursement for authorized travel at the rate of $10 per day for 59 days. McMurray apparently did not accompany the majority of the galvanized unit to the west. He entered Ocmulgee Hospital in Macon on April 18, 1865, and was captured in Macon on April 21.[2]

CAPTAIN LEWIS R. CLARK

Gen. Hood assigned Captain Lewis R. Clark to the galvanized 10th Tennessee under Special Order #130 on October 11, 1864. Clark had been wounded on August 31, 1864, and was apparently was still convalescing when ordered to join the galvanized 10th in October. No direct details of his service with the galvanized unit have survived. However, the muster roll of April 28, 1865, which enumerated those who surrendered at Greensboro under terms agreed upon by generals Johnston and Sherman, contains the notation "Detached in Command of Division Pioneers" for Captain Clark. It is likely that the "Division Pioneers" were the surviving members of the galvanized unit.[3]

CAPTAINS JOHN L. PRENDERGAST AND BARTLY J. DORSEY

Captains John L. Prendergast and Bartly J. Dorsey of the 10th Tennessee Confederate both received orders to report for duty with the galvanized unit under Special Order #130 on October 11, 1864. Both had been wounded in Atlanta on September 1 and were absent from the 10th under surgeon's orders. Nothing more was found concerning their service with the 10th galvanized.[4]

CAPTAIN HENRY RICE

Captain Henry Rice was one of two officers assigned to the galvanized unit from the 15th Tennessee Infantry. Rice was a resident of Shelby County, Tennessee, with fair complexion, brown hair, grey eyes, and standing 5 feet 8 inches tall. Gen. Hood ordered him to proceed to Millen, Georgia, under Special Order #130 on October 11, 1864. Rice surrendered at Macon on May 4, 1865.

2ND LT. JOSEPH DE'G. EVANS

Second Lieutenant Joseph de'G Evans was declared a supernumery officer by special order of General Hood on October 5, 1864. Hood ordered him to duty with the galvanized 10th on October 11, 1864, under Special Order #130. Evans was captured at Macon on April 21, 1865.[5]

1ST LT. CONRAD NUTZEL

Captain Henry Rice ordered 1st Lieutenant Conrad Nutzel to report to him for special service under Special Order #130 of October 11, 1864. He ordered Nutzel to perform recruiting duty at the "Prison Depots" and to report his progress every 10 days. Nutzel was at Augusta on December 19, 1864, when he submitted a requisition for 70 days of travel at $10 per day. Nutzel was a native of Bavaria. He was 27 years old with light complexion and hair and blue eyes. He stood 5 feet 9 ½ inches tall. He was a resident of Memphis by 1853, where he joined what became the 15th

Tennessee Infantry on June 5, 1861. Elected 2nd Lieutenant, he took part in the Battle of Perryville, Kentucky. After the Battle of Murphreesboro Nutzel joined the staff of Col. Ben Hill, Provost Marshall, and went on to join the galvanized 10th after the fall of Atlanta. He supposedly organized a company made up of German immigrants, which was part of the 10th galvanized. He was promoted to Captain and took part in the Battle of Egypt Station. Nutzel was taken prisoner at Egypt Station and swore an oath of amnesty at Johnson's Island on May 13, 1865. He returned to Memphis after the war and married Rosina Hemmerly in 1870.[6]

2ND LT. GEORGE W. WHARTON

2nd Lt. George W. Wharton was a supernumerary officer from the 18th Tennessee Infantry who served with the galvanized 10th. He was described as 30 years old with fair complexion, dark hair, and grey eyes. He was from Woodbury, Tennessee. Wharton joined the 18th Tennessee in April 1861 and was designated a supernumerary officer by General Bragg in Atlanta on October 8, 1863. He was hospitalized in Jackson, Mississippi, on November 8, 1864, for ambustis (a burn). He was released on December 5, 1865, and was captured at the Battle of Egypt Station. Wharton took the oath and was released from Johnson Island Prison on June 17, 1865.[7]

CONFEDERATE PRIVATES

It appears that several privates on the muster rolls of the 10th Tennessee Infantry were also members of the galvanized unit. The origins of four men captured with the galvanized unit were questioned by Federal authorities after Egypt Station. It would be reasonable to assume that Confederates would chose to mix in some of their own men into the unit to help maintain operational control and watch the galvanized Confederates.[8]

APPENDIX D

Officers of Companies A–D, 5th U.S. Volunteer Infantry

LT. COL. JOHN WANLESS

Lt. Col. John Wanless was a native of Canada. He served as a 2nd Lt and then as Captain in the 3rd Colorado Infantry and as Provost Marshall of Colorado prior to joining the 5th USVI. He joined the 5th USVI on March 27, 1865, and reported to St. Louis. He helped Col. Maynadier recruit five companies of the USVI from among Confederate prisoners at Camp Douglas prior to returning to Denver to take care of his final business as Provost Marshall. Wanless had no real military experience, but because of his prior role in the 3rd Colorado he became Acting District Inspector for the District of Upper Arkansas, Department of Missouri. Wanless took command of Fort Halleck on November 2, 1865. He apparently did not adjust well to military life and resigned his commission on March 9, 1866.[1]

John Wanless became a prominent and wealthy businessman after leaving the army. He spent several years as the sutler at Fort Sanders, Wyoming, and was a contractor for the Denver and Rio Grande Railroad. He spent several years in California, but resided in Colorado Springs towards the end of his life. He passed away of a "paralytic condition" in Hot Springs, Arkansas, on July 21,1886, at age 53.[2]

1ST LT. AND ADJUTANT HENRY P. HUMPHREYS

Henry P. Humphreys left the 66th Illinois Infantry from St. Louis as a private, under Special Order Number 89, in order to join the 5th USVI as a 1st Lt. and Adjutant on April 5, 1865. He had spent the war to that point with the 66th Illinois, having joined in 1862. Humphreys was initially stationed at Fort Riley with the majority of the regiment. He moved to Fort Laramie and became the Acting Assistant Adjutant for the West Sub District of Nebraska by Special Order 6 of October 8, 1865. He became the Acting Assistant Attorney General of the District of the Platte on May 1, 1866, based at Fort Laramie. He left the service with the regiment on October 11, 1866. Humphreys applied for a pension as an invalid in 1891 and 1907, but the disposition of those applications was not determined during the current research.[3]

MAJOR AND SURGEON WILLIAM C. FINLAW

William C. Finlaw served first as an Assistant Surgeon for the 2nd Missouri Light Artillery until February 1965. He joined the 5th USVI as a Major and Surgeon from civilian life on April 4, 1865. He served initially as surgeon of the post hospital at Fort Riley and then Fort MacPherson in the Nebraska Territory, until he left the service on October 11, 1866. A widow's pension application by his wife of February 2, 1903, was rejected because of lack of proof of Finlaw's death. Finlaw died at Santa Rosa, California, on November 17, 1905, at which time his other wife applied for a widow's pension. Finlaw had married his first wife, Jane E. Bradley on May 22, 1862. He soon after went back to Keokuk College of Physicians to complete his education while his wife returned to Dover, Delaware, to live with her parents. He joined the 2nd Missouri Light Infantry in 1863 and apparently claimed to have spent nine months in a Confederate prison. Finlaw never saw his son, born on November 1, 1863. Finlaw told his wife that he was leaving for the Idaho gold fields and never communicated with her again. He married his second wife, Anna Love Snyder, while stationed at Fort Riley. He became a wealthy doctor after the war and left an estate worth $60,000. The suit filed by his first wife against his estate was settled out of court with a cash payment and the assignment of his widow's pension to her.[4]

CHAPLAIN ORLANDO CLARKE

Orlando Clarke, a civilian, was recommended for the post of Chaplain for the 5th USVI. He accepted the nomination on March 28, 1865, but never joined the regiment. He was a member of the Trinitarion Congregational Congregation and remained in St. Louis.[5]

GALVANIZED CONFEDERATES IN THE 5TH USVI

The former members of the galvanized 10th were assigned to companies A, B, C, and D of the 5th. Those companies contained both galvanized Confederates and galvanized Yankees, with each group almost equally represented. All of the officers assigned to those companies were Union officers, enlisted men, or civilians.[6]

COMPANY A

Captain Randall G. Butler commanded Company A. He joined the 5th USVI on April 1, 1865, from the 41st Missouri Infantry, where he had been a 2nd Lt. He was absent from his company on detached duty in St. Louis until August 21, 1865, when he was placed in Command of the Post Lake Sibley. He joined his company at Fort Halleck in Dakota Territory in September. A court martial convicted Capt. Butler of trading a government mule for a horse that he then claimed as his own and for stealing money from the sale of government property. The War Department confirmed his conviction in February 1866, and he was dishonorably discharged from the army.[7]

First Lt. Robert E. Jones was next in command of A Company. He previously served as a private in the 23rd Regiment Veteran Corps and left to become a 1st Lt. in the 5th USVI. He was on detached duty with the 5th until he joined his company in July 1865. He commanded Company A from July through June 1866 and served as Post Adjutant at Fort Kearny toward the end of that term. Jones mustered out as a 1st Lt. with the regiment on October 11, 1866.[8]

Second Lt A. C. Dutcher was discharged from the 66th Illinois Infantry as a private to join Company A as a 2nd Lt. In the absence of Captain Butler and 1st Lt. Jones, he commanded Company A first in Fort Riley and then at Fort Halleck and Fort Kearny from April through June 1865. Dutcher transferred to Company B in October 1865 and assumed command of the company in January 1866. He rejoined Company A at Fort Halleck in February 1866, until removed from duty there and sent to Camp Collins in Colorado Territory in April 1866. He was shot and wounded while in Denver and died of the wound on April 24, 1866. His killer was not found.[9]

COMPANY B

Captain Thomas Mower McDougall commanded Company B. He was to become the most famous officer or enlisted man who served in the 5th USVI during the Indian Wars in later life. McDougall was born to a military family at Fort Crawford on May 21, 1845, in Prairie du Chien, Wisconsin. His major service during the Civil War was with the 48th U.S. Colored Infantry, where he was a 2nd Lt., Aide-de-Camp and Commissary of Musters for General John B. Hawkins, Assistant Commissary of Musters of the post and defenses of Vicksburg, and commissary of musters of the Colored Infantry Division. He participated in a number of battles in Mississippi, Florida, and Alabama. He left the 48th U.S. Colored Infantry on June 1, 1865, to join the 5th USVI. He joined Company B at Fort Riley on June 9, 1865, and remained in command of the company until December 1865. He served at the Headquarters at Fort Laramie until January 1866 on detached duty, until ordered to Camp Collins in Colorado. He served as Assistant Commissary of Musters at the District of the Platte as of May 21. He commanded the Post of Salinas after duty at Camp Collins, was relieved from that duty on June 20, and went from there to Fort Leavenworth. He moved from Fort Leavenworth to Fort Sedgeworth in Colorado Territory and mustered out on August 9. His role, beyond his command of Company B, was to direct the mustering out of regiments throughout the west. McDougall requested a transfer to the 10th Louisiana African Infantry upon mustering out of the 5th, but this request was not granted. McDougall joined the regular army as a 2nd Lt., by way of the 14th Infantry, and then transferred to the 32nd Infantry on September 21, 1866, with a promotion to 1st Lt. He transferred to the 21st Infantry on April 19, 1869. He joined the 7th Cavalry on December 31, 1872, with a promotion to Captain on December 15, 1875. His military service after the 5th USVI was diverse. McDougall's duty posts ranged from Fort Vancouver in Washington to South Carolina. He survived the Battle of Little Big Horn in Montana Territory with Custer on June 25 and 26, 1876. McDougall commanded Company B at the battle, in charge of the rear guard and the regimental pack train. Company B joined three companies under Major Marcus Reno and three more under Captain Frederick Benteen, who managed to fight off American Indian attacks and survived the battle. Custer and the rest of the regiment that accompanied him did not survive. McDougall continued his army career after Little Big Horn. On July 22, 1890, a retirement board found him physically unable to serve and he retired.[10]

First Lt. Charles E. Coloney served as 1st Lt. of Company B. He joined the 5th USVI from the 40th Missouri Infantry, where he had served as a private. His first post was Fort Riley in command of Company B, before leaving on detached duty to Fort Leavenworth. He was back at Fort Riley from August to November, and then served as the Assistant Inspector General and then Assistant Commissary of Musters for the Colorado Territory in March and April 1866. He then moved on to the District of the Platte to serve as Provost Marshall. Coloney resigned his commission, which was approved by the War Department on June 20, with an honorable discharge. Coloney filed for a pension as an invalid on October 13, 1890, and passed away on June 23, 1905.[11]

Howard Williams was a private in the 2nd Battalion of the Veteran Reserve Corps and mustered into Company B as a 2nd Lt. He was present with his company at Fort Leavenworth and then Fort Riley. He was absent with leave during October and November 1865, and he was absent on detached duty at the Headquarters of the Department of Missouri during December 1865 and January 1866. He returned to his company in February only to be assigned to detached duty again on February 28. He served as the Acting Assistant Adjutant General for the Colonel who was in command during March and April. He spent June to September as Acting Ordnance Officer for the Post of Denver City. He was ordered to Fort Kearny to be mustered out with his regiment in September 1866. He remained at the Post of Denver City to complete his duties until November 17 and mustered out on December 12, 1866.[12]

COMPANY C

Captain George W. Williford was the most battle-tested company commander in the 5th USVI. He had earned the rank of Captain in the 66th Illinois Infantry, which had taken part in major campaigns in the western theater, including the battles at Fort Donelson, Shiloh, and Corinth. The 66th also took part in the Atlanta Campaign and Sherman's March to the Sea. Williford completed his enlistment with the 66th and was a civilian when pressed into service with the 5th USVI; his appointment was confirmed on April 1, 1865. Companies C and D were ordered west ahead of the rest of the command on April 20 and proceeded under those orders, first to Fort Leavenworth and then to the mouth of the Niobrara River in

Nebraska Territory. The companies joined a group of engineers and private citizens at that point on the "Sawyer Wagon Road Expedition" to build a wagon road to Virginia City. The command of the two companies was intended for an officer with the rank of Major, but Williford commanded them as "best Captain," as no one with the rank of Major was present. Captain Williford and his command were ordered to Fort Reno (also referred to as Fort Connor), and he took command of the post on September 17, 1865. He and his men stayed at Fort Reno through the winter. He was at Fort Casper, Dakota Territory, on a medical leave of absence when he died on April 28, 1866. The cause of death was a heart attack, and he had earlier stated that he had suffered from heart problems for the previous four years.[13]

Thomas G. Stull mustered into Company C as a 1st Lt. on April 1, 1865. Stull had served as a private in the 23rd New York Infantry until May 22, 1863, but he joined the 5th USVI as a civilian. He was present with his company through its deployment to accompany the Sawyer Wagon Road Expedition and its assignment at Camp Reno. He commanded the company in the absence of Capt. Williford. Stull remained at Camp Reno until his resignation for "pressing private reasons." His resignation, approved by the War Department on March 14, 1866, became effective on August 3, 1866. He applied for a pension as an invalid on December 17, 1897, and died on July 17, 1900.[14]

Michael M. McCann joined Company C as a 2nd Lt. from the 11th Kansas Infantry, where he had served as a private. McCann mustered into the 5th USVI on April 10, but first served on detached duty at Alton Prison. He served on detached duty in command of Company E (a galvanized Yankee company) until he mustered out with the regiment.[15]

COMPANY D

George M. Bailey joined the 3rd Indiana Cavalry in 1861 as a private. He joined the 1st Alabama Cavalry in 1863 and served as a 1st Lt. He first served that unit as an Acting Adjutant before becoming Aide-de-Camp for General Grenville M. Dodge. He left for civilian life in 1864, after his enlistment ended. General Dodge was Bailey's connection to the 5th USVI, and Bailey mustered into that regiment on April 12, 1865. Enlisted as Captain in command of Company D, Bailey was unable to join his command because of illness. He was sick in quarters by April 18, but he was present with his command in June and August as they accompanied the Sawyer Wagon Road Expedition. Bailey served detached service as Acting Commissary of Musters for the District of Nebraska from September 1865 to July 1866, and he served at the Post of Omaha and Fort Kearny during that time. He commanded Company D during August and September 1866. General Order Number 65 from the Adjutant General's Office of the War Department promoted Bailey to Brevet Major and then Brevet Lt. Colonel on June 22, 1867. He received the promotions for "gallant and meritorious conduct" during an American Indian attack, while escorting the Sawyer Wagon Road Expedition. The promotions were effective from

March 13, 1865. Bailey was an engineering officer for the Union Pacific Rail Road Company in its Omaha office when he requested copies of his promotions. He filed for a pension as an invalid on April 27, 1885.[16]

James M. Marshall was discharged as a private in the 1st Wisconsin Cavalry to join Company D of the 5th USVI as a 1st Lt on April 1, 1865,. He was present with his company during the Sawyer Wagon Road Expedition and when it was posted to Fort Reno on September 17, 1865. He served on detached service as post Adjutant from September 17 through March 1866, when he appointed as Aide-de-Camp to Major General Wheaton, who commanded the District of Nebraska. He filled that role through July 1866, until placed on daily duty at Fort Kearny. He mustered out with his regiment on October 11, 1866. Marshall received promotions from brevet to Captain and then to Major by action of the Adjutant General's Office of the War Department on June 22, 1867. Those promotions, like those granted to Captain Bailey, were retroactive to March 13, 1865. Bailey's widow filed an application for a pension on March 19, 1886.[17]

Daniel M. Dana was a private in the 7th Minnesota Infantry when he was discharged in order to join Company D of the 5th USVI as a 2nd Lt. He was mustered into the 5th on April 5, 1865, and proceeded with his company to Fort Leavenworth and then to the mouth of the Niobrara River, joining Company C as escorts for the Sawyer Wagon Road Expedition. Dana commanded Company D at Fort Reno when companies C and D were ordered to that post. He served as Assistant Commissary Subsistence Officer and Acting Assistant Quartermaster at Fort Reno in March 1866. He returned to command of Company D for June and July, until ordered to Fort Laramie on August 3 and Fort Kearny on August 8 to command Company C, which he did until the regiment mustered out on October 11. Dana, like James M. Marshall, submitted a formal request to remain in the army, but no evidence of continued service was found for either man. Dana filed for a pension as an invalid on June 8, 1908, and passed away on September 5, 1928.[18]

NOTES

INTRODUCTION

1. Dee Brown, *The Galvanized Yankees* (Lincoln, NE: University of Nebraska Press, reprinted 1986).

2. Michelle Tucker Butts, *Galvanized Yankees on the Upper Missouri* (Boulder, CO: University Press of Colorado, 2003), discusses the 1st USVI made up of former Confederate prisoners of war; Richard Nelson Current, *Lincoln's Loyalists: Union Soldiers From the Confederacy* (Boston, MA: Northeastern University Press, 1992), 128–33, devotes a few pages to Union prisoners of war who joined the Confederacy; Robert G. Athearn, *Forts of the Upper Missouri* (Omaha. NE: University of Nebraska Press, 1972), 155–74, devoted a chapter to the subject of Confederate soldiers who changed sides; Carl Alexander Retzloff, "*The First Fruits of a Re-United People": The Loyalty Motivation and Allegiance of the Men of the Second United States Volunteer Infantry Regiment* (Honors Thesis, Department of History, Washington and Lee University, 2015) discusses the 2nd USVI.

3. Brown, Galvanized Yankees.

4. Robert Ryal Miller, *Shamrock and Sword: The Saint Patrick's Battalion in the U.S.-Mexican War* (Norman, OK: University of Oklahoma Press, 1989); Michael Hogan, *The Irish Soldiers of Mexico* (Intercambio Press, 2011); Peter F. Stevens, *The Rogue's March: John Riley and the St. Patrick's Battalion, 1846–1848* (Dulles, VA: Brassey's, 1999).

5. David T. Maul, "Five Butternut Yankees," *Journal of the Illinois State Historical Society*, vol. LVI, no. 2 (Summer, 1963): 177–92.

6. Robert B. Angelovich, *Riding for Uncle Samuel: The Civil War History of the 1st Connecticut Cavalry Volunteers* (Grand Rapids, MI: Inner Workings, Inc, 2014), 262; Third Cavalry, Compiled Service Records of Volunteer Union Soldiers Who Served in Organizations from the State of Maryland, National Archives Records Administration, Microfilm M384, Rolls 32–38.

7. Ahl's Independent Company Delaware Heavy Artillery, Compiled Service Records of Volunteer Union Soldiers Who Served in Organizations from the State of Delaware, National Archives Record Administration, Microfilm M1961, Roll 13.

8. George C. Rable, *Damn Yankees! Demonization and Defiance in the Confederate South* (Baton Rouge, LA: Louisiana State University Press, 2015). This book

provides an excellent study of southern attitudes towards the north before, during, and after the war.

9. See Chapter 4.

10. See Chapter 2.

11. See Chapters 5 and 6.

12. See Chapter 7 and 8.

13. See Chapter 7.

14. Paul G. Avery and Patrick H. Garrow, *Phase III Archaeological Investigations at 38FL2, The Florence Stockade, Florence South Carolina* (Knoxville, TN: MACTEC Engineering and Consulting, Inc., Washington. DC: Submitted to the Department of Veterans Affairs, National Cemetery Administration, Washington, D. C., 2008).

15. See Chapter 2 for a discussion of Civil War prisons.

16. See Chapter 9.

17. See Chapter 3.

CHAPTER 1

1. Charles W. Sanders Jr., *While in the Hands of the Enemy: Military Prisons of the Civil War* (Baton Rouge, LA; Louisiana State University Press, 2005), 13–20.

2. Sanders, While in the Hands of the Enemy, 13–20.

3. Sanders, While in the Hands of the Enemy, 20–22; Stevens, Rogue's March.

4. Miller, Shamrock and Sword; Hogan, Irish Soldiers of Mexico; Stevens, Rogue's March.

5. Brutus (Samuel F. B. Morse), *Foreign Conspiracy Against the Liberties of the United States* (New York, NY: Leavitt, Lord & Co., 1835). Stevens, Rogue's March, 19.

6. Stevens, Rogue's March, 32.

7. Stevens, Rogue's March, 7–17.

8. Stevens, Rogue's March, 32.

9. Stevens, Rogue's March, 47.

10. Stevens, Rogue's March, 81–82.

11. Miller, Shamrock and Sword, 32; Stevens, Rogue's March, 93–96.

12. Stevens, Rogue's March, 106–12.

13. Stevens, Rogue's March, 127; Miller, Shamrock and Sword, 41–42.

14. Stevens, Rogue's March, 140–41.

15. Miller, Shamrock and Sword, 45–47; Stevens, Rogue's March, 155–57.

16. Stevens, Rogue's March, 148, 161–65.

17. Stevens, Rogue's March, 234–42; Miller, Shamrock and Sword, 82–91.

18. Stevens, Rogue's March, 262, 267–68, 293; Miller, Shamrock and Sword, 92–112.

19. Stevens, Rogue's March.

20. Thomas D. Cockrell and Michael B. Ballard, eds., *Chickasaw: A Mississippi Scout for the Union* (Baton Rouge, LA: Louisiana State University Press, 2005); Current, Lincoln's Loyalists; David C. Downing, *A South Divided: Portraits of Dissent in the Confederacy* (Nashville, TN: Cumberland House, 2007); Margaret M. Storey, *Loyalty and Loss: Alabama's Unionists in the Civil War and Reconstruction* (Baton Rouge, LA: Louisiana State University Press, 2004).

21. Current, Lincoln's Loyalists, 218.

22. A number of men who had been born in the north and moved to the south prior to the Civil War chose to fight for the Confederacy. See David Ross Zimring, *To Live and Die in Dixie: Native Northerners Who Fought for the Confederacy* (Knoxville, TN: University of Tennessee Press, 2014) for a discussion of some of those men.

23. Jennifer L. Weber, *Copperheads: The Rise and Fall of Lincoln's Opponents in the North* (New York, NY: Oxford University Press, 2006).

24. James M. McPherson, *The Cause and Comrades: Why Men Fought in the Civil War* (New York, NY: Oxford University Press, 1997).

25. Tyler Anbinder, *Five Points* (New York, NY: Free Press, 2001).

26. Kenneth Radley, *Rebel Watchdogs: The Confederate States Provost Guard* (Baton Rouge, LA: Louisiana State University Press, 1989).

27. Brown, Galvanized Yankees.

28. Maul, "Five Butternut Yankees," 177–92.

29. 10th Tennessee Infantry, Compiled Service Records of Confederate Soldiers Who Served in Organizations from the State of Tennessee, National Archives Records Administration, Records Group 109, Microfilm M268, Rolls 156, 157, and 158; Brown, Galvanized Yankees, 56.

30. Brian Temple, *The Union Prison at Fort Delaware: A Perfect Hell on Earth* (Jefferson, NC: McFarland & Company, Inc., 2002), 76; Lonnie R. Speer, *Portals to Hell* (Mechanisburg, PA: Stackpole Books, 1997), 163; Ahl's Independent Company.

31. Ahl's Independent Company.

32. Capt. Van Den Corput's Co., Light Artillery, Compiled Service Records of Confederate Soldiers Who Served in Organizations from the State of Georgia, National Archives Records Administration, Records Group 109, Microfilm M266, Rolls 116, H-Y.

33. Third Cavalry.

34. Third Cavalry.

35. Allison L. Wilmer, J. H. Jarrett, and Geo. W. F. Vernon, *Maryland Volunteers, War of 1861–65* (Baltimore, MD: Gugginheimer, Weil, & Company. Baltimore, Maryland, 1898); Third Cavalry.

36. Third Cavalry.

37. Angelovich, Riding for Uncle Samuel, 262.

38. Horace J. Morse, General Catalogue of Volunteer Organizations With

Additional Enlistments and Casualties to July 1, 1864 (Hartford, CT: Press of Case, Kirkwood & Company, 1864), 79–106.

39. Angelovich, Riding for Uncle Samuel, 104.

40. Angelovich, Riding for Uncle Samuel, 356–57.

41. Butts, Galvanized Yankees on the Upper Missouri, 222.

42. Donald E. Collins, "War Crimes or Justice? George Pickett and the Mass Execution of Deserters in Civil War Kinston, North Carolina," in *The Art of Command in the Civil War*, ed. Steven E. Woodworth (Lincoln, NE: University of Nebraska Press, 1998), 50–53.

43. 10th Tennessee Infantry.

44. Robert I. Alotta, *Civil War Justice* (Shippensburg, PA: The White Mane Publishing Company, 1989), 121–23; 24th Infantry, Compiled Service Records of Volunteer Union Soldiers Who Served in Organizations from the State of Massachusetts, National Archives Records Administration, Record Group 94, Catalog ID 300398, Roll RG94-CMSR-MA-24INF-Bx2221.

45. Brown, Galvanized Yankees.

46. Brown, Galvanized Yankees, 211–16.

47. Roger Pickenpaugh, *Captives in Blue* (Tuscaloosa, AL: University of Alabama Press, 2013), 146–202.

CHAPTER 2

1. 5th U.S. Volunteers, Compiled Service Records of Former Confederate Soldiers Who Served in the 1st Through the 6th Volunteer Regiments 1864–1866, National Archives Microfilm Publications, Roll 41, Br-Cod; "Reformed Outlaw Dead," *New York Times*, February 24, 1921. The Buzzard Gang was the subject of numerous newspaper articles in the second half of the nineteenth century, see "The Buzzard Gang," *New York Times,* October 8, 1881; "At Buzzard's Roost," *Lancaster Intelligencer,* January 28, 1881; "Two of the Buzzard Boys Are Released," *Lancaster Daily Intelligencer,* October 20, 1884; and "The Buzzard Brothers," *Lancaster Intelligencer,* January 17, 1881. A somewhat inaccurate article was written about the Buzzard Gang, "Among the Outlaws of Pennsylvania," *The Wide World Magazine*, vol. IV, no. 21 (December, 1899): 266–71.

2. 5th U.S. Volunteers; 10th Tennessee Infantry.

3. William B. Hesseltine, ed., *Civil War Prisons* (Kent, OH; The Kent State University Press, 1972), 6.

4. Sanders, While in the Hands of the Enemy, 13–20, 39–42.

5. Speer, Portals to Hell, 20–22.

6. Joseph Wheelan, *Libby Prison Breakout* (New York, NY: Public Affairs, 2010), 32.

7. Speer, Portals to Hell, 92–93.

8. Arch Frederic Blakey, *General John H. Winder, C.S.A.* (Gainesville, FL: University of Florida Press, 1990), 21–27.

9. Blakey, General Winder CSA, 70–74.

10. Blakey, General Winder CSA, 100–105; *Wm. Hugh Robarts, Mexican War Veterans: A Complete Roster of the Regular and Volunteer Troops in the War Between the United States and Mexico, from 1846 to 1848: The Volunteers are Arranged by States, Alphabetically* (Washington DC: Brentano's: Reprinted by Leopold Classic Library, n.d.), 14.

11. Blakey, General Winder CSA, 46–65.

12. Leslie Gene Hunter. *Warden for the Union: General William Hoffman (1807–1884)* (PhD Dissertation, University of Arizona, 1971), 13–14. Hunter's unpublished PhD dissertation remains the only substantive biography of Hoffman, and that work focused on Hoffman during the Civil War.

13. Hunter, Warden for the Union, 13–14.; George Levy, *To Live and Die in Chicago: Confederate Prisoners at Camp Douglas* (Gretna LA: Pelican Publishing Company 2008), 40; Benton McAdams, *Rebels at Rock Island: The Story of a Civil War Prison* (DeKalb, IL: Northern Illinois University Press, 2000), 3–5; Sanders, While in the Hands of the Enemy, 67–68; Robarts, Mexican War Veterans, 22.

14. Hunter, Warden for the Union, 18–44

15. Levy, To Live and Die in Chicago.

16. Hattie Lou Winslow and Joseph R. H. Moore, *Camp Morton, 1861–1865: Indianapolis Prison Camp* (Indianapolis IN: Indiana Historical Society, 1940).

17. Sanders, While in the Hands of the Enemy, 96–97.

18. Hunter, Warden for the Union, 95.

19. Hunter, Warden for the Union, 18–44.

20. Dale Fetzer and Bruce Mowday, *Unlikely Allies: Fort Delaware's Prison Community in the Civil War* (Mechanisburg, PA: Stackpole Books, 2000).

21. McAdams, Rebels at Rock Island.

22. Michael P. Gray *The Business of Captivity: Elmira and Its Civil War Prison* (Kent, OH: Kent State University Press, 2001); James I. Robertson Jr., "The Scourge of Elmira." in *Civil War Prisons*, ed. William B. Hesseltine, 80–97.

23. Sanders, While in the Hands of the Enemy, 101–2, 171–72, 246.

24. Sanders, While in the Hands of the Enemy, 122.

25. Speer, Portals to Hell, 97–105.

26. James M. Gillispie, *Andersonvilles of the North* (Denton, TX: University of North Texas Press, 2008), 244–45.

27. Speer, Portals to Hell, 104–5.

28. Sanders, While in the Hands of the Enemy, 160.

29. Martinez, Life and Death in Civil War Prisons, 54–55.

30. Hunter, Warden for the Union, 144.

31. Hunter, Warden for the Union, 165.

32. Sanders, While in the Hands of the Enemy, 122; Speer, Portals to Hell, 165.

33. Luther S. Dickey, *History of the 103rd Regiment: Pennsylvania Veteran Volunteer Infantry* (Chicago, IL: by the Author, 1910), 272–74; Hunter, Warden for the Union, 177.

34. Martinez, Life and Death, 55.

35. Speer, Portals to Hell, 9–10.

36. William O. Bryant, *Cahaba Prison and the Sultana Disaster* (Tuscaloosa, AL: University of Alabama Press, 1990).

37. Blakey, General Winder CSA, 147, 158.

38. Blakey, General Winder CSA, 168.

39. Sandra V. Parker, *Richmond's Civil War Prisons* (Lynchburg, VA.: H. E. Howard, Inc,. 1990), 59.

40. Blakey, General Winder CSA, 170–71; Roger Pickenpaugh, *Captives in Blue: The Civil War Prisons of the Confederacy* (Tuscaloosa, AL.: The University of Alabama Press, 2013), 119.

41. Frances H. Casstevens, *George W. Alexander and Castle Thunder: a Confederate Prison and its Commandant* (Jefferson, NC: Macfarland and Company, Inc., 2004), 48–50.

42. Casstevens, George W. Alexander and Castle Thunder, 53.

43. Casstevens, George W. Alexander and Castle Thunder, 79–80.

44. Casstevens, George W. Alexander and Castle Thunder, 107–24.

45. Casstevens, George W. Alexander and Castle Thunder, 128–31.

46. Casstevens, George W. Alexander and Castle Thunder, 147, 149, 166.

47. Wheelan, Libby Prison Breakout, 31–33.

48. Wheelan, Libby Prison Breakout, 33.

49. Wheelan, Libby Prison Breakout, 74–75.

50. Miscellaneous Records of Federal Prisoners of War of the United States Army Who Escaped from Southern Prisons, Deserted to the Rebel Army, Illegally Paroled by the Rebel Army, and the Survivors of the Sultana, Vol. 1, National Archives Microfilm Publications, Roll 3, Target 2; Alphabetical List of Federal Prisoners on the Sultana, including those who survived or perished, Record Group 240, Entry 109, vol. 1; Lorien Foote and Andrew Fialka, "Fugitive Federals: A Digital Humanities Investigation of Escaped Union Prisoners," (August 2018), www.ehistory.org/projects/fugitive-federals.html; https://usg.maps.arcgis.com/apps/MapJournal/index.html?appid=34fd594c6cc44615 85e905588a6a477b, accessed December 26, 2018.

51. Wheelan, Libby Prison Breakout, 157–87. The prisoners who escaped from Libby Prison, for the most part, were able to make their way to the relatively close Union lines on the Virginia Peninsula. Those who escaped from prisons further to the south often had to travel long distances under very difficult conditions. The hardships faced by many of those escapees late in the war have been documented in Lorien Foote, *The Yankee Plague* (Chapel Hill, NC: The University of North Carolina Press, 2006).

52. Wheelan, Libby Prison Breakout, 218–25.

53. Speer, Portals to Hell, 83. *Richmond Inquirer* (May 13, 1862), 1.

54. Parker, Richmond's Civil War Prisons, 14–15, 19.

55. Parker, Richmond's Civil War Prisons, 23.; "Belle Isle," *Richmond Inquirer* (May 16, 1863), 1.

56. Blakey, General Winder CSA, 168; Parker, Richmond's Civil War Prisons, 59.

57. Parker, Richmond's Civil War Prisons, 65.

58. Speer, Portals to Hell, 259–62.

59. William Marvel, *Andersonville: The Last Depot* (Chapel Hill, NC: The University of North Carolina Press, 1994), 238.

60. Robert H. Kellogg, *Life and Death in Rebel Prisons* (Hartford, CN: 1868); Warren Lee Goss, *The Soldier's Story* (Boston, MA: Lee & Shepard, 1866; Reprinted by Digital Scanning, Inc., Scituate MA, 2001); Mark A. Snell, ed., *Dancing Along the Deadline* (Novato, CA: Presidio Press, 1996); Glenn Robbins, *They Have Left Us Here to Die* (Kent, OH: The Kent State University Press, 2011). These are just a few of the many books published by former inmates at Andersonville. Andersonville was the most well known of the Civil War prisons, and demands for firsthand accounts from former prisoners was high by the late nineteenth century.

61. Ovid Futch, "Prison Life at Andersonville," in *Civil War Prisons,* ed. William B. Hesseltine (Kent OH: The Kent State University Press, 1962); Ovid Futch, *History of Andersonville Prison* (Gainesville, FL: The University of Florida Press, 1968).; Ovid Futch, *History of Andersonville*, rev. ed. (Gainesville, FL: The University of Florida Press, 2011); Marvel, Andersonville; Speer, Portals to Hell; Sanders, While in the Hands of the Enemy; Robert Scott Davis, *Andersonville Civil War Prison* (Charleston, SC: The History Press, 2010); Pickenpaugh, Captives in Blue; The histories authored by Ovid Futch and William Marvel remain the most comprehensive treatments of the prison to date.

62. Benjamin G. Cloyd, *Haunted by Atrocity: Civil War Prisons in American Memory* (Baton Rouge, LA: Louisiana State University Press, 2010). Cloyd does an excellent job in this book detailing the aftereffects of the horrors of Civil War prisons, primarily Andersonville, on the collective memory of our society that has lingered to this day.

63. Futch, History of Andersonville, rev. ed., 19–44.

64. Futch, History of Andersonville, rev. ed., 46–47.

65. Futch, History of Andersonville, rev. ed., 17–18, 46–47.

66. Marvel, Andersonville, 53.

67. Futch, History of Andersonville, rev. ed., 5, 19, 22.

68. Marvel, Andersonville, 169–70.

69. Futch, History of Andersonville, rev. ed., 22, 34, 108–9.

70. Speer, Portals to Hell, 264.

71. Futch, History of Andersonville, rev. ed., 14, 87–88.

72. Albert H. Ledoux, *The Florence Stockade* (Gallitzin, PA: Published by the Author, 2015), 3, 5, 11. Father Ledoux's landmark study of the Florence Stockade was the result of many years of archival research and research on published and unpublished accounts left by former prisoners and remains the most comprehensive study of the Florence Stockade that has been published to date.

73. Futch, History of Andersonville, rev. ed., 112, 116.

74. Ledoux, Florence Stockade, 5, 18, 23, 39.

75. Ledoux, Florence Stockade, 22–27.

76. United States War Department, The War of the Rebellion: A Compilation of the Official Records of the Union and Confederate Armies (hereafter cited as OR), II, VII, 1097–99; Snell, Dancing Along the Deadline, 62; Ledoux, Florence Stockade, 76.

77. Kellogg, Life and Death in Rebel Prisons, 318.

78. Andrews, The South Since the War, 94.

79. Ledoux, Ledoux, Florence Stockade, 115–16.

80. Ledoux, Florence Stockade, 115–16; Kellogg, Life and Death in Rebel Prisons, 326.

81. Tracy Power, "The Confederate Prison Stockade at Florence, South Carolina," (unpublished manuscript, 1991).

82. Miscellaneous Records of Federal Prisoners of War.

83. G. Wayne King, "Death Camp at Florence," *Civil War Times Illustrated*, January 1974, 36.

84. OR II VIII, 855; OR II VII, 900.

85. OR II VII, 972–74.

86. Martinez, Life and Death, 169–70; Snell, Dancing Along the Deadline, 116. Goss, Soldier's Story, 225–26.

87. "Lieut. James Barrett Answers Last Call," *Atlanta Constitution*, September 6, 1910, 1.

88. Florence Military Records, Records of the Military Department, Office of the Confederate Historian, Florence Military Prison Records, 1866–1865, South Carolina Department of Archives and History, Columbia, SC.

89. Kellogg, Life and Death in Rebel Prisons, 318.

90. Andrews, The South Since the War, 95.

91. Andrews, The South Since the War, 93.

92. Thomas J. Eccles. October 7, 1864.

93. Ledoux, Florence Stockade.

94. John L. Hoster, "Adventures of a Soldier," Partial Diary, October 1864-March 1865, Unpublished Diary in Possession of Ms. Ruth G. Deike, Vienna, VA; Anon. National Register of Historic Places File for the Stockade, South Carolina Department of Archives and History, Columbia, SC.

95. Avery and Garrow, Archaeological Investigations. The archaeological

excavations covered nine acres adjacent to and immediately north of the Stockade. The investigations were conducted for the National Cemetery Administration in an area planned for expansion of the Florence National Cemetery. This was the first, and to date only, substantive excavation of a guard camp associated with a Civil War prison.

96. Kellogg, Life and Death in Rebel Prisons 323–25, Snell, Dancing Along the Deadline, 105.

97. Power, "Confederate Prison Stockade," 16.

98. James F. Rusling Report to Brevet Major General M.C. Meigs, Quartermaster General,Office of the Inspector, Quartermaster Department Charleston, S.C., May 27, 1866, RG-92, E-576, Box 27, National Archives, Washington, DC.

99. Ledoux, Florence Stockade, 332.

100. Florence Military Records.

101. Thomas J. Eccles. October 28, 1864, November 24, 1864. Andrews, The South Since the War, 93.

102. Thomas J. Eccles. October 7, 1864.

103. Avery and Garrow, Archaeological Investigations, 113–27, 216–17.

104. OR II VII, 1100, 1197.

105. OR II VII, 121, 218, 225, 451–34.

106. Ledoux, Florence Stockade, 279.

107. Avery and Garrow, Archaeological Investigations, 233–49.

108. Speer, Portals to Hell, 278.

109. OR II VII, 509, 514, 565, 593, 773.

110. John K. Derden, *The Story of Camp Lawton* (Macon, GA: Mercer University Press, 2012), 7.

111. OR II VII, 579.

112. OR II VII, 841, 854, 869–70.

113. OR II VII, 955–56, 993.

114. Derden, Story of Camp Lawton, 52–53.

115. Derden, Story of Camp Lawton.

116. Charles F. Bryan Jr. and Nelson D. Lankford, eds., *Eye of the Storm: A Civil War Odyssey* (New York, NY: The Free Press, 2000); Charles F. Bryan Jr., James C. Kelly, and Nelson D. Lankford, eds., *Images from the Storm: 300 Images from the Author of Eye of the Storm* (New York, NY: The Free Press, 2001).

117. William Giles, ed., Disease, Starvation & Death: Personal Accounts of Camp Lawton (Lulu Press, 2005).

118. Derden, Story of Camp Lawton, 65–68.

119. Derden, Story of Camp Lawton, 204.

120. OR II VII, 1130–31; 1137, 1138, 1145.

121. Derden, Story of Camp Lawton, 73–74, 79.

122. Derden, Story of Camp Lawton, 75–81.

123. OR II VII, 1113–14.

124. Derden, Story of Camp Lawton, 204.

125. OR II VII, 869, 993.

126. Derden, Story of Camp Lawton, 102.

127. U.S. Congress, House of Representatives, Report on the Treatment of Prisoners of War by the Rebel Authorities During the War of the Rebellion to Which are Appended the Testimony Taken by the Committee and the Official Documents and Statistics, etc., 40th Cong., 3rd sess. 1969, Rep. No. 45, 750–51.

128. Miscellaneous Records of Federal Prisoners of War.

129. OR II VII, 1145.

130. Speer, Portals to Hell, 279–80.

131. Derden, Story of Camp Lawton, 155–56.

132. Louis A. Brown, *The Salisbury Prison: A Case Study of Confederate Military Prisons 1861–1865* (Wilmington, NC: Broadfoot Publishing Company. 1992), 17–18.

133. Brown, Salisbury Prison, 17, 19, 71–72.

134. Speer, Portals to Hell, 33.

135. Brown, Salisbury Prison, 27–28.

136. Brig. General Archibald C. Godwin, Compiled Service Records of Confederate General and Staff Officers and Nonregimental Enlisted Men, National Archives Microfilm Publications, Roll 108, Go-Goo; Brown, Salisbury Prison, 28.

137. Speer, Portals to Hell, 209.

138. Casstevens, George W. Alexander and Castle Thunder, 133.

139. Colonel John A. Gilmer, Jr, 27th North Carolina Infantry, Compiled Service Records of Confederate Soldiers Who Served in Organizations from the State of North Carolina, Record Group 15, Roll F-He, National Archives Microfilm Publications, Washington, DC.

140. OR II VII, 401.

141. Gilmer, 27th North Carolina Infantry.

142. OR II VII, 401.

143. OR II VII, 586–87.

144. OR II VII, 674.

145. Speer, Portals to Hell, 210.

146. OR II VII, 1127.

147. OR II VII, 1128–30.

148. Miscellaneous Records of Federal Prisoners of War.

149. For a discussion of the incarceration of southern civilians by the Confederate government see, Mark E. Neely Jr., *Southern Rights: Political Prisoners and the Myth of Confederate Constitutionalism* (Charlottesville, VA: The University of Virginia Press, 1999).

150. "The Escaped Correspondents; Safe Arrival at Nashville of Mssers. Richardson and Brown of the Tribune, Accompanied by Mr. Davis, Correspondent of the Cincinnati Gazette. Escaped Union Prisoners at Knoxville." *New*

York Times, January 17, 1865; Brown, Salisbury Prison, 98; Foote, Yankee Plague, 143–47.

151. OR II VII, 1230.

152. OR II VII, 1222.

153. OR II VII, 1240. Brown, Salisbury Prison, 29.

154. OR II VIII, 167.

155. OR II VIII, 198, 179.

156. OR II VIII, 198, 211–12.

157. OR II VIII, 245–49.

158. OR II VIII, 264–65.

159. OR II VIII, 455.

160. OR II VIII, 411–13.

161. OR II VIII, 476.

162. OR II VIII, 956–60; Marvel, Andersonville, 79, 247.

CHAPTER 3

1. General Order No. 26, March 1, 1864, General Orders Nos. 1–87, Volume 4, 1864, National Archives Microfilm Publications; see Albert Burton Moore, *Conscription and Conflict in the Confederacy* (Columbia, SC: The University of South Carolina Press, 1996) for a discussion of conscription and the manpower crisis in the Confederate Army that became more acute as the war progressed. This source, first published in 1926, remains the definitive source on Confederate conscription.

2. Patrick Cleburne's Proposal to Arm Slaves, January 2, 1864, American Battlefield Trust, https://www.battlefields.org/learn/primary-sources/patrick-cleburnes-proposal-arm-slaves-0.

3. James M. McPherson, *For Cause and Comrades: Why Men Fought in the Civil War* (New York, NY: Oxford University Press, 1997), 171.

4. OR II VII, 1099.

5. Hoster, "Adventures of a Soldier," October 1864-March 1865.

6. Goss, Soldier's Story, 322–23.

7. Ledoux, Florence Stockade; OR II VII, 1098.

8. "Morning Report", Florence Military Records, Records of the Military Department, Office of the Confederate Historian, Florence Military Prison Records (Columbia, SC: South Carolina Department of Archives and History, 1866–1865); OR II VII, 1099.

9. OR II VIII, 821–22.

10. Marvel, Andersonville, 147–49; Futch, History of Andersonville, 45.

11. OR IV III II, 694.

12. OR I XL III, 781; OR I XLII II, 529; 1200. OR I XLIII II, 29.

13. George C. Rabble, *Damn Yankees! Demonization and Defiance in the Confederate South* (Baton Rouge, LA: Louisiana State University Press, 2015), 37–39.

14. Letter from Assistant Adjutant General Jno. Blair Hoge to Adjutant General Samuel Cooper, November 21, Tucker's Regiment, Compiled Service Records of Confederate Soldiers Who Served in Organizations Raised Directly by the Confederate Government, Record Group 109, Microfilm 258, Roll 76, E-Z, National Archives Record Administration; Letter From Adjutant General S. Cooper to James A, Seddon, November 21, 1864, Records of Confederate War Department Staff Departments, Confederate Adjutant General Outgoing Correspondence, Record Group 109, Microfilm M627, Pages 196–97, National Archives Records Administration.

15. Brigadier General Zebulon York, Compiled Service Records of Confederate General and Staff Officers and Nonregimental Enlisted Men Who Did Not Belong to Any Company or Comparable Unit or Special Corps, Record Group 109. Microfilm 331. Wu-Z, National Archives Records Administration.

16. Lynda Laswell Crist, ed., *The Papers of Jefferson Davis, Volume 11* (Baton Rouge, LA: Louisiana State University Press, 2003), 100–101.

17. OR II VII, 973–74.

18. OR II VII, 1014; Brooks Battalion, Compiled Service Records of Confederate Soldiers Who Served in Organizations Raised Directly by the Confederate Government, Record Group 109, Microfilm 258, Roll 72, National Archives Record Administration.

19. First Artillery, Compiled Service Records of Volunteer Union Soldiers Who Served in Organizations from the State of South Carolina, Microfilm Publication 267, Rolls 67–64, National Archives Microfilm Publications.

20. "8th New York Cavalry," Annual Report of the Adjutant General of the State of New York, vol. 2 (1893), 1105.

21. Telegram From Gen. W. J. Hardee to Adjutant General S. Cooper, November 7, 1864.

22. OR II VII, 1120–21.

23. William A. Bowers Jr., comp., *The 47th Georgia Volunteer Infantry Regiment* (Global Authors Publications, 2013), 108–12, 132.

24. Forty-Seventh Infantry, Compiled Service Records of Volunteer Union Soldiers Who Served in Organizations from the State of Georgia, Records Group 109, Microfilm M266, Rolls 484–487, National Archives Records Administration.

25. James Harvey McKee, *Back in War Times: History of the 144th New York Volunteer Infantry* (Unadilla, NY: Lieut. Horace E. Bailey Publisher, 1908), 200.

26. Luis F. Emilio, *History of the Fifty-Fourth Regiment of Massachusetts Volunteer Infantry* (Boston, MA: The Boston Book Company, 1894), 255–56.

27. Barry Sheehy and Cindy Wallace, *Savannah: Immortal City. Volume I Civil War Savannah* (Austin, TX: Emerald Book Company), 430–31.

28. Capt. Daniell's Battery, Compiled Service Records of Confederate Soldiers Who Served in Organizations Raised Directly by the Confederate Government,

Record Group 109, Microfilm M266, Roll 315, National Archives Record Administration.

29. Charles Colcock Jones, *The Siege of Savannah in December, 1864, and the Confederate Operations in Georgia and the Third Military District of South Carolina during General Sherman's March from Atlanta to the Sea*: Electronic Edition, Academic Affairs Library, UNC-CH University of North Carolina at Chapel Hill, 1998, http://closouthunc.edu/fpn/JonesCharles/jones.html.

30. Capt. Daniell's Battery.

31. Joseph Liptrot, Pension Applications for Service in the U.S. Army Between 1861 and 1900, Grouped According to the Units in which the Veteran Served, Record Group 15, T289, Roll _pub57_synthroll 1164_.

32. OR II VIII, 1086.

33. Tucker's Regiment.

34. Tucker's Regiment.

35. Major Garnett Andrews, Compiled Service Records of Confederate General and Staff Officers and Nonregimental Enlisted Men Who Did Not Belong to Any Company or Comparable Unit or Special Corps, Record Group 109, Microfilm 331, Anderson, R-Andr, National Archives Records Administration.

36. OR II VII, 821; 8th Confederate Infantry, Compiled Service Records of Confederate Soldiers Who Served in Organizations Raised Directly by the Confederate Government, Record Group 109, Microfilm M258, Roll 0067, National Archives Record Administration.

37. Garnett Andrews, Undated typescript on file with the Andrews Papers at the University of Tennessee-Chattanooga; G. Brown Goode, *Virginia Cousins: A Study of the Ancestry and Posterity of John Goode of Whitby A Virginia Colonist of the Seventeenth Century* (Richmond, VA: J. W. Randolph & English, 1888).

38. 8th Confederate Infantry.

39. Brigadier General Zebulon York.

40. OR IV III II, 822–23, 824–25.

41. OR IV III II, 1029–30. Brigadier General Zebulon York.

42. Fourteenth Infantry. Compiled Service Records of Volunteer Union Soldiers Who Served in Organizations from the State of Louisiana. National Archives Records Administration, Records Group 109, Microfilm M320, Roll 261. Mi-N.

43. Letter From Adjutant General S. Cooper to James A, Seddon, November 21, 1864.

44. Letter From Adjutant General S. Cooper to James A, Seddon, November 21, 1864; 20th Infantry, Compiled Service Records of Volunteer Union Soldiers Who Served in Organizations from the State of Louisiana, Records Group 109, Microfilm M320, Roll 315, National Archives Records Administration.

45. OR IV III II, 694.

46. 10th Infantry, Compiled Service Records of Volunteer Confederate Soldiers

Who Served in Organizations from the State of Tennessee, Records Group 109, Microfilm M268, Roll 0156. A-Z, National Archives Records Administration; 15th Infantry, Compiled Service Records of Volunteer Confederate Soldiers Who Served in Organizations from the State of Tennessee, Records Group 109, Microfilm M268, Roll 0178, National Archives Records Administration.

47. 10th Tennessee Infantry.

48. 10th Tennessee Infantry.

49. Telegram from Major G. S. Buford to General Beauregard, November 2, 1864, George W. Brent Papers 1863–1865, Subseries 55-X-2, Box 12, Folder 3: Telegram Book 1864 October 18–1865 March 10, Louisiana Historical Association Collection, Manuscript Collection 55, Louisiana Research Collection, Howard-Tilton Memorial Library, Tulane University, New Orleans, Louisiana.

50. Crist, Papers of Jefferson Davis, 256.

51. Giles, Disease, Starvation & Death.

52. Kellogg, Life and Death in Rebel Prisons, 392; John B. Vaughter (as Sgt. Oates), *Life and Death in Dixie* (Chicago, IL: Central Book Concern, 1880), 139.

53. James McClean, *John Cain's Andersonville Testimony*, http://www.2mass.reunioncivilwar.com/References/cains_andersonville.htm, Accessed September 6, 2018; Record of Enlisted Federals Who Joined the Federal Army, Records Reflecting the April 27, 1865, Explosion of the Steamer "Sultana", Including Lists of Those Aboard the Ship, Record Group 249, Microfilm M1878, National Archives Records Administration.

54. OR II VII, 1113–14.

55. Marvel, Andersonville, 223.

56. Speer, Portals to Hell, 279–80.

57. Marvel, Andersonville, 223.

58. Michael Dougherty, *Prison Diary of Michael Dougherty: Late Company B, 13th., PA. Cavalry While Confined in Pemberton's, Barrett's, Libby, Andersonville, and Other Southern Prisons Sole Survivor of 127 of his Regiment Captured the Same Time, 122 Dying in Andersonville* (Bristol, PA: Charles A. Dougherty Printer, 1908), 65.

59. Register of Departures of Federal Prisoners of War Confined at Andersonville, GA, February 1864 to April 1865, Record Group 249, Microfilm M1303, National Archives Records Administration.

60. Register of Departures of Federal Prisoners of War Confined at Andersonville.

61. Thirteenth Infantry, Compiled Service Records of Volunteer Union Soldiers Who Served in Organizations from the State of Louisiana, Records Group 109, Microfilm M320, Roll 251, S-Tr, National Archives Records Administration.

62. OR IV III II, 1011–12.

63. Bryant, Cahaba Prison, 65.

64. See J. Mathew Gallman, *Defining Duty in the Civil War: Personal Choice,*

Popular Culture, and the Union Home Front (Chapel Hill, NC: The University of North Carolina Press, 2015), for a discussion of efforts to instill a sense of duty and patriotism in the troops as they went off to war; also see Eugene Converse Murdock, *Patriotism Limited, 1862–1865: The Civil War Draft and Bounty System* (Kent, OH: The Kent State University Press, 1967) for a discussion of the Civil War draft and bounty systems in New York State and the corruption that was rampant as a result.

65. Ella Lonn, *Desertion During the Civil War* (Big Byte Books, 1928, reprinted 2016), 140–41.

66. OR I LIII, 1054

67. Alotta, Civil War Justice.

CHAPTER 4

1. Brooks Battalion.

2. U.R. Brooks, ed., Memoirs of the War of Secession From the Original Manuscripts of Johnson Hagood (Columbia, SC: The State Company, 1910), 472.

3. Norman Vincent Turner, *Confederate Military Executions (Soldiers Shot By the Firing Squad) at Savannah, Georgia, During the Civil War, Which led to the Trial of General Hugh W. Mercer* (Springfield, GA: Published by the Author, 2007), 34–35.

4. Hoster, "Adventures of a Soldier," October 1864-March 1865.

5. John K. Burlingame, comp., *History of the Fifth Regiment of Rhode Island Heavy Artillery During Three and a Half Service in North Carolina, January 1862-June 1865* (Providence, RI: Snow & Farnham Printers and Publishers, 1892), 205–29; Case File 3632, Hugh Mercer, Case Files of Investigations by Levi C. Turner and Lafayette C. Baker 1861–1866. Turner Files 3601–700. National Archives Records Administration, Civil War Subversion Files, Record Group 94, Microfilm M794, Roll 0102; Turner, Confederate Military Executions, 26.

6. Charles Geissler, Alphabetical card index to the compiled service records of volunteer Union soldiers belonging to units from the State of New Jersey, Record Group 94, M550, Roll 0009, National Archives Records Administration Microfilm; Case File 3632, Hugh Mercer; Turner, Confederate Military Executions, 29.

7. Kellogg, Life and Death in Rebel Prisons, 319–320.

8. Thomas J. Eccles 1864–1865 "From the State Reserves." Articles Submitted to the *Yorkville Enquirer*, York, South Carolina from Florence Stockade.

9. Stevens, Rogue's March.

10. Vincent F. Martin, 313; OR II VII, 900.

11. Brooks Battalion, National Park Service, *Soldiers and Sailors Database*. Accessed February 10, 2018, http://www.itd.nps.gov/cwss/Soldier_Results.cfm.

12. Incomplete and Updated List of Federal Prisoners With Birthplace, Name, Unit, and Company (October 1864-Februart 1865). Florence Military Records,

Records of the Military Department, Office of the Confederate Historian, Florence Military Prison Records (Columbia, SC: South Carolina Department of Archives and History, 1866–1865).

13. OR II VII, 900.

14. U.S. Congress, House of Representatives, Testimony of Warren Lee Goss, 1869, Report on the Treatment of Prisoners of War by the Rebel Authorities During the War of the Rebellion, Reports on Committees of the House of Representatives Made During the Third Session of the Fortieth Congress, 983.

15. John H. Cosart, Brooks Battalion, April 1875, *Home Mail*, Vol. 2, No. 4, pp. 50–52; Miscellaneous Records of Federal Prisoners of War of the United States Army Who Escaped from Southern Prisons, Deserted to the Rebel Army, Illegally Paroled by the Rebel Army, and the Survivors of the Sultana, Vol. 1. National Archives Records Administration, Roll 3, Target 2; Alphabetical List of Federal Prisoners on the Sultana, including those who survived or perished, Record Group 249, Entry 109, Vol. 1; John H. Cosart, New York Regiment 27, Company B. Civil War Pensions Index, Record Group 109, Publication T289, National Archives Records Administration; U.S. Bureau of the Census, *Eighth Census of the United States*, 1860 Population Schedules, Wayne County, Lyons Village, New York, Records Group 29, Microfilm M653, Roll 877, National Archives Records Administration; *Ninth Census of the United States*, 1870 Population Schedules, Wayne County, Lyons Village, New York, Records Group 29, Microfilm M1280, Roll 877, National Archives Records Administration; *Tenth Census of the United States*, 1890 Population Schedules, Wayne County, Lyons Village, New York, Records Group 29, Microfilm 55, National Archives Records Administration; Florence Military Records.

16. Cosart, Brooks Battalion, April 1875, 50.

17. Eighth Battalion Confederate Infantry, Compiled Service Records of Confederate Soldiers Who Served in Organizations Raised Directly by the Confederate Government, Record Group 109, Microfilm 258, Roll 67, National Archives Records Administration.

18. Brooks Battalion.

19. See Joanne B. Freeman, *The Field of Blood: Violence in Congress and the Road to the Civil War* (New York, NY: Picador Farrar, Straus and Giroux, 2018) for an excellent discussion of the Brooks caning and other acts of violence in Congress that heightened tensions between North and South prior to the war.

20. D. Augustus Dickert, *History of Kershaw's Brigade* (Elberton, SC: Elbert C. Aull Company, 1899), 481–82.

21. John Hampton Brooks, Seventh South Carolina Infantry, Compiled Service Records of Confederate Soldiers Who Served in Organizations from the State of South Carolina, Records Group 109, Microfilm M267, Roll 213, National Archives Records Administration.

22. Brooks, Memoirs of the War of Secession, 310–12.

23. Dickert, History of Kershaw's Brigade, 481–82; Vincent F. Martin, 327.

24. Vincent F. Martin, 325, 327.

25. Vincent F. Martin, 325, 327.

26. Vincent F. Martin, 327.

27. Vincent F. Martin, 314, 325, 327; Texas Bar Association, *Proceedings of the 24th Annual Session of the Texas Bar Association* (Austin, TX: Printed By Order of the Association, 1905), 64–66.

28. Brooks Battalion.

29. Brooks Battalion; Major General James H. Trapier, Compiled Service Records of Confederate Officers and Enlisted Men Who Did Not Belong to Any Particular Regiment, Separate Company of Comparable Unit, or Special Corps, Record Group 109, Microfilm M331, Roll 250, Tr-Tro, National Archives Records Administration.

30. Vincent F. Martin, 314, 325, 327.

31. Tucker's Regiment, Confederate Infantry, Compiled Service Records of Confederate Soldiers Who Served in Organizations Raised Directly by the Confederate Government, Record Group 109, Microfilm 258, Roll 79, National Archives Records Administration.

32. Sixth Cavalry, Compiled Service Records of Confederate Soldiers Who Served in Organizations from the State of South Carolina, Records Group 109, Microfilm M267, Roll 39, National Archives Records Administration; Brooks, Memoirs of the War of Secession.

33. Cosart, Brooks Battalion, April 1875, 50.

34. Cosart, Brooks Battalion, April 1875, 50.

35. Hoster, "Adventures of a Soldier," October 1864-March 1865; National Register of Historic Places File for the Stockade, South Carolina Department of Archives and History, 118, 120–21.

36. Cosart, Brooks Battalion, April 1875, 52.

37. Vincent F. Martin, 50–51.

38. Cosart, Brooks Battalion, April 1875, 51; N.C. Hughes Jr., "Hardee's Defense of Savannah," *Georgia Historical Quarterly*, Volume XLVII, No. 1, 49–50.

39. H. W. Mercer, Letter of August 11, 1865, from Captain George A Mercer to Brevet Major General J. H. Brannon, Compiled Service Records of Confederate Officers and Enlisted Men Who Did Not Belong to Any Particular Regiment, Separate Company of Comparable Unit, or Special Corps, Record Group 109, Microfilm M347, Roll 272, National Archives Records Administration.

40. Cosart, Brooks Battalion, April 1875, 51; Miscellaneous Records of Federal Prisoners of War of the United States Army Who Escaped from Southern Prisons, Deserted to the Rebel Army, Illegally Paroled by the Rebel Army, and the Survivors of the Sultana, Vol. 1. National Archives Records Administration,

Roll 3, Target 2; Alphabetical List of Federal Prisoners of the Sultana, including those who survived or perished. Record Group 249, Entry 109, Vol. 1; Foote and Fialka, "Fugitive Federals."

41. Cosart, Brooks Battalion, April 1875, 51; Turner, Confederate Military Executions, 26.

42. Turner, Confederate Military Executions, 15.

43. Vincent F. Martin, 315.

44. Cosart, Brooks Battalion, April 1875, 52.

45. Vincent F. Martin, 315.

46. Case File 3632, Hugh Mercer; Turner, Confederate Military Executions, 26–27.

47. Cosart, Brooks Battalion, April 1875, 52.

48. Miscellaneous Records of Federal Prisoners of War of the United States Army Who Escaped from Southern Prisons, Deserted to the Rebel Army, Illegally Paroled by the Rebel Army, and the Survivors of the Sultana.

49. Miscellaneous Records of Federal Prisoners of War of the United States Army Who Escaped from Southern Prisons, Deserted to the Rebel Army, Illegally Paroled by the Rebel Army, and the Survivors of the Sultana.

50. Case File 3632, Hugh Mercer.

51. Cosart, Brooks Battalion, April 1875, 51.

52. Case File 2718. Francis C. Schrenk. Case Files of Investigations by Levi C. Turner and Lafayette C. Baker 1861–1866. Turner Files 3601–3700. National Archives Records Administration, Civil War Subversion Files, Record Group 94, Microfilm M797.

53. Vincent F. Martin, 316.

54. Vincent F. Martin, 316.

55. Joseph Sinner, Unfiled Papers and Slips Belonging in Confederate Compiled Service Records, Record Group 109, Microfilm M347, Roll 363, National Archives Records Administration.

56. Joseph Sinner; 4th Infantry, Index to Compiled Service Records of Volunteer Union Soldiers Who Served in Organizations from the State of New Hampshire, Record Group 94, Microfilm M548, Roll 11, National Archives Records Administration.

57. Joseph Sinner; Weekly Returns of Enlistments at Naval Rendezvous Jan. 6, 1855 to August 8, 1891, Record Group 24, Microfilm 1953, Roll 24, National Archives Records Administration.

58. Vincent F. Martin, 316.

59. Vincent F. Martin, 317.

60. Vincent F. Martin, 318.

61. H. W. Mercer. Case File 2718. Francis C. Schrenk.

62. Vincent F. Martin, 318.

63. Vincent F. Martin, 319–21.

64. Cosart, Brooks Battalion, April 1875, 51.

65. Case File 3632, Hugh Mercer.

66. Cosart, Brooks Battalion, April 1875, 51; Case File 3632, Hugh Mercer; Vincent F. Martin, 322.

67. Vincent F. Martin, 322.

68. Report of the Adjutant General (New York) for the Year 1894, Volume V (Albany, NY: James B. Lyon State Printer, 1895), 769.

69. Case File 2718. Francis C. Schrenk.

70. Vincent F. Martin, 322.

71. Horace J. Morse, *General Catalogue of Connecticut Volunteer Organizations With Additional Enlistments and Casualties to July 1, 1864* (Hartford, CT: Lockwood and Company, 1864), 516; Manuel Fernandez, Index to Compiled Service Records of Volunteer Union Soldiers Who Served in Organizations from the State of Connecticut, Record Group 94, Microfilm 535, Roll 5.

72. Vincent F. Martin, 322. Brooks Battalion.

73. Cosart, Brooks Battalion, April 1875, 52.

74. Vincent F. Martin, 322; Case File 2718. Francis C. Schrenk; Case File 3632, Hugh Mercer.

75. Vincent F. Martin, 322–23.

76. Vincent F. Martin, 322–23; Miscellaneous Records of Federal Prisoners of War of the United States Army Who Escaped from Southern Prisons, Deserted to the Rebel Army, Illegally Paroled by the Rebel Army, and the Survivors of the Sultana.

77. Vincent F. Martin, 323–24.

78. Hoster, "Adventures of a Soldier," October 1864-March 1865, 123.

79. Cosart, Brooks Battalion, April 1875, 52.

80. *Reports and Resolutions of the General Assembly of the State of South Carolina at the Regular Session Commencing January 9, 1900* (Columbia, SC: The Bryan Printing Company, 1900), 74.

81. First (Butler's), Infantry Compiled Service Records of Confederate Soldiers Who Served in Organizations from the State of South Carolina, Records Group 109, Microfilm M267, Rolls 110–18, National Archives Records Administration.

82. First Artillery, Compiled Service Records of Confederate Soldiers Who Served in Organizations from the State of South Carolina, Records Group 109, Microfilm M267, Rolls 57–65, National Archives Records Administration.

83. 8th Confederate Infantry.

84. Miscellaneous Records of Federal Prisoners of War of the United States Army Who Escaped from Southern Prisons, Deserted to the Rebel Army, Illegally Paroled by the Rebel Army, and the Survivors of the Sultana.

85. Rev. Albert H. Ledoux, *The Union Dead of the Florence Stockade* (Old Darlington District Chapter, South Carolina Genealogical Society, Inc., 2000).

86. Turner, Confederate Military Executions.

87. Case File 2718. Francis C. Schrenk. Case File 3632, Hugh Mercer.

88. Hugh W. Mercer, Case Files of Applications from Former Confederates for Presidential Pardons (Amnesty Papers) 1865–1867, Record Group 94, Microfilm M1003, Roll 21, National Archives Records Administration.

89. Turner, Confederate Military Executions, 20–21.

90. Case File 2718. Francis C. Schrenk.

91. Case File 3632, Hugh Mercer.

92. Turner, Confederate Military Executions, 25–30; Case File 2718, Francis C. Schrenk.

93. Turner, Confederate Military Executions, 32–39.

94. Hoster, "Adventures of a Soldier," October 1864-March 1865.

95. Avery and Garrow, Archaeological Investigations.

96. Turner, Confederate Military Executions, 33–34.

97. Turner, Confederate Military Executions, 34.

98. William M. Gibbons, Confederate Papers Relating to Citizens or Business Firms 1861–1865, Record Group 109, Microfilm 348, Roll 346, National Archives Records Administration.

99. Turner, Confederate Military Executions, 35–36.

100. Vincent F. Martin, 327.

101. Mercer, Case Files of Applications from Former Confederates for Presidential Pardons, 1865–1867.

CHAPTER 5

1. Tucker's Regiment, Compiled Service Records of Confederate Soldiers Who Served in Organizations Raised Directly by the Confederate Government, Record Group 109, Microfilm 258, Roll 76, National Archives Record Administration.

2. Tucker's Regiment.

3. Allardice, Confederate Colonels, 377; 10th Cavalry, Compiled Service Records of Confederate Soldiers Who Served in Organizations from the State of Virginia, Record Group 109, Microfilm M324, Roll 0109.

4. Allardice, Confederate Colonels, 377.

5. Tucker's Regiment.

6. Tucker's Regiment.

7. Judith A. Scharle, 33; Tucker's Regiment.

8. Tucker's Regiment.

9. Tucker's Regiment

10. Isabella D. Martin and Mary Lockett Avery, eds., *A Diary From Dixie* (New York, NY: D. Appleton & Co., 1906), 33.

11. Marli F. Weiner, ed., *A Heritage of Woe: The Civil War Diary of Grace Brown Elmore, 1861–1868,* Southern Voices from the Past: Women's Letters, Diaries, and Writings (Athens, GA: University of Georgia Press, 1997), 92.

12. Walter Brian Cisco, *Wade Hampton: Confederate Warrior, Conservative Statesman* (Washington, D.C.: Potomac Books, Inc., 2004), 148.

13. Letter from Lt. Col. Julius Tucker to Secretary of War James A Seddon, December 14, 1864, Letters Received by the Adjutant and Inspector General, 1861–1865, Record Group 109, Microfilm 474, Roll 147, National Archives Records Administration.

14. OR I XLIV, 1004, 1008.

15. OR IV III II, 1030; Tucker's Regiment.

16. Tucker's Regiment.

17. Tucker's Regiment.

18. Tucker's Regiment.

19. Tucker's Regiment.

20. George G. Kundahl, *Confederate Engineer* (Knoxville, TN: The University of Tennessee Press, 2000), 161–62.

21. Tucker Regiment.

22. Judith A. Scharle, 33–34

23. Jim Miles, *To The Sea: A History and Tour Guide of the War in the West, Sherman's March Across Georgia and Through the Carolinas, 1864–1865* (Nashville, TN: Cumberland House Publishing, Inc., 2002); Steven E. Woodworth, *Nothing But Victory: The Army of Tennessee 1861–1865* (New York, NY: Alfred A. Knopf, 2005).

24. Robert Paul Broadwater, *Battle of Despair: Bentonville and the North Carolina Campaign* (Macon, GA: Mercer University Press, 2004), 6; Michael Chearis Hughes, *Bentonville: The Final Battle of Sherman and Johnston* (Chapel Hill, NC: University of North Carolina Press, 1996), 22.

25. OR I XLVII III, 1069–71.

26. United Daughters of the Confederacy, *War Days in Fayetteville, North Carolina Reminiscences of 1861–1865* (Fayetteville, NC: Judge Printing Company, 1910), 46.; Broadwater, Battle of Despair, 23–24.

27. Mark L. Bradley, *This Astounding Close: The Road to Bennett Place* (Chapel Hill, NC: The University of North Carolina Press, 2000), 438.

28. Tucker Regiment.

29. Tucker Regiment.

30. Jacob D. Cox, *The March to the Sea: Franklin and Nashville* (New York, NY: Charles Scribners Sons, 1886), 242.

31. Cox, March to the Sea, 242.

32. OR II VIII, 246; Mark L. Bradley, *Last Stand in the Carolinas: The Battle of Bentonville* (Campbell, CA: Savas Woodbury Publishers, 1996). 63–64.

33. Bradley, This Astounding Close, 88.

34. Michael B. Ballard, *A Long Shadow: Jefferson Davis and the Final Days of the Confederacy* (Athens, GA: University of Georgia Press, 2013), 24; Bradley, This Astounding Close, 68–69, 71.

35. Robert M. Dunkerly, *The Confederate Surrender at Greensboro: The Final Days of the Army of Tennessee, April, 1865* (Jefferson, NC: McFarland and Company Publishers, 2013), 36–37, 40–41.

36. Dunkerly, Confederate Surrender at Greensboro, 188–89; Bradley, Last Stand in the Carolinas, 158–59.

37. Bradley, Last Stand in the Carolinas, 136, 154; Chris J. Hartley, *Stoneman's Raid, 1865* (Winston-Salem, NC: John F. Blair Publisher, 2010), 256, 288.

38. Bradley, This Astounding Close, 153–54.

39. Dunkerly, Confederate Surrender at Greensboro, 93–106.

40. Bradley, This Astounding Close, 225–26.

41. Bradley, This Astounding Close, 300; Tucker's Regiment

42. Tucker's Regiment.

43. Tucker's Regiment.

CHAPTER 6

1. 8th Confederate Infantry.

2. OR II VII, 821. 8th Confederate Infantry.

3. Eliza Francis Andrews, *The Wartime Journal of a Georgia Girl, 1864–1865* (New York, NY: Appleton and Company, 1908).

4. Garnett Andrews, Undated typescript on file with the Andrews Papers at the University of Tennessee-Chattanooga; Goode, Virginia Cousins, 307–8.

5. Garnett Andrews.

6. 10th Tennessee Infantry.

7. OR II VIII, 254.

8. Brigadier General Zebulon York.

9. Garnett Andrews. Undated typescript.

10. Brooks Battalion, Compiled Service Records of Confederate Soldiers Who Served in Organizations Raised Directly by the Confederate Government, Record Group 109, Microfilm 258, Roll 72, National Archives Record Administration; 8th Confederate Infantry.

11. Pickenpaugh, Captives in Blue, 168.

12. Robert T. Fouche, Compiled Service Records of Confederate Officers and Enlisted Men Who Did Not Belong to Any Particular Regiment, Separate Company or Comparable Unit, or Special Corps, Record Group 109, Microfilm M331, Roll 0097; 8th Confederate Infantry; "Major Fouche Dies at Rome," *Constitution*, March 2, 1908.

13. 8th Confederate Infantry.

14. 8th Confederate Infantry.

15. John B. Jones, *A Rebel War Clerk's Diary*, Vol. II (Philadelphia, PA: J. B. Lippincott & Co., 1869), 423.

16. Woodworth, Nothing But Victory, 610; Broadwater, Battle of Despair, 132–52.

17. 8th Confederate Infantry.

18. "Six Members . . ." *Western Democrat*, March 7, 1865.

19. 8th Confederate Infantry.

20. Miscellaneous Records of Federal Prisoners of War of the United States Army Who Escaped from Southern Prisons, Deserted to the Rebel Army, Illegally Paroled by the Rebel Army, and the Survivors of the Sultana; "Fugitive Federals: A Digital Humanities Investigation of Escaped Union Prisoners," Texas A&M University, Accessed December 26, 2018, https://usg.maps.arcgis.com/apps/MapJournal/index.html?appid=34fd594c6cc4461585e905588a6a477b.

21. Hartley, Stoneman's Raid 1865.

22. Garnett Andrews. Undated typescript.

23. 8th Confederate Infantry; 58th Massachusetts Infantry, Compiled Service Records of Volunteer Union Soldiers Who Served in Organizations From the State of Massachusetts, Record Group 95, Catalog ID 300398, Roll RG94-CMSR-MA-58INF-Bx3414, National Archives Records Administration.

24. OR I LIII, 1054

25. OR I XLIX, 324

26. OR I XLIX, 328–29, 330–37.

27. Hartley, Stoneman's Raid 1865, 214.

28. Robert L. Beall, "Stoneman's Raid War Riot of Ruin," *North Carolina Review*, October 2, November 11, and December 4, 1910.

29. Margaret Wright Hollingsworth, ed., *The Confederate Diary of Wesley Olin Connor of Cave Spring, Georgia* (np: self-published, 2006), 63.

30. William H, Knauss, *The Story of Camp Chase* (Nashville, TN: Publishing House of the Methodist Episcopal Church, 1906), 118.

31. OR I LIII, 1054.

32. Andrews, Wartime Journal of a Georgia Girl, 190.

33. Andrews, Wartime Journal of a Georgia Girl, 208.

34. James R. Jackson, *History of Littleton, New Hampshire*, Vol I (Cambridge, MA: University Press, 1905), 872; Andrews, Wartime Journal of a Georgia Girl, 215.

35. 8th Confederate Infantry.

36. 8th Confederate Infantry.

37. 8th Confederate Infantry; James W. McCorkle, Virginia Military Institute Historical Roster; George Baber, ed., *Decisions of the Department of the Interior, In Cases Relation to Prison Claims and the Laws of the United States Governing Pensions, With An Appendix Containing Certain Acts Relating to Pensions Passed by the Fifty-First Congress.* Volume IV. (Washington, D.C.: U.S. Government Printing Office, 1891), 143.

CHAPTER 7

1. 10th Infantry, Compiled Service Records of Volunteer Union Soldiers Who Served in Organizations from the State of Tennessee, Records Group 109, Microfilm M268, Roll 0156, A-Z, National Archives Records Administration; 15th

Infantry, Compiled Service Records of Volunteer Union Soldiers Who Served in Organizations from the State of Tennessee, Records Group 109, Microfilm M268, Roll 0178, National Archives Records Administration; 1st Infantry, Compiled Service Records of Volunteer Union Soldiers Who Served in Organizations from the State of Missouri, Records Group 109, Microfilm M322, Roll 0098, National Archives Records Administration; McP. B. Eve, Compiled Service Records of Confederate General and Staff Officers and Nonregimental Enlisted Men Who Did Not Belong to Any Company or Comparable Unit or Special Corps, Record Group 109, Microfilm 331, National Archives Records Administration; William R. Scaife and William Harris Bragg, *Joe Brown's Pets: The Georgia Militia, 1861–1865* (Mercer, GA: Mercer University Press, 2004), 2–3.

2. Captain Patrick H. Griffin, "The Famous Tenth Tennessee," *Confederate Veteran*, Vol. XIV, No. 12 (December 1905), 553–60; Captain Thomas Gibson, "Experiences of the Tenth Tennessee With a Special Tribute to Capt. James P. Kirkman," *Confederate Veteran*, Vol. XX, No. 6 (June 1912), 274; Lewis R. Clark, "Tenth Tennessee Infantry," 1912, *Donelson Campaign Sources: Supplementing Volume 7 of the Official Records of the Union and Confederate Armies in the War of the Rebellion*, Army Service Schools Press, 115–16; Ed Gleeson, *Rebel Sons of Erin* (Indianapolis, IN: Guild Press of Indiana, 1993).

3. Gleeson, Rebel Sons of Erin, 10–20; Tenth Tennessee Infantry, 554.

4. James R. Knight, *The Battle of Fort Donelson* (Charleston, SC: The History Press, 2011), 74–79.

5. Knight, Battle of Fort Donelson, 98–109, 143.

6. Knight, Battle of Fort Donelson, 91–130.

7. Griffin, "The Famous Tenth Tennessee," 554.

8. Griffin, "The Famous Tenth Tennessee," 115.

9. Griffin, "The Famous Tenth Tennessee," 554.

10. 10th Tennessee Infantry.

11. 10th Tennessee Infantry.

12. 10th Tennessee Infantry, 116; Griffin, "The Famous Tenth Tennessee," 554.

13. OR II III, 335.

14. OR II III, 170, 172.

15. OR II III, 174; 10th Tennessee Infantry; Brigadier General J. N. Reese, *Report of the Attorney General of the State of Illinois, Vol. II, 1861–1865* (Springfield, IL: Phillips Brothers, 1886), 244–75.

16. David T. Maul, "Five Butternut Yankees," *Journal of the Illinois State Historical Society*, Civil War Centennial Issue, Volume LVI, Number 2 (Summer 1963), 177–92.

17. 10th Tennessee Infantry.

18. OR II III, 360.

19. OR II III, 388.

20. 10th Tennessee Infantry.

21. 10th Tennessee Infantry.

22. 5th South Carolina Reserves, Compiled Service Records of Volunteer Confederate Soldiers Who Served in Organizations from the State of South Carolina, Records Group 109, Microfilm M267, Roll 0202, National Archives Records Administration.

23. Record of Enlisted Federals Who Joined the Federal Army; 10th Tennessee Infantry.

24. Bruce S. Allardice, *Confederate Colonels* (Columbia, MO: University of Missouri Press, 2008), 294–95; Bruce S. Allardice, Personal Communication (e-mail), August 28, 2018.

25. 1st and 4th (Consolidated) Missouri Infantry, Compiled Service Records of Volunteer Confederate Soldiers Who Served in Organizations from the State of Missouri, Records Group 109, Microfilm M322, Roll 0098, National Archives Records Administration; Allardice, Personal Communication (e-mail), August 28, 2018.

26. 1st and 4th (Consolidated) Missouri Infantry.

27. Samuel Shriver, Virginia Military Institute Historical Rosters Database, 2013, Virginia Military Institute Archives, Lexington, Virginia, http://www9.vmi.edu/archiverosters/show.asp?page=details&ID2875; McP. B. Eve, Compiled Service Records of Confederate Officers and Enlisted Men Who Did Not Belong to Any Particular Regiment, Separate Company or Comparable Unit, or Special Corps, Record Group 109, Microfilm M331, Roll 0089; Scaife and Bragg, Joe Brown's Pets, 2–3.

28. OR IV III II, 694.

29. "An Old Bible," *Atlanta Constitution*, August 1, 1915.

30. Telegram from Col. George William Brent to Captain John Perry of December 15, 1864, Col. George Brent Papers, Civil War Collection, Series 55-X, Box 12, Folder 3, Telegrams, Louisiana Historical Society Collections, Louisiana Research Collections, Tulane University, New Orleans.

31. Col. George Brent Papers. Col. George William Brent to Captain John Perry of December 15, 1864.

32. OR I XLV, Part 2, 724.

33. Michael B. Ballard, *Civil War in Mississippi: Major Campaigns and Battles* (Jackson, MS: University Press of Mississippi, 2011), 260.

34. "'Galvanized Yankee' Battalion Let Loose in Georgia," *Cleveland Morning Leader*, January 13, 1865.

35. Wilber W. Caldwell, *The Courthouse and the Depot: A Narrative Guide to Railroad Expansion and Its Impact on Public Architecture in Georgia 1833–1910* (Macon, GA, 2001), 242–43.

36. Bruce J. Dinges and Shirkey A. Leckie, eds., *A Just and Righteous Cause:*

Benjamin H. Grierson's Civil War Memoir (Carbondale, IL: Southern Illinois Press, 2008), 134–86; "The Horse Soldiers," accessed October 12 2018, http://www.tcm.com/this-month/article/30040%7C0/The-Horse Soldiers.html.

37. OR I XLV, Part 1, 844–47; Cockrell and Ballard, Chickasaw, 142–45.

38. OR I XLV I, 861.

39. OR I XLV I, 870. 5th Infantry State Troops, Compiled Service Records of Volunteer Confederate Soldiers Who Served in Organizations from the State of Mississippi, Record Group 109, Microfilm M269, Roll 0153.

40. OR I XLV I, 861, 861, 864.

41. OR I XLV I, 862.

42. OR I XLV I, 862.

43. OR I XLV I, 845–46, 848; 10th Tennessee Infantry; Pvt. P. W. Murphy was supposedly recruited at Andersonville, but that cannot be confirmed since many enlisted Federals gave Andersonville as their place of recruitment, presumably to receive more understanding and forgiveness when they returned to their original units or to home; 52nd New York Infantry, "Rosters of the New York Regiments During the Civil War," https://dmna.ny.gov/historic/reghist/civil/rosters/rostersinfantry.htm.

44. OR I XLV I, 854.

45. OR I XLV I, 867.

46. Major General Franklin Gardner, Compiled Service Records of Confederate Officers and Enlisted Men Who Did Not Belong to Any Particular Regiment, Separate Company or Comparable Unit, or Special Corps, Record Group 109, Microfilm M331, Roll 0102.

47. OR I XLV I, 848; J. Harvey Mathes, 178.

48. Thomas Brownrigg, Brownrigg Family Papers #2226, Southern Historical Collection, Wilson Library, University of North Carolina Chapel Hill.

49. Thomas Brownrigg, Brownrigg Family Papers #2226.

50. Thomas Brownrigg, Brownrigg Family Papers #2226; OR I XLV, Part 1, 849, 857.

51. Thomas Brownrigg, Brownrigg Family Papers #2226; Cockrell and Ballard, Chickasaw, 150; OR I XLV, Part 1, 851.

52. OR I XLV, Part 1, 848–49, 857; Thomas Brownrigg, Brownrigg Family Papers #2226.

53. OR I XLV I, 857, 860.

54. OR I XLV I, 857.

55. OR I XLV I, 849, 863.

56. OR I XLV I, 870–71.

57. OR I XLV I, 846.

58. Thomas S. Cogley, *History of the Seventh Indiana Cavalry Volunteers* (Laporte, IN: Herald Company, Steam Printers, 1876), 140–43.

59. OR I XLV I, 849, 857, 871.

60. OR I XLV I, 872–73.

61. OR I XLV I, 857; Cockrell and Ballard, Chickasaw, 150.

62. Major General Gardner, 247.

63. OR I XLV I, 872–73.

64. OR I XLV I, 867; Major General Gardner, 250–51.

65. OR I XLV I, 867; Major General Gardner, 204, 250, 259.

66. Major General Gardner, 204, 250–51, 269.

67. Richard A. Baumgartner, ed., *Blood & Sacrifices: The Civil War Journal of a Confederate Soldier* (Huntington, WV: Blue Acorn Press, 1994), 190.

68. Baumgartner, Blood & Sacrifices, 190–97.

69. 10th Tennessee Infantry.

70. Dunkerly, Confederate Surrender at Greensboro, 184.

71. W. J. McMurray, MD, *History of the Twentieth Tennessee Regiment Volunteer Infantry* (Nashville, TN: The Publication Committee, 1904), 148.

72. McMurray, History of the Twentieth Tennessee, 432.

73. Bradley, This Astounding Close, 307.

74. Lt. Marcus W. Bates, "The Battle of Bentonville," in *Glimpses of the Nation's Struggle, Fifth Series. Papers Read Before the Minnesota Commandery of the Military Order of the Loyal Legion of the United States, 1897–1902,* eds. Captain J. C. Donahower, Lt. Silas H. Towles, and Lt. David L. Kingsbury (St. Paul, MN: Review Publishing Company, 1908), 147.

75. Major General Henry W. Slocum, "Sherman's March from Savannah to Bentonville," in *Battles and Leaders of the Civil War*, Vol. IV, eds. Robert Underwood Johnson and Clarence Cough Buell (New York, NY: The Century Company, 1884), 692.

76. *Medal of Honor Recipients, 1863–2013* (Washington, D.C.: U.S. Government Printing Office, 2013).

77. McP. B. Eve.

78. Records of Federal Soldiers Who Joined the Confederate Army, Records of the Sultana Disaster, Compiled 1865–1865, Record Group 249, Microfilm M1878, Roll 0003; Register of Departures of Federal Prisoners of War Confined at Andersonville, GA, February 1864 to April 1865, Record Group 249, Microfilm M1303, National Archives Records Administration.

79. Register of Departures of Federal Prisoners of War.

80. "Our Women in the War," *Intelligencer*, July 31, 1884.

81. C.Q.M., "Travels Through the South," *Buffalo Commercial Advertiser*, April 3, 1865.

CHAPTER 8

1. Brown, Galvanized Yankees.

2. Marvel, Andersonville, 8–9, 83–84, 233; Register of Departures of Federal Prisoners of War; William Child, A History of the Fifth Regiment, New

Hampshire Regiment, New Hampshire Volunteers, In the American Civil War, 1861–1865, Volume II (London, U.K.: Forgotten Books, 2018), 97.

3. 5th U.S. Volunteer Infantry, Compiled Service Records of Former Confederate Soldiers (Galvanized Yankees) who served in the 1st through 6th U.S. Volunteer Infantry Regiments, 1864–1866, Record Group 94, Microfilm M1017, Roll 0045; Child, A History of the Fifth Regiment, 97.

4. Marvel, Andersonville, 300; Child, A History of the Fifth Regiment; Hiram Jepperson, November 14, 1892, Organization Index to Pension Files of Veterans Who Served Between 1861 and 1900, compiled 1949–1949, documenting the period 1861–1942, Record Group 15, Publication Number T289, Roll 294; Thomas Mulvey, November 14, 1892, Organization Index to Pension Files of Veterans Who Served Between 1861 and 1900, compiled 1949–1949, documenting the period 1861–1942, Record Group 15, Publication Number T289, Roll 294.

5. 10th Tennessee Infantry.

6. OR II VIII, 124.

7. OR II VIII, 125, 201.

8. OR II VIII, 125; OR I XLV, Part 2, 849.

9. OR II VIII, 125; OR I XLV, Part 2, 861.

10. OR II VIII, 125–26.

11. OR II VIII, 358–59.

12. OR II VIII, 358–59; 5th U.S. Volunteer Infantry.

13. OR II VIII, 554.

14. 5th U.S. Volunteer Infantry.

15. 5th U.S. Volunteer Infantry.

16. 5th U.S. Volunteer Infantry; Henry E. Maynadier, Letters Received by the Attorney General's Office, 1860–70, During and After the Civil War Period, Record Group 94, Microfilm M619, Roll 0279; General George W. Collum, "Cullum's Biographical Register of the Officers and Graduates of the United States Military Academy at West Point, New York, Since its Establishment in 1802. Class of 1851," penelope.uchicago.edu/Thayer/E/Gazetteer/Places/.../USMA/.../Classes/1851.htm.

17. 5th U.S. Volunteer Infantry; Julia B. Maynadier, Approved Pension Applications of Widows and Other Veterans of the Army and Navy Who Served Mainly in the Civil War and the War With Spain, Compiled 1861–1834, Record Group 15, Catalogue Id 300020, Roll WC126444-WC126476, National Archives Records Administration.

18. 5th U.S. Volunteer Infantry.

19. 5th U.S. Volunteer Infantry.

20. OR I XLVIII, 149.

21. 5th U.S. Volunteer Infantry.

22. 5th U.S. Volunteer Infantry; Leroy R. Hafen and Ann W. Hefen, *Powder River Campaigns and Sawyers Expedition of 1865* (Glendale, CA: The Arthur H.

Clark Company, 1961), 226; R Eli Paul, "A Galvanized Yankee Along the Niobrara River," *Nebraska History*, 70 (1989): 146–57, http://www.nebraskahistory.org/publish/publicat/history/full-text/NH1989Niob_Ynkee.pdf.

23. 5th U.S. Volunteer Infantry.

24. Hafen and Hefen, Powder River Campaigns, 221–23; 7th Iowa Cavalry, Index to Compiled Service Records of Volunteer Union Soldiers Who Served in Organizations from the State of Iowa, Record Group 94, Microfilm M541, Roll 0023, National Archives Records Administration; Millards Sioux City Cavalry, Index to Compiled Service Records of Volunteer Union Soldiers Who Served in Organizations from the State of Iowa, Record Group 94, Microfilm M541, Roll 0023, National Archives Records Administration.

25. Paul, "A Galvanized Yankee Along the Niobrara River."

26. Hafen and Hefen, Powder River Campaigns, 224–81, 282–85, 286–87, 286–346.

27. Paul, "A Galvanized Yankee Along the Niobrara River," 147. Brown, Galvanized Yankees, 122; 5th U.S. Volunteer Infantry.

28. Hafen and Hefen, Powder River Campaigns, 245.

29. Hafen and Hefen, Powder River Campaigns, 225–28.

30. Hafen and Hefen, Powder River Campaigns, 228.

31. Paul, "A Galvanized Yankee Along the Niobrara River," 295.

32. Hafen and Hefen, Powder River Campaigns, 228–29.

33. Paul, "A Galvanized Yankee Along the Niobrara River," 148; 5th U.S. Volunteer Infantry.

34. Paul, "A Galvanized Yankee Along the Niobrara River," 150, 153; 5th U.S. Volunteer Infantry.

35. Paul, "A Galvanized Yankee Along the Niobrara River," 153–55; Hafen and Hefen, Powder River Campaigns, 287.

36. Hafen and Hefen, Powder River Campaigns, 289, 287.

37. Paul, "A Galvanized Yankee Along the Niobrara River," 156.

38. W. Turrentine Jackson, *Wagon Roads West* (Lincoln, NE: University of Nebraska Press, 1979), 292–96; 5th U.S. Volunteer Infantry.

39. Brown, Galvanized Yankees, 133–35; 5th U.S. Volunteer Infantry.

40. 5th U.S. Volunteer Infantry.

41. 5th U.S. Volunteer Infantry.

42. OR I XLVIII, 306, 411, 873.

43. OR I XLVIII, 1144.

44. 5th U.S. Volunteer Infantry.

45. 5th U.S. Volunteer Infantry.

46. 5th U.S. Volunteer Infantry.

47. 5th U.S. Volunteer Infantry.

48. 5th U.S. Volunteer Infantry.

49. The question of loyalty and treason during the war has been thoroughly

investigated and reported by William A. Blair, *With Malice Towards Some Treason and Loyalty in the Civil War Era* (Chapel Hill, NC: University of North Carolina Press, 2014).

50. 5th U.S. Volunteer Infantry.

51. 5th U.S. Volunteer Infantry.

52. Brown, Galvanized Yankees, 119–42.

CHAPTER 9

1. Cosart, Brooks Battalion, April 1875, 50–52; "John H. Cosart," *Democrat and Chronicle*, April 12, 1932.

2. Edward McQuade, Case Files of the investigations by Levi Turner and Lafayette C. Baker 1861–1866, Turner Files, Case File 3632, Record Group 15, Microfilm 797, Roll 0070, National Archives Records Administration.

3. Edward McQuade; *1870 Census*, New York Ward 19 District 24, New York, New York, Roll M593_1005, Page 469A: Family History Library Film 552504; 1880 Census, Brooklyn, Kings, New York, Roll 848; Page: 429A, Enumeration District 125; "Bush's Blow Was It Responsible For Edward McQuade's Death?" *Brooklyn Daily Eagle*, July 27, 1889,.

4. Francis Schrenk.

5. John Y. Simon, ed., *The Papers of Ulysses S. Grant*, Volume 16 (Carbondale, IL: Southern Illinois University Press, 1988). 493–94; 5th U.S. Volunteer Infantry.

6. John Kirkwood, Pension Applications for Service in the U.S. Army Between 1861 and 1900, Grouped According to the Units in Which the Veterans Served, Record Group 15, T289, Roll _pub57_synthroll570_, National Archives Records Administration.

7. 5th U.S. Volunteer Infantry; Elias Bare, Pension Applications for Service in the U.S. Army Between 1861 and 1900, Grouped According to the Units in Which the Veterans Served, Record Group 15, T289, Roll _pub57_synthroll570_, National Archives Records Administration; Dennis W. Brendt, *Home Guards to Heroes: The 87th Pennsylvania and Its Civil War Community* (Columbia, MO: University of Missouri Press, 2006), 138–39.

8. 8th Confederate Infantry; "Bannon," *El Dorado Republican*, March 11, 1904; "January 15th," *Girard Press*, January 23, 1890; Franklin Bannon, Pension Applications for Service in the U.S. Army Between 1861 and 1900, Grouped According to the Units in Which the Veterans Served, Record Group 15, T289, Roll _pub57_synthroll570_, National Archives Records Administration.

9. 5th U.S. Volunteer Infantry.

10. John W. Bixler, ed., *Decisions of the Department of the Interior of Appealed Pension and Bounty Land Claims Also a Table of Cases Reported, Cited, Overruled, and Modified and of Statutes Cited and Construed*, Volume XVIII (Washington, D.C.: U.S. Government Printing Office, 1912), 339–41.

11. 5th U.S. Volunteer Infantry; *Miscellaneous Documents of the Senate of the United States for the Second Session Fortieth Congress 1867–'68* (Washington, D.C.: U.S. Government Printing Office, 1868), Miscellaneous Document 78; Peter J. Knapp, Pensions Indexed By Number for Army of Navy Service in the Civil War and Later, 1860–1934, Record Group 15, A1158, Roll A1158_0118, National Archives Records Administration.

12. James R. Jackson, *History of Littleton, New Hampshire.* Vol II (Cambridge, MA: University Press, 1905), 872; Andrews, *Wartime Journal of a Georgia Girl*, 208.

13. *Report of Committees of the Senate of the United States for the First Session of the Forty-Fourth Congress, 1975–'76,* Volume I (Washington, D.C.: U.S. Government Printing Office, 1876), Report No. 83.

14. *Reports of Committees of the Senate of the United States for the First Session of the Fifty-First Congress, 1989–'90,* Volume II (Washington, D.C.: U.S. Government Printing Office, 1876), Report No. 558.

15. John McFarland, Pension Applications for Service in the U.S. Army Between 1861 and 1900, Grouped According to the Units in Which the Veterans Served, Record Group 15, T289. Roll _pub57_synthroll1194_, National Archives Records Administration; "Short Illness is Fatal to Veteran," *New-Journal*, November 12, 1918.

16. Capt. Daniell's Battery; *1870 Census,* Philadelphia Ward 23 District, Philadelphia, Pennsylvania, Roll M593_410, Page 179B; Joseph Liptrot, Pension Applications for Service in the US Army Between 1861 and 1900, Grouped According to the Units in Which the Veteran Served, Record Group 15, T289, Roll _pub 57 _synthroll1164_, National Archives Records Administration; "Pension Certificates," *Philadelphia Inquirer*, December 6, 1897; "Soldier's Pensions," *Evening Republican*, December 7, 1897.

17. Michael Nelligan, Pension Applications for Service in the US Army Between 1861–1934, Record Group 15, MA1158, Roll A1158–214, National Archives Records Administration; 20th Massachusetts Infantry, Compiled Service Records of Volunteer Union Soldiers Who Served from in Organizations the State of Massachusetts, Record Group 94, Catalogue Number 300398, Roll RG-94-CMSR-MA-20INF-Bx1979, National Archives Record Administration; Tucker's Regiment. Compiled Service Records of Confederate Soldiers Who Served in Organizations Raised Directly by the Confederate Government. National Archives Record Administration. Record Group 109, Microfilm 258, Roll 76.

18. See Chapter 1.

19. See Chapter 1.

20. See Foote and Fialka, "Fugitive Federals," for an excellent discussion of escaped Union prisoners of war. See Foote, Yankee Plague, for specific case studies.

21. See Chapter 2 for a discussion of the exchange protocols and the reasons for its eventual collapse.

22. See Chapter 2 for a discussion centered primarily on Florence Prison.

23. See Chapters 4 and 5.

24. See Chapter 2.

25. Francis Schrenk.

26. Benjamin G. Cloyd, *Haunted by Atrocity Civil War Prisons in American Memory* (Baton Rouge, LA: Louisiana State University, 2010), presents a persuasive case for the role played by memories of Civil War prisons in delaying reconciliation between North and South well into the 20th century. The treatment of prisoners at Andersonville Prison and the many prisoners who did not survive played a major role in that narrative.

27. *Miscellaneous Documents of the Senate of the United States*; Peter J. Knapp, Pensions Indexed By Number for Army of Navy Service in the Civil War and Later, 1860–1934, Record Group 15, A1158, Roll A1158_0118, National Archives Records Administration

28. *Reports of Committees of the Senate of the United States for the First Session of the Fifty-First Congress, 1989-'90*, Volume II (Washington, D.C.: U.S. Government Printing Office, 1876), Report No. 558.

29. Marvel, Andersonville, 8–9, 83–84, 233.

30. John Kirkwood, Pension Applications for Service in the U.S. Army Between 1861 and 1900, Grouped According to the Units in Which the Veterans Served, Record Group 15, T289, Roll _pub57_synthroll570_, National Archives Records Administration; Elias Bare, Pension Applications for Service in the U.S. Army Between 1861 and 1900; Brendt, Home Guards to Heroes, 138–39.

31. Baber, Decisions of the Department of the Interior, 143.

32. Baber, Decisions of the Department of the Interior, 141–43.

33. Frederick Thatcher, Approved Pension Applications of Widows and Other Dependents of U.S. Navy Veterans Who Served Between 1861 and 1910, Record Group 15, Microfilm M1279, Roll 00801–0900, National Archives Records Administration.

34. 2nd West Virginia Cavalry, Compiled Military Service Records of Volunteer Union Soldiers Belonging to Units Organized for Service From the State of West Virginia, Record Group 94, Microfilm M508, Roll 0021, National Archives Records Administration; Register of Departures of Federal Prisoners of War; Baber, Decisions of the Department of the Interior, 145.

35. Baber, Decisions of the Department of the Interior, 149–50.

36. Baber, Decisions of the Department of the Interior, 151.

APPENDIX A

1. Henry B. Christian, Compiled Service Records of Confederate Officers and Enlisted Men Who Did Not Belong to Any Particular Regiment, Separate Company or Comparable Unit, or Special Corps Record Group 109, Microfilm M331, Roll 0055.

2. Tucker's Regiment.
3. Tucker's Regiment.
4. Tucker's Regiment.
5. Tucker's Regiment.
6. Tucker's Regiment; 3rd Infantry, Local Defense, Compiled Service Records of Confederate Soldiers Who Served in Organizations from the State of Virginia. Record Group 109, Microfilm M324, Roll 0398.
7. 2nd Virginia Artillery, Compiled Service Records of Confederate Soldiers Who Served in Organizations from the State of Virginia, Record Group 109, Microfilm M234, Roll 0216.
8. 3rd Infantry, Local Defense; Tucker's Regiment; 2nd South Carolina Cavalry, Compiled Service Records of Confederate Soldiers Who Served in Organizations from the State of South Carolina, Record Group 109, Microfilm 267, Roll 0010.
9. W. A. James, Unfiled Papers and Slips Belonging in Confederate Compiled Service Records, Record Group 109, M347, Roll 0203.
10. Tucker's Regiment.
11. Benjamin Azariah Colonna, Virginia Military Institute Historical Rosters Database, Virginia Military Institute Archives, Lexington, Virginia, 2013, http://www9.vmi.edu/archiverosters/show.asp?page=details&ID2875; Judith A. Scharle, comp. *The Life and Times of Benjamin Azariah Colonna,* 1999. http://www.colonnapapers.com/COLONNAPAPERSUP/BenAColonnaHistory_-_Vol_2.html. Accessed February 1, 2014; Tucker's Regiment.
12. Walker Baron Bolling, Virginia Military Institute Historical Rosters Database, Virginia Military Institute Archives, Lexington, Virginia, 2013, http://www9.vmi.edu/archiverosters/show.asp?page=details&ID2875; 7th South Carolina Cavalry, Compiled Service Records of Confederate Soldiers Who Served in Organizations from the State of South Carolina, Record Group 109, Microfilm 267, Roll 0045.
13. 7th South Carolina Cavalry.
14. James K. Cleary, Captain Moore's Co., Light Artillery, Compiled Service Records of Confederate Soldiers Who Served in Organizations from the State of Virginia, Record Group 109, Microfilm M324, Roll 0322.
15. Tucker's Regiment.
16. Capt Walter's Co, Light Artillery (Washington Artillery), Compiled Service Records of Confederate Soldiers Who Served in Organizations from the State of South Carolina, Record Group 109, Microfilm M267, Roll 0107.
17. Tucker's Regiment. 3rd Infantry, Local Defense.
18. 3rd Infantry, Local Defense.
19. 2nd Infantry, Compiled Service Records of Confederate Soldiers Who

Served in Organizations from the State of South Carolina, Record Group 109, Microfilm M267, Roll 0154.

20. Jennings C. Wise, *The Military History of the Virginia Military Institute from 1839 to 1865* (Lynchburg, VA: J. P. Bell Company, Inc., 1915), 306; Tucker's Regiment.

21. S. O. Kirk, Unfiled Papers and Slips Belonging in Confederate Compiled Service Records, Record Group 109, Microfilm M347, Roll 0221, National Archives Record Administration; Blakey, General Winder C.S.A., 120–74, 190.

22. W. H. Heyward, Unfiled Papers and Slips Belonging in Confederate Compiled Service Records, Record Group 109, Microfilm M347, Roll 0183, National Archives Record Administration.

23. H. H. Dinwiddie, Letters received by the Adjutant General's Office, 1860–70, during and after the Civil War period, Record Group 94, Microfilm M619, Roll 0619, National Archives Record Administration; Tucker's Regiment.

24. Tucker's Regiment.

25. W. J. Duncan, Lt. Moorehead's Company Local Defense, Compiled Service Records of Confederate Soldiers Who Served in Organizations from the State of Virginia, Record Group 109, Microfilm M324, Roll 1071, National Archives Record Administration.

26. Tucker's Regiment.

27. John Setze, Capt Walter's Co, Light Artillery; Moses Ezekiel, Virginia Military Institute Historical Rosters Database, Virginia Military Institute Archives, Lexington, Virginia, 2013, http://www9.vmi.edu/archiverosters/show.asp?page=details&ID2695; William J. Hubbard, Tucker's Regiment; Sue Eisenfeld, "Hidden in Plain Sight," *Civil War Times*, February, 2019, 38–44; Tucker Regiment.

28. Tucker's Regiment.

29. 3rd Infantry Local Defense; Robert L. Brockenbrough, Virginia Military Institute Historical Rosters Database; Brooks Battalion, Compiled Service Records of Confederate Soldiers Who Served in Organizations Raised Directly by the Confederate Government, Record Group 109, Microfilm 258, Roll 72, National Archives Record Administration; Tucker Regiment.

30. Capt. Walter's Co, Light Artillery; 1st Infantry, Compiled Service Records of Confederate Soldiers Who Served in Organizations from the State of Virginia, Record Group 109, Microfilm M324, Roll 0357; Tucker's Regiment; 4th South Carolina Cavalry, Compiled Service Records of Confederate Soldiers Who Served in Organizations from the State of South Carolina, Record Group 109, Microfilm 267, Roll 0024.

31. 3rd Infantry Local Defense; Tucker's Regiment.

APPENDIX B

1. John L. Lyerly, 42nd Infantry, Compiled Service Records of Volunteer Confederate Soldiers Who Served in Organizations from the State of North Carolina, Record Group 109, Microfilm M270, Roll 0423; John F. Hanna, Virginia Military Institute Historical Roster, https://archivesweb.vmi.edu/rosters/record.php?ID=1668.

2. John Rigdon, *The Boys of the Fifth: Regimental History of the Georgia 5th Infantry Regiment* (Clearwater, SC: Eastern Digital Resources, 2008), 89; 5th Georgia Infantry, Compiled Service Records of Volunteer Confederate Soldiers Who Served in Organizations from the State of North Carolina, Record Group 109, Microfilm M266, Roll 0197; 8th Confederate Infantry.

3. Warren Lee Goss, *The Soldier's Story of His Captivity at Belle Island, Andersonville, and Other Prisons* (Boston, MA: Lee and Shepard, Publishers, 1866), 225–26; Robert H. Kellogg, *Life and Death in Rebel Prisons* (Hartford, CT: L. Stebbins, 1868), 341; Mark A. Snell, ed., *Dancing Along the Dead Line: The Andersonville Memoir of a Prisoner of the Confederacy* (Novato, CA: Presidio Press, 1996), 116–17.

4. OR II VIII, 782–883.

5. "Lieutenant James Barrett," *New York Tribune*, September, 1910; "Lieut. James Barrett Answers Last Call," *Atlanta Constitution,* September 6, 1910.

6. William Beamish Crawford, Virginia Military Institute Historical Roster, https://archivesweb.vmi.edu/rosters/record.php?ID=2848; 8th Confederate Infantry.

7. 5th Infantry, Compiled Service Records of Volunteer Confederate Soldiers Who Served in Organizations from the State of Texas, Record Group 109, Microfilm M323, Roll 0301; 8th Confederate Infantry.

8. 1st Infantry; 2nd Infantry, Compiled Service Records of Volunteer Confederate Soldiers Who Served in Organizations from the State of Texas, Record Group 109, Microfilm M323, Roll 0255; 8th Confederate Infantry; C. H. Marks, Virginia Military Institute Historical Roster, https://archivesweb.vmi.edu/rosters/record.php?ID=2945.

9. 60th Infantry, Compiled Service Records of Volunteer Confederate Soldiers Who Served in Organizations from the State of Georgia, Record Group 109, Microfilm M266, Roll 0552; 8th Confederate Infantry.

10. James W. McCorkle, Virginia Military Institute Historical Roster, https://archivesweb.vmi.edu/rosters/record.php?ID=2954.

11. H. C. Mosely, Confederate Papers Relating to Citizens or Business Firms, compiled 1874–1899, documenting the period 1861–1865, Record Group 109, Microfilm M348, Roll 0719; Capt. W. P. Carter's Co., Light Artillery, Compiled Service Records of Volunteer Confederate Soldiers Who Served in Organizations from the State of Compiled Service Records of Volunteer Confederate Soldiers

Who Served in Organizations from the State of Virginia, Record Group 109, Microfilm M324, Roll 0274; 7th Battalion Reserves, Compiled Service Records of Volunteer Confederate Soldiers Who Served in Organizations from the State of Virginia, Record Group 109, Microfilm M324, Roll 0264.

12. Samuel Sprigg, Virginia Military Institute Historical Roster, https://archivesweb.vmi.edu/rosters/record.php?ID=1727; John F. Hanna.

13. Henry C. Stacker, Unfiled Papers and Slips Belonging in Confederate Compiled Service Records, Record 109, Microfilm M347, Roll 0376.

14. Edward Lumpkin Hamlin, Virginia Military Institute Historical Roster, https://archivesweb.vmi.edu/rosters/record.php?ID=2896; *Memphis Daily Appeal,* August 27, 1870.

15. Alexander Hamilton Leftwich, Virginia Military Institute Historical Roster, https://archivesweb.vmi.edu/rosters/record.php?ID=2935. 8th Confederate Infantry.

16. 8th Confederate Infantry.

APPENDIX C

1. 10th Infantry, Compiled Service Records of Volunteer Union Soldiers Who Served in Organizations from the State of Tennessee, Records Group 109, Microfilm M268, Roll 0156, National Archives Records Administration; J. Harvey Mathes, *The Old Guard in Gray: Researches in the Annals of the Confederate Historical Society* (Memphis, TN: Press of S. C. Toof & Co, 1897), 173.

2. 10th Tennessee Infantry.; OR II VIII, 254.

3. 10th Tennessee Infantry.

4. 10th Tennessee Infantry.

5. 10th Tennessee Infantry.

6. 10th Tennessee Infantry; Mathes, Old Guard in Gray, 172–74; *Memphis Daily Appeal,* 3 June, 1870.

7. 18th Tennessee Infantry, Compiled Service Records of Volunteer Confederate Soldiers Who Served in Organizations from the State of Tennessee, Records Group 109, Microfilm M368, Roll 0195, National Archives Records Administration.

8. 10th Tennessee Infantry.

APPENDIX D

1. 3rd Infantry, Compiled Service Records of Volunteer Union Soldiers Who Served in Organizations from the State of Colorado, Records Group 94, Catalog Id 300398, Roll RG94-CMSR-CO-3INF-Bx0015, National Archives Records Administration; 5th USVI.

2. "Death of a 59er," *Colorado Springs Daily Gazette,* July 23, 1886; *Laramie Sentinel Weekly,* July 21, 1886; *Wanless Web,* http://www.wanlessweb.org/TNG/getperson.php?personID=I895&tree=3. Accessed 11/13/18.

3. 5th USVI; Henry P. Humphreys, T289, National Archives Records

Administration; Pension applications for service in the U.S. Army Between 1861 and 1900, Grouped According to the Units in Which the Veterans served, Record Group 15, T289, Roll 680, National Archives Records Administration.

4. 5th USVI; William C. Finlaw, Pension Applications, Record Group 15, T289, Roll _pub57_synthroll5636, National Archives Records Administration; "Fortune and a Second Widow Revealed by Two Applications for Pension," *Cincinnati Enquirer*, October 8, 1909; "Widows Agree Upon a Settlement Claims Against the Estate of Dr. W. C. Finlaw Settled Out of Court," *San Francisco Chronicle*, June 7, 1910.

5. 5th USVI.

6. 5th USVI.

7. 5th USVI.

8. 5th USVI.

9. 5th USVI.

10. 5th USVI; William H. Powell and Edward Shippen, eds., *Officers of the Army and Navy Who Served in The Civil War* (Philadelphia, PA: L. R. Hamersly & Co., 1892), 263.

11. 5th USVI; Charles E. Colony, Pension Applications, Record Group 15, T289, Roll _pub57_synthroll5955, National Archives Records Administration.

12. 5th USVI.

13. "66th Illinois Infantry History," *Illinois Civil War Project.* Accessed Nov 25, 2018, https://civilwar.illinoisgenweb.org/history/066.htm; 5th USVI.

14. Record of the Adjutant General (New York) For the Year 1899 (Albany, NY: James B. Lyon State Printer, 1900), Page 522; 5th USVI; Pension Applications, Record Group 15, T289, Roll _pub57_synthroll4698 and 656, National Archives Records Administration.

15. 5th USVI.

16. 3rd Cavalry, Index to Compiled Service Records of Volunteer Union Soldiers Who Served in Organizations from the State of Indiana, Records Group 94, Microfilm M540, Roll 0003, National Archive Records Administration; 1st Cavalry, Index to Compiled Service Records of Volunteer Union Soldiers Who Served in Organizations from the State of Alabama, Records Group 94, Microfilm M276, Roll 0001, National Archive Records Administration; 5th USVI; George M. Bailey, Pension Applications, Record Group 15, T289, Roll _pub57_synthroll233, National Archives Records Administration.

17. 5th USVI; James M. Marshall Pension Applications, Record Group 15, T289, Roll _pub57_synthroll5955, National Archives Records Administration.

18. 5th USVI; Daniel Dana, Pension Applications, Record Group 15, T289, Roll _pub57_synthroll5955_, National Archives Records Administration; Daniel M. Dana. Letters and Their Enclosures Received by the Commission Branch of the Adjutant General's Office, 1863–1870, Record Group 94, Microfilm M1064, Roll 0252, National Archives Record Administration.

BIBLIOGRAPHY

PRIMARY SOURCES

Andrews, Garnett. Undated typescript on file with the Andrews Papers at the University of Tennessee-Chattanooga.

Bixler, John W., ed. *Decisions of the Department of the Interior in Appealed Pension and Bounty-Land Claims,* Volume VIII. July 14, 1908–August 6, 1912. Washington, D.C.

Crist, Lynda Laswell, ed. *The Papers of Jefferson Davis*, Volume 11. Baton Rouge, LA: Louisiana State University Press, 2003.

Hoster, John L. "Adventures of a Soldier," Partial Diary, October 1864-March 1865. Vienna, VA: Unpublished Diary in Possession of Ms. Ruth G. Deike, Columbia, SC.

Miscellaneous Documents of the Senate of the United States for the Second Session Fortieth Congress 1867-'68. Washington, D.C.: U.S. Government Printing Office, 1868.

Morse, Horace J. *General Catalogue of Volunteer Organizations With Additional Enlistments and Casualties to July 1, 1864.* Hartford, CT: Press of Case, Kirkwood & Company, 1864.

Record of the Adjutant General (New York) For the Year 1899. Albany, NY: James B. Lyon State Printer, 1900.

Reese, Brigadier General J. N. *Report of the Attorney General of the State of Illinois.* Vol. II, 1861–1865. Springfield, IL: Phillips Brothers, 1886.

Report of Committees of the Senate of the United States for the First Session of the Forty-Fourth Congress, 1975-'76. Volume I. Washington, D.C.: U.S. Government Printing Office, 1876.

Report of the Adjutant General (New York) for the Year 1894. Albany, NY: James B. Lyon State Printer, Volume V, 1895.

Report on the Treatment of Prisoners of War by the Rebel Authorities During the War of the Rebellion to Which are Appended the Testimony Taken by the Committee and the Official Documents and Statistics, etc. United States House of Representatives. 40th Congress, 3rd Session. Report Number 45. Washington DC: Government Printing Office, 1969.

Reports and Resolutions of the General Assembly of the State of South Carolina at the Regular Session Commencing January 9, 1900. Columbia, SC: The Bryan Printing Company, 1900.

Reports of Committees of the Senate of the United States for the First Session of the Fifty-First Congress, 1989–'90. Volume II. Washington, D.C.: U.S. Government Printing Office, 1876.

Robarts, Wm. Hugh. *Mexican War Veterans: A Complete Roster of the Regular and Volunteer Troops in the War Between the United States and Mexico, from 1846 to 1848: The Volunteers are Arranged by States, Alphabetically.* Washington DC: Brentano's: Reprinted by Leopold Classic Library, n.d.

Rusling James F. *Report to Brevet Major General M.C. Meigs, Quartermaster General,Office of the Inspector, Quartermaster Department Charleston, S.C.* May 27, 1866. National Archives, RG-92, E-576, Box 27. Washington, DC. Columbia, SC: Copy on File with the South Carolina Department of Archives and History.

Scott, Captain Robert N., preparer. *The War of the Rebellion: A Compilation of the Official Records of the Union and Confederate Armies.* United States War Department, Washington, DC.

Texas Bar Association. *Proceedings of the 24th Annual Session of the Texas Bar Association.* Austin, TX: Printed By Order of the Association 1905.

GOVERNMENT DOCUMENTS

1st (Butler's) Infantry. Compiled Service Records of Confederate Soldiers Who Served in Organizations from the State of South Carolina. National Archives Records Administration, Records Group 109. Microfilm M267, Rolls 110–18.

1st Alabama Cavalry. Index to Compiled Service Records of Volunteer Union Soldiers Who Served in Organizations from the State of Alabama. National Archives Records Administration, Records Group 94, Microfilm M276, Roll 0001.

1st Missouri Infantry. Compiled Service Records of Volunteer Union Soldiers Who Served in Organizations from the State of Missouri. National Archives Records Administration, Records Group 109, Microfilm M322, Roll 0098.

1st South Carolina Artillery. Compiled Service Records of Volunteer Confederate Soldiers Who Served in Organizations from the State of South Carolina. National Archives Records Administration, Records Group 109, Microfilm M267, Rolls 67–64.

1st Texas Infantry. Compiled Service Records of Confederate Soldiers Who Served in Organizations from the State of Texas. National Archives Records Administration, Record Group 109, Microfilm M323, Roll 0255.

1st Virginia Infantry. Compiled Service Records of Confederate Soldiers Who Served in Organizations from the State of Virginia. National Archives Records Administration, Record Group 109, Microfilm 329, Rolls 0352-0396.

1st and 4th (Consolidated) Missouri Infantry. Compiled Service Records of Volunteer Confederate Soldiers Who Served in Organizations from the State of

Missouri. National Archives Records Administration, Records Group 109, Microfilm M322, Roll 0098.
2nd South Carolina Cavalry. Compiled Service Records of Confederate Soldiers Who Served in Organizations from the State of South Carolina. National Archives Records Administration, Record Group 109, Microfilm M267, Rolls 0010–0013.
2nd South Carolina Infantry. Compiled Service Records of Confederate Soldiers Who Served in Organizations from the State of South Carolina. National Archives Records Administration, Record Group 109, Microfilm M267, Roll 0154.
2nd Virginia Artillery. Compiled Service Records of Confederate Soldiers Who Served in Organizations from the State of Virginia. National Archives Records Administration, Record Group 109, Microfilm M234, Roll 0216.
2nd West Virginia Cavalry. Compiled Military Service Records of Volunteer Union Soldiers Belonging to Units Organized for Service From the State of West Virginia. National Archives Records Administration, Records Group 94, Microfilm M508, Roll 0021.
3rd Colorado Infantry. Compiled Service Records of Volunteer Union Soldiers Who Served in Organizations from the State of Colorado. National Archives Records Administration, Records Group 94, Catalog Id 300398. Roll RG94-CMSR-CO-3INF-Bx0015.
3rd Indiana Cavalry. Index to Compiled Service Records of Volunteer Union Soldiers Who Served in Organizations from the State of Indiana. National Archive Records Administration, Records Group 94, Microfilm M540, Roll 0003.
3rd Local Defense Troops. Compiled Service Records of Confederate Soldiers Who Served in Organizations from the State of Virginia. National Archives Records Administration, Record Group 109, Microfilm 324, Roll 0396.
3rd Maryland Cavalry. Compiled Service Records of Volunteer Union Soldiers Who Served in Organizations from the State of Maryland. National Archives Records Administration, Records Grou 94, Microfilm M384, Rolls 32–38.
3rd South Carolina Cavalry. Compiled Service Records of Confederate Soldiers Who Served in Organizations from the State of South Carolina. National Archives Records Administration, Record Group 109, Microfilm M267, Rolls 0015.
4th South Carolina Cavalry. Compiled Service Records of Confederate Soldiers Who Served in Organizations from the State of South Carolina. National Archives Records Administration, Record Group 109, Microfilm M267, Rolls 0024.
4th New Hampshire Infantry. Index to Compiled Service Records of Volunteer Union Soldiers Who Served in Organizations from the State of New Hampshire. National Archives Records Administration, Record Group 94, Microfilm M548, Roll 11.

5th Mississippi Infantry State Troops. Compiled Service Records of Volunteer Confederate Soldiers Who Served in Organizations from the State of Mississippi. National Archives Records Administration, Record Group 109, Microfilm M269, Roll 0153.

5th South Carolina Reserves. Compiled Service Records of Volunteer Confederate Soldiers Who Served in Organizations from the State of South Carolina. National Archives Records Administration, Records Group 109, Microfilm M267, Roll 0202.

5th Texas Infantry. Compiled Service Records of Confederate Soldiers Who Served in Organizations from the State of Texas. National Archives Records Administration, Record Group 109, Microfilm M267, Roll 0024.

5th U.S. Volunteers. Compiled Service Records of Former Confederate Soldiers Who Served in the 1st Through the 6th Volunteer Regiments 1864–1866. National Archives Records Administration, Records Group 94. Microfilm M017, Roll 40.

6th South Carolina Cavalry. Compiled Service Records of Confederate Soldiers Who Served in Organizations from the State of South Carolina. National Archives Records Administration, Records Group 109. Microfilm M267, Roll 39.

7th Iowa Cavalry. Index to Compiled Service Records of Volunteer Union Soldiers Who Served in Organizations from the State of Iowa. National Archives Records Administration Record Group 94, Microfilm M541, Roll 0023.

7th South Carolina Cavalry. Compiled Service Records of Confederate Soldiers Who Served in Organizations from the State of South Carolina. National Archives Records Administration, Record Group 109, Microfilm 267, Roll 045.

7th South Carolina Infantry. Compiled Service Records of Confederate Soldiers Who Served in Organizations from the State of South Carolina. National Archives Records Administration, Record Group 109. Microfilm M267, Roll 213.

7th Virginia Reserves. Compiled Service Records of Confederate Soldiers Who Served in Organizations from the State of Virginia. National Archives Records Administration, Record Group 109, Microfilm 324, Roll 0464.

8th Confederate Infantry. Compiled Service Records of Confederate Soldiers Who Served in Organizations Raised Directly by the Confederate Government. National Archives Record Administration, Record Group 109, Microfilm 258, Roll 067.

8th Georgia Infantry. Compiled Service Records of Confederate Soldiers Who Served in Organizations from the State of Georgia. National Archives Records Administration, Record Group 109, Microfilm M266, Roll 0228.

10th Tennessee Infantry. Compiled Service Records of Confederate Soldiers Who Served in Organizations from the State of Tennessee. National Archives Records Administration, Record Group 109, Microfilm M268, Rolls 156, 157, and 158.

10th Virginia Cavalry. Compiled Service Records of Confederate Soldiers Who

Served in Organizations from the State of Virginia. National Archives Records Administration, Record Group 109, Microfilm 324, Roll 0107.

13th Louisiana Infantry. Compiled Service Records of Volunteer Union Soldiers Who Served in Organizations from the State of Louisiana. National Archives Records Administration, Record Group 109, Microfilm M320, Roll 251.

14th Connecticut Infantry. Compiled Service Records of Volunteer Union Soldiers Who Served in Organizations from the State of Connecticut. National Archives Records Administration, Record Group 94, Microfilm 535, Roll 5.

14th Louisiana Infantry. Compiled Service Records of Volunteer Union Soldiers Who Served in Organizations from the State of Louisiana. National Archives Records Administration, Record Group 109, Microfilm M320, Roll 261.

15th Tennessee Infantry. Compiled Service Records of Volunteer Union Soldiers Who Served in Organizations from the State of Tennessee. National Archives Records Administration, Record Group 109, Microfilm M268, Roll 0178.

18th Tennessee Infantry. Compiled Service Records of Volunteer Confederate Soldiers Who Served in Organizations from the State of Tennessee. National Archives Records Administration, Record Group 109, Microfilm M368, Roll 0195.

20th Louisiana Infantry. Compiled Service Records of Volunteer Union Soldiers Who Served in Organizations from the State of Louisiana. National Archives Records Administration, Record Group 109, Microfilm M320, Roll 315.

20th Massachusetts Infantry. Compiled Service Records of Volunteer Union Soldiers Who Served from in Organizations the State of Massachusetts. National Archives Record Administration. Record Group 94, Catalogue Number 300398, Roll RG-94-CMSR-MA-20INF-Bx1979.

24th Infantry, Compiled Service Records of Volunteer Union Soldiers Who Served in Organizations from the State of Massachusetts. National Archives Records Administration, Record Group 94, Catalog ID 300398, Roll RG94-CMSR-MA-24INF-Bx2221.

27th North Carolina Infantry. Compiled Service Records of Confederate Soldiers Who Served in Organizations from the State of North Carolina. National Archives Records Administration, Record Group 109 Microfilm Publications M333, Roll 106.

47th Georgia Infantry, Compiled Service Records of Volunteer Confederate Soldiers Who Served in Organizations from the State of Georgia. National Archives Records Administration, Record Group 109, Microfilm M266, Rolls 484-487.

52nd New York Infantry. *Rosters of the New York Regiments During the Civil War.* https://dmna.ny.gov/historic/reghist/civil/rosters/rostersinfantry.htm.

58th Massachusetts Infantry, Compiled Service Records of Volunteer Union Soldiers Who Served in Organizations From the State of Massachusetts. National Archives Records Administration, Record Group 95, Catalog ID 300398, Roll RG94-CMSR-MA-58INF-Bx3414.

60th Georgia Infantry. Compiled Service Records of Volunteer Confederate Soldiers Who Served in Organizations from the State of Georgia. National Archives Records Administration, Record Group 109, Microfilm M266, Roll 0552.

60th Texas Infantry. Compiled Service Records of Confederate Soldiers Who Served in Organizations from the State of Texas. National Archives Records Administration, Record Group 109, Microfilm M323, Rolls 0295-303.

Ahl's Independent Company Delaware Heavy Artillery. Compiled Service Records of Volunteer Union Soldiers Who Seved in Organizations from the State of Delaware. National Archives Record Administration, Record Group 94, Microfilm M1961, Roll 13.

Andrews, Major Garnett. Compiled Service Records of Confederate General and Staff Officers and Nonregimental Enlisted Men Who Did Not Belong to Any Company or Comparable Unit or Special Corps. National Archives Records Administration. Record Group 109. Microfilm 331. Roll 1007.

Bailey, George M. Pension Applications. Record Group 15, National Archives Records Administration, T289, Roll _pub57_synthroll233.

Bannon, Franklin. Pension Applications for Service in the U.S. Army Between 1861 and 1900. Grouped According to the Units in Which the Veterans Served. Record Group 15, National Archives Records Administration, T289. Roll _pub57_synthroll570_.

Bare, Elias. Pension Applications for Service in the U.S. Army Between 1861 and 1900. Grouped According to the Units in Which the Veterans Served. Record Group 15, National Archives Records Administration, T289. Roll _pub57_synthroll570_.

Brooks Battalion. Compiled Service Records of Confederate Soldiers Who Served in Organizations Raised Directly by the Confederate Government. National Archives Records Administration, Record Group 109, Microfilm 258, Roll 72

Brooks Battalion. National Park Service, *Soldiers and Sailors Database* Accessed February 10, 2018. (http://www.itd.nps.gov/cwss/Soldier_Results.cfm).

Carter's Co., Capt. W. P. Light Artillery. Compiled Service Records of Confederate Soldiers Who Served in Organizations from the State of Virginia. National Archives Records Administration, Record Group 109, Microfilm M324, Roll 1071.

Christian, Henry B. Compiled Service Records of Confederate Officers and Enlisted Men Who Did Not Belong to Any Particular Regiment, Separate Company or Comparable Unit, or Special Corps. National Archives Records Administration, Record Group 109, Microfilm M331, Roll 0055.

Cleary, James K. Captain Moore's Co., Light Artillery. Compiled Service Records of Confederate Soldiers Who Served in Organizations from the State of

Virginia. National Archives Records Administration, Record Group 109, Microfilm M324, Roll 0322.

Collum, General George W. *Cullum's Biographical Register of the Officers and Graduates of the United States Military Academy at West Point, New York, Since its Establishment in 1802. Class of 1851.* penelope.uchicago.edu/Thayer/E/Gazetteer/Places/.../USMA/.../Classes/1851.htm. Accessed December 15, 2018.

Colony, Charles E. Pension Applications. National Archives Records Administration, Record Group 15, T289, Roll _pub57_synthroll5955.

Cosart, John H. New York Regiment 27, Company B. Civil War Pensions Index, National Archives Records Administration, Record Group 94, Publication T289.

Daniel M. Dana. Letters and Their Enclosures Received by the Commission Branch of the Adjutant General's Office, 1863–1870. National Archives Records Administration, Record Group 94, Microfilm M1064, Roll 0252.

Dana, Daniel. Pension Applications. National Archives Records Administration Record Group 15, T289, Roll _pub57_synthroll5955_.

Dinwiddie, H. H. Letters Received by the Office of the Adjutant General, Main Series, 1861–1870. National Archives Records Administration, Record Group 94, Microfilm M619, Roll 0619.

Capt. Daniell's Battery. Compiled Service Records of Confederate Soldiers Who Served in Organizations Raised Directly by the Confederate Government. National Archives Records Administration, Record Group 109, Microfilm M266, Roll 315.

Duncan, W. J. Lt. Moorehead's Company Local Defense. Compiled Service Records of Confederate Soldiers Who Served in Organizations from the State of Virginia. National Archives Records Administration, Record Group 109, Microfilm M324, Roll 1071.

Eve, McPherson B. Compiled Service Records of Confederate General and Staff Officers and Nonregimental Enlisted Men Who Did Not Belong to Any Company or Comparable Unit or Special Corps. National Archives Records Administration, Record Group 109, Microfilm 331, Roll 0089.

Fernandez, Manuel. Index to Compiled Service Records of Volunteer Union Soldiers Who Served in Organizations from the State of Connecticut. National Archives Records Administration, Record Group 94, Microfilm 535, Roll 5.

Florence Military Records. Records of the Military Department, Office of the Confederate Historian, Florence Military Prison Records. 1864–1865. South Carolina Department of Archives and History, Columbia, SC.

Fouche, Robert T. Compiled Service Records of Confederate General and Staff Officers, and Nonregimental Enlisted Men. National Archives Records Administration, Record Group 109, Microfilm M331, Roll 0097.

Gardner, Major General Franklin. Compiled Service Records of Confederate Officers and Enlisted Men Who Did Not Belong to Any Particular Regiment. Separate Company or Comparable Unit, or Special Corps. National Archives Records Administration, Record Group 109, Microfilm M331, Roll 0102.

Geissler, Charles. Alphabetical card index to the compiled service records of volunteer Union soldiers belonging to units from the State of New Jersey. National Archives Records Administration, Record Group 94, Microfilm M550, Roll 0009.

Gibbons, William M. Confederate Papers Relating to Citizens or Business Firms 1861–1865. National Archives Records Administration, Record Group 109, Microfilm 348, Roll 346.

Gilmer, Jr., Colonel John A. 27th North Carolina Infantry. Compiled Service Records of Confederate Soldiers Who Served in Organizations from the State of North Carolina. National Archives Records Administration, Record Group 109, Roll 333, F-He.

Godwin, Brig. General Archibald C. Compiled Service Records of Confederate General and Staff Officers and Nonregimental Enlisted Men. National Archives Records Administration, Record Group 109, Roll 108, Go-Goo.

Heyward, W. H. Unfiled Papers and Slips Belonging in Confederate Compiled Service Records. National Archives Records Administration, Record Group 109, Microfilm M347, Roll 0183.

Humphreys, Henry P. Pension applications for service in the U.S. Army Between 1861 and 1900, Grouped According to the Units in Which the Veterans served. National Archives Records Administration. Record Group 15, T289, Roll 680.

James, W. A. Unfiled Papers and Slips Belonging in Confederate Compiled Service Records. National Archives Records Administration, Record Group 109. M347, Roll 0203.

Jepperson, Hiram. November 14, 1892. Organization Index to Pension Files of Veterans Who Served Between 1861 and 1900, compiled 1949–1949, documenting the period 1861–1942, National Archives Records Administration, Record Group 15, Publication Number T289, Roll 294.

Kirk, S. O. Unfiled Papers and Slips Belonging in Confederate Compiled Service Records. National Archives Records Administration, Record Group 109. Microfilm M347, Roll 0221.

Kirkwood, John. Pension Applications for Service in the U.S. Army Between 1861 and 1900, Grouped According to the Units in Which the Veterans Served. National Archives Records Administration, Record Group 15, T289. Roll _pub57_synthroll570_.

Knapp, Peter J. Pensions Indexed By Number for Army of Navy Service in the Civil War and Later, 1860–1934. National Archives Records Administration, Record Group 15, A1158, Roll A1158_0118.

Letter from Adjutant General S. Cooper to James A, Seddon, November 21,

1864. Records of Confederate War Department Staff Departments, Confederate Adjutant General Outgoing Correspondence. National Archives Records Administration, Record Group 109, Microfilm M627, Pages 196–97.

Letter from Assistant Adjutant General Jno. Blair Hoge to Adjutant General Samuel Cooper, November 21, Tucker's Regiment. Compiled Service Records of Confederate Soldiers Who Served in Organizations Raised Directly by the Confederate Government. National Archives Records Administration, Record Group 109, Microfilm M258, Roll 76, E-Z.

Liptrot, Joseph. Pension Applications for Service in the U.S. Army Between 1861 and 1900, Grouped According to the Units in which the Veteran Served. National Archives Records Administration, Record Group 15, T289, Roll _pub57_synthroll 1164_.

Marshall, James M. Pension Applications. National Archives Records Administration, Record Group 15, T289, Roll _pub57_synthroll5955.

Maynadier, Henry E. Letters Received by the Attorney General's Office, 1860–70, During and After the Civil War Period. National Archives Records Administration, Record Group 94, Microfilm M619, Roll 0279.

Maynadier, Julia B. Approved Pension Applications of Widows and Other Veterans of the Army and Navy Who Served Mainly in the Civil War and the War With Spain, Compiled 1861–1834. National Archives Records Administration, Record Group 15, Record Catalogue Id 300020, Roll WC126444-WC126476.

McFarland, John. Pension Applications for Service in the U.S. Army Between 1861 and 1900, Grouped According to the Units in Which the Veterans Served. National Archives Records Administration, Record Group 15, T289. Roll _pub57_synthroll1194_.

Mercer, H. W. Letter of August 11, 1865, from Captain George A Mercer to Brevet Major General J. H. Brannon. Compiled Service Records of Confederate Officers and Enlisted Men Who Did Not Belong to Any Particular Regiment, Separate Company of Comparable Unit, or Special Corps. National Archives Records Administration, Record Group 109. Microfilm M347, Roll 272.

Mercer, Hugh. Case File 3632, Case Files of Investigations by Levi C. Turner and Lafayette C. Baker 1861–1866. Turner Files 3601-3700. National Archives Records Administration, Record Group 94, Microfilm M797, Roll 0102.

Mercer, Hugh W. Case Files of Applications from Former Confederates for Presidential Pardons (Amnesty Papers) 1865–1867. National Archives Records Administration. Record Group 94, Microfilm M1003, Roll 21.

Millards Sioux City Cavalry. Index to Compiled Service Records of Volunteer Union Soldiers Who Served in Organizations from the State of Iowa. National Archives Records Administration, Record Group 94, Microfilm M541, Roll 0023.

Miscellaneous Records of Federal Prisoners of War of the United States Army Who Escaped from Southern Prisons, Deserted to the Rebel Army, Illegally

Paroled by the Rebel Army, and the Survivors of the Sultana, Vol. 1. National Archives Records Administration, Alphabetical List of Federal Prisoners on the Sultana, including those who survived or perished. National Archives Records Administration, Record Group 249, Microfilm 1878, Roll 3, Vol. 1.

Moorehead's Company, Local Defense. Compiled Service Records of Confederate Soldiers Who Served in Organizations from the State of Virginia. National Archives Records Administration, Record Group 109, Microfilm M324, Roll 0275.

Moore's Company Light Artillery, Captain. Compiled Service Records of Confederate Soldiers Who Served in Organizations from the State of Virginia. National Archives Records Administration, Record Group 109, Microfilm 324, Roll 0322.

Morning Report, Florence Military Records, Records of the Military Department, Office of the Confederate Historian, Florence Military Prison Records (Columbia, SC: South Carolina Department of Archives and History, 1864–1865).

Mosely, H. C. Confederate Papers Relating to Citizens or Business Firms, Documenting the Period 1861–1865. National Archives Records Administration, Record Group 109, Microfilm M346, Roll 0719.

Mulvey, Thomas. November 14, 1892. Organization Index to Pension Files of Veterans Who Served Between 1861 and 1900, compiled 1949–1949, documenting the period 1861–1942, National Archives Records Administration, Record Group 15, T289, Roll 294.

National Register of Historic Places File for the Stockade, South Carolina. Columbia, SC: South Carolina Department of Archives and History, n.d.

Nelligan, Michael. Pension Applications for Service in the U.S. Army Between 1861–1934. National Archives Records Administration, Record Group 15, Microfilm MA1158, Roll A1158-0214.

Organization Index to Pension Files of Veterans Who Served Between 1861 and 1900. National Archives Records Administration, Record Group 15, Roll 265.

Record of Enlisted Federals Who Joined the Confederate Army. Records Reflecting the April 27, 1865 Explosion of the Steamer "Sultana", Including Lists of Those Aboard the Ship. National Archives Records Administration, Record Group 249, Microfilm M1878.

Register of Departures of Federal Prisoners of War Confined at Andersonville, GA February 1864 to April 1865. National Archives Records Administration. Record Group 249, Microfilm M1303.

Rusling, James F. Report to Brevet Major General M.C. Meigs, Quartermaster General, Office of the Inspector, Quartermaster Department Charleston, S.C. May 27, 1866. National Archives Records Administration, Record Group 92, E-576, Box 27.

Schrenk, Francis C. Case File 2718. Case Files of Investigations by Levi C. Turner and Lafayette C. Baker 1861–1866. Turner Files 3601-3700. National Archives Records Administration, Record Group 94, Microfilm M797, Roll 0070.

Shriver, Samuel Sprigg. Compiled Service Records of Confederate General and Staff Officers, and Nonregimental Enlisted Men. National Archives Records Administration, Record Group 109, Microfilm M331, Roll 0225.

Sinner, Joseph. 4th Infantry, Index to Compiled Service Records of Volunteer Union Soldiers Who Served in Organizations from the State of New Hampshire. National Archives Records Administration, Record Group 94, Microfilm M548, Roll 11.

Sinner, Joseph. Unfiled Papers and Slips Belonging in Confederate Compiled Service Records. National Archives Records Administration, Record Group 109, Microfilm M347, Roll 363.

Sinner, Joseph. Weekly Returns of Enlistments at Naval Rendezvous Jan. 6, 1855 to August 8, 1891. National Archives Records Administration, Record Group 24, Microfilm 1953, Roll 24.

Stacker, Henry C. Unfiled Papers and Slips Belonging in Confederate Compiled Service Records. National Archives Records Administration, Record Group 109, Microfilm M347, Roll 0376.

Testimony of Warren Lee Goss, *Report on the Treatment of Prisoners of War by the Rebel Authorities During the War of the Rebellion*. Reports on Committees of the House of Representatives Made During the Third Session of the Fortieth Congress. (Washington, DC: Government Printing Office, 1869).

Thatcher, Frederick. Approved Pension Applications of Widows and Other Dependents of U.S. Navy Veterans Who Served Between 1861 and 1910. National Archives Records Administration, Record Group 15, Microfilm M1279, Roll 00801-00900.

Trapier Major General James H. Compiled Service Records of Confederate Officers and Enlisted Men Who Did Not Belong to Any Particular Regiment, Separate Company of Comparable Unit, or Special Corps. National Archives Records Administration, Record Group 109. Microfilm M331, Roll 250.

Tucker's Regiment, Confederate Infantry, Compiled Service Records of Confederate Soldiers Who Served in Organizations Raised Directly by the Confederate Government. National Archives Records Administration, Record Group 109, Microfilm 258, Roll 79.

Van Den Corput's Co., Light Artillery,Capt. Compiled Service Records of Confederate Soldiers Who Served in Organizations from the State of Georgia. National Archives Records Administration, Record Group 109, Microfilm M266, Roll 116.

Walter's Co., Light Artillery (Washington Artillery), Captain. Compiled Service

Records of Confederate Soldiers Who Served in Organizations from the State of South Carolina. National Archives Records Administration. Record Group 109, Microfilm M267, Roll 0107.

York, Brigadier General Zebulon. Compiled Service Records of Confederate General and Staff Officers and Nonregimental Enlisted Men Who Did Not Belong to Any Company or Comparable Unit or Special Corps. National Archives Records Administration, Record Group 109. Microfilm 331. Wu-Z.

U.S. BUREAU OF THE CENSUS

1870 Census. Philadelphia Ward 23 District, Philadelphia, Pennsylvania. National Archives Records Administration, Roll M593_410; Page 179B.

1880 Census. Brooklyn, Kings, New York, Roll 848; Page: 429A. Enumeration District 125

Eighth Census of the United States, 1860 Population Schedules. Wayne County, Lyons Village, New York. National Archives Records Administration, Records Group 29, Microfilm M653.

Ninth Census of the United States, 1870. Population Schedules, Wayne County, Lyons Village, New York. National Archives Records Administration, Records Group 29, Microfilm M1280.

Tenth Census of the United States, 1890. Wayne County, Lyons Village, New York. Records Group 29. Population Schedules, Wayne County, New York. National Archives Records Administration, Records Group 29.

PRIVATE PAPERS

Andrews, Garnett. Undated typescript on file with the Andrews Papers, University of Tennessee-Chattanooga.

Brent, George W. Papers 1863–1865. Subseries 55-X-2, Box 12, Folder 3: Telegram Book, 1864 October 18–1865 March 10. Louisiana Historical Association Collection, Manuscript Collection 55, Louisiana Research Collection, Howard-Tilton Memorial Library, Tulane University, New Orleans, Louisiana.

Brownrigg, Thomas. Brownrigg Family Papers #2226. Southern Historical Collection, Wilson Library, University of North Carolina Chapel Hill.

NEWSPAPERS AND MAGAZINES

"At Buzzard's Roost." *Lancaster Intelligencer.* January 28, 1881.

"Bannon." *El Dorado Republican.* March 11, 1904.

"Belle Isle." *Richmond Inquirer.* May 16, 1863, p. 1.

"Bush's Blow Was It Responsible For Edward McQuade's Death?" *Brooklyn Daily Eagle.* July 27, 1889, p. 4.

"Buzzard Brothers, The." *Lancaster Intelligencer.* January 17, 1881.

"Buzzard Gang, The." *New York Times.* October 8, 1881.

Cosart, John H. "Brooks Battalion." *Home Mail,* Vol. 2, No. 4 (April, 1875): 50–52.
C.Q.M. "Travels Through the South." *Buffalo Commercial Advertiser.* April 3, 1865.
"Death of a 59er." *Colorado Springs Daily Gazette.* July 23, 1886. *Laramie Sentinel Weekly,* Laramie, Wyoming, July 21, 1886.
Eccles, Thomas J. "From the State Reserves." Articles Submitted to the *Yorkville Enquirer,* York, South Carolina from Florence Stockade 1864–1865.
"Edward Lumkin Hamlin." *Memphis Daily Appeal.* June 3, 1870.
"Edward Lumpkin Hamlin." *Memphis Daily Appeal.* August 27, 1870.
Eisenfeld, Sue. "Hidden in Plain Sight." *Civil War Times.* February, 2019.
"Escaped Correspondents; Safe Arrival at Nashville of Mssers. Richardson and Brown of the Tribune, Accompanied by Mr. Davis, Correspondent of the Cincinnati Gazette. Escaped Union Prisoners at Knoxville, The." *New York Times.* January 17, 1865.
"Fortune and a Second Widow Revealed by Two Applications for Pension." *Cincinnati Enquirer.* October 8, 1909, p. 14.
"'Galvanized Yankee' Battalion Let Loose in Georgia." *Cleveland Morning Leader.* January 13, 1865.
"January 15th." *The Girard Press.* January 23, 1890.
"Lieut. James Barrett Answers Last Call." *Atlanta Constitution.* September 6, 1910.
"Lieutenant James Barrett." *New York Tribune.* September, 1910.
"*Major* Fouche Dies at Rome." *Atlanta Constitution.* March 2, 1908.
"Notorious Buzzard Gang, The." *Wide World Magazine,* vol. IV, no. 21 (December 1899): 266–71.
"Old Bible, An." *Atlanta Constitution.* August 1, 1915, p. 8.
"Our Women in the War." *Intelligencer.* July 31, 1884.
"Reformed Outlaw Dead." *New York Times.* February 24, 1921.
"Pension Certificates." *Philadelphia Inquirer.* December 6, 1897, p. 6.
"Short Illness is Fatal to Veteran." *New-Journal.* November 12, 1918.
"Six Members . . ." *Western Democrat.* March 7, 1865, p. 1.
"Soldier's Pensions." *Evening Republican.* December 7, 1897, p. 2.
"Two of the Buzzard Boys Are Released." *Lancaster Daily Intelligencer.* October 20, 1884.
"Widows Agree Upon a Settlement Claims Against the Estate of Dr. W. C. Finlaw Settled Out of Court." *San Francisco Chronicle.* June 7, 1910, p. 9.

SECONDARY SOURCES

"8th New York Cavalry." *Annual Report of the Adjutant General of the State of New York,* vol. 2, 1893.
"66th Illinois Infantry History." *The Illinois Civil War Project.* https://civilwar.illinoisgenweb.org/history/066.html. Accessed Nov 25, 2018.

Allardice, Bruce S. *Confederate Colonels: A Bibliographic Register.* Columbia MO: University of Missouri Press, 2008.

Allardice, Bruce S. Personal Communication (e-mail). August 28, 2018.

Alotta, Robert I. *Civil War Justice.* Shippensburg, PA: The White Mane Publishing Company, 1989.

Anbinder, Tyler. *Five Points.* New York, NY: Free Press, 2001.

Andrews, Eliza Francis. *The Wartime Journal of a Georgia Girl, 1864–1865.* New York, NY: D. Appleton and Company, 1908.

Andrews, Sidney. *The South Since the War.* Baton Rouge, LA: Louisiana State University Press, 2004.

Angelovich, Robert B. *Riding for Uncle Samuel: The Civil War History of the 1st Connecticut Cavalry Volunteers.* Grand Rapids, MI: Inner Workings, Inc, 2014.

Anon. Columbia, SC: National Register of Historic Places File for the Stockade, South Carolina Department of Archives and History, n.d.).

Avery, Paul G. and Patrick H. Garrow. *Phase III Archaeological Investigations at 38FL2, The Florence Stockade, Florence South Carolina.* Knoxville, TN: MACTEC Engineering and Consulting, Inc., Washington. DC: Submitted to the Department of Veterans Affairs, National Cemetery Administration, Washington, D. C. 2008.

Baber, George, ed. *Decisions of the Department of the Interior, In Cases Relation to Prison Claims and the Laws of the United States Governing Pensions, With An Appendix Containing Certain Acts Relating to Pensions Passed by the Fifty-First Congress,* vol. IV. Washington, D. C.: U.S. Government Printing Office, 1891.

Ballard, Michael B. *A Long Shadow: Jefferson Davis and the Final Days of the Confederacy.* Athens, GA: University of Georgia Press, 2013.

Ballard, Michael B. *Civil War in Mississippi: Major Campaigns and Battles.* Jackson, MS: University Press of Mississippi, 2011.

Bates, Marcus W., Lt. "The Battle of Bentonville." In *Glimpses of the Nation's Struggle, Fifth Series. Papers Read Before the Minnesota Commander of the Military Order of the Loyal Legion of the United States, 1897–1902*, edited by Captain J. C. Donahower, Lt. Silas H. Towles, and Lt. David L. Kingsbury. St. Paul, MN: Review Publishing Company, 1908.

Baumgartner, Richard A. ed. *Blood & Sacrifices: The Civil War Journal of a Confederate Soldier.* Huntington, WV: Blue Acorn Press, 1994.

Beall, Robert L. "Stoneman's Raid War Riot of Ruin." *North Carolina Review.* October 2, November 11, and December 4, 1910.

Blair, William A. *With Malice Towards Some: Treason and Loyalty in the Civil War Era.* Chapel Hill, NC: University f North Carolina Press, 2014.

Blakey, Arch Frederic. *General John H. Winder, C.S.A.* Gainesville, FL: University of Florida Press, 1990.

Bolling, Walker Baron. Virginia Military Institute Historical Rosters Database.

Virginia Military Institute Archives, Lexington, VA. 2013. http://www9.vmi.edu/archiverosters/show.asp?page=details&ID2875.

Bowers, William A., Jr., comp. *The 47th Georgia Volunteer Infantry Regiment.* Global Authors Publications, 2013.

Bradley, Mark L. *Last Stand in the Carolinas: The Battle of Bentonville.* Campbell, CA: Savas Woodbury Publishers, 1996.

Bradley, Mark L. *This Astounding Close: The Road to Bennett Place.* Chapel Hill, NC: The University of North Carolina Press, 2000.

Brendt, Dennis W. *Home Guards to Heroes: The 87th Pennsylvania and Its Civil War Community.* Columbia, MO: University of Missouri Press, 2006.

Broadwater, Robert Paul. *Battle of Despair: Bentonville and the North Carolina Campaign.* Macon, GA: Mercer University Press, 2004.

Brockenbrough, Robert L. Virginia Military Institute Historical Rosters Database. Virginia Military Institute Archives, Lexington, VA. 2013. http://www9.vmi.edu/archiverosters/show.asp?page=details&ID2667.

Brooks, U.R., ed. *Memoirs of the War of Secession: From the Original Manuscripts of Johnson Hagood.* Columbia SC: The State Company, 1910.

Brown, Dee. *The Galvanized Yankees.* Lincoln, NE: University of Nebraska Press, reprinted 1986.

Brown, Louis A. *The Salisbury Prison: A Case Study of Confederate Military Prisons 1861–1865.* Wilmington, NC: Broadfoot Publishing Company. 1992.

"Brutus" (Samuel F. B. Morse). *Foreign Conspiracy Against the Liberties of the United States.* New York, NY: Leavitt, Lord & Co., 1835.

Bryan, Charles F., Jr., James C. Kelly, and Nelson D. Lankford, eds. *Images from the Storm: 300 Images from the Author of Eye of the Storm.* New York, NY: The Free Press, 2001.

Bryan, Charles F., Jr., and Nelson D. Lankford, ed. *Eye of the Storm: A Civil War Odyssey.* New York, NY: The Free Press, 2000.

Bryant, William O. *Cahaba Prison and the Sultana Disaster.* Tuscaloosa, AL: The University of Alabama Press, 1990.

Burlingame, John K., comp. *History of the Fifth Regiment of Rhode Island Heavy Artillery During Three and a Half Service in North Carolina January 1862–June 1865.* Providence, RI: Snow & Farnham Printers and Publishers, 1892.

Butts, Michelle Tucker. *Galvanized: Yankees on the Upper Missouri.* Boulder, CO: The University Press of Colorado, 2003.

Caldwell, Wilber W. *The Courthouse and the Depot: A Narrative Guide to Railroad Expansion and Its Impact on Public Architecture in Georgia 1833–1910.* Macon, GA: 2001.

Casstevens, Frances H. *George W. Alexander and Castle Thunder: A Confederate Prison and its Commandant.* Jefferson, NC: MacFarland and Company, Inc., 2004.

Chesnut, Mary Boykin, Isabella D. Martin and Myrta Lockett, eds. *A Diary from Dixie.* New York, NY: D. Appleton and Company, 1905.

Child, William. *A History of the Fifth Regiment, New Hampshire Regiment, New Hampshire Volunteers, In the American Civil War, 1861–1865.* Volume II. Bristol, NH: R.W. Musgrove, Printer, 1893.

Cisco, Walter Brian. *Wade Hampton: Confederate Warrior, Conservative Statesman.* Washington, D.C.: Potomac Books, Inc., 2004.

Clark, Lewis R. "Tenth Tennessee Infantry." Donelson Campaign Sources Supplementing Volume 7 of the Official Records of the Union and Confederate Armies in the War of the Rebellion. (Army Service Schools Press, 1912), 115–16

Cloyd, Benjamin G. *Haunted by Atrocity: Civil War Prisons in American Memory.* Baton Rouge, LA: Louisiana State University Press, 2010.

Cockrell, Thomas D. and Michael B. Ballard, eds. *Chickasaw: A Mississippi Scout for the Union.* Baton Rouge, LA: Louisiana State University Press, 2005.

Cogley, Thomas S. *History of the Seventh Indiana Cavalry Volunteers.* Laporte, IN: Herald Company, Steam Printers, 1876.

Collins, Donald E. "War Crimes or Justice? George Pickett and the Mass Execution of Deserters in Civil War Kinston, North Carolina." In *The Art of Command in the Civil War*, edited by Steven E. Woodworth. Lincoln, NE:University of Nebraska Press, 1998.

Colonna, Benjamin Azariah. Virginia Military Institute Historical Rosters Database. Virginia Military Institute Archives, Lexington, Virginia, 2013. http://www9.vmi.edu/archiverosters/show.asp?page=details&ID2875.

Cox, Jacob D. *The March to the Sea: Franklin and Nashville.* New York, NY: Charles Scribners Sons, 1886.

Crawford, William Beamish. Virginia Military Institute Historical Rosters Database. Virginia Military Institute Archives, Lexington, Virginia. Accessed January 8, 2018. http://www9.vmi.edu/archiverosters/show.asp?page=details&ID2848.

Current, Richard Nelson. *Lincoln's Loyalists: Union Soldiers From the Confederacy.* Boston, MA: Northeastern University Press, 1992.

Davis, Robert Scott. *Andersonville Civil War Prison.* Charleston, SC: The History Press, 2010.

Derden, John K. *The Story of Camp Lawton.* Macon, GA: Mercer University Press, 2012.

Dickert, D. Augustus. *History of Kershaw's Brigade.* Elberton, SC: Elbert C. Aull Company, 1899.

Dickey, Luther S. *History of the 103rd Regiment: Pennsylvania Veteran Volunteer Infantry.* Chicago, IL: by the Author, 1910.

Dinges, Bruce J., and Shirkey A.Leckie, eds. *A Just and Righteous Cause: Benjamin H. Grierson's Civil War Memoir.* Carbondale, IL: Southern Illinois Press, 2008.

Dougherty, Michael. *Prison Diary of Michael Dougherty Late Company B, 13th., PA. Cavalry While Confined in Pemberton's, Barrett's, Libby, Andersonville, and Other Sothern Prisons Sole Survivor of 127 of his Regiment Captured the Same Time, 122 Dying in Andersonville.* Bristol, PA: Charles A. Dougherty Printer, 1908.

Downing, David C. *A South Divided: Portraits of Dissent in the Confederacy.* Nashville, TN: Cumberland House, 2007.

Dunkerly, Robert M. *The Confederate Surrender at Greensboro: The Final Days of the Army of Tennessee, April, 1865.* Jefferson, NC: McFarland and Company Publishers, 2013.

Emilio, Luis F. *History of the Fifty-Fourth Regiment of Massachusetts Volunteer Infantry.* Boston, MA: The Boston Book Company, 1894.

Evans, Clement A., ed. *Confederate Military History*, Vol. V. Atlanta, GA: Confederate Publishing Company, 1899.

Ezekiel, Moses. Virginia Military Institute Historical Rosters Database. Virginia Military Institute Archives, Lexington, Virginia, 2013. http://www9.vmi.edu/archiverosters/show.asp?page=details&ID2695.

Fetzer, Dale and Bruce Mowday. *Unlikely Allies: Fort Delaware's Prison Community in the Civil War.* Mechanisburg, PA: Stackpole Books, 2000.

Foote, Lorien. *The Yankee Plague.* Chapel Hill, NC: The University of North Carolina Press, 2016.

Foote, Lorien and Andrew Fialka. *Fugitive Federals: A Digital Humanities Investigation of Escaped Union Prisoners.* August 2018. www.ehistory.org/projects/fugitive-federals.html.

Freeman, Joanne B. *The Field of Blood: Violence in Congress and the Road to the Civil War.* New York, NY: Picador Farrar, Straus and Giroux, 2018.

Futch, Ovid. *History of Andersonville Prison.* Gainesville, FL: The University of Florida Press, 1968.

Futch, Ovid. *History of Andersonville Prison*, Revised Edition. Gainesville, FL: The University of Florida Press, 2011.

Futch, Ovid. "Prison Life at Andersonville." In *Civil War Prisons*, edited by William B. Hesseltine. Kent OH: The Kent State University Press, 1962.

Gallman, J. Mathew. *Defining Duty in the Civil War: Personal Choice, Popular Culture, and the Union Home Front.* Chapel Hill, NC: The University of North Carolina Press, 2015.

Gibson, Captain Thomas. "Experiences of the Tenth Tennessee With a Special Tribute to Capt. James P. Kirkman." *Confederate Veteran*, Vol. XX, No. 6 (June 1912): 274.

Giles, William, ed. *Disease, Starvation & Death: Personal Accounts of Camp Lawton.* Lulu Press, 2005.

Gillispie, James M. *Andersonvilles of the North.* Denton, TX: University of North Texas Press, 2008.

Gleeson, Ed. *Rebel Sons of Erin.* Indianapolis, IN: Guild Press of Indiana, 1993.

Goode, G. Brown. *Virginia Cousins: A Study of the Ancestry and Posterity of John Goode of Whitby A Virginia Colonist of the Seventeenth Century.* Richmond, VA: J. W. Randolph & English, 1888.

Goss, Warren Lee. *The Soldier's Story.* Boston, MA: Lee & Shepard, 1866; Reprinted by Digital Scanning, Inc., Scituate MA, 2001.

Gray, Michael P. *The Business of Captivity: Elmira and Its Civil War Prison.* Kent, OH: The Kent State University Press, 2001.

Griffin, Captain Patrick H. "The Famous Tenth Tennessee." *Confederate Veteran*, Vol. XIV, No. 12 (December 1905): 553–60.

Hafen, Leroy R. and Ann W. Hefen. *Powder River Campaigns and Sawyers Expedition of 1865.* Glendale, CA: The Arthur H. Clark Company, 1961.

Hamlin, Edward Lumpkin. Virginia Military Institute Historical Rosters Database. Virginia Military Institute Archives, Lexington, Virginia, 2013. http://www9.vmi.edu/archiverosters/show.asp?page=details&ID2896.

Hanna, John F. Virginia Military Institute Historical Rosters Database. Virginia Military Institute Archives, Lexington, Virginia, 2013. https://archivesweb.vmi.edu/rosters/record.php?ID=1668.

Hartley, Chris J. *Stoneman's Raid 1865.* Winston-Salem, NC: John F. Blair Publisher, 2010.

Hesseltine, William B., ed. *Civil War Prisons.* Kent, OH: The Kent State University Press, 1972.

Hogan, Michael. *The Irish Soldiers of Mexico.* Intercambio Press in Cooperation With Createspace, 2011.

Hollingsworth, Margaret Wright, ed. *The Confederate Diary of Wesley Olin Connor of Cave Spring, Georgia.* Self-published, 2006.

Horse Soldiers, The. Accessed October 12 2018. http://www.tcm.com/this-month/article/30040%7C0/The-Horse-Soldiers.html.

Hughes, Michael Chearis. *Bentonville: The Final Battle of Sherman and Johnston.* Chapel Hill, NC: University of North Carolina Press, 1996.

Hughes, N.C., Jr. "Hardee's Defense of Savannah." *Georgia Historical Quarterly*, Volume XLVII, No. 1.

Hunter, Leslie Gene. *Warden for the Union: General William Hoffman (1807–1884.)* PhD Dissertation, University of Arizona, 1971.

Jackson, James R. *History of Littleton, New Hampshire.* Cambridge, MA: University Press, Vol I, 1905.

Jackson, W. Turrentine. *Wagon Roads West.* Lincoln, NE: University of Nebraska Press, 1979.

Jones, Charles Colcock. *The Siege of Savannah in December, 1864, and the Confederate Operations in Georgia and the Third Military District of South Carolina during General Sherman's March from Atlanta to the Sea: Electronic Edition.*

Academic Affairs Library, UNC-CH University of North Carolina at Chapel Hill, 1998. http://closouthunc.edu/fpn/JonesCharles/jones.html.

Jones, John B. *A Rebel War Clerk's Diary*, Vol. II. Philadelphia, PA: J. B. Lippincott & Co., 1869.

Kellogg, Robert H. *Life and Death in Rebel Prisons.* Hartford, CN: 1868.

King, G. Wayne. "Death Camp at Florence." *Civil War Times Illustrated*, January 1974.

Knauss, William H. *The Story of Camp Chase.* Nashville, TN: Publishing House of the Methodist Episcopal Church, 1906.

Knight, James R. *The Battle of Fort Donelson.* Charleston, SC: The History Press, 2011.

Kundahl, George G. *Confederate Engineer.* Knoxville, TN: The University of Tennessee Press 2000.

Ledoux, Rev. Albert H. *The Florence Stockade.* Gallitzin, PA: Published by the Author, 2015.

Ledoux, Rev. Albert H. *The Union Dead of the Florence Stockade.* Old Darlington District Chapter, South Carolina Genealogical Society, Inc., 2000.

Leftwich, Lief Alexander H. Family Tree. ancestry.com. Accessed April 3, 2014. http://trees.ancestry.com/Military.aspx?pid=669563.

Levy, George. *To Live and Die in Chicago: Confederate Prisoners at Camp Douglas.* Gretna, LA: Pelican Publishing Company, 2008.

Lonn, Ella. *Desertion During the Civil War.* Big Byte Books, 1928; reprinted 2016. http://www.bigbytebooks.com.

Martin, Isabella D. and Mary Lockett Avery, eds. *A Diary From Dixie.* New York, NY: D. Appleton & Co., 1906.

Martin, Vincent F. "Story of the Brooks Battalion," In S*tories of the Confederacy*, edited by U. R. Brooks. Columbia, SC: The State Company, 1912.

Martinez, J. Michael. *Life and Death in Civil War Prisons.* Nashville, TN: Rutledge Hill Press, 2004.

Marvel, William. *Andersonville the Last Depot.* Chapel Hill, NC: The University of North Carolina Press, 1994.

Mathes, J. Harvey. *The Old Guard in Gray: Researches in the Annals of the Confederate Historical Society.* Memphis, TN: Press of S. C. Toof & Co, 1897.

Maul, David T. "Five Butternut Yankees." *Journal of the Illinois State Historical Society*, Vol. LVI, Number 2 (Summer 1963): 177–92.

McAdams, Benton. *Rebels at Rock Island: The Story of a Civil War Prison.* DeKalb, IL: Northern Illinois University Press, 2000.

McClean, James. *John Cain's Andersonville Testimony.* Accessed September 6, 2018. http://www.2mass.reunioncivilwar.com/References/cains_andersonville.htm.

McCorkle, James William. Virginia Military Institute Historical Rosters

Database. Virginia Military Institute Archives, Lexington, Virginia. Accessed January 8, 2018. http://www9.vmi.edu/archiverosters/show.asp?page=details&ID2954.

McKee, James Harvey. *Back in War Times: History of the 144th New York Volunteer Infantry*. Unadilla, NY: Lieut. Horace E. Bailey Publisher, 1908), 200.

McMurray, W. J., MD. *History of the Twentieth Tennessee Regiment Volunteer Infantry*. Nashville, TN: The Publication Committee, 1904.

McPherson, James M. *The Cause and Comrades: Why Men Fought in the Civil War*. New York, NY: Oxford University Press, 1997.

Medal of Honor Recipients, 1863–2013. Washington, D.C.: U.S. Government Printing Office, 2013.

Miles, Jim. *To The Sea: A History and Tour Guide of the War in the West, Sherman's March Across Georgia and Through the Carolinas, 1864–1865*. Nashville, TN: Cumberland House, 2002.

Miller, Robert Ryal. *Shamrock and Sword: The Saint Patrick's Battalion in the U.S.-Mexican War*. Norman, OK: University of Oklahoma Press, 1989.

Moore, Albert Burton. *Conscription and Conflict in the Confederacy*. Columbia, SC: The University of South Carolina Press, 1996.

Murdock, Eugene Converse. *Patriotism Limited, 1862–1865: The Civil War Draft and Bounty System*. Kent, OH: The Kent State University Press, 1967.

National Register of Historic Places File for the Stockade. South Carolina Department of Archives and History.

Neely, Mark E., Jr. *Southern Rights: Political Prisoners and the Myth of Confederate Constitutionalism*. Charlottesville, VA: The University of Virginia Press, 1999.

Parker, Sandra V. *Richmond's Civil War Prisons*. Lynchburg, VA: H. E. Howard, Inc. 1990.

Paul, R Eli, "A Galvanized Yankee Along the Niobrara River," *Nebraska History*, 70 (1989): 146–57. http://www.nebraskahistory.org/publish/publicat/history/full-text/NH1989Niob_Ynkee.pdf.

Pickenpaugh, Roger. *Captives in Blue: The Civil War Prisons of the Confederacy*. Tuscaloosa, AL: The University of Alabama Press, 2013.

Powell William H., and Edward Shippen, eds. *Officers of the Army and Navy Who Served in The Civil War*. Philadelphia, PA: L. R. Hamersly & Co., 1892.

Power, Tracy. *The Confederate Prison Stockade at Florence, South Carolina* Unpublished Manuscript in the South Carolina Department of Archives and History, Columbia, SC, 1991.

Rable, George C. *Damn Yankees! Demonization and Defiance in the Confederate South*. Baton Rouge, LA: Louisiana State University Press, 2015.

Radley, Kenneth. *Rebel Watchdogs: The Confederate States Provost Guard*. Baton Rouge, LA: Louisiana State University Press, 1989.

Retzloff, Carl Alexander. *The First Fruits of a Re-United People: The Loyalty Motivation and Allegiance of the Men of the Second United States Volunteer*

Infantry Regiment. Honors Thesis, Department of History, Washington and Lee University, 2015.

Rigdon, John. *The* Boys *of the Fifth: Regimental History of the Georgia 5th Infantry Regiment.* Clearwater, SC: Eastern Digital Resources, 2008.

Robarts, Wm. Hugh. *Mexican War Veterans: A Complete Roster of the Regular and Volunteer Troops in the War Between the United States and Mexico, from 1846 to 1848: The Volunteers are Arranged by States, Alphabetically.* Washington DC: Brentano's.

Robbins, Glenn. *They Have Left Us Here to Die.* Kent, OH: The Kent State University Press, 2011.

Sanders, Charles W. Jr., *While in the Hands of the Enemy: Military Prisons of the Civil War* Baton Rouge, LA: Louisiana State University Press, 2005.

Scaife, William R., and William Harris Bragg. *Joe Brown's Pets: The Georgia Militia 1861–1865.* Mercer, GA: Mercer University Press, 2004.

Scharle, Judith A., compiler. *The Life and Times of Benjamin Azariah Colonna.* Accessed February 1, 2014. http://www.colonnapapers.com/COLONNA PAPERSUP/BenAColonnaHistory_-_Vol_2.html.

Sheehy, Barry, Cindy Wallace, and Vaughnette Goode-Walker. *Savannah Immortal City, Volume I Civil War Savannah.* Austin, TX: Emerald Book Co., 2011.

Shriver, Samuel. VMI Alumnus and New Market Veteran, ca. 1865. Virginia Military Institute Archives Digital Collection. Accessed January 8, 2018. http://digitalcollections.vmi.edu/cdm/ref/collection/p15820coll7/id/3030.

Slocum, Henry W., Major General. "Sherman's March from Savannah to Bentonville." In *Battles and Leaders of the Civil War,* Vol. IV, edited by Robert Underwood Johnson and Clarence Cough Buell. New York, NY: The Century Company, 1884.

Snell, Mark A., ed. *Dancing Along the Deadline.* Novato, CA: Presidio Press, 1996.

Speer, Lonnie R. *Portals to Hell.* Mechanisburg, PA: Stackpole Books, 1997.

Stevens, Peter F. *The Rogue's March: John Riley and the St. Patrick's Battalion 1846–1848.* Dulles, VA: Brassey's, 1999.

Storey, Margaret M. *Loyalty and Loss: Alabama's Unionists in the Civil War and Reconstruction.* Baton Rouge, LA: Louisiana State University Press, 2004.

Temple, Brian. *The Union Prison at Fort Delaware: A Perfect Hell on Earth.* Jefferson, NC: McFarland & Company, Inc., 2002.

Texas Bar Association. *Proceedings of the 24th Annual Session of the Texas Bar Association.* Austin, TX: Printed By Order of the Association, 1905.

Turner, Norman Vincent. *Confederate Military Executions (Soldiers Shot By the Firing Squad) at Savannah, Georgia During the Civil War, Which led to the Trial of General Hugh W. Mercer.* Springfield, GA: Published by the Author, 2007.

United Daughters of the Confederacy. *War Days in Fayetteville, North Carolina Reminiscences of 1861–1865*. United Daughters of the Confederacy. Fayetteville, NC: Judge Printing Company, 1910.

Vaughter, John B. (as Sgt. Oates). *Life and Death in Dixie*. Chicago, IL: Central Book Concern, 1880.

Wanless Web. Accessed November 12, 2018. http://www.wanlessweb.org/TNG/getperson.php?personID=I895&tree=3.

Weber, Jennifer L. *Copperheads: The Rise and Fall of Lincoln's Opponents in the North*. New York, NY: Oxford University Press, 2006.

Weiner, Marli F., ed. *A Heritage of Woe: The Civil War Diary of Grace Brown Elmore, 1861–1868. Southern Voices from the Past: Women's Letters, Diaries, and Writings*. Athens, GA: University of Georgia Press, 1997.

Wheelan, Joseph. *Libby Prison Breakout*. New York, NY: Public Affairs, 2010.

Wilmer, Allison L., J. H. Jarrett, and Geo. W. F. Vernon. *Maryland Volunteers, War of 1861–65*. Baltimore MD: Gugginheimer, Weil, & Company. Baltimore, Maryland, 1898.

Winslow, Hattie Lou and Joseph R. H. Moore. *Camp Morton, 1861–1865: Indianapolis Prison Camp*. Indianapolis IN: Indiana Historical Society, 1940.

Wise, Jennings C. *The Military History of the Virginia Military Institute from 1839 to 1865*. Lynchburg, VA: J. P. Bell Company, Inc., 1915.

Woodworth, Steven E. *Nothing But Victory: The Army of Tennessee, 1861–1865*. New York, NY: Alfred A. Knopf, 2005.

Woodworth, Steven E., ed. *The Art of Command in the Civil War*. Lincoln, NE: University of Nebraska Press, 1998.

Zimring, David Ross. *To Live and Die in Dixie: Native Northerners Who Fought for the Confederacy*. Knoxville, TN: University of Tennessee Press, 2014.

INDEX

www.ingramcontent.com/pod-product-compliance
Lightning Source LLC
Chambersburg PA
CBHW031937090426
42811CB00002B/208

* 9 7 8 1 6 2 1 9 0 6 1 7 9 *